Alex. (Alexander) Mackay

Facts And Dates

Alex. (Alexander) Mackay

Facts And Dates

ISBN/EAN: 9783744743747

Printed in Europe, USA, Canada, Australia, Japan

Cover: Foto ©Andreas Hilbeck / pixelio.de

More available books at **www.hansebooks.com**

Second Edition, Crown 8vo, pp. 336, price 4s.

FACTS AND DATES;

OR,

THE LEADING EVENTS IN SACRED AND PROFANE HISTORY,
AND THE PRINCIPAL FACTS IN THE VARIOUS
PHYSICAL SCIENCES:

THE MEMORY BEING AIDED THROUGHOUT BY A SIMPLE
AND NATURAL METHOD.

For Schools and Private Reference.

BY THE

Rev. ALEX. MACKAY, LL.D. F.R.G.S.

Author of 'A Manual of Modern Geography, Mathematical,
Physical, and Political,' &c. &c.

OPINIONS OF THE PRESS.

"A most valuable book of reference, which will be of immense service to students of history His wide knowledge has directed the author at once to the most trustworthy guides in the various departments of the almost illimitable field he has traversed. . . . Every date throughout is embodied in a mnemonic sentence, so happily and tersely illustrative of the event, as to leave us fairly astonished at the patience and ingenuity of the author."—*Papers for the Schoolmaster.*

"This work is a wonderfully elaborate production. . . . 'Facts and Dates,' which in some hands would furnish forth a cyclopædia of tolerable dimensions, have their essence extracted, and here appear in the moderate compass of 317 pages. . . . Great care has been taken to bring the volume in all respects to the point which the material and historical sciences have at present reached, while deep reverence for the Bible breathes through the volume."—*London Weekly Review.*

"'Facts and Dates' is the name of a very neat and well-compiled collection of tables, not exclusively chronological, though all involving numbers. But the chief feature is an extremely simple system of mnemonics, by means of which a few appropriate words attached to each fact or event are made to carry with them a string of figures."—*Guardian.*

"Dr Mackay's book is planned with great ingenuity and skill. It is a text-book of physical science and universal chronology, adapted for scholastic purposes, on a principle of *natural mnemonics*, and gives evidence of much labour and research."—*Nonconformist.*

"A valuable text-book of physical science and universal chronology. . . . The plan is exceedingly ingenious, and at the same time eminently simple and natural."—*London Scotsman.*

"There are certainly the elements of a very desirable auxiliary to students and general readers in this portion of Dr Mackay's volume, and we hope he will expand and elaborate the part alluded to in a future publication."—*Athenæum.*

"There is a most interesting chapter on Scripture chronology, written in an admirable spirit, and displaying much ingenuity and research. . . . Our deliberate opinion is, that it is one of the finest books of the kind we have ever met with."—*Daily Review.*

OPINIONS OF THE PRESS—*Continued.*

"We can aver that this compendium of Facts and Dates contains a vast amount of accurate and well-digested information; and we may add that in the hands of a competent schoolmaster it must prove a most effective instrument of teaching on the subjects to which it relates."—*Edinburgh Courant.*

"The second division deals with historical facts; in other words, it gives the chronology of the leading facts of history, and is subdivided into two parts—the one summarising sacred history in three chapters, and the other, profane history, in nine chapters. This division of the book is also of great value."—*Aberdeen Journal.*

"The research of historic data, and mastery of scientific facts and principles, with the careful manner in which they are tabulated, cannot fail to add yet further to the Author's reputation."—*Aberdeen Free Press.*

"We have not the least doubt that the system can be introduced with much advantage into some of the younger classes in every school, while more advanced students will gladly welcome it as an aid to memory that will be of daily and hourly use."—*Banffshire Journal.*

"A very valuable book for teachers, and still more so for students preparing for public examinations of any kind."—*Ayr Advertiser.*

"The care and labour requisite for the production of such a work are out of all proportion to its size, and we must congratulate the author on the extreme accuracy and comprehensiveness of the scientific part of the work, which is scrupulously written up to the knowledge of the times, and includes the latest discoveries in each of the sciences."—*John o' Groat Journal.*

"The amount of industry, intelligence, and research it represents is something enormous, and the way in which a valuable *comment* on a fact is *made to give up the date* is most ingenious."—*Brighton Herald.*

"It is a work suited to almost all ages—not too far advanced or profound for the schoolroom, and, on the other hand, many engaged in literary pursuits, or preparing for public examination, will find it most useful as a work of reference."—*Dublin Mail.*

"It will be more than valuable to the student and teacher of history as a sort of *vade mecum.* In the division of ancient history it is particularly full, and especially in all that relates to Egypt—the author having obtained for that department of his labours the aid of the most advanced scholars in 'Egyptology.' In this portion of the book there will be found a condensed and deeply interesting account of the discoveries and measurements of the Great Pyramid—that wonder of wonders come down to us from hoary time."—*Montrose Review.*

"The volume is not a bare catalogue of statistics, for every department of the book is prefaced by a very able and interesting introduction, bringing out in a condensed form the prominent and latest discoveries and views in connection with the respective subjects, and also the most reliable sources of information. The labour and research of the author must have been enormous, the fruit of which will be reaped by the reader with the smallest amount of trouble. The volume will be specially valuable as a text-book for advanced classes and students, and as a book of reference in the library."—*Press and St James's Chronicle.*

"Considerable ingenuity has been displayed in making the mnemonic sentences illustrate the character of the various facts; and, mnemonics apart, the book, in an educational sense, is of unquestionable value."—*Weekly Dispatch.*

"No pains have been spared to select the facts most worthy of being remembered, and to determine the dates according to the most approved system of modern chronology. Each chapter is preceded by a longer or shorter discussion of the subject on hand, remarkable for its elaborate learning and great conciseness."—*Glasgow Journal.*

WILLIAM BLACKWOOD & SONS, Edinburgh and London.

FACTS AND DATES

OR

THE LEADING EVENTS IN SACRED AND PROFANE HISTORY
AND THE PRINCIPAL FACTS IN THE VARIOUS
PHYSICAL SCIENCES

THE MEMORY BEING AIDED THROUGHOUT BY A
SIMPLE AND NATURAL METHOD

FOR SCHOOLS AND PRIVATE REFERENCE

BY THE

REV. ALEX. MACKAY, LL.D. F.R.G.S.

AUTHOR OF 'A MANUAL OF MODERN GEOGRAPHY, MATHEMATICAL, PHYSICAL, AND POLITICAL;'
'TLINES OF M⸺
;RAPHY;' ETC

DITION

WILLIAM BLACKWOOD AND SONS
EDINBURGH AND LONDON
MDCCCLXX

PREFACE.

A LIMITED acquaintance with reading, writing, and arithmetic can no longer be regarded as sufficient for the great bulk of the community. It has become imperative that the youth of our land, whether rich or poor, shall acquire some knowledge of history and the physical sciences.

Human life, however, is very short, and the struggle for existence on the part of the many seems to be daily becoming more arduous. Hence it follows that new branches of instruction, however necessary, are practically unattainable, unless they are simplified, condensed, and in every way rendered as attractive as possible. The man, therefore, who in our day produces the *best school-book* on any elementary subject confers an immense boon on the community.

The following pages consist of an earnest and elaborate attempt—prosecuted without intermission for a number of years—to popularise science and history, to enable our boys and girls to *acquire and remember* all the more important events in history, whether sacred or profane, as well as a multitude of interesting facts in most of the physical sciences. To render such a gigantic undertaking practicable within the limits of an ordinary-sized school-book—to enable the student to master the sections in which he may be specially interested in a comparatively brief period, and *to retain through life the knowledge thus acquired*—it became necessary to have recourse to some method of *aiding the memory*. The author could not avail himself of any of the systems of Mnemonics hitherto made public, as they are all, so far as he has seen, *arbitrary, lifeless,* and *extremely unnatural—destitute alike of beauty, simplicity, and truth*. They are also practically *useless;* for however extraordinary the power they appear to impart to the memory, that power is invariably of short duration. The more the acquired information accumulates, the more unwieldy becomes the burden, till at length, the pressure becoming intolerable, the mind shakes off the whole in disgust.

Whatever merit or defect may attach to the method employed in this volume, it is at all events eminently *simple and natural*. The only *artificial* element characterising it is, that the letters of the alphabet are employed to express numbers. But of this feature it will probably be found impossible ever to get rid, and in fact it is rather a help than a hindrance. And such a use of letters need scarcely startle us, for ever since man became possessed of letters, they have been employed to denote numbers.

Yet it would be a serious error to imagine that the present work is a treatise on Mnemonics. The work is solely devoted to SCIENCE and HISTORY, and Mnemonics is merely employed as an *auxiliary*. It is by no means *essential* to the plan of the book; and both teacher and student may always feel themselves at perfect liberty to pass by the mnemonic sentences, should they feel so inclined. In not a few instances this may be done *at first*, owing to the strong prejudice now entertained against everything calling itself Artificial Memory. In many departments of knowledge, however, artificial aid becomes absolutely necessary; and all the objections we have heard expressed are really directed, not against the thing itself, but against the fantastic forms which it has been made to assume. If we can get quit of these, and refuse to aid the memory except by *natural methods*, we need not be apprehensive of any injurious consequences.

Geography and Chronology are justly styled "the eyes of History," and the author has long felt that his labours in the former field would be one-sided and defective did he not give an equal degree of attention to the latter. On his various geographical works the teaching profession have pronounced an emphatic verdict, and he is not without hope that a similar result will follow the publication of his Chronology. In the chronology of the earlier ages he is aware that he has laid himself open to the charge of forsaking the old paths; but he has done this deliberately, after thorough and earnest investigation, and he respectfully craves that his book shall have a fair and unprejudiced trial.

The author finds, as the result of many trials, that young people of about the age of ten are quite competent to understand and employ the method here illustrated, and by its means to treasure up in their minds a vast number of important facts. He has also asked the unbiassed opinion of not a few of the most eminent educationists in the Scottish capital. These, without exception, have expressed their cordial approval of the method here employed, and its perfect adaptability to school purposes; while for students at the university and candidates for the civil service they believe the book will prove invaluable.

GRANGE, EDINBURGH, *Oct.* 1869.

NOTE TO SECOND EDITION.

THE Author returns his sincere thanks to the heads of schools and the public for having so rapidly exhausted the first edition of this work. He also thanks the public journalists of the kingdom for the high encomiums they have bestowed on his labours. In this edition, the few typographical errors that have been observed are corrected, while to page x have been appended a few examples to illustrate the system of mnemonics employed.

EDINBURGH, *Jan.* 1870.

KEY TO THE MNEMONICS.

In the system of mnemonics here adopted, the consonants of the English alphabet are employed to express numbers, the five vowels (a, e, i, o, u) being disregarded, and the half-vowels (w, y) being used to denote the cipher (0), as also the letter x.

This leaves eighteen consonants to express the nine ordinary numerals, or *two consonants to each*. The first two consonants of the alphabet (b, c) will then denote 1; the second pair (d, f) will denote 2; g, h, 3, &c., as shown in the following diagram :—

b, c = 1	j, k, s = 4	p, q, z = 7
d, f = 2	l = 5	r = 8
g, h = 3	m, n = 6	t, v = 9
	w, x, y = 0	

In the above diagram it will be observed that *three* letters are employed to denote 4 and 7 respectively, while to express 5 and 8 there is only *one*. This departure from the rule was found to be practically necessary, as *l* and *r* begin a far greater number of words than *j, k, q, z*, and as it is to the *initial* consonant of a word that we attach a numerical value.

1. When we wish to remember any fact in science, or any event in history, we have merely to form a short sentence bearing on the fact or event, and in such a way that the *first consonants* of *the several words* shall express the figures or numerals in the number we desire to remember.

2. Special care must be taken that the sentence thus con-

structed shall express one or more of the essential features of the fact or event about to be committed to memory. It will be always found that the happier and more appropriate the sentence is, the more easy it will be to remember it.

3. It will greatly facilitate the construction of brief, pointed, and appropriate sentences if we attach *no numerical value to the Article, Pronoun, Preposition, Interjection, and Conjunction,* and confine ourselves to Nouns, Verbs, Adjectives, and Adverbs. For the same reason it will be found necessary to disregard the verb *to be,* on account of its frequent occurrence.

4. A word put within parentheses does not count, such word being introduced merely to render the sentence more striking or intelligible.

5. Silent letters do not count—as, for example, *h* in honour, and *s* in island.

6. When, as occasionally happens, any word must be counted contrary to the foregoing rules, such word is printed in a different type.

7. When absolute accuracy is not required, or is, in fact, unattainable, the mnemonic sentence may be allowed a certain degree of licence. This is especially the case when the number is obviously a *round* one ; but this licence should seldom be allowed beyond the first figure of the number.

8. To avoid all possible misunderstanding as to the precise words which are meant to have a numerical value in any sentence, the student will observe that all such are printed in *italics*.

EXAMPLES.—The distance of the earth from the sun, as stated at p. 9, is 92 (millions of miles, understood), and the mnemonic sentence, intended to yield up this number, is " the world's *true distance:*" here the three first consonants are *w, t, d,* which, according to the diagram at p. ix, denote 0, 9, 2—or simply 92, as the cipher on the *left* has no value. Ex. 2. Date of the Deluge, according to the Septuagint, B.C. 3216 (see p. 71) ; the mnemonic sentence is, "a *general deluge covers* the *mountains:*" here the four first consonants are *g, d, c, m,* which, as the diagram shows, denote 3, 2, 1, 6, or 3216. In each example the *article* is disregarded, according to Rule 3, above.

TABLE OF CONTENTS.

DIVISION I.—SCIENTIFIC FACTS.

CHAP. I.—FACTS IN ASTRONOMY.

		PAGE
Sect. 1.	Mean Distances of the Planets from the Sun,	9
,, 2.	Time of the Planets' Revolution,	9
,, 3.	Distances of the Comets from the Sun,	10
,, 4.	Time of Revolution of the Comets,	11
,, 5.	Number of the Fixed Stars,	11
,, 6.	Distances of the Fixed Stars from our Sun,	12
,, 7.	Proper motion of the Stars,	13

CHAP. II.—FACTS IN CHEMISTRY.

,, 8.	Table of Elementary Substances,	17
,, 9.	Table of Chemical Equivalents,	19
,, 10.	Specific Gravity of Elementary Substances,	20
,, 11.	Freezing-point of Liquids,	21
,, 12.	Boiling-point of Liquids,	22
,, 13.	Fusing-point of Metals,	23

CHAP. III.—FACTS IN NATURAL PHILOSOPHY.

,, 14.	Action of Gravity on Falling Bodies,	26
15.	Various Velocities in Nature compared,	26

CHAP. IV.—FACTS IN BOTANY.

Sect. 16. The Flora of the Globe, ... 27
,, 17. The Flora of some European Countries, ... 28
,, 18. Geological or Fossil Botany, ... 29

CHAP. V.—FACTS IN ZOOLOGY.

,, 19. The Fauna of the Globe, ... 32
,, 20. Distribution of the Mammalia, ... 32
,, 21. The Fauna of some European Countries, . . . 33
,, 22. Palæontology, or Fossil Zoology, ... 34

CHAP. VI.—FACTS IN ETHNOGRAPHY.

,, 23. Races of Mankind, ... 35
,, 24. Religions of Mankind, ... 35
,, 25. Races of Men in Europe, ... 36
,, 26. Religions in Europe, ... 36

CHAP. VII.—FACTS IN GEOGRAPHY.

,, 27. Areas of the different Continents, ... 37
,, 28. Population of the Continents, ... 38
,, 29. Areas of European Countries, ... 38
,, 30. Population of European Countries, ... 40
,, 31. Heights of European Mountains, ... 41
,, 32. Areas of European River-Basins, ... 42
,, 33. Areas of Asiatic Countries, ... 43
,, 34. Population of Asiatic Countries, ... 43
,, 35. Heights of Asiatic Mountain-Chains, ... 44
,, 36. Areas of Asiatic River-Basins, ... 45
,, 37. Areas of African Countries, ... 46
,, 38. Population of African Countries, ... 46
,, 39. Areas of North American Countries, ... 47
,, 40. Population of North American Countries, . . . 48
,, 41. Height of North American Mountains, . . . 48
,, 42. Areas of North American River-Basins, . . . 49
,, 43. Areas of South American States, ... 49
,, 44. Population of South American States, . . . 50
,, 45. Height of South American Mountains, . . . 50
,, 46. Areas of South American River-Basins, . . . 51
,, 47. Areas of Countries in Oceania, ... 52
,, 48. Population of the Countries of Oceania, . . . 52
,, 49. Height of principal Mountains in Oceania, . . . 53
,, 50. Progress of Geographical Discovery, ... 54

DIVISION II.—HISTORICAL FACTS.

PART FIRST.—SACRED HISTORY.

CHAP. I.—OLD TESTAMENT HISTORY.—B.C. 5478-B.C. 4.

Sect.	1. Antediluvian Period,	69
,,	2. Patriarchal Period,	71
,,	3. Period of the Exodus,	73
,,	4. Period of the Judges—from Joshua to Saul,	74
,,	5. Period of the Hebrew Monarchy,	76
,,	6. Kingdom of Israel, or of the Ten Tribes,	77
,,	7. Kingdom of Judah,	81
,,	8. From the Jewish Captivity to Malachi,	85
,,	9. The Jews under the Greeks,	87
,,	10. The Jews under the Romans,	88

CHAP. II.—NEW TESTAMENT HISTORY.—B.C. 4-A.D. 100.

,,	11. From the Birth of Christ to the Ascension,	97
,,	12. From the Ascension to the Introduction of the Gospel into Europe,	99
,,	13. From the Introduction of the Gospel into Europe to the Death of John,	102

CHAP. III.—ECCLESIASTICAL HISTORY.—A.D. 100-476.

,,	14. Early Christian Writers,	107
,,	15. The Twenty Œcumenical Councils,	109
,,	16. The Ten General Persecutions,	110
,,	17. Principal Events in Ecclesiastical History from the Death of John to Constantine,	111
,,	18. Principal Events from Constantine to the Fall of the Western Empire,	116

PART SECOND.—PROFANE HISTORY.

PERIOD FIRST.—ANCIENT HISTORY.

CHAP. I.—HISTORY OF EGYPT.—B.C. 2550-B.C. 30.

Sect.	1. Egypt from the Earliest Time to the Shepherd Kings,	136
,,	2. From the Shepherd Kings to the Exodus of the Israelites,	140
,,	3. From the Exodus to the Death of Alexander the Great,	145
,,	4. From the Death of Alexander to the Conquest of Egypt by the Romans,	149

CHAP. II.—HISTORY OF CHALDÆA, ASSYRIA, AND BABYLONIA.—B.C. 2500-B.C. 538.

,,	5. The Chaldæan or Old Babylonian Monarchy,	155
,,	6. The Assyrian Monarchy,	157
,,	7. Later Babylonian Empire,	161

CHAP. III.—HISTORY OF THE MEDO-PERSIAN EMPIRE.—B.C. 880-B.C. 330.

,,	8. The Median Kingdom to the Fall of Babylon,	163
,,	9. From the Destruction of Babylon to Alexander the Great,	164

CHAP. IV.—HISTORY OF GREECE.—B.C. 2000-B.C. 146.

,,	10. The Heroic or Mythical Period,	168
,,	11. Earliest Historic Period,	171
,,	12. Period of Athenian Supremacy,	173
,,	13. Period of Spartan Supremacy,	177
,,	14. Period of Theban Supremacy,	178
,,	15. Period of Macedonian Supremacy,	178
,,	16. From the Death of Alexander the Great to the Conquest of Greece by the Romans,	180

CHAP. V.—HISTORY OF ROME.—B.C. 2000-A.D. 476.

Sect.	17. Italy from the Earliest Times to the Founding of Rome,	185
,,	18. From the Founding of Rome to the end of the Kingdom,	187
,,	19. The Republic—to the end of the First Punic War,	189
,,	20. From the First Punic War to the end of the Third,	193
,,	21. From the Third Punic War to the Empire,	196
,,	22. The Empire—from Augustus to Aurelius,	200
,,	23. The Empire—from Commodus to Augustulus,	207

PERIOD SECOND.—MEDIÆVAL HISTORY.

CHAP. VI.—FROM THE FALL OF THE ROMAN EMPIRE TO THE DISCOVERY OF AMERICA BY COLUMBUS.—A.D. 476-1492.

,,	24. From Romulus Augustulus to Charlemagne,	220
,,	25. From Charlemagne to the Norman Conquest,	224
,,	26. From the Conquest to the Accession of the Plantagenets,	228
,,	27. From the Plantagenets to the end of the Crusades,	230
,,	28. From the Crusades to the Death of Richard II.,	235
,,	29. From Richard II. to the Accession of Edward IV.,	240
,,	30. From Edward IV. to the Discovery of America,	243

PERIOD THIRD.—MODERN HISTORY.

CHAP. VII.—FROM THE DISCOVERY OF AMERICA TO THE PEACE OF WESTPHALIA.—A.D. 1492-1648.

,,	31. From the Discovery of America to the Reformation,	246
,,	32. From the Reformation to the Death of Luther,	250
,,	33. From Luther to the Accession of Queen Elizabeth,	254
,,	34. From Queen Elizabeth to the Accession of James I.,	255
,,	35. From James I. to the Accession of Charles I.,	259
,,	36. From Charles I. to the Peace of Westphalia,	261

CHAP. VIII.—FROM THE PEACE OF WESTPHALIA TO THE FRENCH REVOLUTION.—A.D. 1648-1789.

Sect. 37. From the Peace of Westphalia to the English Revolution,   264
,, 38. From the English Revolution to the Peace of Utrecht,   269
,, 39. From the Peace of Utrecht to the Treaty of Aix-la-Chapelle,   272
,, 40. From the Peace of Aix-la-Chapelle to the American War of Independence,   276
,, 41. From the American War to the French Revolution,   280

CHAP. IX.—FROM THE FRENCH REVOLUTION TO THE PRESENT TIME.—A.D. 1789-1869.

,, 42. From the Meeting of the States-General to the Death of Louis XVI.,   284
,, 43. From Louis XVI. to the Election of the First Consul,   285
,, 44. From the First Consul to the Battle of Austerlitz,   288
,, 45. From the Battle of Austerlitz to the Burning of Moscow,   290
,, 46. From the Burning of Moscow to the Battle of Waterloo,   293
,, 47. From the Battle of Waterloo to the Accession of George IV.,   295
,, 48. From the Accession of George IV. to William IV.,   297
,, 49. From William IV. to the Accession of Queen Victoria,   301
,, 50. From the Accession of Queen Victoria to the Repeal of the Corn-Laws,   304
,, 51. From the Repeal of the Corn-Laws to the Accession of Louis Napoleon as Emperor of the French,   307
,, 52. From the Accession of Louis Napoleon to the American Secession,   310
,, 53. From the American Secession to the Present Time,   313

INDEX,   319

FACTS AND DATES.

DIVISION I.—SCIENTIFIC FACTS.

CHAP. I.—FACTS IN ASTRONOMY.

WITHIN the last seven years all our previous conceptions regarding the distance of the sun from the earth and the other members of the solar system have been seriously modified. It appears that we can no longer accept of 95,293,000 miles as the true mean distance of our planet from the solar luminary, but something between 91,430,000 and 92,380,000 miles. The best way of determining the sun's distance is by means of the transits of Venus across the sun's disc. These occur very seldom, and at curiously regulated intervals. The first predicted transit took place in 1631, but astronomers failed to observe it; the next happened in 1639, and was witnessed by many scientific observers; the third in 1761; the fourth in 1769; the fifth will occur in 1874, but will be unfavourable for observation; and the sixth in 1882, which will be rather favourable. These intervals, it will be observed, form a series, the terms of which, in years, are 8, 122, 8, 105, 8, 122, 8, &c. The last available transit took place in 1769, exactly one hundred years ago, while the next fully available one will not occur till 1882. It was from the transit of 1769 that astronomers determined the sun's mean distance from the earth to be 95,293,000 miles; and by one of Kepler's "Laws" the distances of all the other planets were thence easily calculated. Very recently, however, it has been shown that serious errors entered into the computations based on that transit—errors, indeed, that have vitiated all the results, and which cannot be corrected by this method till the year 1882. But on a matter so deeply interesting in itself, and so vitally important to humanity, it could not be supposed that the world would willingly remain in suspense for thirteen long years. In the words of the able Astronomer-Royal for Scotland, in his recently-published 'Antiquity of Intellectual Man' (Edinburgh, 1868), "Of all material elements for supporting life on the earth, none are so dominant as those depending on the light and heat of the sun, and of all problems in natural science none is so important as the true distance of the sun. Upon that depends our knowledge of its weight and size, the weight, sizes, and distances of the planets, and even the masses, distances, and illuminating power of the fixed stars themselves. The sun's distance is therefore the great problem, and modern science has spared neither time nor expense in endeavouring to settle it. But the distance is so great, and our base-line for measuring it (the earth's breadth) so comparatively small, that modern science has found her telescopes, micrometers, divided circles, and mathematical methods all taxed beyond their powers in accurately determining *what* the distance is."

How strange that, in the latter half of the nineteenth century—an age so arrogant and boastful of scientific progress—any doubt should remain on a question of such paramount physical importance! To remove this stigma, therefore, from modern science, and to obtain, meanwhile, as near an approximation as possible of the sun's distance, astronomers have exerted themselves to the uttermost, pending their grand preparations for 1874 and 1882. Two principal classes of minor methods lay before them — one by the parallax of Mars in opposition, under the most favourable circumstances, in 1862, and the other by the perturbations of the planets or of the moon. Astronomers strenuously availed themselves of both. The several mean results, each from different observations, showed distances varying mostly between 2½ and 4 millions of miles less than had been theretofore received from the transit of Venus in 1769. So great and so uncertain a reduction of distance induced M. Powalky, in Germany, to perform the important service of making, from the original observations of that transit, an elaborate recomputation, in 1864, founded partly on the recently-determined and more correct longitudes of the places of the original observations. M. Powalky's new result, 92,254,000 miles, was approved in 1867 by Professor Simon Newcombe of the United States, and was confirmed in a general sense by M. Faye's researches on the same transit, and by results advocated by M. Delaunay from other sources. Since the above recomputation was published by M. Powalky and Professor Newcombe, Mr E. J. Stone, of the Royal Observatory, Greenwich, has followed, similarly favouring the scientific world with an independent recomputation from that transit, and more than confirming M. Powalky's diminution of the distance—Mr Stone's result being the yet shorter distance of 91,736,000 miles. Very evenly midway between these two results lies the probable truth, as will be further noticed (p. 8); and the scientific world looks forward with ever-deepening interest to the approaching renewal of that rare astronomical opportunity, as well as to possible improvements in M. Leon Foucault's independent experimental method, of more conclusively solving the great problem.

In connection with this subject we are glad at being able to lay before the student the following interesting facts, chiefly gleaned from a very elaborate but as yet unpublished paper by a man of rare genius, who is destined, no doubt, to leave his mark on the thinking of the age—we refer to William Petrie, Esq., a Civil Engineer, London, whose MS. has been obligingly lent us by Professor C. Piazzi Smyth, himself an indefatigable explorer in the same field, and whose chief work, entitled 'Life and Work at the Great Pyramid,' constitutes an era in modern Egyptology. The paper referred to gives an epitome of the numerous though unsuccessful efforts of human reason to recover, by its own unaided efforts, that fundamental *datum* which the Creator revealed to man in the earliest age of human history—the distance of the earth from the centre of the solar system. Herodotus, "the father of history," who flourished B.C. 500, and consequently near the commencement of the intellectual life of Greece, narrates the first recorded attempts or impressions in this direction. These were made not long before his own day, and were believed in both by himself and his contemporaries, though they placed the sun within the limits of the winds on the surface of the earth, and at a distance therefrom of some eight to ten miles! Anaxagoras, the Ionian, who flourished fifty years later, estimated the sun's absolute size as equal to that of the Peloponnesus. Hence, with the sun's known angular diameter, his distance should be about 18,000 miles. Aristarchus, the astronomer of Samos, who died B.C. 280, made an immense advance in the right direction. Employing a true though rather rough method of observation —viz., the moon's dichotomy—he at once increased the received sun's distance to 5,300,000 miles. With this result the world seems to have been satisfied for four centuries, for we find Claudius Ptolemy, the celebrated astronomer of Alexandria, re-observing and substantially adopting it in A.D. 140. It is unnecessary to follow the blind gropings after truth that characterised the thirteen subsequent centuries, when the human intellect enjoyed its profound and lengthened repose, giving few other proofs of its vitality than the subtle but frivolous sophistries of the schoolmen. After a sleep of more than a millennium, the European mind, like a giant refreshed with wine, was suddenly roused to unprecedented energy. Several grand events marked the period of its awakening — the invention of printing in 1440; the revived study of the ancient classical languages; and the discovery of a new world in 1492. In the beginning of the sixteenth century, Martin Luther began the Reformation in Germany; while, early in the seventeenth, science could boast of such intellectual heroes as Galileo, Kepler, and Tycho Brahe. In 1620 Kepler estimated the sun's distance from the earth at 26,400,000 miles, and at the same time announced the great "law" regulating the distances of all the other planets. This result startled men, on account of the increased size which it gave to the planetary spaces.

Mankind felt a difficulty in expanding their ideas to receive the truth of the vastness of nature that was beginning to open before them. But science was now pursued on correct mathematical principles; and in 1750 the French astronomer, De la Caille, taking Mars in opposition as his subject of observation, and the terrestrial distance between Paris and the Cape of Good Hope as his base-line, more than trebled the distance announced by Kepler, and gave the world the first tolerable approximation to the truth by stating as his result 81,650,000 miles. The first astronomer that calculated the sun's distance from a transit of Venus, and from observations taken from nearly opposite sides of the earth, was the celebrated Delambre. Publishing his observations in 1789, he confidently announced the vastly greater quantity of 96,100,000 miles as the sun's true distance; and for a whole generation his finding was adopted by the scientific world. About the year 1820, Encke, Bessel, and other German astronomers, using refined mathematical processes, corrected Delambre's estimate, and brought it down to 95,293,000 miles; and nearly every astronomer now living accepted this finding, till within the last few years. We must observe, however, that in 1832 Professor Henderson, the first Astronomer-Royal for Scotland, and some time her Majesty's Astronomer at the Cape of Good Hope, from his own observations when there, announced the greatly-reduced quantity of 90,537,000 miles; but could gain no hearing in a world completely given up to the belief that the transit-of-Venus observations, as computed by the great German and French mathematicians of the present century, must be correct. In this uncertainty the question of the sun's distance remained till 1862, when Mars was again in opposition. In that year, accordingly, it was abundantly observed in both the northern and southern hemispheres—Greenwich linking itself with the Cape of Good Hope, and St Petersburg with Australia. Strange to say, when these measurements were computed by the originator of this method (Winnecke, in Russia), they gave, from 26 independent sets of observations, a mean result of 91,184,000 miles, thus remarkably confirming the Scottish astronomer's result, as against the received distance; and thus more than a quarter of a century of progress was needed to aid astronomers in general before they suspected themselves of being in any such error, or would credit Henderson's long prior amendment as being nearer to the difficult truth. The fact, however, was in a great measure confirmed at Greenwich Observatory: 58 sets of observations there computed by E. J. Stone gave a mean result of 91,400,000 miles; afterwards about 100 by Newcombe, in the United States, gave 92,306,000; and some by Hall, United States, 92,442,000 miles. In 1862, M. Foucault, a most ingenious French investigator, made a series of interesting experiments on the velocity of light, and from these, through the agency of the eclipses of Jupiter's satellites, and their difference of time as seen from opposite sides of the earth's orbit, he was enabled to announce the sun's true distance as 92,254,000 miles. We have already mentioned M. Powalky's elaborate recomputation of the calculations connected with the last transit of Venus, and we refer to it here only because we have come up to it in the order of time, and also because we are satisfied of the comparative accuracy of his result. That result, republished in 1867 by Professor Newcombe, amounted, it will be remembered, to 92,254,000 miles, being identical in round numbers with the result obtained by Foucault from data of a wholly different kind, and not very different from that obtained by S. Newcombe from the observations of Mars. Newcombe combined these three recent results, and some from minor methods—in fact, all results that he regarded as available; whence he deduced a grand mean of 92,380,000 miles as the probable truth. But, from other observations and computations, mostly by similar methods, the mean, as adopted at the Greenwich and Paris Observatories since 1864, has been 91,430,000 miles. The advocates of these two grand means group themselves into two sets, suggestive of some bias of party feeling on both sides—a suspicion not without support from the literature of this great discussion. A careful attempt, made by W. Petrie, in 1869, to assign impartially the relative weight due to each of the many mean results composing these two grand means of the rival parties, gives a final grand mean of 92,061,000 miles; but he attaches to this result the probable though insignificant error (not by any arbitrary guesswork, but computed by the recognised laws of probability) of *plus* or *minus* 90,000 miles, or only about $\frac{1}{1000}$ part of the whole quantity. That is to say, the truth is proved to lie probably between 91,970,000 and 92,150,000—unlikely to be much beyond these limits either way, and most likely to be nearly midway between them; and we cannot expect, by purely scientific methods, to attain to a greatly higher degree of accuracy.

But these facts, however interesting, by no means exhaust the subject. The mechanical school of Egyptologists to whom we have referred—the late John Taylor of London, Professor C. Piazzi Smyth of Edinburgh, Mr Petrie, Civil Engineer, London, Mr St John Vincent Day, C.E., Glasgow, with a daily-increasing number of other truth-loving investigators—have within the last five years originated an entirely new branch of the science. From C. Piazzi Smyth's lengthened personal inspection of the most ancient monuments of Egypt, his innumerable and most elaborate measurements of that one amongst them which is confessedly the most ancient, and from enlightened reflection on the results so obtained, they adduce the most satisfactory evidence that, in the earliest postdiluvian age, those of our race who had not degraded themselves with the loathsome idolatries of the nations, and who reverently cherished the primeval revelation vouchsafed by the Creator to our species, were, *by some means or other*, most certainly in possession of that grand secret which, for the last two thousand years, science has in vain been endeavouring to discover for herself, and relying on her own unaided resources.

The most ancient architectural monument now existing on the earth's surface—the Great Pyramid at Jeezeh—demonstrated by astronomy to have been erected B.C. 2170 (or close on 4040 years ago), has now been investigated and explored as no other monument, ancient or modern, ever was; and the indefatigable explorers have been rewarded with an abundant harvest of the most brilliant discoveries. One of these, discovered by Mr Petrie, is the clear indication that the architect of this pyramid knew the mean distance of the sun from the earth with an exactitude to which modern science never approached till within the last seven years. This distance he symbolises as $=$ height $\times 10^9$. The best lineal and angular measurements—

namely, those of M. Jomard, of Col. Howard Vyse, and recently, of Professor C. Piazzi Smyth—have been combined by W. Petrie, who shows therefrom that the original height of the great pyramid, from the pavement at its base, was 486.25 British feet: this multiplied, as above said, by the ninth power of ten— *i.e.*, 1,000,000,000, gives a result of 486,250,000,000 feet, or 92,093,000 *British miles, for the mean distance of the sun.* We have seen that the latest collective result of science reckons the probable truth to be between 91,970,000 and 92,150,000; while the Great Pyramid gives 92,093,000 miles, being completely within these minimum uncertainties of science. Moreover, in a paper to the Royal Society of Edinburgh, 1869, he has well shown that this uncommonly complete numerical coincidence is not merely fortuitous, because, striking as is the coincidence itself, it constitutes but a small part of the evidence discovered, that this was *intended* in the original design of the structure. According, then, to the best historical and monumental evidence, this is the exact mean distance of the sun from our planet. Only a few years ago, there was not an astronomer in Europe who would not have instantly rejected this result, as more than three millions of miles away from the truth; but now—such has been the progress of astronomy within the last decade of years—there is not, perhaps, one among the whole number who would risk his reputation by denying its possible correctness. The brief sketch of the progress of astronomy here given—even were there no other reasons for asserting its absolute exactness—clearly points to such a conclusion; for from the days of De la Caille downwards, all the results of modern science, like the vibrations of a pendulum coming to rest, approach closer and closer to one fixed point; and, strange to say, that fixed point is precisely the number indicated by the Great Pyramid, and therefore, we believe, *revealed* to man ages and generations before science had any existence.

FACTS IN ASTRONOMY. 9

SECT. I.—Mean Distances of the Planets from the Sun.
(In millions of miles.)

13. Vulcan's probable distance.
    a *burning heat.*
36. Mercury: actual distance, 35,649,000.
    glowing Mercury.
67. Venus: actual distance, 66,614,000.
    the *nearest planet.*
92. Distance of the earth, as indicated by the Great Pyramid of Jeezeh: actual distance, 92,093,000.
    the world's *true distance.**
140. Mars: actual distance, 140,322,000.
    the *celebrated Kepler wrought* at it.†
259. The minor planets, 100 in number (*average*).
    they *fill* a *large void.*
479. Jupiter: true distance, 479,141,000.
    satellites appear in his *train.*
878. Saturn: true distance, 878,461,000.
    the *rings* of this *planet* are *remarkable.*
1766. Uranus: true distance, 1,766,565,000.
    a *curious planet* with a *multitude* of *moons.*
2766. Neptune: true distance, 2,766,133,000.
    the *finest proof* of *modern mathematics.*
240. Moon's distance from the earth in thousands of miles.
    distance of our *satellite* from the *world.*

SECT. 2.—Time of the Planets' Revolution.
(In days.)

19. Time of Vulcan's revolution.
    the years are *brief* on *Vulcan.*
87. Time of Mercury's revolution.
    the *revolution* of *Apollo.*

---

* Or, seeing that the ancients gave to the pyramids of Egypt the first place among "the seven wonders of the world," we can express the sun's distance still more exactly thus: *true distance* of the *world*, by the *true height* of the *world's worthiest wonder.*

† Kepler spent twenty years of unremitting study in determining the true orbit of this planet, and in deducing from it his three famous "laws."

224. Time of Venus' revolution.
  the *first descried star* (of eve).

365. Time of the earth's revolution.
  the world's *great annual ellipse.*

686. Time of Mar's revolution.
  the *moonless orb* of *Mars.*

1684. Time of the planetoids' revolution.
  they *career* between *Mar's orbit* and *Jupiter's.*

4333. Time of Jupiter's revolution.
  Jupiter, the *greatest globe* in our *heavens.*

10,759. Time of Saturn's revolution.
  the *central exterior planet,* with his *luminous train.*

30,686. Time of Uranus or Herschel's revolution.
  Herschel wanted to *name* it after the *reigning monarch.*

60,126. Time of Neptune's revolution.
  the *naked eye cannot discern Neptune.*

29½. The moon's period of revolution round the earth.
  a wave of waters *follows* her *everywhere.*

SECT. 3.—Distances of the Comets from the Sun.

(In miles—supply 000.)

538. Perihelion or nearest distance of the comet of 1843 (the smallest known perihelion).
  it *almost grazed* the *sun.*

(Supply 000,000.)

384. Perihelion distance of the comet of 1729 (greatest known perihelion).
  it *grazed* the *orbit* of *Jupiter.*

387. Aphelion distance of Encke's comet (smallest known aphelion).
  goes beyond the *region* of the *planetoids.*

40,121. Aphelion distance of the great comet of 1811.
  shone for a *year,* a *bright* and *flaming comet.*

406,130. Aphelion distance of the comet of 1844 (greatest aphelion known).
  our *system's extremest member counts ages* in his *year.*

FACTS IN ASTRONOMY. 11

SECT. 4.—Time of Revolution of the Comets.

Days.
- **1,210.** Encke's comet (*shortest period known* = 3¼ years).
  this *comet finds* an *obstacle* in his *way*.
- **2,042.** Brörsen's comet (= 5.58 years).
  a *Dane, expert* in *astronomy, discovered* it.
- **2,413.** Biela's comet (= 6.61 years).
  the *disrupted sections* of *Biela gleam*.
- **2,718.** Faye's comet, the least eccentric (= 7.44 years).
  Faye performs the (least) *eccentric orbit*.
- **28,105.** Halley's celebrated comet (= 76.78 years).
  days required to *complete* the *year of Halley*.

Years.
- **2,500.** Donati's comet of 1785.
  Donati's luminous comet, in *years*.
- **3,000.** The great comet of 1811.
  gloriously wends his *way* through the *welkin*.
- **15,864.** Newton's celebrated comet of 1680.
  this *comet long remained* a *marvel to astronomers*.
- **75,000.** The first comet of 1780.
  a *period lasting* a *thousand human lives*.
- **102,050.** The second comet of 1844.
  consider the *extraordinary duration* of *yonder luminary's year*.
- **123,683.** The comet of 1744 (the *longest period known*).
  a *comet demanding* a *hundred millenniums* to *reach* his *goal*.

SECT. 5.—Number of the Fixed Stars.

- **21.** Number of stars of the first magnitude.
  their *distance* is *calculable*.
- **65.** Number of stars of the second magnitude.
  worlds of *inferior luminosity*.
- **190.** Number of stars of the third magnitude.
  a *curious tripling observable*.

FACTS AND DATES.

426. Number of stars of the fourth magnitude.
stars of the *fourth magnitude.*

1,100. Number of stars of the fifth magnitude.
we are *able* to *count yonder worlds.*

3,200. Number of stars of the sixth magnitude.
how distant are *yonder worlds !*

3,206. Stars visible to the naked eye at Berlin.
the *greatest display* of *worlds* in *Prussia.*

4,146. Stars visible to the naked eye at Paris.
stars that *can* be *seen* at *Paris.*

4,638. Stars visible to the naked eye at Alexandria.
see the *nightly galaxy* at *Alexandria.*

5,000. Total number of stars visible at the equator.
the *largest worlds* in the *whole welkin.*

13,000. Number of stars of seventh magnitude (visible only through the telescope).
the *celebrated Galileo first saw* these *worlds.*

40,000. Number of stars of the eighth magnitude.
starry worlds belonging to *class eight.*

142,000. Number of stars of the ninth magnitude.
countless stars dimly shine in *class ninth.*

500,000 (million). Total number of stars visible through the best telescopes).
O *Lord, wondrous* are thy *works,* in *wisdom* thou *madest* them *all !*

SECT. 6.—Distance of the Fixed Stars.

(In billions of miles.)

21. Distance of *Alpha Centauri*, the nearest star known.
distance of *a Centauri.*

56. Distance of 61 *Cygni* (the first measured star).
the *illustrious* (Bessel) *measured* it.

75. Distance of *Vega* (Alpha Lyræ).
welcome a *parallax* for the *lyre !*

85. Distance of *Sirius*, our brightest star.
what a *resplendent luminary !*

147. Distance of *Iota* in Ursa Major (the Plough).
        (Peters) *obtained* this *star's parallax.*
154. Distance of *Arcturus* (α Boötes).
        Boötes' largest star.
292. Distance of *Polaris* (the Pole star) in Ursa Minor.
        directly vertical in *Greenland.*
426. Distance of *Capella.*
        the *extremest star* whose *distance* is *measured.*
33,908. Supposed distance of stars of 16th magnitude.
        ages ago they *transmitted* these *waning rays.*

SECT. 7.—Proper Motion of the Stars.

(In miles per second.)

5. Our sun's motion through space.
        he wends his way round *Alcyonè.*
13. Rate of motion of the nearest star (α Centauri).
        the wandering *bull hunter.*
14. Sirius' rate of motion.
        our *brightest star.*
30. Capella's rate of motion.
        the wandering *goat* of the *waggoner.*
41. Rate of motion of 61 Cygni.
        the wandering *star* of *Cygnus.*
54. Rate of motion of Arcturus (α Boötes).
        the *largest star* (in Boötes.)

CHAP. II.—FACTS IN CHEMISTRY.

NONE of the physical sciences has made greater progress in the last twenty years than Chemistry. To such an extent has this been the case, that the standard works of the past generation have now become almost obsolete. New views have arisen as to the constitution and chemical properties of matter; a reformed chemical notation has thence of necessity ensued; the nomenclature of the science has been simplified and greatly improved; the combining proportions of the elementary substances has been ascertained with far greater precision; and numerous fundamental laws have been discovered. As we are not here writing a treatise on chemistry, we are precluded from entering at large on any of these subjects; but the following particulars, gleaned from a multitude, may not be deemed wholly out of place.

1. The number of simple or elementary substances out of which the whole earth, as well as the other members of the solar system, has been built up, has been raised from 54 to 65. These are divided into two primary groups—viz., METALS, of which there are 52 (the principal of them being gold, silver, platinum, copper, iron, lead, zinc, tin, mercury); and Non-Metals or METALLOIDS, of which there are 13—viz., oxygen, hydrogen, nitrogen, chlorine, carbon, sulphur, phosphorus, iodine, fluorine, bromine, boron, silicon, and selenium.

2. On each of these 65 substances the Creator has stamped, in deep and indelible characters, *a particular and invariable number*, which forms, as it were, the law of its being, and determines in what proportions it shall unite with every other substance, whether simple or compound. Thus 1 is stamped on hydrogen, 12 on carbon, 16 on oxygen, 56 on iron, &c. In the event, therefore, of iron uniting with oxygen, the two substances, as to weight, will be always found in the ratio of 56 and 16. Under the operation of this mysterious principle, the *identity of species* in the mineral world is rigidly preserved, and, notwithstanding the prodigious number of mineral substances, all confusion is avoided.

3. All chemical compounds are definite in their nature, the ratio of the elements being constant. Many substances, however, are capable of uniting with others in several proportions; but, when this is the case, it is invariably found that these proportions bear a very simple ratio to each other. Further, if a body A unites with several other bodies B C D, then the quantities of B C D which respectively unite with A represent also the proportions in which they shall unite among each other. From

this it follows that the combining quantity of a compound is the sum of the combining quantities of its components.

4. Such being the important part which these invisible numbers play, it is obvious that it is of the utmost consequence to chemistry that they be determined with the greatest accuracy. And here the revolution that has taken place in modern chemistry is more easily perceived than anywhere else, for it will be found that during the last twenty years no fewer than 32 of the elementary substances—or precisely one-half of the whole number—have had their atomic weights exactly doubled, while not a few more have been materially modified. The student will find in the table at the end of this Introduction the latest determinations of the combining powers of all the elementary substances, together with their most recently established specific gravities.

5. In regard to changes in the nomenclature of the science, we can here only remark that the smallest quantity of any substance which has the power of uniting with one or more particles of the same or any other substance is called an *atom*. It is now believed that such an atom cannot exist in its separate or isolated state, but must either be linked together with another atom of the same kind, or united with an atom of a different kind of matter. Single atoms, it is maintained, are nowhere found in nature, however low we penetrate into the organic or inorganic world, but invariably atoms in a dual form. Such dual atom is named a *molecule*, and is the smallest quantity of matter that can exist in a separate form.

6. But by far the greatest discovery adorning the annals of modern chemistry remains to be specified. The 65 elementary substances divide themselves, in respect to their combining power, into four great natural groups—named, respectively, Monads, Dyads, Triads, and Tetrads. The MONADS are twelve in number — viz., seven Metals (silver, sodium, potassium, cæsium, lithium, rubidium, thallium), and five Metalloids (hydrogen, chlorine, fluorine, iodine, bromine). Their distinguishing characteristic is, that one atom of any one of them can unite with, or replace, *one* atom of any other, and no more. For example, one atom of hydrogen can combine with one atom

of chlorine, and form hydrochloric acid ; or the atom of hydrogen in the acid may be replaced by one atom of any other monad, as sodium, which, setting free the atom of hydrogen, unites with the atom of chlorine, and forms chloride of sodium (common salt). The DYADS are twenty-five in number, only three of them being non-metallic (oxygen, sulphur, selenium); while twenty-two are metals, the best known of which are—iron, lead, mercury, nickel, zinc, calcium, cobalt, and copper. In regard to combining power, each of this class is equivalent to *two* of the former. For example, an atom of oxygen will readily combine with two atoms of hydrogen, and form water; but it refuses to unite with one atom of hydrogen. Oxygen is, therefore, termed a Dyad, having twice the combining power of hydrogen. In like manner, a TRIAD is an elementary substance which, when it enters into combination, requires *three* Monads to neutralise it, or one Monad and a Dyad. For example, one atom of the chloride of bismuth contains three atoms of chlorine, that element being a Monad, and one atom of the metal, which is a Triad. Should the three atoms of chlorine be set free, and the one atom of bismuth be allowed to unite with any other monad, it would require three atoms of such monad to saturate it. The Triads are only nine in number—viz., six Metals (aluminum, antimony, arsenic, bismuth, gold, rhodium), and three Metalloids (boron, nitrogen, phosphorus). Finally, the TETRADS are substances which have the property of uniting with or replacing *four* combining weights of the class termed Monads, two Dyads, or one Tryad and one Monad. For instance, carbon, which is a Tetrad, has the property of uniting with hydrogen, which is a Monad, in the ratio of 1 to 4, thus forming carburetted hydrogen or marsh gas. There are eight Tetrads—viz., two Metalloids (carbon, silicon) and six Metals, only two of which are common—viz., tin and platinum. The remaining eleven elements still remain undetermined.

7. Closely allied to the preceding is the kindred and equally remarkable laws regulating the combining *volumes* of the elements when reduced to or already existing in the gaseous state. (1.) If we take that number of grains of any two gases which is denoted by their respective atomic weights, we do not find them

occupying an amount of space corresponding to their weight, but precisely *equal spaces*, provided the temperature and pressure are the same: thus, 1 grain of hydrogen gas will occupy the same amount of space as $35\frac{1}{2}$ grains of chlorine gas. (2.) Still more remarkable is the next law: if both the combining gases belong to the class of Monads, then the two equal spaces which the gases occupied when separate are precisely equal to the space they occupy after union; but should one of the gases belong to the class of Monads and the other to that of Dyads— as hydrogen and oxygen, the two constituents of water—union cannot take place until two volumes of the former be brought into contact with one of the latter; and the remarkable thing is, that three spaces or volumes are not occupied by the united gas, as we might have expected, but two volumes only. The same law holds good in regard to the other two classes above referred to. In order to form gaseous ammonia, for example, one volume of nitrogen, which is a Triad, requires three volumes of the Monad hydrogen, and the result is, not *four* volumes of ammonia, but *two*. For a fuller illustration of the several topics here briefly discussed, we must refer the student to Roscoe's 'Lessons in Elementary Chemistry,' Macmillan & Co., 1868; Hofmann's 'Introduction to Modern Chemistry,' Walton & Maberly, 1866; and especially to the eloquent and admirable 'Inorganic Chemistry,' by the late Dr G. Wilson, Professor of Technology in the University of Edinburgh, revised and enlarged by Dr Stevenson Macadam, Edinburgh— W. and R. Chambers, 1866.

SECT. 8.—Number of Elementary Substances.

65. Number of elementary substances.
    existing *number* of *elements*.
52. Number of simple metallic substances.
    their *lustre distinguishes* them.
13. Number of metalloids, or non-metallic substances.
    oxygen, *carbon, hydrogen*, &c.

Table of Elementary Substances.

Names of Elements.	Atomic weight, hydrogen=1.	Specific gravity, water=1.	Names of Elements.	Atomic weight, hydrogen=1.	Specific gravity, water=1.
Aluminum,	27.5	2.56	Molybdenum,	96.	8.62
Antimony,	122.	6.71	Nickel,	59.	8.82
Arsenic,	75.	5.96	Niobium,	97.5	...
Barium,	137.	...	Nitrogen, gas,	14.	0.972
Beryllium or Glucinum,	14.	...	Norium,	...	...
			Osmium,	192.2	21.4
Bismuth,	210.	9.8	Oxygen, gas,	16.	1.103
Boron,	11.	2.68	Palladium,	106.5	11.8
Bromine, liq.,	80.	2.96	Phosphorus,	31.	1.77
Cadmium,	112.	8.69	Platinum,	197.5	21.53
Cæsium,	133.	...	Potassium,	39.	0.86
Calcium,	40.	1.57	Rhodium,	104.4	12.1
Carbon,	12.	3.4	Rubidium,	85.4	1.52
Cerium,	92.	...	Ruthenium,	104.4	11.4
Chlorine, gas,	35.5	2.47	Selenium,	79.5	...
Chromium,	52.5	5.9	Silicon,	28.5	2.49
Cobalt,	59.	8.95	Silver,	108.	10.53
Copper,	63.5	8.95	Sodium,	23.	0.97
Didymium,	96.	...	Strontium,	87.5	2.54
Erbium,	...	...	Sulphur,	32.	2.
Fluorine,	19.	...	Tantalum,	137.5	...
Gold,	197.	19.3	Telurium,	129.	6.25
Hydrogen, gas,	1.	0.069	Terbium,	...	...
Indium,	71.8	...	Thallium,	204.	11.91
Iodine,	127.	4.95	Thorinm,	231.5	...
Iridium,	198.	21.15	Tin,	118.	7.29
Iron,	56.	7.84	Titanium,	50.	...
Lanthanum,	92.8	...	Tungsten,	184.	17.6
Lead,	207.	11.36	Uranium,	120.	18.4
Lithium,	7.	0.59	Vanadium,	137.	...
Magnesium,	24.	1.74	Yttrium,	68.	...
Manganese,	55.	8.01	Zinc,	65.	7.14
Mercury, liq.,	200.	13.59	Zirconium,	90.	...

SECT. 9.—Table of Chemical Equivalents.

($Hydrogen = 1.$)

122. Antimony.
   brittle, with *fine fracture*.
75. Arsenic.
   extremely *prejudicial* to *life*.
210. Bismuth.
   dense, brittle, and *white*.
11. Boron.
   exists in *common borax*.
80. Bromine.
   (mineral) waters *rarely want* it.
40. Calcium.
   exceedingly *useful* when *oxidised*.
12. Carbon.
   charcoal and *diamonds*.
35·5. Chlorine.
   a yellowish *green element*.
64. Copper.
   malachite from *Australia*.
19. Fluorine.
   exists in the *bones* and *teeth*.
197. Gold and platinum.
   common in *Victoria* and *Peru*.
1. Hydrogen.
   exceedingly *buoyant*.
127. Iodine.
   in *colour* and *odour peculiar*.
198. Iridium.
   common in the *valleys* of the *Urals*.
56. Iron.
   largely manufactured.
207. Lead.
   formed into *water pipes*.
24. Magnesium.
   (burns) with *dazzling splendour*.

200. Mercury.
: *freezes* in *winter* at *Yakutsk*.

59. Nickel and cobalt.
: wonderfully *like* each *other*.

14. Nitrogen.
: a *component* of *strychnine*.

16. Oxygen.
: the *breath* of *animals*.

31. Phosphorus.
: exists in *guano* and *bones*.

39. Potassium.
: exists in *granite* and *trap*.

28. Silicon.
: its oxide *forms* the *rocks*.

108. Silver.
: *Copiapo yields* the *richest*.

23. Sodium.
: water is *denser* and *heavier*.

32. Sulphur.
: *Gomorrah destroyed* by it.

118. Tin.
: common *Cornish ore*.

65. Zinc.
: the *main alloy* (in brass).

SECT. 10.—Specific Gravity of Elementary Substances, Water being unity.

21. Platinum, osmium, and iridium, specific gravity of.
: the *densest bodies*.

19. Specific gravity of gold.
: wrought into *costly trinkets*.

14. Mercury.
: warns us of *coming storms*.

11. Silver and lead.
: of a whitish *beautiful colour*.

10. Bismuth.
: *Bohemia yields* it.

9. Copper.
    wrought of yore into war *utensils*.
8. Iron, nickel, cobalt, and manganese.
    oxidise by exposure to *air*.
7. Tin and antimony.
    wrought into *pewter*.
7. Zinc.
    extensively wrought into *pipes*.
6. Arsenic.
    extinguishes *animal* (life).
3. Bromine, chlorine, boron, carbon, and silicon.
    in weight they exceed *glucinum*.
2. Magnesium, sulphur, and phosphorus.
    exceed water in *density*.
1—. Sodium, potassium, and lithium.
    in weight they yield to *ice*.
5·7. Specific gravity of the earth as a whole.
    the weightiest of *all* the *planets* (except Mercury).

SECT. 11.—Freezing-point of Liquids.

(*Fahrenheit's thermometer.*)

— 220°. Greatest artificial cold hitherto produced.
    the *famous frigorific experiment*.
— 56°. Greatest natural cold hitherto observed.
    at Yakutsk, on the *Lena*, is the *maximum*.
— 39°. Mercury freezes.
    (alcohol) *gauges* this *temperature*.
— 25°. Vitriol or sulphuric acid.
    an exceedingly *dense liquid*.
— 7°. Freezing-point of brandy.
    the wonders of the (frigid) *zone*.
0°. The zero of Fahrenheit's thermometer.
    warmer than the winter at *Yakutsk*.
14°. Turpentine freezes.
    it *becomes solid*.
30°. Milk freezes.
    how white it is !

32°. Water freezes.
: *hoar frost.*

36°. Olive-oil freezes.
: the *girls murmur.*

39°·2. Water at maximum density.
: water's *heaviest temperature.*

46°·46. Average mean temperature of Scotland for the ten years 1856-65, ascertained from 55 separate localities by the Scot. Meteorol. Society.
: *Scotland's mean* (temperature).

62°. Zero temperature of British linear measures.
: an *inconvenient degree.*

68°. Mean temperature of the earth's habitable surface.
: the yearly *mean* of the *earth.*

90°. Tallow melts.
: the waste of *tallow* is *excessive.*

154°. Wax melts.
: a wax *candle illuminates sparingly.*

226°. Sulphur melts.
: *friction fires* a *match.*

SECT. 12.—Boiling-point of Liquids.

72°. Boiling-point of water *in vacuo.*
: water from *pressure freed.*

95°. Boiling-point of ether.
: an extremely *volatile liquid.*

140°. Liquids *in vacuo* boil 140° lower than under atmospheric pressure.
: they *boil soon* in an *exhausted* (receiver).

175°. Boiling-point of alcohol.
: the *boiling point* of *alcohol.*

212°. Ordinary boiling-point of water (barometer at 30 in.)
: a *fluid* to *cook* our *food.*

320°. Naphtha, turpentine, and sulphurous ether boil.
: great *danger* of *explosion.*

599°. Fish-oil and tallow.
: *oil* and *tallow* are *tardy.*

640°. Boiling-point of sulphuric acid.
      the *monohydrate* of *sulphuric acid*.

662°. Boiling-point of mercury.
      the *mercury now fumes*.

983°. Heat of incandescence.
      the *temperature* of *red heat*.

SECT. 13.—The Fusing-point of Metals.

— 39°. Fusing-point of mercury.
      (spirit) of wine *gauges* this *temperature*.

136°. Potassium.
      brittle, greyish, and *malleable*.

190°. Sodium.
      (below) the *boiling temperature* of *water*.

442°. Tin.
      so easily fused!

612°. Lead.
      malleable, bluish, and *dense*.

775°. Zinc.
      for water *pipes* it is *preferable* to *lead*.

1873°. Silver fuses.
      in *commerce regarded* as *preferable* to *gold*.

1996°. Copper.
      copper turns thin as *mercury*.

2016°. Gold.
      fine yellow coins are *made* of it.

2786°. Cast iron.
      the *founder pours* his *running metal*.

21,000°. Malleable iron.
      the *furious blast* of *Wedgewood's wind furnace*.

CHAP. III.—FACTS IN NATURAL PHILOSOPHY.

ONLY a very limited number of the facts in this most important branch of science can be recorded in the following sections. For the most part we must content ourselves with a comparison of the various velocities seen existing in nature. We give the velocity of sound travelling through the air as 1130 feet per second, but usually it is regarded as somewhat less. In 1822, the French Board of Longitude instituted experiments to determine the velocity of sound through atmospheric air. For this purpose two heights were selected near Paris, about 11½ miles apart, and a piece of ordnance planted on each. These were fired during the night, at regular intervals of 10 minutes, and the time that elapsed between the discharge at one station and the report at the other was exactly measured by chronometers, when it was found that the distance (20,355 yards) was traversed in 54.6 seconds, being at the rate of 1118 feet per second. During these experiments the temperature of the air was 16° Cent. or 60° Fahr.; but at 10° Cent. the velocity diminished to 1106 feet, and at zero to 1093 feet. By subsequent experiments it appears that the velocity is materially affected by the *kind* of gas through which the sound passes. Thus, at a uniform temperature of 32° Fahr. sound travels through carbonic acid gas at the rate of 856 feet per second; through oxygen gas at the rate of 1040 feet; atmospheric air, 1093 feet; and hydrogen gas, 4163 feet. These facts establish the general law, that *the velocity is in all cases inversely as the square root of the density of the gas.* The velocity is also said to be affected by the *loudness* of the sound, though this is not borne out by experiments continued for many years at the Edinburgh Royal Observatory, where the time-gun—which is fired electrically at the Castle, in all weathers, with reports sometimes loud and startling, and sometimes scarcely audible—shows a velocity always exceeding 1100 feet per second. When sound is made to traverse liquids or solids, the speed is much greater. Colladon and Sturm, in 1827, determined that sound passes through water (at 8°.1 Cent.) at the rate of 4708 feet per second, or four times greater than through the atmosphere; still more recently, experiments give for beams of wood about sixteen times greater; for solid granite, 1664 feet; for cast iron, 11,865; and for the metals generally, between four and sixteen times a greater speed than in air. The velocity of light was first determined by astronomical observation. In 1675, Römer, a Danish philosopher, by observing the eclipse of one of the satellites of Jupiter, calculated the velocity of light at 192,000 miles per second, inasmuch as it traversed the diameter of the earth's orbit, or 190,000,000 of miles, in 16 minutes 36 seconds. We have shown, however, in our preliminary observations on Astronomy, that the distance of the sun from the earth can no longer be regarded as 95,000,000 miles, but 92,000,000. This makes the velocity of light to be 186,000 miles per second. In 1849, M. Fizeau, a Frenchman, made an ingenious experiment to determine the velocity of light, and arrived at the conclusion that it travels at the rate of 196,000 miles per second, a rate not very different from that given by the Danish astronomer. Still later, however, another French philosopher—viz., M. Foucault, in 1862, made his celebrated experiments on the velocity of light by means of a rotating mirror, and announced 185,170 miles per second as the true rate (see p. 6). Still more divergent were the results obtained for the velocity of electricity, until Sir W. Thomson showed that there was a most important correction dependent on the *length of the wire*—the electric speed decreasing in an accelerated ratio with the distance it has to traverse. Thus, were it possible to observe the rate of passage through a wire only 1 foot long, it might exceed 1,000,000 miles per second. In the wire-coil of an experimental apparatus, Professor Wheatstone, upwards of thirty years ago, had found a velocity equal to 288,000 miles per second—or considerably above the highest estimate for the velocity of light. But when astronomers, soon after, began to use the long lines of the electric telegraph from city to city in order to measure the true longitudes of the latter, the practical velocities along the entire lengths were found vastly smaller. Thus, in the new Atlantic Telegraph Cable, 1866 miles long—the facilities for the motion of the electric fluid being unusually great—the time occupied in the passage is $\frac{1.3}{100}$ of a second; while in a still more recent experiment on land-wires, by Mr G. Davidson, an American astronomer, the average velocity has been found to be 10,000 miles per second.

SECT. 14.—Action of Gravity on Falling Bodies.

(Feet per second.)

16. Distance traversed by a body falling from a state of rest, in free space, the *first* second.
    accelerated motion.
32. Velocity at end of *first* second.
    our *globe's force* (of gravity).
48. Distance traversed the *second* second.
    watch the *stone returning.*
80. Distance traversed the *third* second.
    the wind *rarely exceeds* this.
112. Distance traversed the *fourth* second.
    with your watch *observe* a *bird falling.*
256. Total distance traversed in four seconds.
    what a *distance* in a *little moment!*

SECT. 15.—Various Velocities in Nature Compared.

(Feet per second.)

9. Minimum velocity of Newton's comet.
    weary with *travelling.*
32. Velocity of a falling body at end of first second.
    gravitation's force.
1130. Velocity of sound in atmospheric air.
    the *calm celerity* of *gaseous waves.*
1664. Velocity of sound transmitted through solid granite.
    the *commonest masses* a *medium* of *sound.*
1700. Average velocity of shot from modern artillery.
    cannon projectiles excel in *speed.*
4706. Velocity of sound in water.
    sound pervading a *watery medium.*
17,400. Velocity of sound transmitted through wood.
    beams propagate sound with *wondrous expedition.*

Miles.

3. Neptune's orbital motion.
    yonder he wearily *goes.*
18. The earth's orbital motion.
    the world's *course* is *rapid.*

Miles.
30. Mercury's orbital motion.
exultingly hastens on his way.
5. Proper motion of the sun and planets.
they wend their way around Alcyonè.
280. Maximum velocity of Newton's comet.
the fearful rapidity of a comet.

(*Supply* 000.)
10. Velocity of electricity in long land-wires, according to G. Davidson.
by continental wires.
14. Velocity of electricity transmitted through submerged wires.
when the cable is submerged.
185. Velocity of light, as determined by Foucault in 1862.
a bright ray of light.

CHAP. IV.—FACTS IN BOTANY.

LITTLE need be said regarding the interesting subject of the three following sections. Meagre as the facts are, the author found it a somewhat difficult task to collect them. Those in section 16 were mainly obtained from that admirable thesaurus of natural phenomena, Johnston's 'Physical Atlas.' Section 17 is largely indebted to the author's 'Manual of Modern Geography,' and to the elaborate Manuals of Botany by Professors Balfour and Henfrey. For the remaining countries of Europe no recent or reliable data could be found, and even for France and Germany the results can be given, as yet, in only round numbers. Section 18 is the result of much examination, but accurate statistics of the existing number of fossil plants are really not attainable.

SECT. 16.—The Flora of the Globe.
(*Supply* 000.)
1. Species of plants known to Pliny in A.D. 79.
exceeded by Aberdeenshire.

6. Species described by Linnæus in 1753.
   he widely extended the *number*.
20. Species estimated by Wildenow in 1807.
   described by *Wildenow*.
56. Species contained in the Jardin des Plantes in 1820.
   exotics in *large numbers*.
86. Species in the collection of M. Delessert, Paris, in 1847.
   a wondrous *rich muscum*.
93. Species estimated by Lindley in 1846, forming 9000 genera.
   (averaging) *ten* to a *genus*.
120. Number of species known in 1869.
   the *beautiful flora* of the *world*.
103. Known species of flowering plants.
   botanists widely agree on it.
17. Known species of cryptogamia.
   the world's *cryptogamic plants*.
200. Humboldt's estimate of the probable number of existing plants.
   the *flora* of the *whole world*.

SECT. 17.—The Flora of some European Countries.

4400. Species of plants in the British Isles.
   known species in our *own country*.
1600. Flowering plants in the British Isles.
   Balfour's Manual of *Botany exhibits* them.
2800. Cryptogamic plants in the British Isles.
   their *four orders* are *well defined*.
60. Number of ferns in the British Isles.
   many of them are *beautiful*.
300. Number of mosses in the British Isles.
   they *greatly exceed* the *ferns*.
3230. Species common to England and Scotland.
   the *graceful flora* of *Great Britain*.
7000. Estimated number of plants in France.
   its *plants excel* in *beauty* and *variety*.
3660. Number of flowering species in France.
   the *great majority* are *flowering plants*.

7000. Estimated number of plants in Germany.
Prussia comprises the *greater part.*

2700. Number of flowering plants in Germany.
its *flowering plants comparatively few.*

SECT. 18.—Geological or Fossil Botany.

527. Total number of fossil plants known in 1836.
these were *all* the *fossil plants.*

1792. Number known to Gœppert in 1845.
considerable progress in *ten years.*

1932. Number known to Henfrey in 1857.
the *brightest time* in *geological research.*

645. Fossil plants in British Isles in 1854 (Morris's Catal.)
the *number* of *species* in our own *land.*

122. Number of plants in the SILURIAN and DEVONIAN Systems (1867).
club-mosses, ferns, and *fucoids.*

1700. Fossil plants in the CARBONIFEROUS System of all countries (1867).
cryptogamic plants of the *coal measures.*

1100. Fossil plants in the Coal Measures of the British Isles (1867).
chiefly coniferæ, calamites, and *club-mosses.*

183. Number of plants in the PERMIAN System (1867).
collected in *Russia* and *Germany.*

72. Number of plants in the TRIASSIC System (1857).
equisetaceæ and *ferns.*

150. Number of plants in the LIAS (1857).
cycadeæ largely in *excess.*

180 Number of plants in the OOLITIC System (1857).
coniferous plants and *palms.*

128. Fossil Oolitic flora of British Isles (1864).
cycads, ferns, and *pines.*

70. Number of plants in the WEALDEN (1857).
the extinct *plants* of the *weald.*

182. Number of plants in the CRETACEOUS System (1857).
its *beds* are *rich* in *dicotyledons.*

977. Number in the TERTIARY System (Eocene, Miocene, and Pleiocene) in 1859.
tertiary petrified plants.
3639. Total species of fossil plants known to science, the *greater number* of *humble types.*

CHAP. V.—FACTS IN ZOOLOGY.

THE facts enumerated in sections 19, 20, and 21 have been obtained from a great variety of sources, though, as under the last chapter, the chief place must be assigned to the 'Physical Atlas.' The single page on Palæontology or Fossil Zoology, constituting section 22, is the result of considerable correspondence with eminent geologists, and of many months' hard reading. The young student of this fascinating science will accordingly find here, ready to his hand, information which in moderate compass he will probably find nowhere else. The statistics contained in the first half of this section may be wholly relied on, as they have been extracted from the latest edition of Murchison's 'Siluria,' the greatest work of the prince of living geologists. For all that related to the great Palæozoic series of rocks, the first place must always be assigned to this elaborate volume; but it formed no part of the author's plan to discuss the Secondary and Tertiary series. For these, no other work occupying a similar position is known to us, and we therefore experienced much greater difficulty in obtaining the statistics constituting the second half of our section. Having searched in vain for facts sufficiently recent in many other quarters, the author took the liberty of applying to his accomplished friend, Professor Ramsay, now at the head of the geological survey of England and Wales. A speedy answer was received, in the following laconic terms: "London, 15th February 1869.—MY DEAR SIR, I received your letter this morning, and would willingly comply with your request. But the information you require would take a man a year to tabulate, even if he knew all the books containing the scattered information it would be necessary to collect; and then it would be very incorrect, because of the number of fossils that go by different names in different lists. In the mean time I send some papers that may possibly be of a little use; but even these are very imperfect, and already partly out of date. — Believe me, yours very sincerely, AND. RAMSAY." The papers referred to are two lectures read before the Royal Geological Society in 1863 and 1864, and characterised by consummate ability. They discuss the deeply interesting question relative to the number of species common to the successive formations of the great Mesozoic or Secondary series of rocks, from the Permian system to the Tertiary. The facts derived from these masterly essays will be readily distinguished from those preceding them, as they refer only to the geology of the *British Isles*, and have, in each instance, the year 1864 appended to them. The *total number* of species, as given in the last line of our table, is obtained by adding together the fossil species of the various geological systems, some of them being the collected results from all countries, and the remainder those from the British Isles. Of course this gives no true idea of the real number of recorded fossil organisms, which must be greatly in excess of the 14,918 given in our table. This will readily appear when we consider that, in 1867, the fossil Silurian fauna of the British Isles alone amounted to 1186 species; whereas, according to Dr Bigsby's 'Thesaurus Siluricus,' a work of immense industry and research, the Silurian rocks of *all* countries exhibited, in the same year, an array of no fewer than 7553 species, or more than six times that number. Again, in 1864, the Triassic system, as developed in the British Isles, had yielded only 61 species; while on the Continent one single formation (the Muschelkalk) has yielded 222 species, and the St Cassian beds 744 more. We can form, then, a more correct estimate of the probable number of ascertained fossil species, by adding together the results derived from the Palæozoic rocks of all countries (9535 sp.) to about five times the number of Secondary species found in the British Isles alone (2447 sp.), which would give an approximation to the true number of Secondary species hitherto found in all countries: that is to say, we should add 12,235 Secondary species to 9535 Palæozoic species. This gives a result of 21,770 species for these two grand series of rocks. Nothing very definite can be said relative to the number of species derived from the last or Tertiary series of rocks. Upwards of 100 *genera* of mammals alone have been recorded, amounting probably to about 936 species. If we now take the mammalia as forming one-tenth of its entire fauna, we shall have 9360 species as belonging to the Tertiary series; and this number added to our former result gives a grand total of 31,130 species from the entire geological field.

SECT. 19.—Fauna of the Globe.

(Supply 000.)

250. Supposed number of existing species of animals, according to Agassiz.
 the *fauna* of the *land* and *water*.

20. Species of vertebrated animals.
 they exist in *four classes*.

2. Species of known mammals.
 warm-blooded and *four-footed*.

8. Species of known birds.
 they wend their way through the *air*.

2. Species of known reptiles.
 they exist in *four* (orders).

8. Species of known fishes.
 in the world of waters they *roam*.

20. Number of species of known molluscs.
 denizens of the *water*.

5. Number of articulated animals (not including insects).
 wily *lobsters*.

5. Number of radiated animals.
 eyes are *lacking* to them.

200. Estimated number of insects.
 dragon-flies, wasps, and *worker-bees*.

SECT.—20. Distribution of the Mammalia.

223. Number of European mammals.
 flesh-eaters and a *few gnawers*.

FACTS IN ZOOLOGY. 33

632. Number of Asiatic mammals.
    its *mammals* are *highly famed*.
446. Number of African mammals.
    the *known species* are *multiplying*.
260. Number of mammals in North America.
    our *finest mammals* are *wanting*.
518. Number of mammals in Central and South America.
    large carnivora are *rare*.
156. Number of mammals in Oceania.
    characterised by *legions* of *marsupials*.

SECT. 21.—Fauna of some European Countries.

11,000. Number of existing species in the British Isles.
    beasts and *birds existing* in our *own country*.
611. Number of vertebrated species in British Isles.
    number with a *back-bone*.
60. Number of mammals in British Isles, including bats.
    numerous (species) are *extinguished*.
274. Number of birds in British Isles.
    a *few* are *peculiar* to our *islands*.
14. Number of reptiles in British Isles.
    batrachians and *saurians*.
263. Number of fishes in British seas.
    fishes of the *United Kingdom*.
392. Number of molluscs in British waters.
    a *great variety* of (shell) *fish*.
10,000. Articulated animals (including insects) in the British Isles.
    bees, worms, butterflies, beetles, and *crabs*.
67. Mammals of Spain and Portugal.
    mammals in the *peninsula*.
78. Number of mammals in Germany.
    between the *Pregel* and the *Rhine*.
68. Number of mammals in Italy.
    mammals in *Italy*.
65. Number of mammals in Turkey and Greece.
    mainly in *Albania*.

SECT. 22.—Fossil Zoology: Number of Species of Fossil Animals in the different Geological Systems.

7553. Fossil species in the SILURIAN SYSTEM of all countries (1867).
the palæontologists' lengthened labours generalised.

1186. Silurian species in British Isles (1867).
consist chiefly of articulata and mollusca.

2735. Silurian species in Bohemia and Bavaria (1867).
fishes appear in the highest layers.

532. Fossil species in the DEVONIAN SYSTEM of all countries (1867).
land-plants and ganoid fishes.

1100. Fossil species in the CARBONIFEROUS SYSTEM of all countries (1867).
*the coal-measures abound in bony fishes.**

350. Fossil species in the PERMIAN SYSTEM of all countries (1867).
gigantic saurian reptiles.

976. Fossil species in the TRIASSIC SYSTEM of all countries (1864).
Telerpeton-Elginense and pouched mammals.

468. Fossil species in the LIAS of the British Isles (1864).
known by its ammonites and reptiles.

1464. Fossil species in the OOLITE of the B. Isles (1864).
its commonest species of mammals is the kangaroo.

237. Fossil species in the WEALDEN of the B. Isles (1864).
flying-reptiles, iguanodons, and placental (mammals).

1362. Fossil species in the CRETACEOUS SYSTEM of the British Isles (1864).
birds and a genus of monkeys are found in it.

936 Species (or 104 genera) of *mammals* in the TERTIARY SERIES (1868).
the true age of mammals.

14,918. Total fossil species in the whole geological series.
collected species from the Tertiary to the Cambrian rocks.

---

* While these sheets are passing through the press, we learn that Mr T. P. Barcas of Newcastle has detected in the Northumberland coal-measures the jaw of a true mammal ! The effect of this discovery, if confirmed, will be to carry back the mammalian life of the globe for countless ages.

CHAP. VI.—FACTS IN ETHNOGRAPHY.

THE facts enumerated in the four Sections of this chapter require no introduction, as they are derived almost exclusively from the author's former works—viz., the 'Manual of Modern Geography, Mathematical, Physical, and Political,' and 'Elements of Modern Geography,' 6th edition; W. Blackwood and Sons, Edinburgh and London; 1869.

SECT. 23.—Races of Mankind.
(Supply 000,000.)

1215. Population of the globe.
    the *children* of *Adam*, a *countless legion*.

500. Caucasian race.
    the *lords* of the *whole world*.

490. Mongolian race.
    their *skin* of a *tawny colour*.

100. Negro or Ethiopian race.
    black and *woolly haired*.

68. Malays, Papuans, and Maories.
    the *mixed races*.

16. American Indians.
    the *aborigines* of *America*.

SECT. 24.—Religions of Mankind.
(Supply 000,000.)

650. Probable number of heathens (Brahmins, Buddhists, &c.)
    mankind's larger half.

200. Number of Brahmins.
    the *idolatrous worship* of *Brahma*.

350. Number of Buddhists.
    a *gross* and *loathsome worship*.

36 FACTS AND DATES.

130. Number of Mohammedans.
        its *cradle* the *Hedjas* and *Yemen.*
5. Number of Jews.
        wandering exiles, under the *law.*
355. Christians of every name.
        our *God* is *Lord* over *all.*
155. Number of Roman Catholics.
        Christians of the *Latin Church.*
100. Number of Protestants.
        Christ is *worshipped exclusively.*
80. Greek Church.
        the *Russian Church.*

SECT. 25.—Races of Men in Europe.
(Supply 000,000.)

78. Celtic blood, pure and mixed.
        the westernmost *people* in *Europe.*
100. Teutonic blood, pure and mixed.
        civilisers of the *whole world.*
70. Sclavonic blood, pure and mixed.
        Poles and *Wends.*
28. Mongolians and Tartars.
        Finns and *Turks.*
2. Jews.
        the exiles of the *dispersion.*
1. Gipsies, &c.
        wandering *Bohemians.*
282. Total population of Europe.
        a *fine race* of *Caucasians.*

SECT. 26.—Religions in Europe.
(Supply 000,000.)

135. Roman Catholics.
        the *Catholics greatly predominate.*
67. Greek Church.
        as *numerous* as the *Protestants.*

65. Protestants.
> *most* of them *Lutherans.*

8. Mohammedans and Heathens.
> exist in *Roumelia.*

2. Jews.
> the exiles of the *dispersion.*

1. Gipsies, &c.
> wandering *Bohemians.*

CHAP. VII.—FACTS IN GEOGRAPHY.

This chapter—by far the longest in the scientific division of "Facts and Dates"—embraces no fewer than 24 Sections and upwards of 300 important facts connected with the physical geography of all the continents and countries of the world. These cannot fail to prove highly serviceable to the young student of this important and many-sided science: and, by the new method for aiding the memory here introduced, he can easily remember the whole. In every instance he will find the closest harmony between these sections and the corresponding pages of the 'Elements.' The last Section alone—that on the Progress of Geographical Discovery—has been drawn up from other sources, and chiefly from the elaborate history of 'Maritime Discovery,' by Rev. C. G. Nicolay, and contained in the 'Manual of Geographical Science, Mathematical, Physical, Historical, and Descriptive' (J. W. Parker, London, 1859).

SECT. 27.—Areas of the different Continents.

(*Supply* 000.)

Sq. miles.
51,500. Land-surface of the globe.
> *all* the *continents* and *islands* of the *wide world.*

3812. Area of Europe.
> its *greatest river* to the *Caspian flows.*

Sq. miles.
16,626. Asia.
  bigger than *America, North added* to *South.*
12,000. Africa.
  the *continent* of *Africa will yet* be *explored.*
 8335. North America.
  a *raised half* and a *grand level.*
 6634. South America.
  the *mighty Amazon* its *greatest stream.*
 4500. Oceania, including Australia.
  Sumatra lies at its *western extremity.*

SECT. 28.—Population of the Continents.
(Supply 000,000.)

1215. Population of the Globe.
  the *children* of *Adam* a *countless legion.*
 282. Europe.
  a *fine race* of *Caucasians.*
 711. Asia.
  the *people's birth-place* and *cradle.*
 130. Africa.
  Caffres and *Hottentots* at *war.*
  50. North America.
  extreme *liberty* in the *west.*
  22. South America.
  a wondrous *diversity* of *dialect.*
  21. Oceania.
  few aborigines.

SECT. 29.—Areas of European Countries.
(Supply 000.)

Sq. miles.
 122. The British Isles.
  British farming is *famous.*
  58. England.
  the *land* of *roses.*
  31. Scotland.
  her wilds are *heath clad.*

FACTS IN GEOGRAPHY.

Sq. miles.

- 33. **Ireland.**
  a green gem.
- 8600. **The British Empire.**
  the *richest empire* in the *whole world.*
- 35. **Portugal.**
  its *agriculture* is *languishing.*
- 177. **Spain.**
  a cold peninsular plateau.
- 214. **France.**
  a fine climate in the *south.*
- 11. **Belgium.**
  celebrated for its *cultivation.*
- 14. **The Netherlands.**
  beneath the *sea-level.*
- 14. **Denmark (*minus* Schelswig-Holstein).**
  the *capital* is on an *island.*
- 43. **Baden, Würtemberg, and Bavaria.**
  South-western Germany.
- 136. **Prussia (subsequent to the war of 1866).**
  Bismark greatly increased it.
- 240. **Austria.**
  the *Danube solely waters* it.
- 15. **Switzerland.**
  wearily *climb* the *Alps.*
- 118. **Italy (including Venetia).**
  its *beautiful capital* on the *Arno.*
- 20. **Greece.**
  its winters are *fine* and *warm.*
- 204. **European Turkey.**
  a densely wooded surface.
- 2087. **Russia.**
  a dreary expanse of *arid plains.*
- 171. **Sweden.**
  beautiful picturesque cataracts.
- 123. **Norway.**
  celebrated falls and *glaciers.*

SECT. 30.—Population of European Countries.

(Supply 000,000.)

29. Population of the British Isles in 1861.
    famed for *valour.*
20. England.
    dauntless in *war.*
3. Scotland.
    warlike *highlanders.*
6. Ireland.
    wit and *humour.*
224. The British Empire.
    a *full fifth* of our *species.*
4. Portugal.
    they excel the *Spaniards.*
16. Spain.
    chivalrous and *indolent.*
37. France.
    a *gay people.*
5. Belgium.
    wise and excellent *laws.*
4. Netherlands.
    expert workers in *silk.*
2. Denmark (*minus* Schleswig-Holstein).
    war wrested the *Duchies* from it.
8. Baden, Würtemberg, and Bavaria.
    (almost) wholly *Romanists.*
24. Prussia.
    they *defeated* the *Austrians.*
36. Austria.
    in the west, *Germans* are *numerous.*
2. Switzerland.
    the west is wholly *French.*
25. Italy.
    eyes *dark* and *lively.*
1. Greece.
    exceedingly *crafty.*

FACTS IN GEOGRAPHY. 41

16. European Turkey.
    Christians and *Mohammedans*.
64. Russia.
    mainly *Sclavonians*.
4. Sweden.
    they excel in *science*.
2. Norway.
    exceedingly *fair-haired*.

SECT. 31.—Heights of European Mountains.

Feet.
4406. Ben Nevis, the loftiest mountain in the B. Isles.
    a *snowy summit* in the *wilds* of *Inverness*.
11,168. Maladetta, the loftiest summit of the Pyrenees.
    the *cloud capped brow* of *Maladetta rises*.
11,663. Sierra Nevada, the loftiest chain in the Hesperian Peninsula.
    bold *Cerro Mulhaçen's noble height*.
9068. Highest summit in the Sardo-Corsican system.
    the *view* is *extensive* from *Monte Rotondo*.
15,744. Mt. Blanc, highest summit of the Alpine system.
    (Mont) *Blanc lifts* up his *snowy summit*.
10,874. Mt. Etna, highest summit of the Apennines.
    its *burning explosions ravage* the *plains* of *Syracuse*.
9528. Mt. Butschetje, highest summit of the Carpathians.
    a *vast elevation dividing realms*.
9718. Tchar-Dagh, loftiest summit of the Balkan Range.
    Tchar-Dagh, prince of the *Balkan range*.
18,493. Mt. Elburz, loftiest summit of the Caucasus.
    Caucasus reigns supreme, a *towering height*.
5397. Mt. Konjakofski, loftiest summit of the Urals.
    low heights with *veins of platina*.
8670. Mt. Skageslöestinden, h. s. of Scandinavian system.
    remarkable for *numerous plateaux* and *glaciers*.

SECT. 32.—Principal River-Basins of Europe in square miles.

(Supply 000.)

Sq. Miles.

49. Petchora basin.
   it wanders *slowly* through the *tundras*.

106. Dwina.
   its *course* is towards the *White Sea*.

67. Neva.
   waters *Novgorod* and *Petersburg*.

57. Vistula.
   its waters *lave Poland*.

40. Oder.
   waters *Silesia* and *Brandenburg*.

41. Elbe.
   waters *Saxony* and *Bohemia*.

65. Rhine.
   navigable to *Switzerland*.

22. Seine.
   waters the west of *fair France*.

34. Loire.
   winds westward to the *Gulf* of *Gascogne*.

24. Garonne.
   the *Dordogne joins* it.

29. Douro.
   flows to the *Atlantic*.

21. Tagus.
   flows from *Castile*.

24. Ebro.
   flows eastward.

28. Rhone.
   its *fall* is *rapid*.

29. Po.
   flows past *Turin*.

234. Danube.
   flows through *Germany* and *Austria*.

170. Dnieper and Bug.
   they water the *best provinces* on the *Euxine*.

FACTS IN GEOGRAPHY. 43

Sq. miles.
169. Don.
  a canal unites it with the *Volga*.
398. Volga.
  waters the *greatest territory* in *Europe*.
84. Ural.
  between *Russia* and *Siberia*.

SECT. 33.—Areas of Asiatic Countries.
(Supply 000.)

Sq. Miles.
669. Asiatic Turkey.
  mankind's native territory.
1200. Arabia.
  the *coasts* are *fertile* where *water exists.*
552. Persia.
  lofty and *almost desert.*
225. Afghanistan.
  the *Afghan's desert land.*
160. Beloochistan.
  the *country* is *nearly* a *waste.*
1476. Hindustan.
  our *beloved Sovereign* is *Queen* of *India.*
880. Further India.
  the *river Irrawaddy waters* it.
5300. Chinese empire.
  a *long high wall defends* it.
414. Turkestan.
  slopes to the *Caspian Sea.*
5585. Siberia.
  a *low level* from the *Urals* to the *Lena.*
266. Japan.
  a *distant insular empire.*

SECT. 34.—Population of Asiatic Countries.
(Supply 000,000.)

16. Asiatic Turkey.
  the *centre* of *Mohammedanism.*

44 FACTS AND DATES.

    8. Arabia.
        wandering *Arabs*.
  10. Persia.
        its *commerce* is *extensive*.
    6. Afghanistan and Beloochistan.
        warlike *Mohammedans*.
186. Hindostan.
        Brahminism is the *religion* of *India*.
  28. Further India.
        the *idolatrous religion* (of Buddha).
415. Chinese Empire.
        the *stereotyped civilisation* of the *Mongols*.
    4. Turkestan.
        extremely *sterile*.
    4. Siberia.
        Wogulians, exiles, and *Kirghiz*.
  35. Japan.
        an *Ugro-Tartarian language*.

SECT. 35.—Heights of Asiatic Mountain Chains.

(Supply 000.)

Feet.
  19. Highest summit of the Bolor Tagh.
        west of *Chinese Turkestan*.
  19. Hindoo Koosh.
        between *Cabool* and *Turkestan*.
  16. Paropamisan range.
        Bokhara is *north* of it.
  18. Elburz range.
        between the *Caspian* and *Iran*.
  17. Mount Ararat, in Armenia.
        near a *branch* of the *Euphrates*.
  13. Mount Arjish, in Taurus range.
        between the *Black* and the *Great* (Sea).
  12. Lebanon range.
        between *Beirût* and *Damascus*.

FACTS IN GEOGRAPHY. 45

Feet.
29. Mount Everest, in the Himalaya range.
  the white *dome* of *Everest.*

28. Dapsang peak, in the Karakorum range.
  yonder *Dapsang rises.*

22. Kuen-Lun range.
  west of a *dreary desert.*

20. Thian-Shan range.
  between the *Daria* and *Yarkand*

SECT. 36.—Principal River-Basins of Asia.
(*Supply* 000.)

Sq. miles.
197. Basin of Euphrates and Tigris.
  the extensive *basin* of the *Tigris* and *Euphrates.*

312. Indus.
  the *Himalaya* and *Cashmere feed* it.

432. Ganges.
  the *Jumna* its *greatest affluent.*

329. Brahamapootra.
  its *greatest affluents* are from *Tibet.*

331. Irrawaddy and Salwen.
  water the *greater half* of *Burmah.*

216. Menam and Cambodia.
  flow through *Burmah* and *Anam.*

100. Choo-Kiang or Canton river.
  the *Choo-kiang waters Canton.*

784. Yang-tse-kiang.
  the *principal river* of (eastern) *Asia.*

640. Hoang-ho.
  next in *size* to the *Yang-tse.*

583. Amour.
  the *largest river* after the *Hoang-ho.*

594. Lena.
  the *Lena traverses* (eastern) *Siberia.*

784. Yenisei.
  the *principal river* of (central) *Siberia.*

1350. Oby.
  its *basin* is the *greatest* in the *Old World.*

FACTS AND DATES.

SECT. 37.—Areas of the Countries of Africa.

(Supply 000.)

Sq. miles.
578. Egypt, Nubia, and Kordofan.
  the *largest pyramid* is *remarkable*.
245. Abyssinia.
  its *four kingdoms* are *elevated*.
379. Tripoli and Tunis.
  governed by *pachas* from *Turkey*.
151. Algeria.
  the *city Algiers* is the *capital*.
290. Marocco.
  the *dates* of (Mount) *Atlas* are *celebrated*.
2500. The Sahara.
  this *desert* is the *largest* in the *whole world*.
250. Senegambia.
  the *diseases* of the *lowlands* are *deadly*.
2250. Soudan or Nigritia.
  the *far distant land* of the *blacks*.
610. Upper and Lower Guinea.
  the *Niger* and *Congo water* it.
240. Cape Colony and Natal.
  our *famous South-African colonies*.
1000. Eastern Africa.
  contains wide expanses of *water*.
3000. Regions unexplored in the interior.
  great explorations yet to be *made*.
200. Madagascar.
  fertile and *well watered*.

SECT. 38.—Population of the Countries of Africa.

(Supply 000,000.)

5. Egypt, Nubia, and Kordofan.
  extensive exports from *Alexandria*.
4. Abyssinia.
  exports *slaves*.

2. Tripoli and Tunis.
    export excellent *fruits*.
3. Algeria.
    excessive *heat*.
9. Marocco.
    exports wool from *Tangiers*.
10. Senegambia.
    Bathurst is the *capital*.
40. Soudan or Nigritia.
    the *Joliba waters* it.
10. Upper and Lower Guinea.
    constantly at *war*.
1. Cape Colony and Natal.
    owned by *Britain*.
10. Eastern Africa.
    Burton explored it.
31. Regions unexplored in the interior.
    extend westward to the *gorilla country*.
4. Madagascar.
    exports *silk*.

SECT. 39.—Areas of the Countries of North America.
(*Supply* 000.)

Sq. miles.
394. Alaska, formerly Russian America.
    gigantic volcanoes surround it.
380. Greenland, or Danish America.
    glaciers and *rocks cover* it.
3598. British North America.
    gigantic lakes and *vast rivers*.
404. Dominion of Canada (including Canada; New Brunswick, and Nova Scotia).
    joined in the *year sixty-seven*.
42. Newfoundland and Prince Edward Island.
    separate dependencies.
365. Western or Pacific Colonies.
    gigantic mountains line them.

48 FACTS AND DATES.

Sq. miles.
2820. United States.
drained by *rivers* of *formidable dimensions.*

857. Mexico.
rises into a *lofty plateau.*

188. Central America.
the *central region* is *raised.*

97. West Indies.
extend beyond the *Torrid Zone.*

SECT. 40.—Population of the Countries of North America.

(*Supply* 000.)

3550. British North America.
Hudson landed on its *lonely wastes.*

3091. Dominion of Canada (Canada, New Brunswick, and Nova Scotia).
generally exiles from *transatlantic countries.*

204. Newfoundland and Prince Edward Island.
fish exported and *seals.*

31,445. United States.
a *great country stretching* from *sea to sea.*

8295. Mexico.
the *remarkable feather-painting* of the *Toltecs* and *Mexicans.*

2352. Central America.
its *five governments* were *lately dependent.*

3808. West Indies.
a *great archipelago owned* by *Europeans.*

SECT. 41.—Height of North American Mountains.

(*Supply* 000.)

Feet.
6. White Mountain, highest summit of Alleghanies.
White *Mountain.*

15. Mount St Elias, highest summit of North-Western America, now Alaska.
the white *crown* of *Alaska.*

FACTS IN GEOGRAPHY. 49

Feet.
18. **Mount Hood,** highest summit of the United States and of North America.
    in the *Cascade Range.*
16. **Mount Brown,** culminating point of British America.
    a *brown mountain.*
17. **Popocatepetl,** highest summit of Mexico.
    the *burning Popocatepetl.*
14. **Mount Agua,** highest summit of Central America.
    Central-America's summit.
7. **El Cobre,** in Cuba, h. s. of the West Indies.
    a West Indian *peak.*

SECT. 42.—Principal River-Basins of North America.
(*Supply* 000.)

Sq. miles.
297. **Basin of the St Lawrence.**
     falls into the *Atlantic* at *Quebec.*
982. **Mississippi.**
     a *vast region drained* by it.
180. **Rio Grande del Norte.**
     basin of the *Rio Grande.*
169. **Colorado.**
     comes from *New-Mexico* and *Utah.*
194. **Columbia.**
     its *chief tributaries* are *gold-bearing.*
445. **Mackenzie.**
     its *source* is the *Slave Lake.*
360. **Nelson and Saskatchewan.**
     grows maize and *wheat.*

SECT. 43.—Areas of South American States.
(*Supply* 000.)

Sq. miles.
521. **Granadian Confederation.**
     the west is *lofty* and *forest clad.*
425. **Venezuela.**
     the *surface* a *flat llano.*

D

Sq. miles.
- 285. Ecuador.
    the *dreadful eruptions* of *Antisana*.
- 136. Guiana.
    with *Cayenne, Georgetown,* and *Paramaribo*.
- 3138. Brazil.
    the *gigantic basin* of the *greatest river*.
- 508. Peru.
    with *Lima* in the *west*, on the *Rimac*.
- 511. Bolivia.
    its *lake* is *celebrated* for its *height*.
- 116. Chilè.
    with *Aconcagua* in the *Chilian Andes*.
- 543. Argentine Confederation.
    elevated slightly above the *sea*.
- 146. Paraguay and Uruguay.
    the *capitals* are *Asuncion* and *Monte-Video*.

SECT. 44.—Population of South American States.

(Supply 000,000.)

- 5. Granadian Confederation, Venezuela, and Ecuador.
    the whites are *all* (Spaniards).
- 7. Brazil.
    the whites are *Portuguese*.
- 6. Peru, Bolivia, and Chilè.
    extremely wealthy in *minerals*.
- 3. Argentine Confederation, Paraguay, and Uruguay.
    they export *hides*.

(Supply 000.)
- 280. Guiana.
    fertile European colonies.

SECT. 45.—Height of South American Mountains.

Feet.
- 19,137. Antisana, in Ecuador.
    among the *cone-shaped volcanoes* of *Ecuador* is the *gigantic Antisana*.

FACTS IN GEOGRAPHY. 51

Feet.
18,875. Cotopaxi.
  Cotopaxi, renowned among the *roaring volcanoes* of Ecuador.

21,424. Chimborazo.
  the *far-famed Chimborazo* shows his *dome-like shape*.

21,140. Sorata and Illimani, in Bolivia.
  among the *formidable cones* of *Bolivia* are *Sorata* and *Illimani*.

23,910. Aconcagua, in Chilè, the h. s. of the Andes.
  by *far* the *highest* is the *volcano* of *Aconcagua*, in *Chilè*.

22,016. Tupungato, east of Santiago de Chilè.
  frequent destructive explosions in the *Chilian Andes*.

8030. Yanteles, highest summit of the Patagonian Andes.
  the *roaring Yanteles* is *glacier crowned*.

6913. Sarmiento, in Tierra-del-Fuego.
  the *mountains* of *Tierra-del-Fuego* are *crowned* with *glaciers*.

15,800. Limit of perennial snow at the equator.
  the *congelation limit reaches high* at the *equator*.

SECT. 46.—Areas of South American River-Basins.

(Supply 000.)

Sq. miles.
72. Magdalena Basin.
  platinum is *found* in it.

252. Orinoco.
  flows through the *llanos* and *delta*.

1512. Amazon.
  the *basin* of this *leviathan contains* the *selvas*.

284. Tocantins.
  flows through the *region* of the *selvas*.

188. San Francisco.
  its *basin* is *rich* in *ores*.

887. Paranâ.
  the *rainless region* of the *pampas*.

SECT. 47.—Areas of Countries in Oceania.

(Supply 000.)

Sq. miles.
- **3428. Australasia.**
  gigantic islands and *dreary regions.*
- **3000. Australia.**
  a *great wilderness colonised* by the *British.*
- **323. New South Wales.**
  a *great field* for gold.
- **87. Victoria.**
  richer than *Ophir.*
- **383. South Australia.**
  great in *iron* and *copper.*
- **978. Western Australia.**
  a *vast penal reformatory..*
- **678. Queensland.**
  the *mineral products* are *rich.*
- **26. Tasmania.**
  fertile and *mountainous.*
- **106. New Zealand.**
  Britain owns the *Antipodes.*
- **240. Papua or New Guinea.**
  Dutch settlements in the *west.*
- **843. Malaysia.**
  rich in *spices* and *gums.*
- **10. Polynesia.**
  yields *cocoa-nuts* and *bananas.*

SECT. 48.—Population of the Countries of Oceania.

(Supply 000.)

- **2500. Australasia.**
  the *degenerate Alfouries are waning away.*
- **1213. Australia.**
  the *commerce* of its *five colonies* is *great.*
- **366. New South Wales.**
  its *gold* was *anticipated* by *Murchison.*

FACTS IN GEOGRAPHY. 53

566. Victoria.
the alpaca and llama are naturalised.

127. South Australia.
copper of the finest quality.

17. Western Australia.
its capital is Perth.

72. Queensland.
its people are few.

90. Tasmania.
exports timber and wool.

126. New Zealand.
the colonists are afraid of the Maories.

110. Papua or New Guinea.
yields camphor, cocoa-nuts, and yams.

16,750. Malaysia.
the aborigines of Malaysia possess a literature of their own.

220. Micronesia.
fast fading away.

500. Polynesia.
the laborious Williams Christianised them.

SECT. 49.—Height of Principal Mountains in Oceania.

Feet.

5158. Bellenden Ker mountains in Queensland.
the loftiest cone in the Ker range.

5700. Mount Lindsay in New South Wales.
Lindsay Peak, between Brisbane and Clarence.

6000. Mount Seaview, Liverpool range (lat. 31½°).
a mountain west of Port Macquarie.

3300. Mount York in the Blue Mountains (lat. 34°).
greatest height of the Blue Mountains.

7300. Mount Kosciusko, Australian Alps, N.S. Wales.
the peak of greatest height in Australia.

3012. Mount Bryant, Flinder range, South Australia.
the highest in the westerly chain of Flinder.

FACTS AND DATES.

Feet.
5000. Mount Tulbanop, Western Australia.
extreme elevation of the *westmost colony* in *Australia.*

5069. Cradle Mountain, Tasmania.
in *altitude exceeds* the *mountains* of *Victoria.*

13,200. Mt. Cook, the culminating point of New Zealand.
Cook is the *highest* by *far* in *New Zealand.*

SECT. 50.—Progress of Geographical Discovery.

A.D.
1271. Marco Polo, a Venetian, begins his travels.
a *bold adventurer proceeds* to " *Cathay.*"

1286. Oderic of Portenau visits India and China.
courageous Oderic arrives in *India.*

1295. Marco Polo returns to Venice, and writes his travels.
China described by a *traveller* in the *land.*

1302. Gioja of Amalfi introduces the mariner's compass.
the *compass gives* a *wider field.*

1324. John Batuta, a Moor of Tangiers, travels through Asia.
Batuta goes to *Afghanistan* and *Sumatra.*

1330. The Canary Islands discovered by a French vessel.
the *Canary group* is *granted* to *Claramonte.*

1335. Balducci Perzoletti travels from Azov to China.
a *caravan goes* to the *great wall.*

1403. Henry of Castile sends Gonzales to Samarcand, to the Court of Timur the Tartar.
come to *Samarcand, wandering Gonzales.*

1418. The Canaries are colonised by the Portuguese.
the *Canary Isles colonised* by *Europeans.*

1420. Madeira discovered by the Portuguese.
a *beautiful island, adorned* with " *wood.*"

1431. The Azores discovered by Vanderberg of Bruges.
the *Açores* are *seen* with " *hawks* " *abounding.*

1449. Cape Verd Islands discovered by the Portuguese.
a *curious scene,* the *seas* are " *verdant !* "

1486. Bartholomew Diaz, a Portuguese, doubles the Cape of Good Hope without seeing it, and arrives at Delagoa Bay.
the " *Cape* of *Storms* " its *original name.*

1487. Cavilham, a Portuguese, travels to India by Suez and Aden.
Cavilham seeks the *renown* of *Portugal.*

1492. America discovered by Columbus, a Genoese, in the service of Ferdinand of Spain.
Columbus sails athwart the *deep.*

1494. Columbus, on his second voyage, discovers Jamaica and Porto Rico.
Columbus sees vast islands.

,, John Cabot, sent out by Henry VII. of England, discovers Newfoundland.
Cabot seizes a *vast island.*

1497. The Cabots discover Labrador, Nova Scotia, and Virginia, being the first parts of the American continent seen by Europeans.
the *Cabots survey* a *vast peninsula.*

,, Vasco de Gama discovers the Cape of Good Hope.
the *Cape* is *seen* by *Vasco,* a *Portuguese.*

1498. The Orinoco discovered by Columbus on his third voyage.
Columbus sees a *vast river.*

1499. Canada discovered by the Cabots.
Cabot sails to a *vast territory.*

1500. Pinzon, a Spaniard, discovers the river Amazon.
beholds the *leviathan* of the *world's waters!*

1501. Alvarez de Cabral, a Portuguese, discovers Brazil.
Cabral lands on *wide Brazil.*

1502. Columbus, on his fourth voyage, discovers Cen. Amer.
Columbus learns the *way* to *Darien.*

1503. Goa Factory, in India, founded by the Portuguese.
began to *lay* the *walls* of *Goa.*

1507. Almeida, a Portuguese, discovers Madagascar and Ceylon, and subdues Western India.
the *bold Almeida wins* them to *Portugal.*

1511. Velasquez, a Spaniard, sails from Hispaniola, and conquers Cuba.
the *Caribs lament* the *conquest* of *Cuba.*

1512. Ponce de Leon, a Spaniard, discovers Florida and the Gulf Stream.
observes a *land* with *beautiful flowers.*

1513. Balbao crosses the Isthmus of Darien, and discovers the Pacific.
Balbao lights on an *ocean great.*

1514. Juan Diaz de Solis enters the La Plata in South America.
Buenos lies on the *bank* of the *estuary.*

1517. Yucatan discovered by Hernandez Cordoba.
Cordoba lands on the *central peninsula.*

1519. Fernandez Cortez, a Spaniard, proceeds from Cuba to conquer Mexico.
Cortez lands on a *civilised territory.*

1520. Magellan discovers the Strait bearing his name.
he *cautiously led* them by a *dangerous way.*

1521. Magellan discovers the Philippine Islands.
the *courageous leader dies* in *battle.*

,, Magellan's ships visit Borneo, the Celebes, and Moluccas, and return to Spain after circumnavigating the globe.
they *curiously lose* a *day* in their *course.*

1526. Pizarro invades the empire of Peru, now under Huana Capac, the 12th emperor.
Capac, the *last* of the *dynasty* of the *Incas.*

1534. Lima, in Peru, founded by Pizarro.
the *building* of *Lima* by a *gold-hunting Spaniard.*

1535. Jacques Cartier, a Frenchman, explores Canada.
the *Canadian lakes* at the *head* of the (St) *Lawrence.*

1537. Macao granted as a settlement to the Portuguese.
China allows a *haven* to the *Portuguese.*

1541. The Spaniards form their first settlement in Chilè.
they *begin* to *lay Santiago* de *Chilè.*

1542. The Portuguese discover Japan accidentally.
the *civilised land* of *Japan* is *discovered.*

1584. Sir W. Raleigh takes possession of Virginia for England.
a colony leaves for our *earliest settlement*.

1600. The English East India Company established.
a *company* of *merchants yearning* for *wealth*.

1604. Barbadoes, England's first colony, established.
chiefly employed in *exporting sugar*.

1606. Virginia begins to be colonised by the English.
colonists from *England wander* to *America*.

,, The Australian continent discovered by the Dutch.
a *beautiful new world* at the *Antipodes*.

1608. Quebec founded by French colonists.
the *chief emporium* of a *wealthy region*.

1610. Hudson Bay discovered by Captain Hudson, in search of a north-west passage to the Pacific.
the *captain enters* a *cheerless expanse*.

1619. Batavia built and settled by the Dutch.
Batavia, the *emporium* of *commerce* and *trade*.

1642. Tasman, a Dutchman, discovers Van Diemen's Land.
a *bold navigator sent* by the *Dutch*.

1672. The Mississippi discovered by Marquette, a Frenchman.
the *basin* of the *Mississippi* of *peerless dimensions*.

1728. Behring Strait discovered, and Asia proven to be disjoined from the New World.
a *chasm appears dividing* the *Russias*.

1744. Admiral Anson completes his voyage round the world.
Britain promotes her *successful sailor*.

1767. Wallis and Carterel's discoveries in the South Seas.
Carterel proceeds on his *mission* to the *Pacific*.

1768. Capt. Cook explores New Holland and New Zealand.
Cook proceeds on a *mission* of *research*.

1787. New South Wales established as an English colony.
our *convicts proceed* to a *remote penitentiary*.

1795. Mungo Park's first voyage to Africa.
the *celebrated Park travels* in *Ludamar*.

DIVISION II.—HISTORICAL FACTS.

PART FIRST—SACRED HISTORY.

CHAP. I.—OLD TESTAMENT HISTORY.
(B.C. 5478-4.)

In regard to the chronology of the Antediluvian period, and especially the point of time at which human history commences, the Book of Genesis is our only guide. Invaluable as this most precious record is, there are many points of the deepest interest on which it throws but a feeble light. The *absolute* age of our planet, and the precise point of time in that age when man first appeared on its surface, are left wholly undetermined; but the mighty changes through which it had passed before man was introduced, and the order of time (in relation to other species) in which that introduction took place, are indicated with sufficient clearness. Regarding the antiquity of the globe, and the moment of time when it was first peopled by living creatures, the inspired volume is silent; nor is there the least likelihood that human science shall ever satisfactorily determine what the Creator has been pleased to conceal. It will be readily perceived, however, that what is clearly indicated is of vastly greater importance to our race than what has been purposely left in the dark. In the very first sentence of the Book of Genesis we are informed that matter is not eternal; that our world had a beginning; and that it required divine energy to bring it into being. Further on, but still on the same page, we are informed that the planet had been in existence for an undefined period before any living thing was created on its surface; that this creation was gradual and progressive, the humbler forms of life taking the precedence of the more highly organised; and that the last creature that appeared on the scene was man, formed in God's own image, and so bearing His likeness that he could with propriety be called "a son of God;" for he not only resembled his Creator in his moral and intellectual nature, but his body also—so fearfully and wonderfully made—bore the form and lineaments of *that body* which, in the fulness of time, the divine Son was to assume—that body in which He was to give perfect obedience to God's violated law, and perfect satisfaction for the sins of His people.

These infinitely important items of revealed truth, in common with many others, are in perfect harmony with the teachings of science; and though the latter cannot draw aside the veil which obstructs our view in some directions, she has opened up a very fascinating vista in others. For example, she has wellnigh demonstrated—what the inspired record had long ago clearly asserted (compare Heb. xi. 3, *in the original*)—that between each of the "days" of creation,—that is, *between each successive exercise of supernatural power*,—an "æon" or mighty cycle of years intervened, during which the results of the new order of things initiated by the divine Word at its commencement were left to operate, by the continuous and undisturbed routine of natural law, until the earth had thereby become adapted for a new act of supernatural power—as, for example, the introduction of a higher type of organic life. She has shown that the order of sequence in these six periods is identical with the order so graphically detailed in the Book of Genesis. She has shown that our planet had existed for untold ages before it became inhabited by living creatures; that the forms of life that first peopled it were zoophytes and fucoids—the very lowest types of animal and vegetable existence; that many ages then elapsed before molluscs and crustaceans peopled its waters; that whole millenniums of the world's history had passed before fishes—the lowest type of vertebrated animals, and the contemporaries of the first land-plants—were ushered into being; that reptiles—the next higher type of vertebral life—made their first appearance when the continents and islands of the globe waved with the most abundant and gigantic flora that ever adorned its surface; that all these vast changes took place during the great PALÆOZOIC age of its history; and that then some mighty, but hitherto unexplained, catastrophe occurred, which suddenly extinguished all the forms of organic life that had hitherto peopled its oceans and continents. Science further demonstrates that during the Triassic era—the first stage of the world's SECONDARY age—an entirely new series of plants and animals, including birds and marsupial mammals, appeared on the scene; that placental or true mammals come first into view near the end of the Wealden period—the period of the iguanodon and pterodactyl;* that true or exogenous trees, together with quadrumanous mammals, had no existence before the Cretaceous era; that immediately after the completion of that era another tremendous cataclysm took place, which once more extinguished every species of organic life; that the third grand age of the planet's palæontological history—viz., the TERTIARY age—was ushered in with myriads of new and higher forms of existence—forms more closely resembling the fauna and flora of the present day than any that had preceded them; that notwithstanding the great cosmical revolutions that occurred during the lapse of the Tertiary era, not a few of the species that were then created continue to survive till the present day, forming a living bridge between our own times and the immeasurable ages of the past. One item more must finish this enumeration (and it is the clearest and best established of all the teachings of geology) —viz., that no trace of the existence of man is found anywhere till we advance far into the present or POST-TERTIARY age of the world's history, and till this beautiful earth had received the last touches of its Creator's hand, every animal and plant now inhabiting it having been already called into existence.

Such, then, are some of the beautiful harmonies that everywhere abound between Science and Revelation. The globe and the Bible are evidently two volumes by the same Author; and though in some things it is still difficult to reconcile their teachings, they nowhere teach contrary lessons. The author of these remarks is a theologian by profession, and at the same

* See Note, p. 34.

time an ardent student of nature; and he takes this opportunity of affirming, in the most solemn manner of which he is capable, that at this moment he is not aware of a single statement in Scripture that is contradicted by any ascertained fact in either science or history. Let us take a single instance in point. The Old Testament declares that God " created man in His own image" (Gen. i. 27), and the New Testament calls Adam "a son of God" (Luke iii. 38), and adds that all men are God's " offspring" (Acts xvii. 29). Now, though the findings of geology are not equally distinct, they all point, as we have seen, in exactly the same direction. Geology nowhere sanctions the doctrine of the transmutation of species, or that the higher types of organic life have, in the course of ages, been "developed" out of the lower. No trace of such development can be found in the innumerable pages of her stony records. Her entire testimony is opposed to the impious theories of the modern infidel, who tries to show that man has been developed from the ape or the baboon, or that he is the lineal descendant of the gorilla—the most hideous and disgusting of all brutes. It is only when men are opposed in *heart* to God, and when, in consequence, their moral eye hopelessly squints, that they can so read the record of either Genesis or Geology.

The entire space of time intervening between the creation of man and the birth of Christ is usually divided by chronologists into six periods or ages. The *first*, extending from Adam to the general Deluge, is called the Antediluvian age; the *second*, from the Deluge to the call of Abraham, the Postdiluvian age; the *third*, from the call of Abraham to the Exodus, the Patriarchal age; the *fourth*, from the Exodus to the foundation of Solomon's Temple, the Critarchal (*Judge-ruling*) age; the *fifth*, from the founding of the Temple to the Jewish Captivity, the Monarchal age; and the *sixth*, from the Captivity to the birth of Christ, the Hierarchal age. Each of these great periods has its own chronological difficulties, but those connected with the first three greatly exceed in magnitude those attaching to the others. The date when man first appeared on the earth, and the precise time when, owing to its multiplied iniquities, almost the entire race was swept away, are out of sight the hardest to determine in the entire field of chronology. With the exception of the Book of Genesis, we possess no authentic records of these events; and it so happens that even this invaluable document, full as it is of notes of time, conveys much less satisfactory information regarding the two grand events referred to than we could wish. That book comes down to us in three distinct forms—the original Hebrew, the Samaritan, and the Greek or Septuagint translation; and these three, while closely agreeing in almost all other particulars, are amazingly divergent in everything connected with dates. According to the chronology of the Septuagint, Adam was created 5478 years before the Incarnation, and the Deluge occurred 2262 years thereafter. According to our present Hebrew text, the former event took place B.C. 4004, and the latter, 1656 years afterwards. In other words, one edition of the Scriptures assigns to the human race an antiquity of more than 1400 years greater than the other, while it makes the period from Adam to the Flood 600 years longer. These discrepancies are enormous, and make it perfectly obvious that either the one or the other copy, or both, have been seriously tampered with. Modern scholars are now generally of opinion that the serious charge of falsifying the sacred record lies at the door of those intrusted with the custody of the *Hebrew* Scriptures; and that, in order to refute their Christian opponents as to the predicted time of the appearance of the Messiah, they committed the fearful crime of changing the inspired records. It was an ancient tradition among the Jews that the world was destined to last for a period of *seven millenniums,*—the first six corresponding to the six days of creation, and the seventh to the Sabbath or day of rest—and that previous to the last millennium the Messiah should appear in great power and glory. Traces of this tradition may be found in the vaticinations of the Sibylline oracles, and in the writings of the Greek theogonists and cosmogonists; and there can be little doubt that it found its way to the native country of the Magi, and prepared them, at the proper time, for the appearance of the star in the east. We have no doubt that the tradition had its firm foundation in the Hebrew and Greek Scriptures, which, *at the time of our Lord's advent,* were in exact harmony. The date of His birth perfectly agreed with the tradition, and thus a powerful argument was supplied to the Christians that "the Desire of all nations" had actually come, and that it was *He* whom the Jewish rulers and priests had maliciously crucified. Seeing they were capable of perpetrating that unparalleled crime, they would hardly shrink from any other. Having already murdered the Son of God, they now resolved on mutilating His inspired word, in order to make the world believe that Jesus of Nazareth was not the promised Saviour, but an impostor who had appeared fourteen hundred years too soon. "It is acknowledged by Biblical critics," says Professor Wallace, in his admirable and exhaustive treatise, 'The True Age of the World' (Smith, Elder, & Co., London, 1844), "that all the copies of the present Hebrew text were taken from manuscripts of dates later than the ninth century, and that the striking uniformity which all the printed editions exhibit is to be attributed to the fact that they were all copied from the same *codex*. Dr Hales also gives citations from Eusebius, from the Jewish Targums, and from other works, in which decided reference is made to the *larger* numbers as they anciently existed in the Hebrew. Mr Cuninghame, also, in his 'Dissertation on the Apocalypse,' proves, on the authority of ancient Jewish tradition, that Adam was 230 years old when he begat Seth (and not 130, as in our Hebrew text). Consequently, by the argument *ex uno disce omnes*, we conclude that the whole of the *antepaidogonian* ages are correctly given in the Septuagint, and that the true extent of the Antediluvian age is 2262 years." The changes introduced are, for the most part, curiously *systematic*, as will be at once perceived by comparing the Hebrew with the Septuagint in regard to the ages of the Antediluvians at the birth of each eldest son:—

HEBREW, . . .	130	105	90	70	65	162	65	187	182
SEPTUAGINT, . .	230	205	190	170	165	162	165	187	188

It will be seen that in six cases the difference is exactly 100 years, and the result is that, according to the Hebrew, the Antediluvian age is shortened by six centuries.*

* We have already (p. 3) referred with high admiration to the labours of Mr W. Petrie, C.E., London; but we cannot resist this opportunity of lay-

In the second or Postdiluvian age, the result is precisely similar, as will be perceived at a glance by arranging the ten descents, from the Flood to Abraham (Gen. xi. 10-27), in parallel columns. The figures show the age of each patriarch at the birth of his firstborn son—*first*, in the Hebrew, and *second*, in the Septuagint :—

HEBREW,	. .	35	0	30	34	30	32	30	29	70	75
SEPTUAGINT,	.	135	130	130	134	130	132	130	79	70	75

Here, again, there appear clear indications of design; for in six cases out of the ten, the age of each patriarch at the date of his eldest son's birth is, in the Hebrew, precisely 100 years less than in the Septuagint. What is still more extraordinary, the Hebrew entirely omits the name of Cainan II., thereby shortening the chronology to the extent of 130 years, though the genuineness of the Septuagint is fully attested by St Luke in his genealogy of our Lord (Luke iii. 36). Lastly, the following table

ing before our readers his sentiments on the comparative merits of the Hebrew and the Septuagint chronology. In a letter dated 25th June 1869, he says : " As to chronology, I am glad to see that your ideas exactly confirm and justify my own conclusions—namely, that the Septuagint is much more reliable than the Hebrew. This is well shown in ' The True Age of the World,' by Professor Wallace, and is also strongly proved by laying off the ages of maturity or procreation and of death in each generation, from Adam to Christ, in the form of a curve or diagram. The eye then detects incongruities and unnatural or anomalous variations in the Hebrew, and harmonies in the Septuagint, which the mind would not catch on merely reading columns of figures, even when aided by a column of differences. The Septuagint shows *sweeps* or *curves* in its diagram which can hardly have been made by a set of falsified numbers, even by a mathematically-minded forger, unless he had the aid of such a diagram, which, at the time that translation was made, is not likely. Our great hope must now be to find a copy of the Hebrew Scriptures among the remaining Jewish communities in the interior of Persia or China, whose present Scriptures have been copied successively from copies taken with them at the time of the Captivity, or at least obtained from Jerusalem after the partial restoration, but before the Christian era, when the Hebrew Scriptures of Judæa, as we now have them, were sophisticated as to dates. Such a true copy of the original Scriptures will probably justify the Septuagint in most cases; though even the Septuagint, here and there, has probably unintentional miscopyings."

shows the discrepancies of the two texts with regard to the *whole lives* of the ten Postdiluvian patriarchs:—

HEBREW,	.	438	0	433	464	239	239	230	148	205	175
SEPTUAGINT,		538	460	433	404	339	339	330	208	205	175

An important consideration in favour of the Septuagint chronology is that, according to it, the decrease in the duration of human life after the Flood is far more natural and progressive than in the Hebrew, which exhibits great leaps between the different terms of the progression. Leibnitz's celebrated rule, *natura non agit per saltum*, is nowhere more applicable than here. There is a suitable proportion, moreover, in the Greek numbers, between the whole lives of the patriarchs (both before and after the Flood), and their ages at the birth of their eldest sons, which is wholly wanting in the Hebrew. In the period before the Flood, the average of the six *antepaidogonian* ages is to the average of their entire lives in the ratio of 1 to 5 in the Greek, but only as 1 to 9 in the Hebrew. If these ratios be applied to the present average duration of human life, we find that, were the proportions indicated by the Hebrew text to hold good, fathers would beget children at the age of *eight* years! but, according to the Greek, not sooner than at the age of *fourteen*. This argument grows in strength when we come to the Postdiluvian age; for there the Hebrew analogy would allow men now to become fathers at the age of *seven*, but the Septuagint not before the age of *twenty-three*.

Once more, the Hebrew text gives B.C. 2288 as the date of the universal Deluge, but the Septuagint B.C. 3216, or nearly a thousand years earlier. Now we cannot possibly accept the former as the true date, for we have the most indubitable monumental evidence to the contrary. Professor C. P. Smyth has shown, in his recently published 'Antiquity of Intellectual Man,' that the Great Pyramid of Jeezeh, the most ancient and stupendous of all existing monuments, was erected about the year B.C. 2170. Now such a gigantic structure, on which, according to Herodotus, 100,000 men were engaged for 30 years, could not possibly have been erected so early as 118 years after the Deluge, or (according to the same system of chronology) only 41 years after the dispersion of nations.*

Dr Richard Lepsius of Berlin, the most learned and accomplished of all living Egyptologists, has proved, by a rigid comparison of the existing monuments, that the duration of the Egyptian monarchy prior to the exodus of the Israelites (an event which he places B.C. 1314) was 1115 years. According to this computation, Memphis was founded B.C. 2429, a date entirely agreeing with the date of the Flood as given by the Septuagint, but wholly inconsistent with it as given by the Hebrew, by Usher, and by our received text. In this conclusion our own indefatigable William Osburn—whose varied learning and familiar acquaintance with the ancient monuments are not inferior to those of the illustrious German, and whose love of truth and reverence for the inspired record are immeasurably superior—substantially agrees (see his able and highly satisfactory treatise,

* This Pyramid, moreover, in its unique and marvellous system of symbology, gives some very remarkable indications of the true date of the Deluge. These, as interpreted by the Scottish Astronomer-Royal, clearly point to a year close upon B.C. 2800 as the actual time of that grand catastrophe. The evidence, therefore, which this colossal monument supplies, while it confirms the general testimony of both the Hebrew text and the Septuagint, differs from each by only $\frac{1}{17}$th part of the whole time, either way—yet, precisely speaking, indicates a year that lies almost midway between the dates which they assign to that great era in the world's history. A doubt is consequently suggested, whether the chronology of the Septuagint has not, to some extent, been tampered with, as well as that of the Hebrew, though in an opposite direction? We need scarcely inform our readers that many able chronologists, including Usher, Petavius, and Clinton, adduce many weighty arguments against the early chronology of the Greek Scriptures, without being in the least swayed by any evidence obtained from the Pyramid. At the same time, the Pyramid date of the Deluge approaches that of the Septuagint about a hundred years more closely than it does the date of the Hebrew text. Further investigations will, in all likelihood, confirm the testimony of this "sign and wonder in the land of Egypt" (Jer. xxxii. 20), and render it more and more manifest that that unparalleled structure was intended from the beginning to be the grand standard for trying and correcting not only the confused *metrologies* of the nations, but also their equally vitiated *chronologies.*—(*See below, under Egypt.*)

entitled, 'The Monumental History of Egypt,' 2 vols.: London, Trübner & Co., 1854). He also agrees with Lepsius in believing that the first migration into Egypt took place not more than 120 years prior to the building of Memphis and the founding of the Egyptian monarchy. No great interval can have separated this migration from the date of the confusion of tongues, and the consequent dispersion of the nations—events which, therefore, we may safely reckon as having occurred about B.C. 2550. Osburn further shows (i. 377) that the call of Abraham, or rather his visit to Egypt, which must have occurred very soon thereafter, took place in the reign of Pharaoh Achthoes, the 24th or 25th king of that country, about 566 years after the first peopling of the land, and 446 years after the building of Memphis. This would make the call of Abraham—that grand date at which all human history really commences—to have occurred about B.C. 1984. According to Usher, Abraham left Haran, on his way to Canaan, B.C. 1921; Joseph was carried into Egypt in 1728; Jacob, with his family, settled in Goshen in 1706; and the exodus took place in 1491. These dates do not differ very widely from those deduced from the monuments, which indicate that Abraham arrived in Egypt in the reign of Pharaoh Achthoes, of the 11th dynasty, about B.C. 1984; that Joseph was sold as a slave in the reign of Pharaoh Aphophis, a prince of the 16th dynasty, in 1791; that the immigration of the Israelites into the land took place in the reign of the same king, about 1769; and that they finally left the land in the reign of Sethos II. of the 19th dynasty, B.C. 1554. It thus appears that our received text is in perfect accordance with the monuments in assigning 430 years as the entire period between the giving of the promise to Abraham and the exit of his seed from the land of bondage. The two records are also in harmony in indicating that the 430 years are divided into two equal parts by the arrival of Jacob and his family in the Delta, each part having a duration of 215 years. This result, especially when taken in connection with the above dates as they stand in the Septuagint, is of the greatest importance in fixing the chronology of the Old Testament, and in silencing the cavils of influential modern objectors. One serious difficulty, however, still remains—a difficulty, indeed, which to many is all but insuperable. In Gen. xv. 13, God says to Abraham, " Know of a surety that thy seed shall be a stranger in a land that is not theirs, and shall serve them ; and they shall afflict them 400 years. . . . . *But in the fourth generation* they shall come hither again; for the iniquity of the Amorites is not yet full." The actual time was 430 years (Ex. xii. 40, Gal. iii. 17), but the apparent discrepancy here is easily explained. The real difficulty is found in the words, "fourth generation." Most expositors assume that this means the fourth generation from *Jacob;* and they adduce texts to show that, in certain well-known pedigrees, *three* names only appear during the 215 years of the actual sojourn. There can be no doubt, however, that the passage quoted speaks of the fourth generation from *Abraham,* and not from *Jacob.* But even admitting that these generations are to be counted from Jacob, we ask how it is possible that, in *three descents,* seventy persons could have expanded into 600,000 fighting men, besides women, children, and old men, amounting in the aggregate to at least 4,000,000 souls! The thing is utterly absurd, and, in short, could not be. Besides, it was *not* the men of the fourth descent from Jacob that left Egypt in the days of Moses, but those of the *twentieth descent,* as is evident from 1 Chron. vii. 20-27. In this interesting passage we have the full details of the genealogy of Joshua, the son of Nun, who belongs to the nineteenth descent from Ephraim, the younger son of Joseph. The house of Joseph doubtless enjoyed many facilities for preserving their pedigree—facilities that were denied to the other tribes—and hence we have *all* the links of the chain presented to our view; but about the same number of descents must have belonged to each of the other tribes, though, *as is usual in such cases,* only prominent persons are mentioned in their pedigrees when they happen to be cited. This extremely important passage, then, enables us at once to see how, in the course of 215 years, so small a number could have increased to such a mighty host. But then, what becomes of the words, "in the fourth generation they shall come hither again " ? We shall have no difficulty in explaining this; for " generation " does not always signify *descent*—as, for example, Num. xxxii. 13, " And the Lord's anger was kindled against Israel, and He made them wander in the wilderness forty years, until all the *generation that had done evil in the sight of the Lord was consumed.*" Here "generation" means simply "all the souls then living." On account of Jehovah's displeasure, the whole of the mighty host that left Egypt (above the age of twenty) were to perish in 40 years instead of 100 years, which would be the time required for all the adults then living to die a natural death. Let us take a simple illustration. In May 1869, the Registrar-General of England estimated the population of the United Kingdom at 31,015,234. Some of these were infants of one hour's age, others were fully 100 years old ; but in one hundred years hence, or a little more, not one person of these thirty-one millions will be alive ; but fifty or sixty millions of other persons will have come in their room. These, or some of them, will live another 100 years, and *four* such universal displacements will require 400 years, or four generations. The average life of man was much greater in the days of the patriarchs than now. Abraham lived 175 years, Isaac 180, Jacob 148, Joseph 110, Aaron 122, and Moses 120, and their mean age is 142 years. This is probably greatly above the general average of the men of their respective generations, for depravity shortens human life ; yet we cannot suppose that it was less than 120 years. Four such generations would require 480 years. But the people actually entered Canaan 470 years after Abraham left it : and thus the word of the Lord was literally fulfilled ! For this splendid result we are again mainly indebted to the admirable W. Osburn ('Monumental History of Egypt,' ii. 629), whose pious and learned labours cannot fail, ere long, to assume their proper place.

SECT. 1.—Antediluvian Period (B.C. 5478-2348).

B. C.
5478. Creation of man, according to Hales, Josephus, and the Septuagint version (Wallace).
   the *likeness* of *Jesus* his *person reflects.*
4004. Creation of man, according to Archbishop Usher* and the Hebrew text.
   Jehovah awards him the *world's sceptre* (Gen. i. 28).

---

* The chronology of Usher is followed throughout, unless it be otherwise indicated.

FACTS AND DATES.

B.C.
3874. Birth of Seth, Adam's third son.
half of the *race* were the *posterity* of *Seth* (Gen. iv. 25).

3769. Birth of Enos, Seth's eldest son.
in the *human pedigree Enos* is the *third* (Gen. v. 6).

3679. Birth of Cainan.
the *age of men* was *prodigious then* (Gen. v. 9).

3609. Birth of Mahalaleel.
the *age of Mahalaleel yields* to *others* (Gen. v. 12).

3544. Birth of Jared.
the *great longevity* of *Jared* is *astounding* (Gen. v. 20).

3382. Birth of Enoch.
his *heavenly home* he *reached* without *dying* (Gen. v. 24).

3317. Birth of Methuselah.
the *greatest age* on *Bible page* (Gen. v. 27).

3130. Birth of Lamech.
a *great calamity hangs* over the *world* (Gen. v. 29).

3074. Death of Adam.
heaven awards him the *penalty* of *sin* (Gen. v. 5).

3017. Translation of Enoch.
the *heavens welcome* the *beginner* of *prophecy* (Jude 14).

2962. Death of Seth.
the *first triumph* of *natural death* (Gen. v. 8).

2948. Birth of Noah, the tenth from Adam.
Adam's tenth son rescued (Gen. v. 28).

2864. Death of Enos, Seth's eldest son.
death results from *nature's sinfulness* (Gen. v. 11).

2469. Noah commanded to construct the ark.
fabricates a *ship* for the *mountain tops* (Gen. vi. 14).

2448. Birth of Japheth, Noah's eldest son.
the *family* of a *saint* is *saved* from *ruin* (Gen. vi. 10).

2349. Death of Methuselah, one year before the Flood.
a *fearful gathering storm terrifies* him (Gen. v. 27).

2348. The universal Deluge, according to Usher.
a *deluge high*, the *surges rise !* (Gen. vii. 20).

2288. The Deluge, according to the Hebrew text.
a *flood destroys* the *rebel race* (Gen. vii. 23).

SECT 2.—Patriarchal Period (B.C. 3216-1574).

B.C.
3216. The Deluge, according to the Septuagint (Wallace).
a general deluge covers the *mountains* (Gen. vii. 20).

2800. The Deluge, as indicated by the Great Pyramid of Jeezeh (C. P. Smyth).
the *floods arise*, the *world expires* (Gen. vii. 21).

2550. Dispersion of nations, and colonisation of Egypt from Shinar by the Mizraites (Osburn).
a *family lands* in the *lonely west*.

2473. Hebron erected, seven years before Zoan in Egypt.
the *first settlement* in *Palestine* was *Hebron* (Num. xiii. 22).

2429. Menes, a native of Tanis, or Zoan, and first king of Egypt, builds Memphis (Osburn).
the *first king* once *dwelt* at *Tanis*.

2346. Birth of Arphaxad, Shem's third son (Usher).
destined to *grace* our *Saviour's ancestry* (Gen. x. 22).

2281. Birth of Heber, grandson of Arphaxad.
father of the *famous race* of *Abraham* (Gen. xi. 14).

2247. Tower of Babel built, and confusion of tongues.
a *famous edifice situated* on the *Euphrates* (Gen. xi. 9).

„ Birth of Peleg, Heber's eldest son, fifth in descent from Noah, and dispersion of nations.
the *divine fiat scatters* the *people* (Acts xvii. 26).

2218. Nimrod, grandson of Ham, founds Nineveh, Calah, Resin, and Rehoboth.
four famous cities erected by him (Gen. x. 11, margin).

2188. Mizraim, or Menes, first king of Egypt, founds This.
the *first beginning* of *royalty* in the *realm* (Usher).

2170. The Great Pyramid at Jeezeh erected (C. P. Smyth).
its *founder characterised* by *profound wisdom*.

2126. Birth of Terah, the fifth from Peleg.
the *father* of *Abraham dwelt* in *Mesopotamia*.

2071. True date of the call of Abraham, according to Wallace.
the *finest example* of *pure obedience*.

2000. The Pelasgi arrive in Greece about this time.
a *family wends* its *way westward* (Philip Smith).

1998. Death of Noah.
ceases to *testify* to *truth* and *righteousness* (Gen. ix. 26).

FACTS AND DATES.

B.C.
1996. Birth of Abraham, the tenth from Shem.
born to *travail* and to *trust* his *Maker* (Gen. xi. 27).

1926. Chedorlaomer reduces Sodom to subjection.
Chedorlaomer vanquishes five nations (Gen. xiv. 11).

1921. Call of Abraham, and his departure from Haran, 430 years before the exodus (Ex. xii. 40).
Abraham trusts to *find* a *country* (Gen. xii. 4).

1920. Abraham visits Egypt in a famine (11th dynasty).
Abraham visits the *Delta* with his *wife* (Gen. xii. 10).

1920. Birth of Ishmael.
Abraham tempted by the *advice* of his *wife* (Gen. xvi. 2).

1912. Chedorlaomer carries Lot captive.
Abraham valiantly confronts the *foe* (Gen. xiv. 14).

1897. Destruction of Sodom and Gomorrah.
brimstone ruins the *vile pentapolis* (Gen. xix. 24).

1896. Birth of Isaac.
Abraham rewarded for *trusting* his *Maker* (Gen. xxi. 2).

1871. Abraham commanded to sacrifice Isaac.
Abraham resolves to be *perfectly obedient* (Gen. xxii. 3).

1859. Death of Sarah.
Abraham refuses the *loan* of a *tomb* (Gen. xxiii. 2).

1856. Isaac marries Rebekah (Gen. xxiv. 67).
they *brought Rebekah* from the *land* of her *nativity.*

1837. Birth of Jacob and Esau.
birth of a *righteous* and a *godless progeny.*

1822. Death of Abraham.
begin thy *rest, father* of the *faithful !* (Gen. xxv. 8.)

1782. Job probably flourished about this time.
born in *Uz,* in *Arabia Deserta* (Job i. 1).

1760. Jacob, escaping from Esau, goes to Mesopotamia.
the *blessing procured* by his *mother wrongfully.*

1758. Birth of Reuben, Jacob's eldest son (Gen. xxix. 32).
the *blessing* of *primogeniture* is *lost* by *Reuben.*

1755. Birth of Judah (Gen. xxix. 35).
obtains the *pre-eminence* in the *lineage* of our *Lord.*

1745. Birth of Joseph (Gen. xxx. 24).
the *blessing* of *primogeniture* on *Joseph lies* (Gen. xlix.)

B.C.
1739. Jacob returns from Padan-aram, and meets Esau.
coming to *Peniel,* he is *greatly troubled* (Gen. xxxii. 11).
1733. Death of Rachel.
at *Bethlehem Ephrath* she *gives* up the *ghost* (Gen. xxxv.)
1728. Joseph sold into Egypt by his brethren.
a *conscientious prisoner finds* his *reward* (Gen. xxxvii.)
1715. Joseph becomes Governor under Phiops (16th dyn.)
a *captive promoted* to be *chief* in the *land* (Gen. xli. 45).
1706. Jacob and his family remove to Egypt.
come to *Pharaoh, youthful nation !* (Gen. xlvi. 28).
1689. Death of Jacob in Goshen.
the *cave* of *Machpelah receives* him in *trust* (Gen. l. 13).
1635. Death of Joseph.
his *body embalmed* in *Egypt lay* (Gen. l. 26).
1619. Death of Levi (Ex. vi. 16).
his *children* were *ministers* in *charge* of the *tabernacle.*

SECT. 3.—Period of the Exodus (B.C. 1574-1413).

B.C.
1574. Birth of Aaron, great-grandson of Levi (Usher).
called by the *Lord* to *propitiate* for *sin* (Ex. vi. 20).
1571. Birth of Moses.
behold he *lies,* what *piteous crying* (Ex. ii. 2).
1531. Moses slays an Egyptian, and flees to Midian.
he *cheerfully loses* the *Egyptian crown* (Heb. xi. 25).
1491. Exodus of the Israelites from Egypt, 430 years after the call of Abraham (Gal. iii. 17).
the *cloven sea avenged* the *bondmen* (Ex. xiv. 13).
1490. Moses receives the law on Mount Sinai.
burning Sinai trembles exceedingly (Ex. xx. 18).
1471. Death of Korah, Dathan, and Abiram.
consume Korah's presumptuous company (Num. xxvi. 10).
1453. Death of Miriam.
her *cymbal sounded* with *loud hosannas* (Ex. xv. 21).
1452. Moses writes the Pentateuch.
the *book* of *Jehovah's law* was the *first* (Ex. xvii. 14).
,, Death of Aaron ; Eleazar becomes high priest.
the *brother* of *Israel's lawgiver dies* (Num. xx. 28).

B.C.
1451. Balaam summoned to curse Israel.
Balak sends his elders to Balaam (Num. xxii. 7).

„ Death of Moses.
beyond Jordan the Lord concealed him (Deut. xxxiv. 6).

„ The Israelites cross the Jordan under Joshua.
observe 'twas Joshua led them across (Rom. vii. 4).

„ The fall of Jericho (Josh. vi. 20).
they compassed Jericho at the Lord's command.

„ Five kings of Canaan are subdued (Josh. x. 13).
at the command of Joshua the luminaries obeyed.

1450. The seven nations destroyed, and whole land subdued
courageous Joshua lays them waste (Josh. x. 40).

1445. Canaan divided among the tribes.
obtained their several shares by lot (Josh. xiv. 2).

1427. Death of Joshua, 110 years old.
obedient Joshua dies in peace (Josh. xxiv. 29).

1426. Death of Eleazar; Phinehas becomes high priest.
bequeaths to his son the office of minister (Judges xx. 28).

1417. The Book of Joshua written.
the Book of Joshua was completed by Phinehas.

SECT. 4.—Period of the Judges—from Joshua to Saul (B.C. 1413-1095).

B.C.
1413. Israel becomes tributary to *Mesopotamia*.
the Book of Judges begins here.

1406. The tribe of Benjamin nearly exterminated.
Benjamin smitten for wanton iniquity (Judges xx. 48).

1405. Othniel, the first Judge, delivers Israel from Mesopotamia.
a brave Judge wins his laurels (Judges iii. 9).

1396. Era of the First Jubilee.
blow the gladsome trumpet now (Lev. xxv. 11).

1343. Israel becomes tributary to the *Moabites*.
cruel Eglon subjects them to hardships (Judges ii. 14).

1325. Ehud slays Eglon, King of Moab, and delivers his country.
crafty Ehud the despot levels (Judges iii. 21).

OLD TESTAMENT HISTORY. 75

B.C.
1322. Naomi and Ruth return from the land of Moab.
    a *beautiful history* of *devoted affection* (Ruth i. 6).

1303. Shamgar delivers Israel from the *Philistines*.
    beats them *ignominiously* with an *ox goad* (Judg. iii. 31).

1285. Barak and Deborah deliver Israel from the *Canaanites*.
    Barak and *Deborah rescue* the *land* (Judges iv. 15).

1273. Tyre built by a colony of Sidonians (Isa. xxiii. 12).
    the *beautiful daughter* of "*Zidon* the *Great*."

1252. Israel cruelly oppressed by the *Midianites*.
    caves and *dens* their *last defence* (Judges vi. 2).

1245. Gideon saves Israel from the Midianites.
    a *curious dream saves* the *land* (Judges vii. 13).

1236. Abimelech slays his seventy brothers.
    Abimelech destroys a *host* without *mercy* (Judges ix. 5).

1232. Tola and Jair judge Israel.
    their *countrymen adore heathen deities* (Judges x. 6).

1201. The Fifth Jubilee celebrated.
    celebrate the *fifth year* of *freedom* (Lev. xxv. 11).

1194. The Trojan war commences.
    a *band* of *confederates* for *Troy set* out.

1188. Jephthah saves Israel from the *Ammonites*.
    a *courageous chief's remarkable resolution* (Judges xi. 30).

1182. Ibzan succeeds Jephthah as Judge of Israel.
    Ibzan begat a *regiment* of *daughters* (Judges xii. 9).

1175. Elon succeeds Ibzan (Judges xii. 11).
    the *chronology* is *obscure* in the *period* of *Elon*.

1165. Abdon succeeds Elon.
    Abdon comes next after *Elon* (Judges xii. 13).

1157. Eli, the high priest, judges Israel.
    after *Abdon comes Eli* the *priest* (Judges xviii. 31).

1155. Birth of Samson.
    a *child* is *born* to *liberate* the *land* (Judges xiii. 24).

1137. Samson becomes Judge, and plagues the *Philistines*.
    a *brave champion governs* the *people* (Judges xv. 20).

B.C.
1137. Birth of Samuel, son of Elkanah.
  a *child chosen* of *God* for the *priesthood* (1 Sam. i. 20).

1117. Death of Samson.
  a *blind captive chastises* the *Philistines* (Judges xvi. 30)

1116. The Philistines capture the Ark: death of Eli.
  a *child called "Ichabod"* by his *mother* (1 Sam. iv. 21).

1114. Samuel becomes Judge of Israel.
  a *child chosen* to *become* a *Judge* (1 Sam. vii. 6).

1101. The Seventh Jubilee.
  come and *celebrate* the *year* of *deliverance* (Lev. xxv. 11).

1096. The Philistines overthrown in battle at Mizpeh.
  "*Ebenezer*" *witnessed* the *victory* at *Mizpeh* (1 Sam. vii).

SECT. 5.—Period of the Hebrew Monarchy (B.C. 1095-975).

B.C.
1095. Saul anointed king at Ramah.
  they *choose* a *young* and *timid leader* (1 Sam. x. 1).

1085. Birth of David.
  birth of the *young ruler* of the *land* (Ruth iv. 22).

1063. Saul, sent against Amalek, is disobedient (1 Sam. xv).
  commissioned to *exterminate Amalek* and *Agag*.

 ,, David is anointed king, Saul being rejected.
  a *bard* and *warrior anointed* to *govern* (1 Sam. xvi. 13).

 ,, War with the Philistines: David slays Goliath.
  a *courageous youth encounters* a *giant* (1 Sam. xvii. 49).

1062. David escapes from Saul, and takes refuge in Gath.
  Achish welcomes a *mad fugitive* (1 Sam. xxi. 10).

 ,, Death of Samuel (1 Sam. xv. 35).
  courageously warned the *monarch* of his *fate*.

1055. Battle of Gilboa: death of Saul and Jonathan.
  consults a *witch*, being *left* of the *Lord* (1 Sam. xxxi. 6).

 ,, David begins to reign in Hebron.
  they *crown* the *youth* whom the *Lord loves* (2 Sam. ii. 4).

1051. The Eighth Jubilee.
  they *bless* the *year* that *liberates* the *captives*.

OLD TESTAMENT HISTORY. 77

B.C.
1047. David reigns over all Israel at Jerusalem.
begins to wield the sceptre in Zion (2 Sam. v. 5).

1045. The Ark removed from Kirjath-jearim to Jerusalem.
a *cordial welcome* is *shouted* by *all* (1 Chron. xv. 28).

1033. Birth of Solomon (2 Sam. xii. 24).
he *chose wisdom* before *greatness* and *glory*.

1024. Absalom's rebellion.
Absalom wins the *affections* of *Israel* (2 Sam. xv. 4).

1023. Death of Absalom.
a *beautiful youth found hanging* (2 Sam. xviii. 10).

1017. David numbers the people.
chastised for *wilfully counting* the *people* (2 Sam. xxiv. 2).

1016. Birth of Rehoboam.
birth of an *exacting* and *cruel monarch* (1 Chron. iii. 10).

1015. Solomon's accession, and death of David.
a *crown* of *wisdom* his *chosen laurels* (1 Kings ii. 12).

1014. Solomon marries Pharaoh's daughter (Sheshouk).
betroths a *wife* of *coloured skin* (1 Kings iii. 1).

1012. Solomon lays the foundation of the Temple, 480 years after the exodus (1 Kings vi. 1).
carefully executes a *celestial design* (Ex. xxv. 40).

1004. Dedication of the Temple.
accept our *willing work, Jehovah !* (1 Kings viii. 63).

992. Solomon erects a royal palace.
a *throne* of *ivory adorned* it (1 Kings vii. 1).

990. The Queen of Sheba visits Solomon.
attracted by the *tale* of his *wisdom* (1 Kings x. 1).

980. Jeroboam escapes from Solomon-to Shishak, King of Egypt.
takes refuge in *exile* (1 Kings xi. 40).

975. Death of Solomon, and dismemberment of the empire.
the *tribes petition* for *liberty* (1 Kings xii. 4).

SECT. 6.—Kingdom of the Ten Tribes (B.C. 975-721).

B.C.
975. Jeroboam chosen king by the ten tribes.
ten parts are *alienated* (1 Kings xii. 20).

B.C.
974. Jeroboam establishes idolatrous worship.
      the *vilest persons* are *set* (apart) (1 Kings xii. 28).
957. Jeroboam at war with Abijah—500,000 men are slain.
      a *terrible loss* of *people* (2 Chron. xiii. 17).
956. Jeroboam sends his queen to Ahijah the prophet.
      in *Tirzah lamentation* and *mourning* (1 Kings xiv. 13).
954. Nadab succeeds his father Jeroboam.
      a *trusted lieutenant slays* him (1 Kings xiv. 20).
953. Baasha succeeds Nadab.
      the *vengeance* of the *Lord haunts* him (1 Kings xvi. 3).
940. Baasha, at war with Asa, is defeated by the Syrians.
      he *terrifies Asa* by his *wiles* (1 Kings xv. 32).
930. Elah succeeds his father Baasha.
      a *traitor gives* him his *wages* (1 Kings xvi. 10).
929. Zimri, Elah's captain, slays him, and reigns 7 days.
      the *traitor destroys* himself in *Tirzah* (1 Kings xvi. 18).
 ,, Omri succeeds Zimri, but is opposed by Tibni.
      Tibni is *defeated* at *Tirzah* (1 Kings xvi. 22).
924. Omri builds Samaria, the future capital of Israel.
      Tirzah forsaken for *Samaria* (1 Kings xvi. 29).
918. Ahab succeeds his father Omri.
      the *evil climax* is *reached* (1 Kings xvi. 33).
 ,, Jericho rebuilt by Hiel the Bethelite.
      a *terrible curse rewards* him (1 Kings xvi. 34).
910. Elijah prophesies a drought of three years.
      the *Tishbite begins* to *warn* (1 Kings xvii. 1).
906. Elijah slays 450 prophets of Baal on Mt. Carmel.
      the *Tishbite exterminates* the *impostors* (1 Kings xviii. 40).
901. Benhadad II., King of Syria, besieges Samaria.
      a *terrible waste* of *blood* (1 Kings xx. 21).
900. Benhadad invades Israel a second time.
      he is *twice worsted* in the *war* (1 Kings xx. 26).
899. Ahab covets the garden of Naboth.
      reproved by the *Tishbite* in the *vineyard* (1 Kings xxi. 15).

B.C.

897. Ahab is slain at Ramoth-gilead.
  Ramoth tries the *prophets* (1 Kings xxii. 19).

,, Ahaziah succeeds his father Ahab.
  reproved by the *Tishbite* for *apostasy* (2 Kings i. 8).

896. Elijah is caught up into heaven: Elisha succeeds.
  the *rapture* of the *testifying* (witnesses) *anticipated.*

,, Jehoram succeeds his father: Moab rebels.
  the *rebellion* of *turbulent Moab* (2 Kings iii. 5).

895. The Kings of Israel, Judah, and Edom invade Moab.
  rescued from *overthrow* by *Elisha* (2 Kings iii. 9).

894. Naaman the Syrian cured of his leprosy by Elisha.
  he *rejected* the *talents* of *silver* (2 Kings v. 14).

,, The Syrians besiege Samaria: a great famine.
  a *rumour terrifies* the *Syrians* (2 Kings xvii. 4).

884. Jehu is elected king by the army.
  he *rides rapidly* to *Jezreel* (2 Kings ix. 16).

860. Hazael, King of Syria, greatly oppresses Israel.
  a *ruthless monster* of *wickedness* (2 Kings viii. 12).

856. Jehoahaz succeeds his father Jehu.
  his *repentance elicited mercy* (2 Kings xiii. 4).

842. Israel delivered from the Syrian oppression.
  rescued from the *Syrians* by a *deliverer* (2 Kings xiii. 5).

839. Jehoash succeeds his father Jehoahaz, and thrice defeats Benhadad III., King of Syria.
  the *arrow* is *hurled thrice* (2 Kings xiii. 18).

838. Death of Elisha.
  he *receives* his *great reward* (2 Kings xiii. 20).

826. Jonah, the prophet, is sent to Nineveh.
  ruin is *doomed* to *Nineveh* (Jonah iii. 4).

825. Jeroboam II. succeeds his father Jehoash.
  he *ruled* from the *Dead-Sea* to *Lebanon* (2 Kings xiv. 25).

784. The prophets Amos and Hosea flourish.
  they *prophesy* to *rebellious Israel.*

,, Interregnum of eleven years.
  princes are *removed* in *judgment.*

B.C.

776. Era of the First Olympiad.
   a prime epoch with the *ancients*.

773. Zachariah succeeds Jeroboam II., his father.
   he *perishes* by the *prediction* of *Hosea* (Hosea i. 4).

772. Shallum succeeds Zachariah, and reigns one month.
   this *prince quickly departs* (2 Kings xv. 13).

„ Menahem succeeds Shallum.
   a *prophet's prediction fulfilled* (Amos vii. 9).

771. Pul, King of Assyria, invades Israel in his reign.
   he *pays* to *Pul* a *contribution* (2 Kings xv. 19).

761. Pekahiah succeeds his father Menahem.
   Pekahiah murdered by his *captain* (2 Kings xv. 23).

758. Pekah, one of his captains, succeeds him.
   Pekah's lamentable reign (2 Kings xv. 25).

753. Rome founded by Romulus.
   its *position learned* by *augury*.

741. Pekah, and Rezin King of Syria, invade Judah.
   Ephraim and *Syria* are *confederate* (Isa. vii. 1).

740. Tiglath-pileser II., King of Assyria, seizes Gilead, and carries the inhabitants into captivity.
   a *part* of the *Israelites exiled* (1 Chron. v. 26).

„ Tiglath-pileser slays Rezin, and destroys the kingdom of Syria.
   the *power* of *Syria exterminated* (2 Kings xvi. 9).

739. Death of Pekah; interregnum of eight years.
   perishes by the *hand* of a *traitor* (2 Kings xv. 31).

730. Hoshea, last king of Israel, begins to reign.
   the *patience* of *God* is *exhausted* (2 Kings xv. 30).

724. Hoshea solicits aid from So (Shebek II.), King of Egypt, against Assyria.
   petitions for *aid* from *So* (2 Kings xvii. 4).

„ Shalmaneser, King of Assyria, invades Israel, and besieges Samaria.
   a *prolonged defence* at *Samaria* (2 Kings xvii. 3).

721. Shalmaneser carries the Israelites captive to Assyria.
   Ephraim departs into *captivity* (2 Kings xvii. 6).

B.C.
721. The Ten Tribes arrive in Halah, Habor, Gozan, &c., near the Caspian.
Ephraim's destination is the *Caspian* (2 Kings xviii. 11).

677. Esarhaddon, son of Sennacherib, King of Assyria, colonises Israel with heathen nations.
Medes and *Persians* in *Ephraim* (Ezra iv. 2).

SECT. 7.—The Kingdom of Judah (B.C. 975-588).

B.C.
975. Accession of Rehoboam, first King of Judah.
two parts are *loyal* (1 Kings xiv. 21).

971. Shishak, King of Egypt, captures Jerusalem.
vast plunder acquired (2 Chron. xii. 2).

958. Abijah succeeds his father Rehoboam.
a *vain* though *long oration* (1 Kings xv. 1).

957. Great battle between Abijah and Jeroboam.
a *terrible loss* of *people* (2 Chron. xiii. 3).

955. Asa succeeds his father Abijah.
a *true* and *loyal leader* (1 Kings xv. 8).

951. The Tenth Jubilee.
the *trumpet loudly calls* (Lev. xxv. 11).

942. Zerah (Osorkhon I.) the Ethiopian invades Judah.
the *triumph* of *Asa's faith* (2 Chron. xiv. 9).

940. Asa bribes Benhadad to aid him against Baasha.
trusts in the *assistance* of an *auxiliary* (1 Kings xv. 18).

917. Asa, being sick, applies to human physicians.
takes counsel of the *physicians* (2 Chron. xvi. 12).

914. Jehoshaphat succeeds his father Asa.
teaches backsliding Judah (1 Kings xv. 24).

901. The Eleventh Jubilee.
the *trumpet's welcome blast* (Lev. xxv. 11).

898. Jehoshaphat shares his throne with his son Jehoram.
the *heir* is *taught* to *reign* (2 Kings viii. 16).

897. Jehoshaphat accompanies Ahab to Ramoth-gilead.
Ramoth tries the *prophets* (1 Kings xxii. 19).

896. Jehoshaphat equips a fleet to go to Ophir.
an *argosy* to *visit India* (1 Kings xxii. 48).

B.C.
- **889.** Jehoram sole monarch : revolt of Edom.
  his *rule a reign of terror* (2 Kings viii. 20).
- **888.** The Philistines and Arabians invade Judah.
  the *Arabians ravage* the *realm* (2 Chron. xxi. 16).
- **887.** Jehoram receives a letter from Elijah the prophet.
  receives a *remarkable epistle* (2 Chron. xxi. 12).
- **885.** Ahaziah succeeds Jehoram : war with Hazael.
  he *rues* a *rash alliance* (2 Chron. xxii. 7).
- **884.** Athaliah, his mother, usurps the throne.
  the *royal race* is *slain* by her (2 Chron. xxii. 10).
- **878.** Jehoash, the infant son of Ahaziah, begins to reign.
  they *rescue* the *pious heir* (2 Chron. xxii. 11).
- **856.** Jehoash repairs the Temple.
  he *repairs* the *Lord's mansion* (2 Chron. xxiv. 4).
- **853.** Carthage, a Tyrian colony, founded by Queen Dido, one hundred years before the founding of Rome.
  its *ruins lie* in *heaps*.
- **851.** The Twelfth Jubilee.
  the *redemption* of the *land* and the *captive* (Lev. xxv. 11).
- **840.** Zechariah the priest stoned by order of Jehoash.
  the *reward* of *Jehovah's witnesses* (2 Chron. xxiv. 20).
- **839.** The Syrians invade Judah : murder of Jehoash.
  the *retribution* of *God* is *terrible* (2 Chron. xxiv. 24).
- ,, Amaziah succeeds his father Jehoash.
  rewards the *guilty traitors* (2 Chron. xxv. 3).
- **827.** Amaziah hires an Israelitish army against Edom.
  he *receives advice* from a *prophet* (2 Chron. xxv. 7).
- **826.** Amaziah is victorious in Edom.
  remembers Edom's enmity (2 Chron. xxv. 11).
- ,, Amaziah establishes idolatry in Judah.
  rejects the *admonition* of the *messenger* (2 Chron. xxv. 16).
- **825.** Amaziah challenges the King of Israel to war.
  he *receives* the *fool's lesson* (2 Chron. xxv. 18).
- **810.** Uzziah succeeds his father Amaziah.
  the *righteous becomes wicked* (2 Chron. xxvi. 16).
- **801.** The Thirteenth Jubilee.
  release is *welcome* to the *captive* (Lev. xxv. 11).

B.C.
784. Uzziah is smitten with leprosy.
    the *priests reprove* him for *sacrilege* (2 Chron. xxvi. 18).

776. Era of the First Olympiad.
    an *epoch* of *prime importance*.

774. The prophets Isaiah and Zechariah flourish.
    the *prophets Zechariah* and *Isaiah* (Isa. i. 1).

758. Jotham succeeds his father Uzziah.
    a *prince loving righteousness* (2 Chron. xxvii. 2).

753. Rome founded by Romulus.
    its *position learned* by *augury*.

751. The Fourteenth Jubilee.
    proclaim liberty to the *captives* (Isa. lxi. 1).

746. The prophets Joel and Micah flourish.
    the *prophets Joel* and *Micah*.

742. Ahaz succeeds his father Jotham.
    this *prince served idols* (2 Chron. xxviii. 1).

,, The Kings of Israel and Syria invade Judah.
    the *proffered sign* is *declined* (Isa. vii. 12).

741. Ahaz asks aid from Tiglath-pileser II., King of Assyria, who destroys Damascus.
    propitiates the *Assyrians* with a *bribe* (2 Kings xvi. 7).

740. The Edomites and Philistines invade Judah.
    they *punish Judah's wickedness* (2 Chron. xxviii. 17).

726. Hezekiah succeeds his father Ahaz.
    he *zealously destroys* the *images* (2 Kings xviii. 4).

721. Shalmaneser, King of Assyria, carries the Ten Tribes into captivity.
    Ephraim departs into *captivity* (2 Kings xvii. 6).

713. Sennacherib, King of Assyria, attacks Hezekiah.
    he *places* his *confidence* in *God* (Isa. xxxvii. 20).

,, Hezekiah is miraculously healed of his sickness.
    in *prayer* he *beseeches God* (Isa. xxxviii. 3).

712. Merodach Baladan, King of Babylon, sends messengers to Hezekiah.
    a *prophecy* of the *coming departure* (Isa. xxxix. 5).

B.C.
710. Sennacherib sends Rabshakeh against Jerusalem: his army is miraculously destroyed.
pronounces blasphemous words (2 Kings xviii. 35).

710. Tirhakah, King of Ethiopia, marches against Sennacherib (2 Kings xix. 9).
Pharaoh is *beaten* in the *war*.

701. The Fifteenth Jubilee.
peace to the *weary captive* (Isa. lxi. 1).

698. Manasseh succeeds his father Hezekiah.
Manasseh's evil reign (2 Kings xxi. 1).

677. Manasseh carried captive to Babylon by Esarhaddon, who brings heathen colonists to Samaria.
Manasseh punished for *apostasy* (2 Chron. xxxiii. 11).

676. Manasseh repents, and returns to Jerusalem.
Manasseh prays for *mercy* (2 Chron. xxxiii. 13).

674. Manasseh re-establishes the true religion.
Manasseh zealous for *Jehovah* (2 Chron. xxxiii. 16).

651. The Sixteenth Jubilee.
announce liberty to the *captive* (Isa. lxi. 1).

643. Amon succeeds his father Manasseh.
murdered by his *servants* in his *house* (2 Chron. xxxiii. 24).

641. Josiah succeeds his father Amon.
the *meek Josiah* an *iconoclast* (2 Chron. xxxiv. 1).

629. Jeremiah, Habakkuk, and Zephaniah flourish.
they *mourn* the *degeneracy* of the *times* (Jer. ii. 5).

625. Fall of Nineveh; Saracus burns himself to death.
Nineveh destroyed by the *allies*.

624. The Temple repaired, and the Law of Moses discovered.
the *monarch discovers* the *Scriptures* (2 Kings xxii. 8).

623. Josiah holds a great Passover at Jerusalem.
never a *feast* so *honoured* (2 Chron. xxxv. 18).

610. Josiah marches against Pharaoh-Necho, King of Egypt.
at *Megiddo* he is *badly wounded* (2 Kings xxiii. 29).

„ Jehoahaz, or Shallum, succeeds Josiah.
Necho carries him *away* (2 Chron. xxxvi. 4).

B.C.
610. Jehoiakim, or Eliakim, succeeds his father Shallum.
the *monarch behaves wickedly* (2 Kings xxiii. 34).

606. Jerusalem taken by Nebuchadnezzar, joint king with his father Nabopolassar.
Nebuchadnezzar wastes the *nation* (2 Kings xxiv. 7).

,, The *first* deportation to Babylon : Daniel a captive : Nebuchadnezzar sole king.
Nebuchadnezzar wonders at his *understanding* (Dan. i. 19).

599. Jehoiachin, or Coniah, reigns three months : *second* deportation.
they *lead* the *vassal* in *triumph* (2 Kings xxiv. 12).

,, Zedekiah succeeds his father Coniah.
lived in *troublous times* (2 Chron. xxxvi. 11).

594. Ezekiel begins his prophecy in Mesopotamia among the Jews on the river Chebar.
lived among *transported Jews* (Ezek. i. 1).

588. *Third* deportation to Babylon : the Temple destroyed.
the *Lord's residence* is in *ruins* (2 Chron. xxxvi. 19).

SECT. 8.—From the Captivity of the Jews to Malachi (B.C. 588–416).

B.C.
580. Shadrach, Meshach, and Abed-nego, cast into the furnace by Nebuchadnezzar.
the *Lord rescues* his *witnesses* (Dan. iii. 26).

568. Nebuchadnezzar, insane, is driven from his kingdom.
he *learns* that the *Most-High ruleth* (Dan. iv. 33).

562. Jehoiachin liberated from prison in Babylon.
they *liberate* the *monarch* from *durance* (Jer. lii. 31).

560. Jehoiachin, the last Jewish monarch, dies in Babylon.
the *last* of their *monarchs expires* (Jer. lii. 34).

559. Cyrus the elder founds the Medo-Persian empire.
lead thy *legions* to *victory !* (Isa. xliv. 28).

555. Daniel's dream of the four beasts.
lo ! a *lion* and a *leopard* (Dan. vii. 3).

B.C.
- **538.** Belshazzar's feast: Cyrus the elder, and Darius the Mede, son of Cyaxares II., seize Babylon.
  the *Lord* of *heaven's revenge* (Dan. v. 23).

- ,, Daniel is cast into the den of lions.
  the *Lord honours* those that *reverence* Him (Dan. vi. 16).

- **536.** Zerubbabel the priest, in the seventieth year of the captivity, leads back 42,000 Jews to Jerusalem by command of Cyrus.
  liberates the *holy nation* (Ezra ii. 2).

- **535.** Zerubbabel lays the foundation of the second Temple.
  they *lament* that the *house* is *lowlier* (Ezra iii. 8).

- **517.** Ahasuerus (Darius Hystaspes) marries Esther.
  a *lovely captive* is *preferred* (Esther ii. 17).

- **515.** Dedication of the second Temple.
  they *loudly bless* the *Lord* (Ezra vi. 16).

- **510.** Haman, the enemy of the Jews, slain by Ahasuerus.
  allured to a *banquet* of *wine* (Esther vii. 10).

- **485.** Xerxes I. succeeds his father Darius as King of Persia.
  Xerxes *succeeds* him as *ruler* of the *land*.

- **465.** Artaxerxes I., his son, becomes king.
  known by the *name* of *Longimanus* (Ezra iv. 7).

- **457.** Ezra brings back a second company from Babylon.
  a *scribe leads* back a *part* (Ezra viii. 1).

- **452.** Ezra writes the two books of Chronicles.
  the *kings* of the *land described* in them.

- **444.** Nehemiah becomes Governor of Judæa for ten years.
  sent by the *king* to *Jerusalem* (Neh. ii. 5).

- **434.** Nehemiah's second journey to Jerusalem.
  the *Jew* is *grieved* at the *sacrilege* (Neh. xiii. 6).

- **416.** Malachi prophesies: the Old Testament completed.
  the *Scriptures conclude* with *Malachi*.

- **401.** Cyrus the younger defeated and slain by Artaxerxes Mnemon at Cunaxa.
  Xenophon *joined* the "*Expedition* of *Cyrus.*"

- **359.** Philip ascends the throne of Macedon.
  as a *hostage* he *learned* his *tactics*.

SECT. 9.—The Jews under the Greeks (B.C. 356-63).

B.C.
356. Birth of Alexander the Great.
    the *great Leviathan* of *antiquity*.
336. Alexander succeeds to the throne of Macedon.
    the *greatest hero* a *monarch*.
332. Alexander marches against Jerusalem.
    the *God* of the *Hebrews* is *adored* (Josephus' Antiq.)
320. Jerusalem taken by Ptolemy Soter: 100,000 Jews captured.
    the *Egyptians drive* them into *exile*.
314. Antigonus wrests Judæa and Phœnicia from Ptolemy.
    greatly curtails the *kingdom*.
284. The Septuagint translation completed at Alexandria.
    the *first rendering* of the *Scriptures*.
263. Berosus of Babylonia writes the history of his country in Greek.
    a *famous native historian*.
216. Ptolemy Philopater slays 50,000 Jews at Alexandria.
    a *frightful carnage* at *Alexandria*.
204. The sect of the Sadducees formed.
    they *denied* the *existence* of *spirits* (Acts xxiii. 8).
198. Antiochus the Great recovers Palestine from Egypt.
    Canaan is *triumphantly restored*.
170. Antiochus-Epiphanes, King of Syria, takes Jerusalem and plunders the Temple.
    a *cruel persecutor wastes* it (1 Mac. i. 20-24).
168. Epiphanes dedicates the Temple of Jehovah to Jupiter.
    a *blasphemer's impious revenge*.
165. Judas Maccabeus begins his insurrection.
    courageous Maccabeus the *liberator*.
160. Death of Judas: composition of "The Maccabees."
    the *Book* of *Maccabees written*.
155. Palestine freed from the yoke of Syria.
    a *breathing allowed* it for a *little*.

B.C.
146. Third Punic War: Carthage destroyed.
  the *Carthaginian kingdom annihilated.*
144. Jonathan the high priest slain by Iryphon.
  butchery of *Jonathan* by the *Syrians.*
125. Antiochus VII. besieges Jerusalem.
  conquers the *Holy Land.*
130. John Hyrcanus subdues Idumæa.
  compels the *Gentiles* to *worship.*
107. Aristobulus, his son, assumes the title of king.
  a *crown worn* by a *priest.*
95. The Pharisees provoke an insurrection in Jerusalem.
  the wonted *troublers* of the *land.*
88. Anna, the prophetess, begins to reside in the Temple.
  waiting for the *era* of *redemption* (Luke ii. 37).
70. Aristobulus II. deposes his brother Hyrcanus.
  excited by *Pompey* to the *war.*

SECT. 10.—The Jews under the Romans (B.C. 63-4).

B.C.
63. The Romans, under Pompey, take Jerusalem.
  the Western *Empire grasps* it.
54. Crassus plunders the Temple, and overruns Judæa.
  he wastes the *land* of the *Jews.*
48. Antipater becomes Governor of Judæa.
  Judæa is under the *Romans.*
40. Herod the Great, son of Antipater, becomes King of Judæa.
  the *senate exalts* him.
37. The Romans, under Herod, take Jerusalem, and slay multitudes of the inhabitants.
  the wicked *Herod persecutes* them.
31. An earthquake destroys 30,000 persons in Judæa.
  a *great convulsion.*
28. The Roman republic ends: Augustus becomes emperor.
  the *fall* of the *republic.*
17. Herod begins to rebuild the Temple.
  the wiles of a *crafty prince.*

B.C.
11. Herod builds the city of Cæsarea.
   he builds Cæsarea.
5. Birth of John the Baptist.
   he walks in the ways of Elijah (Luke i. 57).
4. Birth of Jesus Christ.
   welcome the world's Saviour ! (Luke ii. 7).
3. Death of Herod : Archelaus becomes Ethnarch of Judæa, Samaria, and Idumæa.
   woe to the wicked Herod ! (Matt. ii 22.)
„ Herod Antipas (son of Herod the Great) becomes Tetrarch of Galilee and Peræa.
   his wife was the wicked Herodias (Mark vi. 14).
2. Jesus returns with his parents from Egypt to Nazareth.
   exodus of the Deliverer (Matt. ii. 23).

CHAP. II.—NEW TESTAMENT HISTORY.

(B.C. 4.-A.D. 100.)

WE cannot be expected here to discuss all the difficulties connected with New Testament chronology, for, however interesting in themselves, they are insignificant when compared with those we encountered under the last chapter. There the discrepancies sometimes amounted to several centuries, whereas here they usually embrace only a very few years. By far the most important is the true date of our Lord's birth. This is the central point of human history—the grand era from which all other events are counted by Christian nations. Hence this era—when "the Word became flesh," and when the Creator eternally allied Himself to the creature—is significantly termed "the fulness of time." But just as we cannot determine that point in past *eternity* when God called the physical universe into existence ; or that point in past *time* when living creatures first peopled the earth; or that greatly more recent date when God created man in His own image; or, finally, that other point, still future, when "an angel shall swear by Him that liveth for ever and ever that time shall be no longer;"—so also we cannot determine, at least with undoubted accuracy, the precise time when the Word became flesh, and when our ruined species became linked, by indissoluble bonds, to the Eternal.

The New Testament writers—closely following the example of Moses—give us two distinct genealogies of our Lord (Matt. i. 1-16; Luke iii. 23-38), the one being his lineage through Joseph, his supposed father, and the other his real pedigree through Mary. These genealogies sufficiently determine the order of time in which the "Desire of all nations" appeared, but they do not fix the precise year. As the genealogy given by Matthew was specially meant for Jewish readers, it begins with Abraham their renowned ancestor; while that of Luke, whose main purpose was to show that Jesus is the kinsman of the entire race, is extended backward to Adam, who is emphatically styled "the son of God." Matthew appends a very curious summary to his genealogy, apparently for *mnemonic* purposes: "So all the generations from Abraham to David are fourteen generations; and from David until the carrying away into Babylon are fourteen generations; and from the carrying away into Babylon unto Christ are fourteen generations." This remarkable summary, besides being helpful to the memory, is eminently *suggestive;* for here the God of Israel is represented as marching gloriously through the ages in stately, measured steps, disposing at pleasure of all events in Israel's history, and, through Israel, of the fortunes of all mankind. It will be perceived that the passage does not refer to *all* past time, but simply to *Israel's* past; not to the five thousand years that had already elapsed of human history, but to the two thousand years that had elapsed since God singled out one family from among all the families of our species to be a peculiar people unto Himself. Here God is seen descending from heaven to earth, and the precise spot which His feet first touch is UR OF THE CHALDEES, the native city of him who is, ere long, honoured with the appellation of "the friend of God."

"Arise," said God, "get thee out of thy country, and from thy kindred, unto a land that I will show thee; and I will make of thee a great nation; and I will bless thee, and make thy name great: and in thee and thy seed shall all families of the earth be blessed" (Gen. xii. 1-3). Subsequently he greatly enlarges this promise by adding, "And I will establish my covenant between me and thee, and thy seed after thee, in their generations, for an everlasting covenant, to be a God unto thee, and to thy seed after thee. And I will give unto thee and to thy seed after thee the land wherein thou art a stranger, all the land of Canaan, for an *everlasting possession;* and I will be their God" (Gen. xvii. 7, 8). These exceeding great and precious promises are afterwards solemnly confirmed by an oath, when Abraham by self-sacrificing obedience has demonstrated the vitality of his faith. "And the angel of the Lord called unto Abraham out of heaven the second time, and said, By myself have I sworn, saith the Lord, because thou hast done this thing, and hast not withheld thy son, thine only son, that in blessing I will bless thee, and in multiplying I will multiply thy seed as the stars of heaven, and as the sand which is upon the sea-shore; and thy seed shall possess the gate of his enemies; and in thy seed shall all the nations of the earth be blessed, because thou hast obeyed my voice" (Gen. xxii. 15-18). We give these passages at length, because they constitute Israel's title-deeds to the land out of which he has, for a time, been ejected, and because the time is approaching when the original charter will speak for itself.

The inspired apostle next sees the Ancient of days beginning to walk down, in solemn tread, athwart the centuries. His feet first meet the ground at HEBRON—where Abraham once purchased a field and a cave in which to deposit the sacred remains of his beloved Sarah, thus affording to his posterity a new ground of hope that at a future day they would obtain possession of the entire land — and at the moment that the man after God's own heart is being crowned king of the covenant people. This stupendous step embraces a period of 866 years, or, according to the authentic pedigree from which the

apostle is quoting, it embraced "fourteen generations" of men *
(including events till then unparalleled in the world's history),
and terminated with the full establishment of the Israelitic
kingdom, and the erection of the Temple where the God of
Israel dwelt among them after the manner of an earthly sovereign. The next step spans the entire period of the kingdom—
embracing 467 years, or fourteen generations—and Jehovah's
foot is seen to rest on "the rivers of Babylon," where captive
Judah, the last of the tribes of expatriated Israel, sits on the
ground weeping, with her harp hung up on the willows, remembering Zion, and refusing to be comforted (Ps. cxxxvii. 2).

One step more, and the Eternal plants his foot on the most
interesting point of the earth's surface, and at the moment when
the most memorable event in the world's annals is being enacted
—even when the Eternal Son, now incarnate, lies a little babe in
the manger at BETHLEHEM, and when an angel is heard proclaiming, "Fear not: for, behold, I bring you good tidings of great joy,
which shall be to all people. For unto you is born this day, in
the city of David, a Saviour, which is Christ the Lord." The
event is not merely of infinite importance to Israel and to "all
people," but it necessitates a grand jubilee in the realms of
glory; for "suddenly there was with the angel a multitude of
the heavenly host praising God, and saying, Glory to God in the
highest, and on earth peace, goodwill toward men." This, truly,
is the divine fruit of that wondrous tree which, ages before,
Jehovah had planted, but which has not yet produced its destined fruit.

---

* In reality this period (from Abraham to David) embraced about 36
generations — viz., 5 from Abraham to Ephraim; 19 from Ephraim to
Joshua the son of Nun (see 1 Chron. vii. 20-27); and about 12, at least,
from Joshua to David. That there were 19 generations—that is, *descents*
—from Ephraim to Joshua, we have fully demonstrated in our remarks on
the chronology of the Old Testament (p. 68). Doubtless the "fourteen
descents" recorded by St Matthew were all the names *recorded* in the
genealogy of the tribe of Judah in the period referred to; but, as in almost all similar cases, this genealogy records only well-known outstanding names.

Here the Almighty pauses as if to contemplate the glory yet to be revealed—that eternal revenue of glory which He will infallibly derive from this unparalleled event. Assuredly, however, though He pauses, He does not mean to halt. His face is still steadfastly directed towards the future, and we are led confidently to expect that He will take as many steps more as He has already taken. Indeed we cannot but anticipate that His future steps shall, like all His past, be both *measured* and *majestic;* and that they shall, in the same way, correspond with the critical junctures in Israel's future. The two millenniums He has already traversed consisted, as we have seen, of three great periods, commencing respectively with Abraham, David, and the Captivity; and doubtless three other periods, not less eventful, have yet to be traversed ere all God's purposes regarding His covenant people shall have been consummated. The Cross of Christ stands in the centre of all the ages. The three former periods terminated *there;* and *there* must the three periods that follow begin. Not only does St Matthew *suggest* this in his famous mnemonic sentence (for *mnemonic* it is, in the highest sense of the term), but near the end of his Gospel (Matt. xxiv. 3-41) He shows how the Lord Himself, as He sat on the Mount of Olives, and immediately before His last sufferings, filled up St Matthew's outline with details of the most momentous character. St Luke in the first chapter of the Acts, St Paul in his two epistles to the Thessalonians, and especially St John in that wonderful " Revelation" which so appropriately closes the canon of Scripture (particularly chap. xx.), furnish us with many further particulars. In short, all the writers of the New Testament agree in assigning to the portion of Israel's history then future THREE GRAND PERIODS, which, on account of their main characteristics, we may denominate the Period of the Dispersion, the Period of the Kingdom, and the Period of Consummation, after which time shall cease and the eternal ages begin. But all the periods in Israel's history, whether past or future, will be more clearly apprehended by our employing a simple diagram.

THE SIX PERIODS OF ISRAEL'S HISTORY.

A	Abraham.
1.	Israel's preparation, or the planting and training.
B	David.
2.	Israel under kings.
C	Captivity.
3.	Israel in subjection.
D	Christ.
4.	Israel dispersed among the nations, or, "the times of the Gentiles."
E	Second Advent.
5.	Israel restored to the kingdom, or, "the times of restitution."
F	Satan loosed.
6.	The age of consummations.
G	General Judgment.

It will be observed that the periods are separated from each other by double lines enclosing narrow *spaces*—for the ages of history, and especially those of Israel's history, glide into one another as gradually and imperceptibly as the colours of the rainbow. Or, taking another illustration, a man can measure the length he traverses on the sea-shore by merely counting the number of his footprints on the sand; but the measurement must include not simply the distance between the footprints, but also the length of the footprint itself. Each of the double lines (A, B, C, &c.), denotes, therefore, not a single point of time, but a considerable number of years. Thus, when the evangelist says, "from the captivity to Christ are fourteen generations," it would be impossible to say which of the *three deportations* he alludes to; and whether he refers to the incarnation, birth, baptism, death, resurrection, or ascension of the Lord. As a matter of fact, all these events separate the present age from that which preceded it; and it will be found, in all cases, that the brief period that separates one age from another is crowded with events having a vital bearing on the character of the later age. Thus the PRESENT PERIOD (marked 4 in the diagram) derives all its peculiarities from the events that took place immediately prior to the Lord's ascension (D); for that people for whom, above all others, the Son of God died—that people who nailed Him to the tree, exclaiming, "His blood be on us and on our children"—have for the last eighteen hundred years been wandering among the nations as fugitives and vagabonds. That fearful imprecation, taken in conjunction with the unparalleled crime to which it had reference, was so heinous and aggravated, that the heavens became black at the spectacle, the rocks rent, and all nature reeled to its foundations. Such was the crime, that although the divine sufferer looked up to heaven and cried, "Father, forgive them, for they know not what they do," no response has been given to the prayer until this day. But that prayer was as unparalleled as the crime; and though God in His wrath has delayed the answer, yet that answer lies among the absolute certainties of the future, "for God hath not cast away His people which He foreknew." "Blindness in part is happened to Israel, until the fulness of the Gentiles be come in;

and so all Israel shall be saved: as it is written, There shall come out of Zion the Deliverer, and shall turn away ungodliness from Jacob" (Rom. xi. 25, 26). Till that eventful day arrives (we have no hesitation in affirming it), all the pious efforts of Christians to induce Israel to acknowledge their Messiah cannot fail, except in individual cases, to end in disappointment. The period or age now existing is emphatically termed by the Lord "the times of the Gentiles," and these "times" are to continue until the Lord's second advent (E). During this period, "this gospel of the kingdom shall be preached in all the world for a witness unto all nations, and then shall the end come" (*i.e.*; the end of the *age*, Matt. xxiv. 14). All the nations, however, it appears, are not to be saved by such preaching, for the passage indicates the contrary, and *that* result will never be attained till the seed of Abraham become the preachers; but the heralds of salvation are now sent to every land to proclaim salvation through Christ to all nations, "as a *testimony against them*," and in order to leave all men without excuse. A limited number, however, from all nations, will give heed to the good tidings, and surrender themselves to Him who is now seated at God's right hand. These, in their aggregate, are called in Scripture "the fulness of the Gentiles;" for though a very small body in comparison with the mighty host "whom the God of this world (*age*) hath blinded," they will doubtless form an immense multitude.

Before the age terminates, or the millennial era commences, Christianity will everywhere become adulterated—the impure leaven will have thoroughly changed the character of the "three measures of meal" (Matt. xiii. 33), and the faithful witnesses shall be hated of all nations, and be everywhere persecuted. The true Church, in deepest distress, shall look upward and cry, "Lord, how long!" and then, as when He delivered His covenant people from Egypt, " the Lord himself shall descend from heaven with a shout, with the voice of the archangel, and with the trump of God; and the dead in Christ shall rise first: then we which are alive and remain shall be caught up together with them in the clouds, to meet the Lord in the air" (1 Thess. iv. 16). It would appear that immediately after the removal of the saints the wrath of the Almighty shall descend in unparalleled judgments on the earth, yet the inhabitants shall not learn righteousness. On the contrary, wickedness shall abound, and the love of many wax cold. Then, also, shall the long-predicted Antichrist—that "wicked one," who is to be as really an incarnation of Satan as the Redeemer was of the divine nature—appear, "with all power and signs and lying wonders, opposing and exalting himself above all that is called God, or that is worshipped; so that he, as God, shall sit in the temple of God, showing himself that he is God." His reign, however, is destined to be of short duration; for the Lord "shall consume him with the spirit of His mouth, and destroy him with the brightness of His coming" (2 Thess. ii. 3, 12).

"The times of the Gentiles" shall thus suddenly come to an end, and a new age begin (Period 5 of our diagram). Judah and Ephraim shall then suddenly be brought back to their own land in a state of unfeigned repentance; for "it shall come to pass in that day that I will pour on the house of David and on the inhabitants of Jerusalem the spirit of prayer and of supplication; and they shall look on me whom they have pierced, and shall mourn for him as one mourneth for his only son, and shall be in bitterness as one is in bitterness for his first-born" (Zech. xii. 9).

SECT. 11.—From the Birth of Christ to the Ascension (B.C. 4-A.D. 31).

B.C.
4. Birth of Christ, four years before the vulgar era.
A.D.   welcome, the world's *Saviour* (Matt. i. 25).

1. Birth of Christ, according to Dionysius Exiguus.
      Exiguus's wrong *computation*.

6. Augustus makes Palestine a Roman province.
      extinguished its *nationality* (Luke ii. 1).

7. Archelaus, Ethnarch of Judæa and Samaria, is banished by the emperor to Gaul.
      the weary exile of the *prince*.

„ Coponius becomes first procurator of Judæa.
      it is under the yoke of *procurators*.

A.D.
- 8. Jesus at Jerusalem among the doctors.
    a young reasoner (Luke ii. 46).
- 14. Tiberius succeeds his stepfather Augustus.
    this *Cæsar* is the *second*.
- ,, Valerius Gratus, fifth procurator of Judæa.
    he *commanded Judæa*.
- 18. Herod Antipas builds Tiberias, on the margin of the Sea of Galilee.
    on the western *coast erected*.
- 19. Tiberius banishes the Jews from Rome.
    they are *banished* by *Tiberius*.
- 26. Pontius Pilate becomes the sixth procurator of Judæa.
    awed by the *fear* of *man* (Luke xxiii. 24).
- ,, John the Baptist begins his ministry.
    the *forerunner* of the *Messiah* (John i. 6).
- 27. The baptism of Jesus by John.
    a *dove appears* (John i. 32).
- ,, Commencement of Christ's ministry.
    the *divine Preacher* (John i. 38).
- ,, Caiaphas becomes high priest.
    a *famous prophecy* (John xi. 51).
- ,, Jesus at the marriage of Cana in Galilee.
    wine *fills* the *pots* (John ii. 7).
- 28. Jesus, at the first passover, cleanses the Temple.
    The oxen and *doves* are *removed* (John ii. 16).
- ,, Jesus discourses with Nicodemus.
    He *discourses* with a *ruler* (John iii. 2).
- ,, Jesus discourses with the woman of Samaria.
    she *denies* His *request* (John iv. 5).
- ,, Jesus preaches his first sermon at Nazareth.
    His words *fill* them with *rage* (Luke iv. 16).
- ,, John beheaded by Herod Antipas.
    a *damsel's request* (Matt. xiv. 8).
- 29. The Sermon on the Mount.
    He expounds *divine truth* (Matt. v. 1).
- ,, The twelve disciples are sent forth to preach.
    the *disciples* on a *tour* (Matt. x. 5).

A.D.
29. Peter's famous confession.
   a *fisherman's theology* (Matt. xvi. 16).
30. The transfiguration of Jesus.
   His *glory* was *wonderful* (2 Pet. i. 17).
,, The seventy disciples sent out.
   worthy of his *hire* is the *workman* ! (Luke x. 7.)
,, The disciples taught how to pray.
   they wanted a *heavenly example* (Matt. vi. 9).
,, The raising of Lazarus.
   at yonder *grave* He *weeps* (John xi. 43).
31. The counsel of Caiaphas.
   the *high-priest's counsel* (John xi. 47).
,, Jesus beyond Jordan : parable of the prodigal son.
   exemplifies *God's compassion* (Luke xv. 11).
,, Jesus blesses little children.
   extending His *hands* He *blessed* them (Matt. xix. 15).
,, Two blind men healed at Jericho.
   He willingly *heals* the *blind* (Mark x. 46).
,, The Lord's last appearance in the Temple.
   warns His *guilty censors* (Matt. xxiv. 1).
,, The fourth passover : the Lord's Supper instituted.
   the *Holy Communion* (Luke xxii. 15).
,, Judas Iscariot betrays Jesus.
   in *Gethsemane* he *betrayed* Him (Luke xxii. 47).
,, The crucifixion.
   the *God-man crucified* (Luke xxiii. 46).
,, The resurrection of Jesus.
   yield, O *grave*, thy *Captive* ! (Matt. xxviii. 6.)
,, The ascension into heaven.
   He wears a *glorious crown* (Acts i. 9).

SECT. 12.—From the Ascension to the Introduction of the Gospel into Europe (A.D. 31–51).

A.D.
31. Feast of Pentecost and descent of the Holy Ghost.
   welcome, *Holy Comforter* ! (Acts ii. 1.)

A.D.
31. Peter and John heal an impotent man.
    they *heal a cripple* (Acts iii. 1).

,, Peter and John before the Jewish Sanhedrim.
    exhibit *great courage* (Acts iv. 6).

,, The disciples practise community of goods.
    the whole of their *goods* in *common* (Acts iv. 32).

32. Ananias and Sapphira are struck dead.
    hypocrites are *frightened* (Acts v. 11).

,, The disciples are arraigned before the Sanhedrim.
    wary *Gamaliel's advice* (Acts v. 34).

,, The seven deacons are chosen.
    wise and *holy deacons* (Acts vi. 5).

,, Stephen, the first martyr, stoned.
    witness his *heavenly face!* (Acts vii. 54.)

,, Great persecution at Jerusalem—the disciples dispersed.
    a *general flight* (Acts viii. 1).

,, Philip, one of the seven, preaches at Samaria.
    wins a *host* from *death* (Acts viii. 5).

33. Simon Magus seeks to purchase the Holy Ghost.
    wanted the *Gift* for *gold* (Acts viii. 18).

,, Philip baptises the Ethiopian eunuch.
    on his way *home* by *Gaza* (Acts viii. 36).

34. Saul vehemently persecutes the Church.
    extreme *hatred* to the *saints* (Acts viii. 3).

35. Saul, on his way to Damascus, is converted.
    witnessed a *heavenly light* (Acts ix. 1).

36. Peter's vision at Joppa: conversion of Cornelius.
    the *Gentiles* to be *invited* (Acts x. 9).

,, Pontius Pilate and Caiaphas deposed: Pilate is succeeded by Marcellus.
    the *guiltiest* of *mankind*.

37. Birth of Josephus, the historian.
    wrote the *history* of his *people*.

,, Death of Tiberius, and accession of Caligula.
    hated by his *people*.

A.D.

37. Paul, at Jerusalem, is sent to preach to the Gentiles.
    the *Gentile's apostle* (Acts ix. 15).

38. Paul preaches to the Gentiles at Tarsus, his native city.
    welcomes the *heathen* to the *Redeemer* (Acts xi. 25).

41. Claudius, fourth Roman emperor, ascends the throne.
    he *succeeds Caligula* (Acts xi. 28).

,, Herod Agrippa becomes king of Palestine.
    wields the *sceptre* of *Canaan* (Acts xii. 1).

,, Paul leaves Tarsus for Antioch in Syria.
    they are *known* as "*Christians*" (Acts xi. 26).

42. Herod slays the Apostle James and imprisons Peter.
    James is *decapitated* (Acts xii. 2).

43. Paul and Barnabas go from Antioch to Jerusalem with a collection.
    they went to *Jerusalem* with a *gift* (Acts xi. 30).

44. Paul goes to Asia Minor on his first missionary journey.
    exhorts them to *seek salvation* (Acts xiii. 38).

45. Paul and Barnabas in Cyprus.
    the *sorcerer Elymas* (Acts xiii. 8).

46. Paul and Barnabas go to Antioch in Pisidia.
    they *set* out for *Antioch* (Acts xiii. 14).

,, Paul and Barnabas visit Iconium and Lystra.
    "*Jupiter* and *Mercury!*" (Acts xiv. 8.)

,, Paul and Barnabas go to Antioch in Syria.
    they *sail* to *Antioch* (Acts xiv. 26).

47. Paul sees a heavenly vision.
    a wondrous *sight appears* (2 Cor. xii. 2).

48. Disputation at Antioch regarding circumcision.
    a war for *Jewish rites* (Acts xv. 1).

,, Paul and Barnabas sent to Jerusalem to consult the Apostles.
    a *synod's resolutions* (Acts xv. 2).

49. Paul and Barnabas return to Antioch in Syria.
    the *Judaisers* are *vanquished* (Acts xv. 22).

50. Peter, at Antioch, is rebuked by Paul for dissimulation.
    what a *lamentable example!* (Gal. ii. 11.)

A.D.
51 Paul leaves Antioch for Cilicia.
   leaves for *Cilicia* (Acts xv. 41).

 ,, Paul, at Lystra, becomes acquainted with Timothy.
   the wanderer *lights* on a *companion* (Acts xvi. 1).

SECT. 13.—From the Introduction of the Gospel into Europe to the Death of John (A.D. 51–100).

A.D.
51. Paul at Troas sees a remarkable vision.
   yonder the *Lord* is *beckoning* us! (Acts xvi. 9.)

 ,, Paul and Timothy arrive at Macedonia.
   Lydia is *converted* (Acts xvi. 11).

52. Felix becomes procurator of Judæa.
   wantonly *loved Drusilla* (Josephus).

 ,, Paul visits Athens, and preaches on Mars' Hill.
   laments their *idolatry* (Acts xvii. 22).

53. Paul at Corinth is arraigned before Gallio.
   a *liberal-minded governor* (Acts xviii. 12).

 ,, Paul writes to the Thessalonians and Galatians.
   "the *Lord* is at *hand*" (Phil. iv. 5).

54. Paul sets out for Jerusalem, and sails by Ephesus.
   he *leaves* for *Jerusalem* (Acts xix. 21).

 ,, Paul returns to Antioch in Syria.
   he *leaves* for *Syria*.

 ,, Paul leaves Antioch on his third missionary journey.
   a *long journey*.

 ,, Nero, the fifth Roman emperor, succeeds Claudius.
   a wretched *life* of *sensuality*.

55. St Matthew writes his Greek Gospel.
   exhibits our *Lord's lineage*.

 ,, St Mark writes his Gospel at Rome.
   exhibits our *Lord's life*.

 ,, St Paul, at Ephesus, writes 1st Corinthians.
   he excommunicates a *lawless libertine*.

56. St Paul leaves Ephesus for Troas and Philippi.
   he *leaves* for *Macedonia* (Acts xx. 1).

57. St Paul composes his 2d Epistle to the Corinthians.
   writes them a *letter* from *Philippi*.

A.D.
58. Returns to Corinth, and writes to the Romans.
        wholly excludes *legal righteousness.*

59. Paul, at Miletus, sends for the Ephesian elders.
        they wept at *leave taking* (Acts xx. 37).

,, Paul, at Jerusalem, is assaulted in the Temple.
        they *lay* hold on him in the *Temple* (Acts xxi. 27).

,, Lysias sends Paul by night to Cæsarea.
        Lysias evades them (Acts xxiii. 23).

,, Paul tried by Felix, then left in prison two years.
        the *eloquent Tertullus* (Acts xxiv. 2).

60. Felix is recalled, and is succeeded by Porcius Festus.
        Nero expels him (Acts xxiv. 27).

,, Paul pleads his cause before Agrippa and Bernice.
        what *noble witnessing!* (Acts xxvi. 27.)

,, Paul is sent to Rome, but is shipwrecked.
        at *Malta* they *winter* (Acts xxviii. 1).

61. Paul arrives in Rome, where he remains two years.
        the *missionary* in the *capital* (Acts xxviii. 30).

62. Festus dies, and is succeeded by Albinus.
        he witnessed *many disorders.*

63. Paul, in Rome, writes Ephesians, Colossians, Philemon,
        and perhaps Philippians and Hebrews.
        what *noble gems!*

,, St Luke writes his Gospel and the Acts at Rome.
        matchless histories.

64. Paul tried and acquitted by Nero.
        Nero justifies him.

,, Rome set on fire by Nero, who blames the Christians.
        Nero himself *kindled* it.

,, First general persecution of the Christians.
        an awful *massacre* of the *saints.*

,, Paul escapes from Rome, and goes to Macedonia and
        Asia Minor.
        an expedition to *Macedonia* and *Asia* (Acts xx. 1).

A.D.

64. Paul leaves Macedonia and sails to Spain.
    went from Macedonia to Spain (Rom. xv. 28).

65. Rebellion in Judæa against the Romans breaks out.
    a *mutiny* in the *Land*.

,, Many prodigies are seen at Jerusalem.
    the wonders in *nature* are *alarming* (Josephus).

,, Paul leaves Spain for Crete, Miletus, Corinth, &c.
    this *mission* is his *last*.

66. The Jewish war begins under Flavius Vespasian.
    a war *unparalleled* in *annals*.

67. Paul sets out for Nicopolis in Epirus, and writes his Epistle to Titus.
    what a *noble pastoral!* (Tit. iii. 12.)

,, Paul is arrested at Nicopolis and sent to Rome.
    his *end* is *approaching* (Acts xxvii. 1).

,, Paul arrives in Rome and is confined in the Mamertine prison.
    the awful *Mamertine prison* (Acts xxviii. 16).

,, Paul writes his 2d Epistle to Timothy.
    he *ends* his *epistles*.

,, Massacre of the Jews at Cæsarea, Ptolemais, and Alexandria.
    monstrous proceedings.

68. Paul and Peter are tried, and condemned to be slain.
    executed by *Nero* at *Rome* (Josephus).

,, Death of Nero, who is succeeded by Galba.
    the execrable *Nero* is *removed*.

69. Flavius Vespasian, the ninth emperor, proclaimed at Alexandria.
    next after *Vitellius*.

70. Jerusalem destroyed by Titus Vespasian, the emperor's son, and a million of Jews massacred.
    what a *piteous wail!*

73. Palestine finally subdued by the Romans.
    the wicked *people* are *humbled*.

A.D.
79. Titus Vespasian, tenth emperor of Rome.
   this *prince* is the *tenth*.
81. Domitian, the eleventh emperor (but the twelfth Cæsar).
   a *reign* of *cruelty*.
95. St John banished to Patmos by Domitian; second general persecution.
   tribulation is *allotted* him (Rev. i. 9).
96. The Book of Revelation written by St John.
   it expounds the "*time* of the *end*" (Rev. i. 1).
„ Domitian assassinated: Nerva succeeds him.
   the *twelfth emperor*.
98. Trajan, the thirteenth emperor of Rome.
   Trajan restores (the empire).
99. Death of John (?), the last of the apostles.
   He *outlived* the other *twelve*; or, "what is *that* to *thee?*" (John xxi. 22.)
100. Third general persecution, under Trajan.
   the *Christians* are *wantonly exterminated*.

CHAP. III.—ECCLESIASTICAL HISTORY.

In dealing with this great subject, our limits compel us to confine our attention to the first five centuries, or, more accurately speaking, to the period preceding the downfall of the Roman empire. Section 14 enumerates all the principal Christian writers from the last surviving apostle to Gregory the Great; or all those who, by their writings, either adorned and defended the kingdom of God in its infancy, or who, by advocating perverse opinions, sought to corrupt and undermine it. Many of their works are now hopelessly lost, while of those that are extant a great many are weak and puerile in the extreme, especially when compared with the grave and venerable style of the New Testament writers. The gap which, in this respect, separates St John from his contemporary, Clement of Rome, is almost immeasurable. Childish as they are, however, these ancient writers have their use; and in our day, when all things are being examined anew, the republication of their principal works cannot fail to lead to exceedingly important results. On this ground we hail with deep satisfaction the resolute, though we fear often ill-remunerated, efforts of Mr T. Clark of this city, who, not content with introducing the reading public of this country to many of the noble scholars of Germany, is now engaged in publishing vigorous and elegant translations of all the principal extant productions of the Ante-Nicene Fathers.

Section 15 enumerates the twenty General or Œcumenical Councils recognised by the Roman Catholic Church. Of these the Greek Church regards only the first eight as binding; the Church of England the first six; while Christians in general bow to the authority of only one Council—not reckoned among the twenty—the Apostolic Council held at Jerusalem, A.D. 48. Section 16 is occupied with an enumeration of the so-called Ten General Persecutions, all of which occurred during the first three centuries, when the Church, unprotected and unbefriended, resolutely and persistently endeavoured to subjugate the world to the dominion of Christ, her King. These were the purest and best days of the kingdom of God, though the impure leaven had already begun to work; and hence heathenism, in its expiring agonies, convulsively endeavoured to destroy its superhuman adversary, which was every hour thinning its ranks. At length, in the providence of God, and in answer to the continued supplications of His people, a Christian emperor ascended the throne of the Cæsars, when immediately the religion of Jesus was tolerated throughout the bounds of the Roman empire. Section 17 records all the other principal events in ecclesiastical history from the death of St John to the age of Constantine, or the first development of the Church under external oppression; while the last section traces the history from Constantine to the fall of the Western empire, or the development of Christianity as the prevailing religion of the state, from A.D. 325 to 476.

SECT. 14.—Early Christian Writers (A. D. 101 – 604).

[NOTE.—*b.* denotes *birth; f. flourished; d. death.*]

A.D.
101. *d.* Death of Clement, Bishop of Rome.
   Clement who *wrote* to the *Corinthians.*
106. *d.* Death of Ignatius, Bishop of Antioch.
   a *bishop exposed* in the *amphitheatre.*
112. *f.* Papias, Bishop of Hierapolis.
   companion of the "*beloved disciple.*"
165. *d.* Justin Martyr beheaded at Rome.
   a *Christian martyr learnèd.*
167. *d.* Death of Polycarp, Bishop of Smyrna.
   they *burn* the *noble Polycarp.*
169. *f.* Athenagoras of Athens flourished.
   by *birth,* a *native* of *Athens.*
170. *f.* Hermias, the Christian philosopher.
   criticises the *pagan writers.*
176. *f.* Hegesippus writes his Church History.
   begins to *prepare* his *annals.*
177. *d.* Tatian, the Assyrian.
   abuses the *Platonic philosophy.*
181. *d.* Theophilus, Bishop of Antioch.
   boldly argues for *Christianity.*
185. *b.* Origen, the eminent commentator.
   birth of *Origen* of *Alexandria.*
196. *f.* Tertullian, presbyter of Carthage.
   became a *violent Montanist.*
202. *d.* Irenæus, Bishop of Lyons.
   the *first writer* in *France.*
218. *d.* Clement of Alexandria.
   a *devout Christian rhetorician.*
242. *f.* Gregory Thaumaturgus, Bishop of Neo-Cæsarea.
   first sacred edifices.
248. *f.* Dionysius, Bishop of Alexandria.
   a *few suspect* his *orthodoxy.*

FACTS AND DATES.

A.D.
254. *d.* Death of Origen.
   death of the *Alexandrian scribe.*
258. *d.* Death of Cyprian, Bishop of Carthage.
   Africa laments her *apostle.*
269. *d.* Death of Gregory Thaumaturgus.
   funny miracles these!
270. *b.* Eusebius, the Church historian.
   the *famous presbyter* of *Cæsarea.*
296. *b.* Athanasius, Bishop of Alexandria.
   a *decisive victory* at *Nice.*
307. Arnobius writes his treatise against the Gentiles.
   a *great writer* against *paganism.*
314. *b.* Cyril, Bishop of Jerusalem.
   great *Cyril* of *Jerusalem.*
321. *f.* Lactantius writes his Institutes.
   a *grand defence* of *Christianity.*
332. *b.* Epiphanius, Bishop of Salamis.
   an *honest Greek father.*
338. *d.* Death of Eusebius.
   the *great historian* of *religion.*
361. *f.* Chrysostom, Bishop of Constantinople.
   the "*golden mouthed*" *bishop.*
362. *f.* Gregory, Bishop of Nazianzen.
   Gregory of *Nazianzen flourished.*
368. *d.* Hilary, Bishop of Poitiers.
   Hilary menaced the *Arians.*
371. *f.* Basil the Great, Bishop of Cæsarea.
   a *great* and *pious bishop.*
372. *f.* Gregory of Nyssa.
   Gregory the *philosophic divine.*
373. *d.* Death of Athanasius.
   goes quietly to the *grave.*
374. *d.* Ephræm the Syrian.
   good *Ephræm* the *Syrian.*
385. *f.* Jerome translates the Hebrew Scriptures into Latin.
   the *Hebrew rendered* into *Latin.*

A.D.
395. *f.* Augustine, Bishop of Hippo.
   the *hero* of *theological literature.*
396. *f.* Rufinus, Presbyter of Aquileia.
   the *great Italian monk.*
397. *d.* Death of Ambrose, Archbishop of Milan.
   the *great Italian archbishop.*
415. *f.* Cyril, Archbishop of Alexandria.
   the *austere bishop* of *Alexandria.*
461. *d.* Leo the Great claims to be Vicar of Christ.
   sets up an *impious claim.*
518. *f.* Fulgentins, Bishop of Raspina.
   the *learned bishop* of *Raspina.*
531. *f.* Procopius of Gaza.
   a *learned historian* and *commentator.*
562. *d.* Cassiodorus, the Italian monk.
   the *learned monk* of *Calabria.*
„ *f.* Gregory, Bishop of Tours, author of a 'History of France.'
   the *learned prelate* of *France.*
604. *d.* Gregory the Great, Pope of Rome, dies.
   missionaries wander to *Kent.*

SECT. 15.—The Twenty Œcumenical Councils.

A.D.
325. Council of Nicæa or Nice—the Arian controversy.
   they *agree* in *defining* the "*Logos.*"
382. First Council of Constantinople — divinity of the Holy Ghost.
   the *Holy Ghost reckoned divine.*
431. Council of Ephesus—Pelagianism and Nestorianism condemned.
   sailors guard Cyril.
451. Council of Chalcedon—the Eutychian controversy.
   the *separate elements* of *Christ's* (person).
553. Second Council of Constantinople.
   we *learn little here!*

A.D.
680. Third Council of Constantinople.
the Monothelites are reckoned wrong.

787. Second Council of Nice.
Popish rites approved of.

869. Fourth Council of Constantinople.
the Roman emperor attended it.

1123. First Council of Lateran.
clerical celibacy first agreed on.

1139. Second Council of Lateran.
convoked to condemn heretical tenets.

1179. Third Council of Lateran.
the Church claims the power to torture.

1215. Fourth Council of Lateran.
the council determines to condemn the Albigenses.

1245. Council of Lyons.
condemns Frederick the Second at Lyons.

1274. Second Council of Lyons.
convoked in France by Pope Gregory.

1311. Council of Vienne.
a council in Gaul condemns "the beggars."

1409. Council of Pisa: two rival Popes.
the Church, scandalised, excommunicates the two.

1414. Council of Constance: John Huss and Jerome of Prague condemned.
courageous Jerome consigned to the stake.

1431. Council of Basil.
this Council seeks to heal the breach.

1512. Fifth Council of Lateran.
claims to limit Christian freedom.

1545. Council of Trent.
Calvinism and Lutheranism judged illegal.

SECT. 16.—The Ten General Persecutions.

A.D.
64. The Christians' First Persecution under Nero.
Nero slays them.

A.D.
95. The Second Persecution under Domitian.
   tribulations allotted them.

104. The Third Persecution under Trajan.
   the *Christians wantonly exterminated.*

119. The Fourth Persecution under Adrian.
   their *blood calls* for *vengeance.*

197. The Fifth Persecution under Severus.
   they are *cruelly tortured* by *persecutors.*

235. The Sixth Persecution under Maximinus.
   the *fury* of the *heathen let* loose.

249. The Seventh Persecution under Decius.
   by *far* their *severest trial.*

257. Eighth Persecution under Valerian: death of Cyprian.
   Africa laments her *apostle.*

272. The Ninth Persecution under Aurelian.
   the *edict* to *persecute* is *departed* from.

302. The Tenth Persecution under Diocletian.
   a *general extermination decreed.*

SECT. 17.—Principal Events in Ecclesiastical History from the Death of John to the Age of Constantine.

A.D.
101. Death of Clement, Bishop of Rome.
   Clement wrote to the *Corinthians.*

106. Death of Ignatius, Bishop of Antioch.
   a *bishop exposed* in the *amphitheatre.*

107. Symeon, Bishop of Jerusalem, crucified.
   a *bishop executed* in the *persecution.*

109. Pliny the younger, Procurator of Bithynia, asks advice from the emperor how he is to deal with the Christians.
   the *Consul writes* to *Trajan.*

112. Cerinthus, a Gnostic heretic, flourishes.
   a *contemporary* of the "*beloved disciple.*"

A.D.

115. The Lord's Day now generally observed by Christians.
Christians observe the *Lord's-Day.*

119. Fourth General Persecution under Adrian.
their *blood calls* for *vengeance.*

133. Valentine founds a new sect of Gnosticism.
a *bold Egyptian Gnostic.*

135. Basilides develops Gnosticism more fully.
Basilides, the *Gnostic* of *Alexandria.*

136. Adrian builds Ælia Capitolina on the site of Jerusalem.
bestows on it a *heathenish name.*

141. Marcion completes the first canon of Scripture.
the *canon* of *Scripture completed.*

143. The Syrian Gnostics Saturninus, Tatian, Bardesanes, and Marcion flourish.
a *band* of *Syrian heretics.*

144. The Ophites, another sect of Gnostics, appear.
the *basis* of their *system* was a "*serpent.*"

147. Justin Martyr writes his First Apology for Christianity.
courageous Justin's apology.

152. The Council of Pergamos, the first on record.
begin to *legislate* on *doctrine.*

158. Celsus, Lucian, and Arrian write against Christianity.
Celsus, Lucian, and *Arrian.*

161. Anicetus, Bishop of Rome, and Polycarp, dispute about the time of observing Easter.
controversies menace the *Church.*

166. Montanism and Monarchianism appear in the East.
the *beginning* of *Montanism* and *Monarchianism.*

167. Persecution of the Christians at Smyrna.
they *burn* the *martyr Polycarp.*

174. War with the Marcomanni: the Christians pray for the emperor.
the *Christians pray* for his *success.*

176. Hegesippus writes his Church History.
he *begins* to *prepare* his *annals.*

177. Persecution at Lyons and Vienne.
Bishop Pothinus perishes.

A.D.
185. Birth of Origen, the eminent Commentator.
  the *celebrated Origen* of *Alexandria.*
189. The Saracens, who now first appear in history, defeat the Romans.
  bands of *Arabians vanquish* them.
194. The Scriptures translated into Syriac (*Peshito*).
  the *Bible translated* into *Syriac.*
195. The Scriptures translated into Latin (*Itala*).
  the *Bible translated* into *Latin.*
196. Tertullian writes his Apology for Christianity.
  became a *violent Montanist.*
 ,, Byzantium taken by the Emperor Severus.
  Byzantium is *taken* by the *emperor.*
197. Fifth General Persecution under Septimius Severus.
  they are *cruelly tortured* by *persecutors.*
202. Severus issues an Edict prohibiting Christians from disseminating their doctrines.
  an *edict* to *exterminate* the *faith.*
 ,, Death of Irenæus, Bishop of Lyons.
  the *first writer* in *France.*
204. Origen appointed Catechist at Alexandria.
  a *famous expounder* of *Scripture.*
211. Caracalla becomes Emperor: the persecution ceases.
  favour bestowed on the *Christians.*
215. A council held at Carthage respecting baptism.
  an *African council legislates.*
217. Callistus and Hippolytus, rival bishops at Rome.
  a *furious contest* between *popes.*
218. Death of Clement of Alexandria.
  a *devout Christian rhetorician.*
 ,, Heliogabalus seeks to blend the Christian religion with heathenism.
  a *foolish blending* of *religions.*
220. Death of Tertullian.
  death of a *famous writer.*
222. Urban I., Bishop of Rome: Alex. Severus, Emperor.
  a *fearless defender* of the *faith.*

H

A.D.
230. Noetus excommunicated at Smyrna.
a famous heretic excommunicated.

,, Pontianus, Bishop of Rome: the schism of Hippolytus healed.
the *faction* of *Hippolytus extinguished.*

235. Sixth general persecution, under Maximinus.
the *fury* of the *heathen let-loose.*

240. Hippolytus, Bishop of Portus-Romanus, suffered martyrdom.
doubtful where his *see existed.*

242. Churches first used by Christians.
the *first sacred edifices.*

249. Seventh general persecution, under Decius.
by *far* their *severest trial.*

251. Schism of Novatian begins at Rome.
dispute about the *"lapsed"* commences.

254. Death of Origen: accession of Valerian, the 35th emperor.
death of the *Alexandrian scribe.*

257. Eighth general persecution, under Valerian: martyrdom of Cyprian, and Sixtus II., Bishop of Rome.
Africa laments her *apostle.*

261. The Sabellian controversy: synod of Alexandria: Dionysius the Great.
he *denied* the *incarnation* of *Christ.*

266. Paul of Samosata, Bishop of Antioch.
defends Monarchianism at *Antioch.*

270. Birth of Eusebius, Bishop of Cæsarea: Aurelian, emp.
the *famous presbyter* of *Cæsarea.*

272. The ninth general persecution, under Aurelian.
the *designs* of the *persecutors frustrated.*

274. Mani, or Manichæus, the heretic, put to death in Persia.
the *founder* of a *pernicious sect.*

284. Diocletian and Maximian, joint-emperors; Diocletian takes the East, and Maximian the West: era of Diocletian.
a *famous era* in the *East.*

A.D.
286. The Northmen attack the Roman Empire in the West, and the Persians in the East.
the frontiers ravaged by invaders.

292. Partition of the Roman Empire into four kingdoms, under Diocletian, Maximian, Constantius Chlorus, and Galerius.
four temporary divisions.

295. Alexandria taken by Diocletian.
Diocletian takes Alexandria.

302. The tenth persecution, under Diocletian.
a general extermination decreed.

,, Schism of Meletius of Lycopolis.
an Egyptian excites a disturbance.

305. The Council of Elvira enjoins celibacy on the clergy.
gainsay the written law.

306. Constantine, emp. in the West, Licinius in the East.
they halve the whole empire.

307. Arnobius issues his treatise against the Gentiles.
a great writer against paganism.

311. The Donatist schism.
the great controversy about Cicilianus.

312. Constantine the Great embraces Christianity.
the history of Christianity is affected by it.

313. Edict of Milan : Constantine grants toleration to the Christians.
a grand change in their history.

318. The Arian controversy begins : the Emperor becomes an Arian.
the head of the Church an Arian!

321. Constantine commands the observance of Sunday on all his subjects.
the holy day to be observed.

324. Constantine becomes sole emperor in East and West.
a great date in sacred (history).

,, Christianity becomes the religion of the State.
the holy faith established.

**SECT. 18.—From Constantine to the Fall of the Western Empire.
(324-476.)**

A.D.
325. Council of Nice condemns Arianism.
they agree in defining "the Logos."
330. Constantinople becomes the cap. of the Roman emp.
the government is gone from the West.
336. Death of Arius.
the greatest heretic of antiquity.
337. Death of Constantine the Great.
a great gap produced.
339. The Council of Antioch deposes Athanasius.
the heretics have a triumph.
350. Constantius strictly prohibits heathen sacrifices.
heathenism at last on the wane.
356. Athanasius expelled by force from his see by Constantius.
he gained his laurels at Nice.
359. The Gospels translated into Mœso-Gothic by Bishop Ulphilas.
the Gothic Ulphilas a translator.
361. Julian the Apostate becomes emperor.
a heathen monarch's accession.
371. Pelagius, founder of Pelagianism, born in Britain about this time.
the great Pelagian controversy.
373. Death of Athanasius, Bishop of Alexandria.
a great opponent of heresy.
375. Apollinaristic Controversy.
the heresy of Apollinarus of Laodicæa.
379. Theodosius the Great becomes emperor: advances Christianity.
heathenism persecuted in turn.
382. First General Council, of Constantinople: Macedonius condemned.
the Holy-Ghost reckoned divine.

ECCLESIASTICAL HISTORY. 117

A.D.
385. Jerome translates the Hebrew Scriptures into Latin.
the Hebrew rendered into Latin.

387. Valentinian II. embraces Catholicism: great triumph over Arianism.
the heresy of Arius put-down.

391. Ambrose induces the Emperor Theodosius to do penance for the massacre at Thessalonica.
a great triumph to the Church.

392. The temple of Serapis at Alexandria destroyed, and the final overthrow of Paganism in the East.
the heathen temples are demolished.

395. Augustine appointed Bishop of Hippo.
the hero of theological literature.

„ Final division of the empire between the sons of Theodosius.
a great event is looming.

397. Death of Ambrose, Archbishop of Milan.
the great Italian prelate.

„ Theophilus of Alexandria anathematises Origen, and denounces the Anthropomorphites.
a harsh and violent prelate.

407. Death of Chrysostom, Patriarch of Constantinople.
sinks on the way to Pityus.

410. Rome sacked and burned by Alaric, king of the Visigoths.
they sack the capital of the West.

411. The Pelagian controversy begins at Carthage.
a serious controversy commences.

415. Cyril becomes Bishop of Alexandria.
the austere bishop of Alexandria.

428. Nestorius becomes Patriarch of Constantinople: the Nestorian controversy begins.
serious differences arise.

430. Death of Augustine.
the saintly Augustine expires.

A.D.

431. Third General Council, at Ephesus, condemns Pelagian and Nestorian tenets.
sailors guard Cyril.

439. The Vandals overrun Africa, patronise the Arians, and persecute the Orthodox.
savage Genseric the *Vandal.*

443. The Huns, under Attila, lay waste the Roman Empire, after conquering the Germans.
savage Scythian hordes.

447. Simon Stylites, the hermit of Syria, founder of the sect of the Stylites.
Simon stands on his *pillar.*

449. The Jutes and Saxons arrive in Britain, and nearly extirpate Christianity.
the *Jutes* and *Saxons* in *Thanet.*

451. Fourth General Council (Chalcedon) condemns the tenets of Eutyches, and ratifies the doctrine of two natures and one person in Christ: Monophysite controversy.
the *separate elements* of *Christ's* (person).

461. Leo the Great, Pope of Rome, claims to be vicar of Christ.
sets-up an *impious claim.*

476. Monophysite doctrine declared the religion of the Eastern Empire.
the *State patronises the Monophysites.*

„ Extinction of the Western Empire by the Goths.
the *succeeding period* is *Mediæval.*

PART SECOND.—PROFANE HISTORY.

PERIOD I.—ANCIENT HISTORY.

CHAP. I.—HISTORY OF EGYPT.
(B.C. 2550-30.)

[The Author deems himself peculiarly fortunate in those whose co-operation he has secured in preparing the following introduction to his Chronology of Ancient Egypt. The portion bearing on the History of Egypt is from the pen of Mr W. Osburn, R.S.L., the author of many learned works on Egyptology, and who, from having devoted the greater part of his laborious life to the elucidation of the monuments of that country, and to the testimony which they afford to the truthfulness of the books of Moses, now occupies the foremost place among British Egyptologists. The second portion—that bearing on the Great Pyramid—bears the peculiar impress of its esteemed author, further mentioned in the final note. This paper cannot fail to be appreciated by the Christian who, with soundness in the faith and loyalty to the Master, combines a scientific interest in the order and history of the wonderful Cosmos which He has created.]

PART I.—THE HISTORY OF ANCIENT EGYPT.

THE early history of Egypt is older by centuries than that of any other nation with which we are acquainted. The natural and physical causes which account for this lie at the threshold of the inquiry. The situation of Egypt on the surface of the globe is in the driest parallels of latitude all round the earth, and in both hemispheres. To the eastward and westward of Egypt, and for nearly 3000 miles in each direction, it is closely hemmed in by sandy deserts, through which the river Nile forces its way all but due northward and southward. The periodical overflow of this river, consequent upon the tropical rains, has in the course of ages reclaimed from the desert, on each bank, a thin strip of land of extreme fertility, seldom exceeding half a mile in breadth on each side, and nowhere reaching further than eight or ten miles on both sides.

The mountain-ranges which bound this very narrow valley are composed of rocks of limestone, red sandstone, and granite of every variety of tint, offering everywhere to its inhabitants a perfectly inexhaustible treasure of the hardest and most permanent materials for the construction of magnificent buildings.

The inhabitants of Ancient Egypt had evidently considered these advantages when they invented the remarkable system of writing which is so well known by the name of Hieroglyphics, and with engraven inscriptions of which the walls of their public buildings were absolutely covered. Every character of this singular system is the representation of some physical object; and great artistic power is often displayed both in the outline and details of the birds, animals, &c., which so frequently stand for letters, or the symbols of sounds in it; so that these inscriptions, far from being an unsightly defacement, as on the Greek temples, constitute, in effect, a most important part of the ornature of their public buildings.

That the hieroglyphic mode of writing was invented in Egypt by the Egyptians, and with a special view to the perpetuation of the memories and exploits of the kings and nobles by whom their temples, &c., were constructed, we have elsewhere shown at considerable length. Everywhere throughout the land of Egypt, whether we read these singular inscriptions, magnificently executed on the walls and pillars of gorgeous temples, or attempt to decipher the coarse daubs and splashes of colour which cover the rudest mummy-cases, we shall find that the one object of both has been to procure for the writers an eternal remembrance upon the earth. Nothing in Ancient Egypt was too great or too small not to be deemed worthy of these attempts at perpetual memory.

Far from being, therefore, as a Greek inscription on a temple, unsightly, the constructions of Ancient Egypt—whether obelisks, propyla, temples, tombs, mummy-cases, or bandages—were all hewn from the mountain, or made by the labours of slave artificers, or dug in the bowels of the earth, with the especial view of their being covered with coloured hieroglyphics and reliefs representing gods and sacred animals.

There is another point to which we beg to call the attention of the reader. The first colonists of Egypt evidently reached it from the eastward, bringing with them the worship of Adam, the father of mankind, whom they identified with the setting sun—that is, the sun in the twelfth hour of the day. On, or Heliopolis, at the head of the Delta, is exactly the point at which travellers from the East would be most likely to first touch the land of Egypt. It is well worthy of note that everywhere in the tombs and the papyrus inscriptions of Egypt, the west is called the "blessed" west, and the east the "filthy" east; whereas in the books of the Burmahs and other Trans-Gangetic peoples, this order is inverted, the west being with them the "filthy" west, and the east the "blessed" east. That the point whence these two widely separated races began their first emigration lay somewhere between Egypt and India beyond the Ganges is the inevitable, and, as we submit, the highly important, inference which must be drawn from this fact.

There is yet another circumstance which is not without its importance in the elucidation of the Ethnography. Men and women with black complexions are frequently depicted on the tombs and temples of kings of Egypt contemporary with Abraham and his descendants, but they have merely the *swarthy hue* which is inevitable to exposure to the rays of the sun in countries to the southward of Egypt. They have still the straight noses and regular features of the inhabitants of Egypt and of Syria. But seven hundred years afterwards, in the reign of the king "who knew not Joseph," we see for the first time in the paintings of Ancient Egypt the flat nose and thick lips of the true negro. The period of seven hundred years is just about the time which we might have assumed would be required fully to negrify the European countenance. Surely this fact is not an unimportant one in the science of Ethnography.

We have already dwelt upon the very remarkable fact that the monumental history of Egypt begins with Suphis, the builder of the Great Pyramid, and his contemporaries or immediate predecessors. The names of a few of these predecessors occur occasionally, it is true, in the tombs of the princes that formed the court of Suphis and his nearest successors; but it is only as the reclaimers of tracts of land which afterwards fell into the hands of those nobles that they are so distinguished; or, still more rarely, they stand engraven in the genealogical tables, whereby a very few of their descendants justified their titles to be Pharaohs in Egypt. But nowhere in Egypt has any monument been discovered which it is possible to assign to any earlier epoch than that which may now be safely entitled the Suphic Period.

These earliest memorials of Ancient Egypt embody yet another strange peculiarity. When compared in point of execution with those of the later epochs in the long and varied history of that first of kingdoms, they are, in power and freedom of hand, in delicacy of finish, and in truth to nature, equal to the best of them—perhaps even superior. Where, then, did these first colonists acquire their artistic and constructive powers? Not in Egypt, certainly. No trace can be found there of those rude first attempts which so eloquently and instructively tell the history of the arts in all other countries. As masons or builders, the hardest stones the earth produces were quarried and adorned by them in gorgeous pillars and colossal blocks. As artists, their implements sculptured the entire surfaces, exterior and interior, of their constructions with pictures of physical objects, graven as exquisitely as jewels, finished as delicately as cameos. Where, we ask again, are the first crude attempts which long practice at length matured into this perfection of arts so difficult? We answer unhesitatingly, certainly not in Egypt.

Once more: how came these first settlers, who so clearly invented their picture-writing with an especial view to their own artistic proficiency, to have lost the mode of writing they had formerly possessed, and even the articulations of their former language, so that they had to invent a new language, making the pictures of birds, animals, &c., to represent the first intonation of the cries they naturally uttered? There is but one answer possible to these inquiries. The Scripture account of the dispersion of mankind from Babel, through the confusion of their language, is the only known fact in human history that can account for these strange circumstances (Gen. xi.)

The fact that the lists of kings of Egypt, constructed about the third century B.C. by Manetho and other Alexandrian Greeks, are so hopelessly discrepant among themselves that though the summation of the reigns of 30 dynasties amounts to 6000 years, yet their author has himself to tell us that their real sum is only 3555 years—this latter proving, on closer investigation, to be more than 1600 years too many—is surely not to be lost sight of in this inquiry.

The key to this difficulty is not far to seek; but it opens a dreary page in the annals of fallen man. To record historical truth—the facts that actually took place—formed but an insignificant part of the purpose of these historians. A far more important point in their estimation was to magnify the antiquity of their own country, so as to establish undeniably their assertion that Egypt was the oldest of kingdoms. Accordingly, they preface the human history of Egypt with a deafening trumpet-blast! When Menes, the first of mortal kings, ascended the throne, Egypt had already been a kingdom, under the sceptre of gods, demi-gods, and heroes, for 24,925 years! Yet of these 25 millenia not a trace, not a scratch, in the way of monumental memorial, remains; while the men of the two millenia that followed have absolutely covered Egypt with monuments of masonry and sculpture to an extent unparalleled in any other country. The workmen, moreover, exercised their art with a delicate perfection of finish and freedom of touch rarely equalled, and never surpassed. Now in Egypt, as we have seen, no monument ever perishes from the effects of climate. The necessary inference is, that the people known to us as Egyptians *did not* inhabit the valley of the Nile till the time indicated by the Mosaic record, and that the 24,925 years that, according to Manetho, preceded Menes, is a mere fable. According to Moses, moreover, the age that produced by far the most remarkable of those monuments was one in which the Almighty had frequent and familiar intercourse with man, as in the case of the Patriarchs, Abraham, Melchizedek, and Job; while the monument itself evinces innumerable evidences of a knowledge and a wisdom to which unaided humanity has nowhere ever attained.

PART II — SOME OF THE PECULIARITIES OF THE GREAT PYRAMID SYNOPTICALLY CONSIDERED.

In a compendium of historic and scientific facts, such as the present publication, no apology is needed for noticing that monument which is, strictly speaking, unique—*par excellence*, THE WONDER OF THE WORLD—being at once the most ancient of all in existence, and yet the most intellectually designed, and the highest as well as the most massive that man has ever erected, even by the aid of modern civilisation and wealth : that compendious " sign and wonder set in the land of Egypt unto this day." There being really in existence such a monument, and one only, replete with facts just such as we covet for this volume,—data of wondrous precision, signalled to us across the dark valley of forty centuries of comparative ignorance, during which it has remained an impenetrable enigma in the face of all the world,—apology would indeed be due *if we were to omit* noticing it. Only a portion of the significant facts of the structure (which we shall term its *references*) can be noticed in this synoptic manner; especially must its internal details, its astronomical references, and that order of symbolism in it that is of a more transcendent kind, be here omitted. Further, this being little more than a catalogue of results, no evidences or explanations can be here attempted, however needful these may be to the reader before he can decide for himself on the validity of the results. See notice of publications, &c., at end of this synopsis.

SECT. 1.—General Construction and Form of the Monument.

Art. 1.—Its Materials :—

A. The Coffer is of hardest and toughest granite, and not intended for a dead body, as in other pyramids.

B. Internal passages and the so-called Queen's chamber, of white Mokattam limestone, carefully selected, for parts exposed to wear ; joints wonderfully close ; King's (or Coffer) chamber of red granite.

C. Internal mass, not of rubbish, like many other massive structures, but of well-cut blocks, cemented ; these, and the foundation rock, are of nummulitic limestone, completely pervaded with fossil tokens of organic life.

D. Externally of white Mokattam limestone, of remarkable finish originally; it probably surpasses any building material since selected by man : * any exposed surface of it generates spontaneously, by the action of the weather, an efficient mineral protecting coat, of a buff tint: its durability in the open air, even at its finest edges, is incomparably greater than that of granite selected for subsequent pyramids by even the more experienced " wisdom of Egypt."

E. The cement of the fine joints is of astonishing tenacity.

2. *The correctness and discretion shown in its workmanship:* —There is abundant precision, wherever it is important for scientific data, &c., but a utilitarian economy of such workmanship, in proportion as it can be dispensed with, having regard to the meaning of the parts, and the securing of durability ; * while parts not to be metrically reckoned are made ostentatiously rough.

3. *Its metric standard,*

A. For parts cosmically and symbolically significant, is the sacred cubit (25.025 British inches), exactly one ten-millionth of earth's polar radius—the only natural standard of both unique and extreme precision ; a standard of divine origination, primæval, and preserved in the least disturbed line of Abraham's family (the Arabs) to the present day.

B. Other parts of the structure, not significant, are made in terms of quite another unit, of different origin—the earliest Gentile cubit (20.700 British inches), called the cubit of Memphis, popularly confused with the above-named.

C. National standards in general have originated in one or other of these, by various divisions, &c. * Organic objects (as foot, arm, cane, reed), approximating in length, were the usual origin of the national *names* of the later derived standards, but not of the *dimensions* of those later standards.

4. *Its form :*—

A. Its height, 233.1660 (being very approximately *seven-thirds* of a hundred) sacred cubits, equal to 486¼ British feet, is the

---

* The facts marked by asterisks have not been published previously.

radius whose circle, horizontally on the ground, determines the length of its square base-circuit.

B. The resulting slope of the sides, the π angle of the pyramid, is 51° 51′ 14″.3.

C. Base area $= \pi \times$ the direct vertical section of the pyramid.†

D. The *Azimuth trenches*, cut in the rock near the east side of the pyramid, show this π angle ; also its complement, and the position of the base-circle of the internal core—thus proving that it was made on these principles, and not on less mathematical principles accidentally producing *nearly* that form, as has been suggested in depreciation of its intellectuality.

5. *Allied peculiarities associated with the structural angle, but in a secondary way—that is, pertaining to, practically or approximately, the same form in masonry, though not with theoretical exactitude, as are the preceding :—*

A. The direct angle 51° 51′ 14″.3, is 144 pyramid degrees of 1000 to the circle.

* **B.** The diagonal angle is *seven-sixths* of 100 pyramid degrees.

* **C.** The direct rise is 9 vertical to the square root of 50 horizontal.

D. The diagonal rise is 9 vertical to 10 horizontal.

* **E.** The *ratio* of direct to diagonal *angle* is the square of the ratio 10 : 9; while the ratio of direct to diagonal *rise* is, as in any pyramid of whatever slope, the square of 2 : 1.

* **F.** The *difference* of slope between the direct and diagonal aspect of the pyramid, 0.02744 of a circle, cannot be exceeded—that is, any pyramid, either materially steeper or flatter, would show less difference between the two aspects of it.

* **G.** One-tenth of this angular difference in an entire circle represents the day in an entire *tropical year*.

H. The *surface of a side* is found to be (as Herodotus says) *the square of its height*, or radius of construction—*i.e.*, its *total surface* visible equals the square circumscribing its base-circle already explained.

* **I.** Its π angle, approximately, has its *sine = co-tangent,* and *tangent = co-secant :* this implies some curious facts.

---

* The facts marked by asterisks have not been published previously.
† St John Vincent Day's discovery.

* **J, K, L**. A length of 144 sacred cubits is found to be indicated by points determined by three different mathematical constructions of lines, measuring horizontally along its face from a mid-section plane.

* **M**. The whole form of the Great Pyramid is the same in every side and angle as a natural crystal; one of the definite forms in which the opaque mineral *wolfenite* is found.

6. *The coffer in the pyramid is similar to it in lineal proportions, exhibiting externally the π ratio of height to the length of two adjacent sides.*†

7. *The cubic ratios of the coffer :—*

A. The volume of the bottom = half that of its four sides.

B. The volume of its entire material, bottom and sides together, is equal to its internal content.

C. Its content or capacity is 71,250 cubic inches, pyramid measure. For the meaning of this quantity, see the cosmic references.—Sec. 3, Art. 7.

D. The content of the chamber where the coffer is, up to a marked level, is *fifty* times the coffer's content.

E. This chamber and its coffer stand on the *fiftieth* course of masonry from the base.

8. *The courses of masonry :—*

A. Level throughout, like horizontal strata; not dipping inwards, square with external face, in the more proper way for security. A special reason is perceptible : * as it is built, every external stone of its now ruined surface shows the original slope, and therefore height or radius of construction and the π ratio of base—the roots, in short, of the structure's references and meaning.

* **B**. Partly for the same important reason, the blocks of the core of the structure were set off, accurately in the long run, to the same slope as the batter of the finished casing was to be.

* **C**. There are indications that the horizontal joints of some important courses divided the direct slope, or measurement up the face, in terms of the sacred cubit as a unit.

9. *Their numbers :—*The 25th course is the level of the so-called

---

* The facts marked by asterisks have not been published previously.
† St John Vincent Day's discovery.

Queen's chamber : the 50th course, that of the King's chamber. The 209th course completed the pyramid, and shows the number of pyramid degrees subtended by all the courses, from the axis at the level where the entrance passage intersects the east and west vertical mid-section plane.

* 10. *The vertical axis* is UNINTERCEPTED : all the chambers, passages, &c., are made so as to manifest that they were to avoid interrupting the axis.

11. *The dominant number throughout the pyramid is* FIVE :
Subordinately, *five* is associated with *ten:*
Less specially, *three* in connection with *seven:*
And *nine* with *ten*.

Each have symbolic meanings determining their occurrence and domination.

SECT. 2.—Astro-chronologic references of the Structure.

Art. 1.—*A quinary system of facts.*—(**A**) The direction of the straight entrance-passage, inclining at 26° 20' into the north side of the pyramid, was such, that at (**B**) the date of its establishment (B.C. 2170) this direction was that of the primæval Polestar *a* Draconis, when at (**C**) its lower culmination; while the then chief star of the Pleiades, Alcyone, then near the celestial equator, was at (**D**) its upper culmination, or on the same meridian at midnight of (**E**) the autumnal equinox. This definite combination cannot recur for 25,898 years; it marked the date of the pyramid and of "the year of the Pleiades"—a commencement of a natural chronologic era, traditions of which have remained in most times and countries. This combination shows much evidence of original intention and unrestricted knowledge in designing the Great Pyramid, especially so when the following facts are remembered :—

2. *Facts of Astronomy.*—Those two stars were eminently suitable :

A. They were more rigorously *fixed stars* than most so called, especially more so than Sirius, so much preferred by the less profound wisdom of subsequent times.

* The facts marked by asterisks have not been published previously.

B. Those two were formerly more brilliant.

* C. That primæval and the present or ultimæval pole-star, the *Dracontos-* and *Cynos- ura*, and no others, are remarkably associated together in various mundane aspects: details, however, cannot be here given.

D. Alcyone, a primæval name of the star, means "*the centre,*" and has quite recently been discovered to be really the centre around which even our whole Solar System (amongst others) revolves.

E. The meridian of the primæval pole-star passed with maximum rapidity around the zodiac, through *Aquarius* (the Waterman), at the date of the Deluge; it became rigidly stationary on Alcyone at the date of the Great Pyramid, "the year of the Pleiades," after which it commenced to retrograde. These facts, noted by the pyramid, are confirmed and explained by Scripture, by ubiquitous tradition in all ages, and by mythology. * However divergent these witnesses be in other respects, all three agree in connecting the septenary constellation of the Pleiades—especially its leading star Alcyone—with " halcyon days," a commencement of a new era in calm and sunshine, in restoration and resurrection-life, out of the waters of death.

3. *Facts in the Pyramid :*—The angles of its other passages, and the direction of mathematical lines between various points in the structure, when considered in detail, confirm the reality and intention of the above-named references in the pyramid.

SECT. 3.—Other Cosmic References in the Structure.

REFERENCE BY MULTIPLE.—1. *OF LENGTH.*

1. *Solar distance by pyramid height :*—$10^9 \times$ (*i.e.*, a thousand million times) the pyramid radius or height (233.1660 sacred cubits, or $486\frac{1}{4}$ feet British) is the length of the sun's radius-vector, or mean distance of earth = 92,093,000 miles. That this reference was intentional in the design of the structure is evidenced by several other considerations, quite independently of the nume-

---

* The facts marked by asterisks have not been published previously.

rical coincidence itself. The same is more or less the case in each of the following references.

2. *Earth's mean orbit by pyramid base:*—10^9 × the pyramid base-circuit, is the length of earth's orbit.

3. *Earth's sidereal day's mean march in orbit, during one true rotation on its axis* (1,580,000 miles), is shown by the length of a suitably directed diagonal at the corner of S.E. part of base-circuit; * also of two other suitably placed lines along the base-circuit, 4 sacred cubits in length, symbolically significant, multiplied by 10^9.

4. *Earth's polar radius by the pyramid cubit:*—10^7 × (*i.e.*, ten million times) this cubit (25.025 inches British) is the length of earth's polar radius = 3949.65 miles.

5. *To express important cosmic quantities in general, this cubit seems to be curiously adapted beyond other standards, on whatever principle.*—In terms of this cubit many expressions are either integral or in neat simple ratios, surprising our ideas of probability. This has been already exemplified here, and even the recent discovery of the thermo-dynamic ratio supplies an illustration.—See Art. 10 of this section.

2. OF WEIGHT.

•6. *Earth's mass by pyramid's mass:*—$10^{3 \times 5}$ × (*i.e.*, a thousand billion times) the pyramid's weight, carefully computed, is the mass of the whole earth—namely, six thousand and fifty trillions of tons British. Thence we can deduce the mean specific gravity of the whole earth to be 5.7 × that of water, at pyramid standard temperature.

7. *Weight of a cubic unit* (50 inches pyramid measure in the side, or 25 pyramid inches = 1 cubit each way from its centre) of the mean of the whole earth, is 10 × coffer full of water, at pyramid standard temperature—namely, 2570 pounds British, and constituting the pyramid ton. Weight of 40 cubic cubits of earth (mean density of the whole) is the weight of water in the King's or coffer's chamber, up to the marked level, constituting the pyramid "sea," or largest unit of weight and

---

* The facts marked by asterisks have not been published previously.

measure. From each of these references we can again deduce the mean specific gravity; and these methods give 5.7, the same as by the former method. This identity of results, by itself, confirms the probable reality of both of these references; but much more so, as it is the same specific gravity as is inferred by the methods of physical science alone, as nearly as their uncertainties enable us to know it therefrom.

3. OF TIME.

8. *A year, or annual circuit of earth*, is represented by the length of the base-circuit of the pyramid — namely, a circle drawn with the pyramid height as its radius. Each sidereal day, or interval of true (not apparent) rotation of earth on its axis, becomes, on this same scale, represented by the 100 pyramid inches; each duration of light and darkness, the great natural binary subdivisions, by the *double cubit* each. The next binary natural subdivisions—the intervals between mid-day or night and sunrise or sunset—by *cubits;* the smallest primæval division—the watch—by the half-cubit or *pyramid foot*.

9. *The period of equinoctial precession* — *i.e.*, of tilting of earth's axis, in a complete circle (at 23° 28′ angle) around the mean position of the ecliptic axis—is represented by the length from base-centre to any base-corner, 258.9824 sacred cubits. Each century, on this same scale, becomes represented by a cubit. In other words, taking all of these diagonals (instead of any one), each year becomes represented by a pyramid inch.

* 10. *The period of tilting of the ecliptic axis,* similarly, in a complete circle (at 1° 21′ angle) around its mean position, is (uncertainly) represented by the length from base-centre to apex, *viâ* a base-corner, 607.4632 sacred cubits. Each century, on this same scale, becomes represented by a cubit.

4. REFERENCES BY SAMPLE.

11. *The direction of the poles and of the earth's rotation*—*i.e.*, of the lines of longitude and latitude—*i.e.*, of the cardinal points of azimuth—are respectively shown by the sides of the pyramid base.

* The facts marked by asterisks have not been published previously.

* 12. *The mean terraqueous level*—that is, of both land and water throughout the globe—is probably marked by the level of the pavement constituting the base-surface of the Great Pyramid.

This most difficult but important datum is in advance of modern physicists: they have regarded sea level alone in defining a mean level.

13. *Pyramid thermology.*— Its thermic standard, thermic scales, and thermo-dynamic equivalent :—

A. The natural mean, being also the standard temperature (68° Fahr.) of all inhabited parts of the earth,—best for the functions of man, intellectually and corporeally—best for organic life in general—and the *one-fifth* part of the thermic scale of water,—is marked by the (undisturbed) temperature constant in the interior of the Great Pyramid.

B. On the pyramid principles of subdivision, a thermic scale is found harmonising with cosmic nature, as follows :—

Fahrenheit Scale.	Pyramid Scale.	Cosmical Phenomena.
Degrees.	Degrees.	
32.	0.	Water freezes.
39.2	10.	Water at maximum density.
68.	50.	STANDARD TEMPERATURE relative to man and his cosmos.—See A.
104.	100.	High summer temperature at pyramid, and mean isothermal equator.
212.	250.	Water boils.
752.	1000.	Red heat to human eyes. A full exhibition of spontaneous luminosity of solids in general.

C. The thermo-dynamic equivalent.—Water passing vertically through $\frac{2}{3} \times 10^5 \times$ the pyramid cubit, represents one thermic unit of temperature in that water, with the recognised limitation of the ratio to the pyramid or natural standards of both temperature and level. This is exact, so far as the uncertainties of science enable us to test it.

* The facts marked by asterisks have not been published previously.

SECT. 4.—The Standard Measure of the Pyramid, as having originated National Standards.

*Without here detailing the peculiar circumstances, before and about the pyramid date, that suggest that the Gentile cubit was more freely retained in practical use than the sacred cubit by the then scattering and multiplying nations, and only glancing at the empire of Solomon as an event that produced an impression more world-wide, deeper, and more lasting than is commonly realised by modern Western nations, and that the Jewish (*i.e.*, the pyramidally preserved) weights and measures were thereby extensively adopted by the rulers and traders among the nations at that period—just preceding the great renewal of migrations which determined the present races of European countries—we proceed to condense this part of the subject into a few illustrations of the identity of the standards of the pyramid and of primæval times with the long subsequent Jewish and modern standards.

600 years after the pyramid, we find the standards which were divinely recognised through Moses to be the same as those of the pyramid. The sacred cubit was the pyramid cubit; the four homers, and the sacred ark, were each equal to the pyramid coffer-content.

1200 years after the pyramid (*i.e.*, under Solomon), the measures were the same as the foregoing, and the sacred "molten sea," besides, was of the same capacity as that marked in the pyramid's chief chamber, or 50 of its coffer measures; and the lavers were each equal to one coffer measure.

3000 and 4000 years after the pyramid—that is to say, in modern times—its standards are still found represented. The Arabian *guz* is the pyramid cubit; and in Western Europe, where peopled by migrations of Goths from the countries north of Palestine, we find that their old national measures (before the well-known modern alterations) were counterparts of the pyramid measures, many of them even undisguised by the processes of division and re-multiplication before mentioned, and quite as accurately preserved as could be expected during migration

* The facts marked by asterisks have not been published previously.

and the lapse of time. Thus, the pyramid *pound* (of 50^3 in the coffer) is 1.003 old German pounds; 1.040 ancient French; 1.073 of Denmark; and 0.973 of Britain. Again, the pyramid *foot* or half-cubit is represented by 0.995 of the Bohemian foot (this has been a generally undisturbed country), and by 1.022 of the ancient French foot. The pyramid *inch* is represented by the British inch, within a thousandth part; hence its remarkable scientific property of earth-commensurability (by a minute and simple correction), far better in this respect, as Sir John Herschel has forcibly demonstrated, than the badly-contrived and mistakenly-defined French metre, which is in these days being urged into the place of the rightful standard—our primæval and inherited *inch* and its multiples, decimal or duodecimal. The pyramid coffer-measure is represented by 1.007 of four *quarters* British. The pyramid *gallon*, *pint*, and *mile*, each being a multiple on the regular pyramid system (*i.e.*, 250 and 2500 in its coffer and cubit), are represented by the old British ale gallon, wine pint, and mile, respectively, to an 80th part.

*SECT. 5.—Its Chronologic and Ætiologic place.

Its *date*, relatively with other connected works, and the *causes* of its being built, and of the connected changes in operation amongst the human race at that time (with the allusions to it in Scripture), its corresponding symbols of divine dealings, and its visible and historical opposition to all idolatry,—these considerations, too wide to be given here, show in detail special connections between this structure and others built for the sake of their connected symbolism as well as for utility, and with the same cubit for their unit of measure—*e. g.*, the Ark of Noah, the Tabernacle of Moses, the Temple of Solomon, and the one specified prophetically by Ezekiel.—See above, p. 65, 66.

SECT. 6.—Its Geographic place.

*A. It is the *centre* of the measured area of *human energies* in the old hemisphere (throughout the period of that monument's presence), by a radius of the significant length of just one-tenth

* The facts marked by asterisks have not been published previously.

of a great circle of the earth : the definition north and south has meanings, indeed, but that of east and west is palpable and impressive. Moreover, this circle northward sweeps exactly to the verge of the habitable earth, as defined in God's covenant with Noah, and previously in the Scriptural account of the preparation of the Cosmos—uninterrupted alternation of day and night throughout each year.

*B. That it is on the *circle* of *terrestrial maxima* in relation to man. That is to say, by its latitude (an idea independently betokened in its structure) it marks the dividing line between the two diverse meteorologic zones of this hemisphere : also the maximum of *air* (*i.e.*, greatest mean barometric height, about 100 sacred cubits more air of surface density than at 30° north or south): also the maximum length of *land*, 114 equatorial degrees in the old hemisphere, and 137¼ in the whole circle of the pyramid latitude, including the American hemisphere. This length of land is beyond that of every other latitude on the earth. Further, by specific angular measures, east and west of the pyramid, both the maximum of *mountain* range is noted, and the maximum *points* or *debouchements* into or without deltas of the four *rivers* (including the Jordan at the pyramid date, and of the prophetic future), having a *maximum* of importance in connection with the energies of intellectual man, from the Deluge to the end.

The higher ideas which gather up and connect the foregoing apparently diverse facts and references into a harmonious system, with a unity of signification, cannot be usefully subjected to the rigorous compression implied in a synoptic view.

NOTE.—The foregoing synopsis is by W. Petrie, who, in acceding to our request for it, desires us to say that his investigations and results are the consequence of his following the clue supplied by Professor C. Piazzi Smyth, after the latter had brought the light of modern science to bear more fully on the ideas originated by John Taylor of London, recognising the Holy Scriptures as being words from the Creator, irrespectively of human intellect, and yet in perfect harmony with all that is true in modern science.

See 'Life and Work at the Great Pyramid,' 3 vols., with plates.

---

* The facts marked by asterisks have not been published previously.

Also 'Antiquity of Intellectual Man,' 1 vol., with a diagram, comparing the architectural remains, from the earliest example, onward through each century, in various countries : both by Professor C. Piazzi Smyth, F.R.S., &c., Astronomer - Royal for Scotland (Edmonston & Douglas, Edinburgh).

See also 'Plates and Notes on Structures called Pyramids,' 1 vol. fol., a valuable illustrated work, by St John Vincent Day, C.E., Glasgow (Hamilton & Adams, London).

And 'The Monumental History of Egypt,' by William Osburn. An eminently trustworthy work (Trübner & Co., London).

Of the true method of interpretation of that unique monument—given in the three first named of these works, and here condensed—the germ, so speedily fruitful, was found in a work entitled 'The Great Pyramid, Why was it Built, and Who Built it?' 1860 (second edition, 1864), by JOHN TAYLOR, London.

SECT. 1.—Egypt from the Earliest Time to the Reign of the Shepherd Kings (B.C. 2550-1900).

B.C.

2800. The Universal Deluge, as indicated by the Great Pyramid of Jeezeh (Professor C. P. Smyth).
the floods arise, the world expires.

2552.* Confusion of Tongues, and Dispersion of Nations.
the families leave the land of their fathers.

2550. Colonisation of Egypt and Canaan by the descendants of Ham.
a family lands in the lonely west.

2534. Babylon founded by Nimrod.
a famous lawless hunter established it.

2500. China first colonised.
a family learns the way to "Cathay."

2481. On, or Heliopolis, the first city in Egypt, built by the colonists, and dedicated to the setting sun.
the first settlers erect their capital.

2473. Hebron, the first city in Palestine, erected by the Canaanites.
the first settlement in Palestine was Hebron.

---

* In Sections 1, 2, 3, we follow the chronology of the monuments, as deduced by Mr W. Osburn in his elaborate 'Monumental History of Egypt.'

HISTORY OF ANCIENT EGYPT. 137

B.C.
2467. Zoan or Tanis, Bubastis, and Mendes erected in the eastern delta, seven years after Hebron.
its first king was a native of Zoan.

2460. The worship of Adam, Noah, Ham, and Mizraim established in Egypt about this time.
their first superstition, ancestral worship.

2458. The Median, or first human dynasty of Berosus, begins in Chaldæa.
a dynasty of Scythians in league with Aryans.

2429. Menes crosses the Nile, defeats the Phutim; builds Memphis, and establishes the first dynasty of kings.
founding of the kingdom by a dynasty of Tanites.

2421. Second dynasty (contemporary with the first) begins at Sebennytus, in the eastern delta: Bochus the first king.
founded Sebennytus, a famous city.

2403. Thoth or Athotes, one of the early settlers, invents hieroglyphics at Heliopolis.
the first system of writing was hieroglyphic.

2401. Cechous (second king of second dynasty) introduces animal worship.
the first to establish the worship of bulls.

2397. Psemempses (fifth king of first dynasty) begins to assume the title of Pharaoh.
the first to hold the title of Pharaoh.

2329. Aches founds the third dynasty at Memphis.
his fame is handed down by tradition.

2236. Sephuris (eighth king of third dynasty) unites the rival crowns of Egypt, and establishes the worship of Apis.
famed as the founder of Egyptian unity.

2228. Soris begins the fourth dynasty at Memphis.
famed as the first deified ruler.

,, Usercheres I. builds Abydos, and founds there the fifth dynasty (contemporary with the fourth).
the founder of the fifth dynasty a rebel.

B.C.
2170. Suphis (Cheops), aided by Philites, a shepherd-prince, builds the Great Pyramid at Jeezeh.
its founder characterised by profound wisdom.

2147. Sephres, or Chephrenes (third king of fifth dynasty), builds the second pyramid, and fabricates the Sphynx.
the famous builder of the second pyramid.

2130. Mencheres,* son of Sephres, attempts to collect the scattered limbs of Osiris (Mizraim), and to establish the worship of Osiris over all Egypt: a great religious war ensues, which continues for a century.
the first coloniser of Egypt worshipped.

---

* The history of Egypt, on the death of Mencheres, becomes involved and obscure in the highest degree. During the fierce and long-continued civil war which his religious reforms gave rise to, the archives of the kingdom were imperfectly kept; the authoritative temple-lists of the kings presented numerous gaps, which were filled in at an after period without regard to historical accuracy. For the glorification of Egypt, and to make its antiquity appear greater than that of any other kingdom, whole dynasties came to be inserted into these *lacunæ;* hence to the modern historian the confusion at this period is utterly hopeless. It appears, however, that several rival dynasties reigned at the same time in different parts of the land. Thus, the sixth, seventh, and eighth dynasties reigned at Memphis, if they reigned at all; the ninth and tenth certainly reigned at Sebennytus (Heracleopolis), in Lower Egypt, at the very time that the eleventh and twelfth governed Upper Egypt. The monarchs of both Egypts were the lineal descendants of Menes, the first king, but were at deadly variance with each other. The kings of Heracleopolis determined to preserve the ancient religion uncorrupted, while the Theban monarchs, with equal determination, sought to make all Egypt adhere to the reforms of Mencheres. The Sebennyte Pharaohs were generally the losers, until at last (near the end of the tenth dynasty) they were hemmed in on all sides, and confined to one solitary province. In this crisis of their fortunes they sought to enter into alliances with the Canaanitish and Phœnician princes, whose territories lay on their north-eastern frontier. Othoes, for example, the last king of the *tenth* dynasty, was the father of Saites or Salates, the founder of the *sixteenth* dynasty. Saites gave his daughter in marriage to Mœris, who appears to have been one of

B.C.
2107. Senucheres, first king of eleventh dynasty, succeeds Mencheres at Abydos, and founds Coptos.
the founder of Coptos, west of the Nile.

2059. Menthesuphis (second king of eleventh dynasty) founds Thebes, in Upper Egypt.
its fame excelled all other (cities).

2003. Achthoes (sixth king of eleventh dynasty) founds Eilethja and Crocodilopolis.
his famous wars yielded him glory.

2000. The Pelasgi arrive in Greece about this time.
a family wends its way westward.

1984. Abraham visits Egypt, and aids Achthoes in forming a treaty with his rival to terminate the religious war.
a celebrated treaty is ratified in *Egypt.*

1980. Abraham teaches the King of Egypt the true chronology, after which the inscriptions bear the name of the year and month.
Abraham teaches them *to reckon* by *years.*

---

the princes of Canaan. By his aid Saites overcame the Upper Egyptian Pharaoh, Amenemes III. (also known as Amuntomeus), and captured Memphis, one of his capitals. After a brief peace, war again broke out, and Saites, with his son-in-law, took first Abydos, and afterwards Crocodilopolis, from the rival dynasty, whom they ultimately expelled from Thebes and Upper Egypt. Seeing that these victories were obtained by the *aid* of the *nomadic princes* of Canaan, Saites and his descendants were for ages afterwards stigmatised as the Hycsos or Shepherd Kings, and every imaginable barbarity attributed to them. The monuments demonstrate, however, that both these representations were foul calumnies. In place of being foreigners and shepherds, they were better entitled to the throne of Egypt than their rivals of Upper Egypt; and in place of being barbarians, their names will bear favourable comparison with the wisest and best sovereigns that ever occupied the Egyptian throne. The Christian feels a deeper interest in these so-called Shepherd Kings than in any other Egyptian dynasty, as it was to them that Phiops belonged, the patron of Joseph and the friend of Israel.

FACTS AND DATES.

B.C.
1965. Amenemes (seventh and last king of eleventh dynasty) captures Memphis, and makes Thebes the capital of Egypt.
a bold attempt to unify the land.

1919. Sesortosis I., son of Amenemes, begins the twelfth dynasty at Thebes.
the *building* of *temples begins* at *Thebes.*

1916. Sesortosis expels the Cushites from Nubia, or reduces them to slavery.
the *celebrated tablet of Abydos mentions* it.

1877. Amenemes II. succeeds Sesortosis at Thebes.
a *celebrated reign* of *prosperity* and *peace.*

1868. Sesortosis II. succeeds Amenemes.
brief records of an *inglorious reign.*

1829. Sesortosis III. slain in the hour of victory at Semneh.
a *celebrated ruler falls* in *Ethiopia.*

1815. Amenemes III. (Amuntimæus) expelled from Memphis by Saites of Sebennytus, son of Othoes.
the *celebrated ruler* who *built* the *labyrinth.*

SECT. 2.—From the Shepherd Kings to the Exodus of the Israelites (B.C. 1900-1554).

B.C.
1900. Saites (son of Othoes of the tenth dynasty) begins the sixteenth dynasty at Heliopolis, and wages war with Amuntimæus, of the twelfth dynasty, at Thebes.
his *celebrated victories win* our *admiration.*

1887. Saites solicits aid from Mœris, a Phœnician prince.
calls to the *rescue* an *Arvadite prince.*

1886. Mœris marries Saites' daughter, and captures Memphis from Amuntimæus.
the *courageous Arvadite recovers Memphis.*

1884. Syphoas introduces the common letters into Egypt.
characters representing articulate sounds.

1882. Probable date of the death of Abraham and Job.
Abraham receives the *reward* of his *faithfulness.*

B.C.
1872. Saites and Mœris seize Abydos in Upper Egypt.
  they *capture* the "*resting place* of the *dead.*"
1851. Mœris succeeds Saites, captures Crocodilopolis, excavates Lake Mœris, and completes the unfinished labyrinth.
  a *celebrated reservoir* and *labyrinth completed* by him.
1816. Phiops or Aphophis, son of Mœris, crowned King of Lower Egypt, while Mœris reigns in Upper Egypt.
  a *celebrated ruler* is *crowned* at *Memphis.*
1791. Joseph sold as a slave by his brethren.
  his *brethren persecute* the *type* of *Christ.*
1778. Joseph becomes Prime Minister of Pharaoh Aphophis.
  a *captive promoted* to *princely rule.*
1777. The seven years of plenty begin in Egypt, probably owing to the bursting of an immense lake in Ethiopia (Osburn).
  corn is *produced* in *prodigious quantities.*
1769. Jacob and his family migrate into Egypt in the 54th year of the reign of Aphophis, and 215th after the visit of Abraham.
  the *covenant people* are *nourished* and *trained.*
1759. Death of Phiops, the patron of Joseph, ten years after the immigration of the Israelites.
  a *celebrated prince, liberal* und *tolerant.*
1742. Melaneres, son of Phiops, takes Thebes from the Upper Egyptians, and becomes sole monarch of all Egypt.
  a *bright epoch* in the *shepherd dynasty.*
1708. Death of Melaneres: Jannes and Asses succeed him as co-regents, the former governing Lower Egypt, and the latter Upper Egypt.
  his *children quarrel* about *who* is to *reign.*
1698. Death of Joseph during the regency of Jannes and Asses.
  his *body embalmed* for the *time* of *release.*

B.C.
1690. Asses defeated by Amosis, King of Thebes (eighteenth dynasty), and Memphis taken from the Shepherd Kings, who retire to the Delta, and make Succoth their capital: end of the Shepherd dynasty.
capture of *Memphis* by a *Theban warrior.*

1674. Amosis having expelled the Shepherd Kings from Memphis, begins the eighteenth dynasty at Thebes.
the *bold Amosis pursues* the *shepherds.*

1662. The Shepherd Kings, after losing Memphis, retire to Arvad (the Delta), where they make Xois or Succoth their capital, and begin the fourteenth or Xoite dynasty, contemporary with the eighteenth and nineteenth dynasties.
the *capture* of *Memphis* a *mighty disaster* to them.

1659. Armais (eighth king of eighteenth dynasty) defeated by the Phutim, who capture Thebes, and place a mulatto on the throne of Upper Egypt.
black-skinned nations in *league* against *Thebes.*

1657. Amenophis (Memnon), son of Armais, marries the daughter of the negro king reigning east of the Nile, and unites the two crowns.
betrothes a *negro lady* for *policy.*

1655. Rameses I. expels the negro population east of the Nile, and begins the nineteenth dynasty* at Thebes.
compels the *negroes* to *leave* the *land.*

1646. Sethos I., son of Rameses, aids the Xoite king against the Hittites, Amorites, and Moabites, who have invaded the Delta.
compels the *invaders* to *sue* for *mercy.*

---

* The honour of founding a new dynasty was frequently conferred on a king who had greatly benefited his country. A new dynasty, therefore, in Ancient Egypt, did not always imply a different *family* from that previously reigning.

B.C.
1644. Sethos succeeds in expelling the invaders, and receives as his reward six cities in the Delta from the Xoite king.
cedes a *number* of *strongholds* to *Sethos.*

„ Rameses II. (Sesostris), son of Sethos I., succeeds to the throne.
the *cruel monarch* who *knew* not *Joseph* (Exod. i. 21).

1639. Siphtha, the infant Xoite king, espoused to Thouoris, the daughter of Rameses II., it being stipulated that, until the death of Rameses, Siphtha is to govern the Delta as a Viceroy, after which he is to succeed to the throne of Egypt.
claims by *marriage* the *Egyptian throne.*

1635. Rameses II. begins to oppress the Israelites, now reduced to slavery.
cities multiply in *Egypt* by their *labours.*

1634. Birth of Moses, who is rescued by Queen Thouoris.
birth of *Moses,* the *Hebrew lawgiver.*

1629. Amenephthes, a younger brother of Thouoris, ascends the throne of Egypt, in violation of the stipulation above specified, but reigns only five years.
the *covenant* was *made* in *favour* of *Thouoris.*

1624. Thouoris and Siphtha become joint monarchs in Egypt: being childless, they propose to inaugurate Moses as their successor on the throne, but Moses refuses.
the *childless monarch adopts* a *son.*

1614. Thouoris devolves the entire government on her husband, and retires to Thebes, the Upper Egyptian capital, after appointing Sethos II., infant son of Amenephthes, as her successor.
the *choice* of *Moses causes* this *sorrow.*

1604. Siphtha, Regent of all Egypt, rules the land mildly, and treats the Israelites with clemency:

B.C.

Moses resides at Rameses, a Prince of the court of Siphtha.
the clemency and mercy of a Xoite king.

1593. Moses slays an Egyptian taskmaster, and flees for safety to Midian.
courageously levels a taskmaster of Egypt.

1587. Death of Siphtha, and accession of Sethos II. to the throne: he greatly oppresses the Israelites.
cruelty and lust his reigning propensities.

1582. The chronology of the Arundelian Marbles begins.
contain a lengthened record of dates.

1556. Cecrops, an Egyptian, arrives in Attica, and founds Athens.
Cecrops leaves the land of Mizraim.

„ Moses returns from Midian with a message from God to Pharaoh: Pharaoh's heart is hardened.
he comes to the lord of the land with a message.

1554. Exodus of the Israelites from Egypt (430 years after the visit of Abraham), embracing 4,000,000 of people.
the bondmen leave the land of their sojourn.

„ Sethos II., with the flower of the Egyptian army, is drowned in the Red Sea.
the cruel lord of the land is smitten.

1553. The whole of the inhabitants of Lower Egypt, smitten with the terror of the Lord, flee to Nubia and Ethiopia.
the curse of the Lord on the land is heavy.

1552. The inhabitants of Canaan, terrified at the approach of Israel, migrate in multitudes into the deserted Delta, and thus effect a second Shepherd invasion (the invasion of the Solymites): they form the twentieth dynasty.
the Canaanites learn what the Lord has done.

SECT. 3.—From the Exodus to the death of Alexander the Great (B.C. 1554-323).

B.C.

1518. The fifth or Arabian dynasty of Berosus expel the Cushites from Chaldæa.
Chaldæa at last conquered by Arabians.

1516. Amenophis II., a descendant of Sethos II., returns from Ethiopia with a great army, expels the Solymites from the Delta, and founds the twenty-first dynasty.
comes to the land of his cruel ancestors.

1514. Death of Moses in the land of Moab.
buried by the Lord beyond the Jordan.

„ The Israelites cross the Jordan and enter Canaan.
observe, they were led into Canaan by Joshua.

1490. Death of Joshua.
courageous Joshua, a type of Christ.

1453. First celebration of the Olympic Games.
competitors strive at the Olympic Games.

1405. Othniel becomes the first Judge of Israel.
a brave judge wins his laurels.

1396. Era of the first jubilee in Canaan.
blow the gladsome trumpet now.

1387. The Hellenes enter Greece, and expel the Pelasgi.
the brave Hellenes rout the Pelasgi.

1273. Ninus founds the sixth or Assyrian dynasty in Chaldæa.
a Cushite dynasty of princes govern it.

„ Tyre built by a colony of Sidonians.
the beautiful daughter of " Zidon the Great."

1250. The Argonautic expedition to Colchis, under Jason.
a band of adventurers leave for the Euxine.

1245. Gideon saves Israel from the yoke of Midian.
a curious dream saves the land.

1194. The Trojan war begins.
a band of confederates for Troy sets out.

K

B.C.
1137. Birth of Samuel.
    a child chosen of God for the priesthood.
1113. Tiglath-pileser I., King of Assyria, invades Egypt.
    conquers Babylonia, Cappadocia, and Egypt.
1100. Most ancient Egyptian mummy known to exist (deposited in the Leeds Museum).
    the *body bituminised exists* for ages.
1095. Saul anointed first king of Israel.
    they *choose* a *young* and *tall leader* (1 Sam. xi. 11).
1085. Twenty-first dynasty begins in Zoan (Lower Egypt).
    considerably extend their *rule* in the *land.*
1055. David anointed king in Hebron.
    they *crown* the *youth* whom the *Lord loves.*
1014. Solomon marries the daughter of Sheshouk (Shishak).
    betroths a *wife* of *coloured skin.*
1009. The twenty-second or Syrian dynasty begins at Bubastis.
    a bold warrior's exploits in *Ethiopia.*
980. Jeroboam escapes from Solomon to Shishak.
    takes refuge in *exile.*
971. Shishak captures Jerusalem, and plunders the Temple.
    vast plunder is *acquired.*
942. Zorah the Ethiopian (Osorkhon I.) invades Judah.
    the *triumph* of *Asa's faith* (2 Chron. xiv. 11).
889. Twenty-third dynasty reigns at Zoan (Tanis).
    rulers reigning at *Tanis.*
853. Carthage founded by a Syrian colony.
    her *ruins lie* in *heaps.*
794. Twenty-fourth dynasty begins with Bocchoris at Saïs.
    perishes by an *Ethiopian king.*
786. Egypt establishes her supremacy over the Mediterranean.
    proudly rules the *Mediterranean.*
753. Rome founded by Romulus.
    its *position learned* by *augury.*
749. Twenty-fifth dynasty begins with Sabaco (Shebek I.)
    the "*Prince of Kesh*" an *Ethiopian.*

B.C.
724. Hoshea, King of Israel, asks aid from Shebek II. (So).
petitions for *aid* from *So.*

723. Tirhakah, the Ethiopian, succeeds Shebek II.
proffers aid to Hezekiah.

721. The Ten Tribes carried captive into Assyria.
Ephraim departs into *captivity* (2 Kings xvii. 6).

710. Tirhakah marches agt. Sennacherib, King of Assyria.
Pharaoh is beaten in the *war.*

709. Sennacherib invades Egypt.
a *pestilence wastes* his *troops.*

685. Egypt is divided into twelve kingdoms.
many rulers in the *land.*

664. Psammeticus establishes twenty-sixth dynasty at Saïs.
united under *one sceptre.*

631. Psammeticus besieges Ashdod twenty-nine years, and takes it from the Assyrians.
the *monarch of Egypt captures* it.

625. Nineveh destroyed: Saracus burns himself to death.
Nineveh destroyed by the *allies.*

612. Pharaoh Necho, aided by a Phœnician fleet, circumnavigates the continent of Africa.
Necho circumnavigates Africa.

611. Pharaoh Necho attempts to unite the Red Sea and Mediterranean.
Necho cuts a *canal.*

610. Josiah, King of Judah, marches against Necho, who is on his way to the Euphrates.
at *Megiddo* he is *badly wounded* (2 Kings xxiii. 29).

605. Necho defeated by Nebuchadnezzar: Judæa overrun, and Jerusalem taken.
Nebuchadnezzar wastes the *land.*

595. Psammeticus II. succeeds his father, Necho.
lays Ethiopia low.

589. Pharaoh-Hophra ascends the throne of Egypt.
elated by a *round* of *triumphs.*

B.C.

588. Jewish Captivity : the Temple destroyed.
the Lord's residence in *ruins.*

586. Nebuchadnezzar overruns Egypt, and takes Thebes.
laid in *ruins* by *Nebuchadnezzar.*

581. Pharaoh-Hophra deposed by Nebuchadnezzar.
lost his *army* at *Cyrene.*

569. Nebuchadnezzar makes Amasis King of Egypt.
he *elevates* Amasis to the *throne.*

554. Solon visits Egypt.
the *illustrious legislator* at *Sais.*

536. Pythagoras visits Egypt.
learns the *Egyptian mysteries.*

535. Cyrus the elder makes Egypt tributary to the Persians.
(Cyrus) the *elder governs* the *land.*

525. Cambyses invades Egypt, and establishes the twenty-seventh dynasty.
the *land* is *devastated* by his *legions.*

515. Dedication of the Second Temple.
they *loudly bless* the *Lord.*

490. The Persians invade Greece : Battle of Marathon.
a *strange event* in *war.*

487. Egypt revolts against Darius Hystaspes.
the *kingdom revolts* against the *Persians.*

484. Xerxes speedily represses the revolt.
he *suppresses* the *revolt* with *ease.*

461. Herodotus of Halicarnassus visits Egypt.
stores of *knowledge* are *collected.*

458. Inarus revolts against Artaxerxes I.
a *successful leader* of *revolt.*

448. The Persians suppress the revolt, and make Egypt a satrapy.
satraps suppress the *revolt.*

416. Age of the prophet Malachi.
the *Scriptures conclude* with *Malachi.*

414. Egypt independent : the twenty-eighth dynasty begins with Amyrtæus.
established his *capital* at *Sais.*

B.C.
403. Achoris, of the twenty-ninth dynasty, repulses a Persian attack.
assisted by *auxiliaries* from *Greece.*

401. Battle of Cunaxa: death of Cyrus the Younger.
Xenophon joined the " *expedition of Cyrus.*"

387. Nectanebo I. ascends the throne: peace of Antalcidas.
Greece recognises Persian (supremacy).

373. Nectanebo defends the land against the Persians.
the *Greeks proved hostile.*

362. Tachos, of the thirtieth dynasty, invades Asia, in concert with the Athenians and Lacedemonians.
Greek mercenaries aid *him.*

353. Artaxerxes Ochus invades Egypt: Nectanebo II. ends the thirtieth dynasty.
Egypt loses her *greatness.*

332. Alexander the Great conquers Egypt, and builds Alexandria.
the " *gem* " of the *hero's diadem.*

323. Death of Alexander at Babylon.
the *hero dies* in *agony.*

SECT. 4.—From the Death of Alexander to the Conquest of Egypt by the Romans (B.C. 323-30).

B.C.
321. Partition of the empire of Alexander between Ptolemy Sóter, Seleucus, Antipater, and Antigonus: Ptolemy receives Egypt.
his *generals divide* his *conquests.*

320. Ptolemy takes Jerusalem, and leads 100,000 Jews captive.
the *Egyptians force* them into *exile.*

314. Antigonus wrests Palestine, Phœnicia, and Cœle-Syria from Egypt.
Egypt curtailed sadly.

311. Ptolemy recovers Phœnicia and Judæa, and takes many captives.
a *host* of *bondmen captured.*

B. C.
301. Battle of Ipsus: Antigonus slain: new division of the empire: Egypt independent.
a great war concluded.

285. Ptolemy Philadelphus succeeds Ptolemy Soter.
a distinguished ruler of the land.

284. The Septuagint translation completed at Alexandria.
first rendering of the Scriptures.

283. Ptolemy founds the Great Library of Alexandria.
the famous repository of Egypt.

280. Manetho, a priest of Heliopolis, writes his history of Egypt.
fragments remain of his work.

274. Ptolemy Philadelphus sends an embassy to Rome.
first premonition of subjection.

264. Rome commences the first Punic War.
fights the mistress of the sea.

247. Ptolemy III. (Euergetes) invades Syria.
defeats Seleucus on the Euphrates.

222. Ptolemy IV. (Philopater) murders his father, and ascends the throne.
detested for diabolical deeds.

217. Ptolemy defeats Antiochus at Raphia, and subjects Palestine.
a famous battle in Palestine.

216. Ptolemy massacres 50,000 Jews at Alexandria.
a frightful carnage at Alexandria.

205. Death of Ptolemy Philopater, and accession of Ptolemy Epiphanes.
his death weakens the land.

203. Egypt concludes an alliance with Rome.
flees to the West for help.

198. Antiochus the Great recovers Syria and Palestine from Egypt.
a conqueror attacks the realm.

196. Date of inscription on the famous Rosetta stone, the key to the Egyptian hieroglyphics.
the celebrated trilingual inscription.

B.C.
181. Ptolemy VI. (Philomeleo) succeeds his father.
    Cleopatra is regent in his childhood.

171. Antiochus-Epiphanes invades Egypt.
    he captures the principal cities.

169. Antiochus invades Egypt again : Rome interferes.
    a band of ambassadors threaten him.

164. Egypt is divided between Philometer and his brother Physcon.
    their contests menace the kingdom.

146. Philometer defeats Alexander Balas : is succeeded by Ptolemy VII. (Physcon).
    the conqueror killed at Antioch.

,, The third Punic War : Carthage laid in ruins.
    the Carthaginian kingdom annihilated.

143. Scipio Africanus visits Egypt, and is received by Physcon with great pomp.
    the celebrated Scipio in Egypt.

131. Physcon divorces Cleopatra, and marries her daughter by his brother.
    his brother's heir is cut off.

129. Physcon flees to Cyprus : murders his sons.
    compelled to demit his authority.

128. Physcon defeats the Egyptian army, recovers his throne, and dies.
    a bloody despot reinstated.

,, Immense swarms of locusts ravage the land, and bring on a deadly pestilence.
    consume the fruits of the earth.

107. Cleopatra compels Ptolemy VIII. (Lathyrus) to return to Cyprus.
    Cleopatra exiles Ptolemy.

82. Revolt in Upper Egypt : Thebes destroyed.
    razed to its foundations.

80. Alexander II. (Ptolemy X.) renders Egypt tributary to Rome.
    the way to ruin and extinction.

B.C.
68. Diodorus Siculus, the Greek historian, visits Egypt.
   a writer of *immense research.*
58. Alexander expelled : Berenice and Tryphæna reign jointly.
   expelled from the *land* in *revenge.*
55. Alexander restored to the throne.
   the exile *lands* at *Alexandria.*
51. Ptolemy XI. (Auletes) reigns with the famous Cleopatra.
   Auletes and *Cleopatra.*
49. Auletes expels Cleopatra.
   expels his *spouse* from the *throne.*
48. Julius Cæsar aids Cleopatra, and burns Alexandria.
   Julius's revenge.
47. Auletes defeated and drowned : Ptolemy XII. and Cleopatra, his sister, reign.
   the wicked *king perishes.*
44. Cleopatra poisons her brother : Cæsar is murdered at Rome.
   she wickedly *slays* the *king.*
42. Mark Antony summons Cleopatra to trial for her crime.
   her *judge* is *fascinated* by her.
36. Antony confers Phœnicia, Cyrene, and Cyprus on Cleopatra.
   the excited *general's magnanimity!*
35. Cleopatra receives from Antony all Asia, from the Mediterranean to the Indus.
   the wanton *general* is *lavish.*
31. Battle of Actium : total defeat of Antony and Cleopatra by Octavius Cæsar Augustus.
   a woeful *humiliation* to *Cleopatra.*
30. Augustus enters Egypt : Antony commits suicide.
   the wretched *general expires.*
,, Egypt becomes a Roman province.
   her *glory* is *extinguished.*

CHAP. II.—HISTORY OF CHALDÆA, ASSYRIA, AND BABYLONIA (B.C. 2500-538.)

[Our limits forbid any lengthened observations on the history of the above-named monarchies, while for the general remarks which follow we are largely indebted to Mr Philip Smith's 'Ancient History;' London, Walton and Maberly, 1864.]

It cannot as yet be positively determined whether the Nile or the Euphrates was the earlier seat of civilisation and empire. In all probability, both regions were colonised about the same time, shortly after the confusion of tongues—an event which we have great confidence in placing about B.C. 2500. Our main reason for putting Egypt in advance of Chaldæa is, that the existing monuments of the former are greatly more numerous, more intelligible, and, generally speaking, in a higher state of preservation, than those of the latter. But other considerations, and especially those connected with physical geography, would lead us to assign the priority to Chaldæa. The basin of the Euphrates and Tigris lies greatly nearer the regions first peopled by Noah and his descendants than the valley of the Nile, and nearer also to the scene of the confusion of tongues. By glancing at a physical map of Asia, it will be readily perceived that the two river-basins now mentioned were the only ones practically within reach of the earliest emigrants. The valley of the Kur, in Transcaucasia, is of very limited extent, with its outlets towards the Caspian and the inhospitable plains of Siberia; while the Indus is too remote, and the route thither all but impracticable in the infancy of the new world.

Like the Sahara and the valley of the Nile, the great basin of the Euphrates and Tigris lies within the limits of that mighty rainless zone which encompasses the Old World like a girdle. Its southern extremity being seven degrees north of the Tropic of Cancer, and its length extending to about ten degrees northward, it is most favourably situated in the north temperate zone. The upper or northern half of this immense valley belongs geologically to the Secondary series of rocks, the lower to the Tertiary; but both sections are level and monotonous, and well adapted for the display of those gigantic piles of architecture by which the race of Ham delighted to supply the lack of striking natural features. Though destitute of rocks and minerals, no country except Egypt ever built on a vaster scale—the absence of stones being fully compensated for by the admirable materials supplied everywhere for the manufacture of bricks. For ordinary purposes these were hardened by the fierce, burning sun; for permanent structures, the kiln made them as durable as granite; while the numerous springs of bitumen yielded an admirable cement. All ancient writers extol the surprising fertility of this region, which in the time of the Persian empire yielded a full third of the royal revenue. The vine, date-palm, and numerous other fruit-trees abound; the cereals are plentiful, and here the wheat-plant is indigenous. The main causes of this great fertility are the intense heat of summer and the periodic inundations of its two gigantic rivers.

Such was the country of which we have the earliest records in the Book of Genesis. The two leading facts there recorded regarding it are the erection of a city and tower, and the establishment of a kingdom by Nimrod, the grandson of Ham, and eldest son of Cush, his first-born. "The beginning of his kingdom was Babel, and Erech, and Accad, and Calneh, in the land of Shinar. Out of that land he went forth into Assyria (*margin*) and built Nineveh, and the city Rehoboth, and Calah, and Resen between Nineveh and Calah: the same is a great city" (Gen. x. 10-12). The marginal reading, as we have given it, is doubtless the true one, as it is corroborated by the authentic records of history and by the existing monuments of the country, both of which unite in making Nimrod a Hamitic chief, who laid the foundations of his kingdom by conquering the original Semitic occupants of the country. Nimrod and his warriors, and not the early Semitic inhabitants, must therefore be regarded as the "Chaldæans" of the ancient writers, notwithstanding the close affinity between the later Babylonian tongue and the Hebrew. The original inhabitants of Babylonia, in common with those of Assyria, belonged, no doubt, to the Semitic stock of nations; but there is ample evidence that, subsequent to the invasion of Nimrod, the language of Babylonia passed through an immense change. The native historian,

Berosus, who wrote at Babylon in the reign of Antiochus II. (B.C. 261-246), and in whose fragments we have remains of records of unknown antiquity, clearly distinguishes the Babylonians from the Assyrians; while the cuneiform inscriptions recently discovered in Lower Mesopotamia, the language of which is clearly Hamitic, and allied to that of the modern Gallas, conclusively settles the question.

The upper half of this great river-basin comprehended Mesopotamia (the region "between the two rivers") in the west, Assyria and Media in the east, and Armenia in the north. The lower half embraced Chaldæa, west of the Tigris, and Elam or Susiana, east of that river. We can only add that this region bears the most marked affinity to the valley of the Nile. Both are situated in the rainless zone of the eastern hemisphere; both are watered by the periodic inundations of mighty rivers, in consequence of which, and the high summer temperature, both were characterised by unrivalled fertility; both were colonised about the same time, and by the same race, in the early dawn of antiquity; both were covered with innumerable monuments of art, of colossal dimensions, at a period long prior to authentic history except the notices supplied by their own inscriptions; both were in possession of the art of writing and of numerous other arts indicative of a very high degree of civilisation, ever since the period of their original colonisation; and, finally, both countries had their histories written by native priests (Berosus and Manetho) who lived about the same time, and whose respective annals, written in Greek, and confessedly made up of fiction and fact, have been handed down to us in scraps and interpolated fragments by Josephus, Eusebius, and other chronographers.

SECT. 5.—The Chaldæan or Old Babylonian Monarchy (B.C. 2534-1554).

B.C.
2800. The universal deluge, as indicated by the Great Pyramid.
    the *floods arise*, the *world expires*.
2552. Confusion of tongues, and dispersion of nations.
    the *families leave* the *land* of their *fathers*.

B.C.
2534. Babylon founded by Nimrod, a descendant of Ham.
a famous lawless hunter established it.
2458. The Median or first human dynasty of Berosus.
a dynasty of Scythians in league with Aryans.
2429. Menes crosses the Nile, and builds Memphis.
founding of the kingdom by a dynasty of Tanites.
2401. Cechous introduces animal worship into Egypt.
the first to establish the worship of bulls.
2329. Aches founds the third dynasty at Memphis.
his fame is handed down by tradition.
2170. Suphis, aided by the advice of Philitis, a Shepherd prince, builds the Great Pyramid at Jeezeh.
its founder characterised by profound wisdom.
2059. Menthesuphis founds Thebes, in Upper Egypt.
its fame excelled all other (cities).
2000. The Pelasgi arrive in Greece about this time.
a family wends its way westwards.
1980. Abraham migrates from Ur of the Chaldees to Canaan, and afterwards to Egypt.
Abraham teaches them to reckon by years.
1976. The Chaldæan or Cushite dynasty of Berosus begins.
Chaldæan tyrants plague the land.
1974. Chedorlaomer reduces Sodom to subjection.
Chedorlaomer vanquishes the pentapolis of Siddim.
1965. Amenemes captures Memphis, and makes Thebes his capital.
a bold attempt to unify the land.
1960. Chedorlaomer's second expedition to Sodom: Lot a captive.
Abraham valiantly marches to the war.
1900. The Shepherd Kings begin to reign at Heliopolis.
their celebrated victories win our admiration.
1897. Destruction of the Cities of the Plain.
brimstone ruins the vile pentapolis.
1882. Death of Abraham.
Abraham receives the reward of his faithfulness.
1851. Mœris, King of Egypt, excavates Lake Mœris.
a celebrated reservoir and labyrinth completed by him.

HISTORY OF CHALDÆA, ASSYRIA, AND BABYLONIA. 157

B.C.
1849. The Temple of Kileh-Shergat, near the Tigris, erected.
 a building erected by an Assyrian viceroy.

1816. Phiops, son of Mœris, and patron of Joseph, reigns in Lower Egypt.
 a celebrated ruler crowned at Memphis.

1791. Joseph carried captive into Egypt.
 his brethren persecute the type of Christ.

1769. Jacob and his family migrate into Egypt.
 the covenant people are nourished and trained.

1698. Death of Joseph in Egypt.
 his body embalmed against the time of release.

1674. Amosis expels the Shepherd Kings from Memphis.
 the bold Amosis pursues the shepherds.

1634. Birth of Moses.
 birth of Moses the Hebrew lawgiver.

1593. Moses slays an Egyptian, and flees to Midian.
 courageously levels a taskmaster of Egypt.

1582. The chronology of the Arundelian Marbles begins.
 contain a lengthened record of dates.

1556. Cecrops, an Egyptian, builds Athens.
 Cecrops leaves the land of Mizraim.

1518. The fifth or Arabian dynasty of Berosus commences.
 Chaldæa at last is conquered by Arabs.

1554. Exodus of the Israelites from Egypt.
 the bondmen leave the land of their sojourn.

SECT. 6.—The Assyrian Monarchy (B.C. 1273-625).

1273. The sixth or Assyrian dynasty begins with Ninus.
 a Cushite dynasty of princes governs it.

1184. The fall of Troy.
 brave Achilles razes Ilium.

1155. Birth of Samson.
 a child is born to liberate the land (Judges xiii. 24).

1113. Tiglath-pileser I. begins to reign, according to the cylinder of Kileh-Shergat.
 conquers Babylonia, Cappadocia, and Egypt.

B.C.
1109. Merodach-adan-akhi, King of Babylonia, invades Assyria.
   a *Babylonian conqueror wastes* his *territory.*
1095. Saul anointed King of Israel.
   they *choose* a *young tall leader* (1 Sam. x. 1).
1046. Asshur-bani-pal, the last powerful king of Assyria.
   closes a *whole series* of *emperors.*
1004. Dedication of Solomon's Temple.
   accept our *willing work, Jehovah !* (1 Kings viii. 22.)
975. Death of Solomon, and dismemberment of the empire.
   the *tribes petition* for *liberty* (1 Kings xii. 4).
892. Sardanapalus I. (Asshur-dani-pal) builds magnificent palaces.
   works of *art* of *vast dimensions* (Ph. Smith).
876. Shalmanubar (Shalmaneser I.) succeeds Sardanapalus.
   erects a *pillar* with an *inscription* (Ph. Smith).
864. Shalmanubar defeats Benhadad II. in three battles.
   routs the *monarch* of *Syria* (Ph. Smith).
859. Shalmanubar defeats Hazael, and subdues Syria.
   renders his *land tributary* (Ph. Smith).
851. Death of Shalmanubar, and accession of Shamas-Iva.
   his exploits are *recorded* on a *large obelisk* (Ph. Smith).
831. Iva-lush III., with Semiramis, reign about this time.
   the *records* of their *age* are *obscure* (Ph. Smith).
826. Jonah the prophet sent to threaten Nineveh.
   ruin is *doomed* to *Nineveh* (Jonah i. 2).
771. Pul invades Israel under Menahem.
   pays to *Pul* a *contribution* (2 Kings xv. 19).
753. Building of Rome by Romulus.
   its *place* was *learned* by *augury.*
747. Tiglath-pileser II. establishes the seventh or Lower Assyrian dynasty.
   Pileser the *Second* is *prince* (Ph. Smith).
„ Nabonassar ascends the throne of Babylon: "Era of Nabonassar."
   a *primitive astronomical epoch.*

HISTORY OF CHALDÆA, ASSYRIA, AND BABYLONIA. 159

B.C.
741. Ahaz, King of Judah, asks aid from Tiglath against Syria.
propitiates the *Assyrian* with a *bribe* (2 Kings xvi. 7).

740. Tiglath slays Resin, King of Syria, invades Gilead, and carries the inhabitants into captivity.
part of the *Israelites* are *exiled* (2 Kings xvi. 7).

729. Shalmaneser II. succeeds Tiglath-pileser.
this *prince follows Tiglath.*

724. Shalmaneser invades Israel and besieges Samaria.
a *prolonged defence* at *Samaria.*

721. Shalmaneser carries Israel into captivity.
Ephraim departs into *captivity* (2 Kings xvii. 6).

721. Sennacherib (Sargon* of the monuments) succeeds Shalmaneser, his father.
Ephraim's deportation is *claimed* by him (Ph. Smith).

719. Sennacherib marches against Babylon, and sets Merodach-Baladan on the throne.
appoints Baladan to the *throne.*

715. Sennacherib defeats the Philistines in the great battle at Rephia.
the *Philistine cities* are *levelled.*

714. Sennacherib takes Tyre, Ashdod, and Cyprus.
places Cyprus in *subjection.*

713. Sennacherib invades Judah under Hezekiah, but returns unsuccessful to Nineveh.
he *places* his *confidence* in *God* (Is. xxxvii. 20).

---

* In modern times Sargon is usually regarded as a usurper who ascended the Assyrian throne during Shalmaneser's absence in Syria and Gilead, and erased his predecessor's name from the monuments, substituting his own name in its place. Others, with more propriety, regard Sargon as merely another name for either Shalmaneser or his son Sennacherib. Others still think Sargon must have reigned for a very short period between Shalmaneser and Sennacherib; but for such a reign there is clearly no room in the history. The only possible solution that we can see is to regard Sargon as identical with Sennacherib. In favour of this hypothesis is the fact that, according to Isaiah xxi. 1, *Tartan* is Sargon's General, while by 2 Kings xviii. 17, he is Sennacherib's General. Whoever he was, he reigned nineteen years, according to the monuments.

B.C.
713. Transparent glass manufactured in Assyria.
pottery and *bottles* of *glass* (Ph. Smith).

712. Merodach-Baladan, King of Babylon, sends messengers to Hezekiah.
a *prophecy* of the *coming departure* (2 Kings xx. 13).

710. Rabshakeh sent by Sennacherib against Jerusalem.
pronounces blasphemous words (2 Kings xviii. 35).

„ Tirhakah, King of Egypt, marches to Lachish against Sennacherib.
Pharaoh is *beaten* in the *war* (2 Kings xix. 8).

709. Sennacherib carries away 200,000 Jewish captives.
a *part* is *exiled* to the *Tigris*.

702. Sennacherib subdues Babylonia, removes Merodach-Baladan, and sets up Belibus as Viceroy.
its *Prince* is *wantonly dethroned*.

699. Merodach endeavours, with the aid of the King of Susiana, to recover the throne, but is defeated.
Merodach's attempts are in *vain*.

680. Sennacherib murdered by two of his sons: his other son, Esarhaddon, becomes king of Assyria and Babylonia.
the *mighty ruler executed* (2 Kings xix. 37).

677. Esarhaddon (Asnapper of Scripture, and the Asshurakh-iddina of the inscriptions) transports heathen colonists into Samaria, and carries Manasseh, King of Judah, to Babylon.
Medes and *Persians* in *Ephraim* (Ezra iv. 2).

667. Death of Esarhaddon, and accession of Sammagher to the throne of Assyria.
his *name* is *mentioned* in *Ezra* (Ezra iv. 2).

660. Sardanapulus II. (Asshur-bani-pal) becomes King of Assyria.
the *might* of the *empire* on the *wane*.

640. Asshur-emit-ili (Saracus?) succeeds Sardanapalus.
the e*mpire of Assyria expiring*.

629. The age of Jeremiah, Habakkuk, and Zephaniah.
they *mourn* the *degeneracy* of the *times*.

B.C.
627. Nabopolassar (Saracus's General), Cyaxares the Mede, and Belesys the Babylonian, besiege Nineveh.
Nineveh's doom was predicted (Nahum iii. 7).

625. Nineveh destroyed: Saracus burns himself to death.
Nineveh destroyed by the allies.

SECT. 7.—Later Babylonian Empire (B.C. 625-538).

B.C.
625. Nabopolassar begins the eighth or Chaldæan dynasty, at Babylon.
Nabopolassar founds a line (of kings).

610. Pharaoh Necho garrisons Carchemish on the Euphrates: Josiah, King of Judah, mortally wounded at Megiddo.
at Megiddo he is badly wounded (2 Kings xxiii. 29).

606. Nebuchadnezzar, joint king with his father, Nabopolassar, defeats Pharaoh Necho, and takes Jerusalem: beginning of 70 years' captivity: first deportation—Daniel, &c.
Nebuchadnezzar wastes the nation.

603. Nebuchadnezzar's dream of the golden image, interpreted by Daniel.
an image of extraordinary height (Dan. ii. 1).

„ Jehoiakim rebels against the King of Babylon.
another exodus at hand.

599. Coniah, son of Jehoiakim, carried captive to Babylon: also Ezekiel and ten thousand other captives, who are set down as a colony on the river Chebar.
they lead the vassal in triumph.

„ Nebuchadnezzar and Cyaxeres commence the siege of Tyre, which last twelve years.
lays a trench around Tyre.

594. Ezekiel begins his prophecy among the Jewish colonists on the river Chebar.
lived among the transported Jews.

B.C.

588. Jerusalem taken and destroyed: third and last deportation: the Temple burned.
the Lord's residence in *ruins*.

586. Tyre taken by Nebuchadnezzar, after a siege of thirteen years: Egypt overrun by the Babylonians.
laid in *ruins* by *Nebuchadnezzar*.

581. Pharaoh-Hophra deposed by Nebuchadnezzar.
lost his *army* at *Cyrene*.

580. Nebuchadnezzar sets up the golden image: Shadrach, Meshech, and Abednego cast into a furnace.
the *Lord rescues* his *witnesses* (Dan. iii. 21).

568. Nebuchadnezzar becomes insane, and is driven from his kingdom.
learns that the *Most-High ruleth* (Dan. iv. 33).

562. Evil-Merodach succeeds his father: Coniah liberated from prison.
he *liberates* the *monarch* from *durance*.

560. Coniah, last Jewish monarch, dies at Babylon.
their *last monarch expires*.

559. Evil-Merodach slain by Neriglissar, who succeeds him.
lost his *life* by *violence*.

 ,, Cyrus the Elder, grandson of Astyages, last king of Media, founds the Medo-Persian empire.
lead thy *legions* to *victory!* (Is. xliv. 28.)

555. Daniel's dream of the four beasts.
lo! a *lion* and a *leopard* (Dan. vii. 3).

 ,, Labynetus, or Nabonidas, comes to the throne.
Labynetus lived long.

541. Belshazzar becomes joint king with Labynetus.
its *last king* is *Belshazzar*.

538. Babylon destroyed by Cyrus and Darius: Belshazzar's dream.
the *Lord* of *heaven's revenge* (Dan. v. 23).

CHAP. III.—HISTORY OF THE MEDO-PERSIAN EMPIRE
(B.C. 880-330).

SECT. 8.—The Median Kingdom from its Origin to the Fall of Babylon. (B.C. 880-538).

B.C.
880. The Medes, an Aryan or Japhetic nation, from beyond the Indus, arrive in Elam.
  the *Aryans arrive* in the *west.*
841. Arbaces, their first king, builds Ecbatana (Achmetha).
  Arbaces is *king* at *Ecbatana.*
776. Media becomes a province of Assyria, under Pul.
  Pul is *prince* at *Nineveh.*
721. Sargon overruns the country, and peoples it with Israelitish captives.
  Ephraim deported to the *Caspian.*
711. Revolt of Media from Assyria : Media a republic.
  their *powerful capital* is *Ecbatana.*
709. The Medes elect Deioces to be their king.
  a *peasant exalted* to the *throne.*
657. Phraortes succeeds his father, Deioces.
  the *Medes elect Phraortes.*
634. Cyaxares, the first powerful King of Media, succeeds Phraortes : the Scythians invade Media.
  Media a *great kingdom.*
625. Cyaxares aids Nabopolassar in taking Nineveh.
  Nineveh destroyed by the *allies.*
624. After the fall of Nineveh, Upper Mesopotamia is added to Media.
  Mesopotamia is *added* to the *kingdom.*
610. Cyaxares at war with Alyattes, King of Lydia : Battle of Halys.*
  an *omen concludes* the *war.*

---

* The date of the battle of Halys cannot be accurately determined, even though we are informed that it was suspended by a total eclipse of the

B.C.

593. Astyages succeeds Cyaxares, and forms a league with Babylonia and Lydia.
a league of three great monarchies.

588. The Jews carried captive to Babylon.
alas for the erring race!

559. Cyrus the Elder, son of Cambyses, dethrones Astyages and founds the Medo-Persian empire.
lead thy legions to victory (Is. xliv. 28).

546. Cyrus takes Sardis, and overthrows the Lydian monarchy.
the Lydian kingdom annihilated.

538. Cyrus and "Darius the Mede" take Babylon, and slay Belshazzar.
the Lord of heaven's revenge!

SECT. 9.—From the Destruction of Babylon to Alexander the Great (B.C. 538-330).

B.C.

536. Cyrus becomes master of all Asia.
the lord of a great empire.

 ,,   Cyrus issues a decree for the return of the Jews.
liberate the holy nation! (Ezek. i. 2.)

535. Cyrus makes Egypt tributary to Persia.
(Cyrus) the elder governs their land.

529. Cambyses succeeds his father, Cyrus.
the Lacedemonians defeated by the tyrant.

525. Cambyses invades Egypt, and sets up the twenty-seventh dynasty there.
the land is devastated by his legions.

522. Cambyses accidentally killed: Smerdis the Magian usurps the throne.
the land is freed of a despot.

---

sun. Astronomers vary in their calculations between B.C. 625 and 583. As the result of calculations based on the newest tables, Ideler, the German chronologer, insists on 30th Sept. 610 B.C.; but Professors Airy and Hind lean to B.C. 585.

HISTORY OF THE MEDO-PERSIAN EMPIRE.

B.C.
521. Smerdis slain by conspirators: Darius Hystaspes (Ahasuerus) succeeds him.
   his *life* is *finished* by *conspirators*.

517. Ahasuerus divorces Vashti, and marries Esther.
   a *lovely captive* is *preferred* (Est. ii. 17).

515. Dedication of the Second Temple at Jerusalem.
   they *loudly bless* the *Lord* (Ezek. vi. 16).

510. Haman, the enemy of the Jews, slain by Ahasuerus.
   allured to a *banquet* of *wine*.

,, Macedonia and Thrace become tributary to Persia.
   Olynthus and *Byzantium* under the *yoke*.

500. Revolt of Miletus against the Persians.
   a *league* among *wily exiles*.

495. Artaphernes defeats the Ionian fleet at Ladé.
   the *Samians treacherously leave* them.

494. Miletus retaken by the Persians: the revolt put down.
   shocking atrocities submitted to.

492. First Persian invasion of Greece.
   they *send* a *vast fleet*.

490. Second Persian invasion: Battle of Marathon.
   a *strange event* in *war*.

487. Egypt revolts against Darius Hystaspes.
   the *kingdom revolts* against the *Persians*.

485. Xerxes I. succeeds Darius Hystaspes, his father.
   Xerxes *succeeds* as *ruler* of the *land*.

484. Xerxes suppresses the revolt of the Egyptians.
   suppresses the *revolt* with *ease*.

480. Third Persian invasion of Greece by Xerxes.
   a *splendid array* for the *war*.

,, Battles of Thermopylæ and Salamis: the Persian army destroyed.
   Salamis ruins his *expectations*.

479. Battles of Platæa and Mycalé: the Persians defeated.
   the *Spartans* at *Platæa* are *victorious*.

B.C.
466. The Persians defeated at the Eurymedon : Ionia again independent.
 a *splendid naval engagement.*
465. Xerxes assassinated : Artaxerxes becomes king.
 known by the *name* of *Longimanus.*
458. Egypt, under Inarus, revolts against Persia.
 a *successful leader* of *revolt.*
457. Ezra returns from Babylon with a company of Jews.
 a *scribe leads* back a *part* (Ezek. viii. 1).
448. The revolt suppressed: Egypt made a Persian satrapy.
 satraps suppress the *revolt.*
444. Nehemiah sent by Artaxerxes to Judea as Governor.
 sent by the *king* to *Jerusalem* (Neh. ii. 5).
434. Nehemiah's second journey from Babylon to Jerusalem.
 the *Jew* is *grieved* at the *sacrilege* (Neh. xiii. 6).
424. Darius Nothus succeeds Artaxerxes.
 his *son Darius succeeds* him.
414. Amyrtæus, King of Egypt, throws off the Persian yoke.
 established his *capital* at *Saïs.*
405. Artaxerxes-Mnemon succeeds Darius Nothus.
 satraps at *war* with their *lord.*
401. Cyrus the Younger attempts to seize the throne : Battle of Cunaxa and death of Cyrus.
 Xenophon *joined* the "*expedition* of *Cyrus.*"
396. Agesilaus, King of Sparta, invades Persia.
 Agesilaus outwits his *antagonist.*
394. The Persians victorious at Haliartus, Cnidus, Corinth, and Coronæa.
 Haliartus turns the *scale.*
387. Peace of Antalcidas : the Greek colonies ceded to Persia.
 Greece recognises Persian (supremacy).
359. Artaxerxes-Ochus succeeds Mnemon.
 a *gross* and *lawless tyrant.*
356. Birth of Alexander the Great.
 the *great leviathan* of *antiquity.*

B.C.
353. Persia subdues Egypt : the thirty-first dynasty.
Egypt loses her *greatness.*

338. Ochus poisoned by Bagoas : Arses succeeds him.
his *guilt gains* its *reward.*

336. Arses is slain : Darius Codomannus succeeds.
the *government* in the *hands* of a *eunuch.*

334. Alexander the Great invades Persia : Battle of the Granicus.
the *Granicus hinders* his *journey.*

333. Battle of Issus : defeat of the Persians.
what *heaps* of *gold* and *gems !*

331. Battle of Arbela or Gaugamela.
great havoc and *carnage.*

„ Alexander captures Babylon, Susa, and Persepolis.
the *hoarded gold* is *captured.*

330. Death of Darius : the Persian empire annihilated.
the *great hero extinguished* it.

263. Berosus, a priest of Belus, at Babylon, writes the History of Babylonia.
a *famous native historian.*

CHAP. IV.—HISTORY OF GREECE.

(B.C. 2000-146.)

THE origin of the Greeks and Latins, in common with that of the Celts, Goths, and Sclaves, is lost in the darkness of the prehistoric period. Modern ethnographic science, however, leaves little doubt that the two nations referred to were, respectively, the earliest inhabitants of Greece and Italy ; that they stood to each other in the closest affinity, both of them being the immediate descendants of the Pelasgi, who formed the first great wave of population that broke on the shores of south-eastern Europe, and that permanently covered Asia Minor, Thrace, Macedonia, Greece, and Italy. This migration probably took place about B.C. 2000, but was succeeded by numerous similar migrations of the same stock of nations (including the Hellenes, who were, no doubt, nearly allied to, if not identical with, the Pelasgi), down to B.C. 1350.

In subsequent centuries other great bodies of colonists appear to have entered Europe from other parts of Asia, forming the ancestors of the Celtic, Teutonic, and Sclavonic nations; but the Pelasgi formed, from the very first, the great bulk of the population of Italy and Greece.

The part of Asia from which the Pelasgi set out appears to have been Northern India; for the Sanscrit, the ancient and sacred language of India, has a marked and very decided affinity to both Greek and Latin. The Greek, especially, is more closely allied to the Sanscrit than any other European tongue. In some respects, however, the Latin surpasses the Greek in retaining the features of its venerable parent, and it is in no way to be regarded as a descendant, far less a corruption, of the language of Greece. They are *sister tongues*, deriving from their common parent every feature in which they resemble each other, but exhibiting many differences, arising from the different fortunes of each.

In the following sections the author has followed the chronology adopted by Dr William Smith in his admirable School-Histories of Greece, and by Mr Philip Smith, in his able and eloquent 'History of the Ancient World.'

SECT. 10.—Heroic or Mythical Period (B.C. 2000-776).

B.C.

2000. The Pelasgi, from the East, arrive in Greece and Italy.
  a *family wends* its *way westward.*

1984. Call of Abraham: the Patriarch visits Egypt.
  Abraham visits the *ruler* of *Sebennytus.*

1900. The Shepherd Kings begin to reign in Lower Egypt.
  their *celebrated victories win* our *admiration.*

HISTORY OF GREECE.

B.C.
1886. Mœris, a shepherd king, captures Memphis.
a courageous Arvadite reduces Memphis.

1856. Argos, the most ancient city in Greece, founded by Inachus, a Pelasgian.
colonise Argos, lordly Inachus!

1791. Joseph, sold as a slave, arrives in Egypt.
his brethren persecute the type of Christ.

1769. Jacob and his family migrate to Egypt.
the covenant people are nourished and trained.

1763. Supposed date of the Deluge of Ogyges.
a celebrated epoch in the annals of Grecce.

1698. Death of Joseph, Prime-minister of Pharaoh Aphophis.
his body embalmed for the time of release.

1635. Birth of Moses in Lower Egypt.
birth of Moses the Hebrew lawgiver.

1582. The chronology of the Arundelian Marbles begins.
contain a lengthened record of dates.

1556. Athens founded by Cecrops, an Egyptian.
Cecrops leaves the land of Mizraim.

1554. Exodus of the Israelites, and destruction of Sethos II., with his army.
the cruel lord of the land is smitten.

1551. Cadmus, a Phœnician, builds Thebes, and introduces the Phœnician alphabet into Greece.
Cadmus learned his letters in Canaan.

1514. Death of Moses: the Israelites enter Canaan.
buried by the Lord beyond the Jordan.

1504. Era of Deucalion's Deluge.
a curious legend of the world's submersion.

1453. First celebration of the Olympic Games.
competitors strive at the Olympic Games.

1387. The HELLENES arrive in Greece, and expel the Pelasgi, a kindred race.
the brave Hellēnēs rout the Pelasgi.

FACTS AND DATES.

B.C.

1326. The Isthmian Games instituted near Corinth.
commencement of *games* of *famous name.*

1313. Mycenæ founded by Perseus of Argos.
the *celebrated Agamemnon* was *born here.*

1300. Pelops, from Asia Minor, arrives in the Peloponnesus.
come to *Greece,* thou *wandering exile!*

1273. Tyre built by a colony of Sidonians.
the *beautiful daughter* of " *Zidon* the *Great.*"

1250. The Argonautic expedition to Colchis, under Jason.
a *band* of *adventurers leave* for the *Euxine.*

1230. Theseus becomes the tenth king of Attica.
achieved famous and *heroic exploits.*

1229. First Theban War, or, " The Seven against Thebes."
the *celebrated fable* of " *Œdipus Tyrannus.*"

1216. Helen married to Menelaus, King of Sparta.
occasioned the *first crusade* of *antiquity.*

1198. Helen elopes with Paris, son of Priam, King of Troy.
her *abduction causes* a *terrible revenge.*

1194. The Trojan War begins.
a *band* of *confederates* for *Troy set* out.

1184. Troy captured: the Trojan War ends.
brave Achilles razes Ilium.

1181. Æneas, setting out for Italy, arrives in Africa.
a *celebrated chief arrives* at *Carthage* (Virgil).

1103. Conquest of the Peloponnesus by the Dorians.
the *brave Achæans expelled* by the *Heraclidæ.*

1095. Saul becomes first king of Israel.
they *choose* a *young* and *tall leader.*

1045. Death of Codrus, last king of Athens: perpetual archons succeed him.
Codrus willingly sacrifices his *life.*

1004. Dedication of the Temple of Solomon.
accept our *willing work, Jehovah!*

975. Dismemberment of the Israelitish Empire.
ten parts are *alienated.*

B.C.
853. Carthage founded by a Tyrian colony, 100 years before the foundation of Rome.
   her *ruins lie* in *heaps*.

850. Supposed age of Homer.
   recites his *Iliad wandering*.

825. Supposed age of Lycurgus, the Spartan legislator.
   a *renowned framer* of *laws*.

783. Phidon, King of Argos, begins to coin silver in Greece.
   Phidon at *Argos* and *Ægina*.

SECT. 11.—Earliest Historic Period (B.C. 776-479).

B.C.
776. Date of the first Olympiad.
   a *prime epoch* with the *ancients*.

753. Rome founded by Romulus.
   its *position learned* by *augury*.

752. Decennial archons at Athens succeed the perpetual.
   the *people elect* them *decennially*.

743. First Messenian War, which lasts 19 years.
   the *people* of *Sparta gain*.

735. Supposed age of Hesiod.
   the *poet Hesiod lived*.

721. The Ten Tribes carried captive to Assyria.
   Ephraim departs to the *Caspian*.

685. Second Messenian War, which lasts 17 years.
   the *Messenian Aristomĕnes illustrious*.

683. Annual archons appointed at Athens.
   annual archons govern it.

677. Esarhaddon colonises Samaria with heathen nations.
   Medes and *Persians* in *Ephraim*.

625. Fall of Nineveh.
   Nineveh destroyed by the *allies*.

621. Draco composes a code of laws at Athens.
   merciless Draco's code.

B.C.
612. Insurrection of Cylo at Athens.
   a novel conspiracy defeated.

600. The seven wise men of Greece (Thales, &c.) flourish.
   men who excelled in wisdom.

594. Solon legislates at Athens.
   legislate, venerable Solon!

588. The Jewish captivity.
   the Lord's residence in ruins.

560. Pisistratus, first tyrant of Athens.
   liberty menaced for a while.

 ,, Crœsus, last king of Lydia, begins to reign.
   the Lydian monarch is wealthy.

559. Cyrus the Elder founds the Medo-Persian Empire.
   lead thy legions to victory! (Is. xliv. 28.)

554. Solon visits Egypt.
   the illustrious legislator at Saïs.

546. Cyrus takes Sardis: the Lydian monarchy overthrown.
   the Lydian kingdom annihilated.

538. Fall of Babylon: the Babylonian Empire overthrown.
   the "Lord of heaven's" revenge.

536. Cyrus becomes master of all Asia.
   the lord of a great empire.

534. Pythagoras of Samos flourished: Tarquin, the last king of Rome, ascends the throne.
   he lived in the age of Superbus.

527. Pisistratus dies: Hippias and Hipparchus succeed.
   they lament the death of Pisistratus.

522. Polycrates of Samos crucified by the Persians.
   they allure the despot to his doom.

515. Dedication of the Second Temple at Jerusalem.
   they loudly bless the Lord.

514. Hipparchus slain by Harmodius and Aristogeiton.
   the elder brother escapes.

B.C.
510. Hippias is expelled from Athens.
the elder brother is expelled.

,, Macedonia and Thrace subdued by the Persians.
Olynthus and Byzantium under the yoke.

507. Cleisthenes reforms Solon's constitution: Athens a democracy.
liberty extended to the people.

500. Revolt of Miletus against the Persians.
a league 'mong wily exiles.

499. Sardis burned by the Athenians: this leads to the Persian invasions of Greece.
Sardis taken by the Athenians.

495. Artaphernes defeats the Ionian fleet at Ladé.
the Samians treacherously leave them.

494. Miletus recovered by the Persians.
shocking atrocities are suffered.

492. First Persian invasion of Greece (by Mardonius).
they send a vast fleet.

490. Second Persian invasion: Battle of Marathon.
the strangest event in war.

489. Death of Miltiades.
a sad reverse to the victor.

483. Ostracism of Aristides.
Ostracism of "Aristides the Good."

480. Third invasion of Greece under Xerxes.
a splendid array for the war.

,, Battles of Thermopylæ and Salamis: the Persian army destroyed.
Salamis ruins his expectations.

479. Battles of Platæa and Mycalé.
the Spartans at Platæa are victorious.

SECT. 12.—The Athenian Supremacy (B.C. 479-404).

B.C.
478. Capture of Sestos, the key of the Hellespont, by the Athenians.
they seize the Persian's refuge.

B.C.

476. Reduction of Scyros by Cimon.
known for its *quarries* of *marble*.

471. Death of Pausanias at Sparta.
they *starve Pausanias* for *conspiracy*.

469. Themistocles ostracised.
the *sad end* of a *traitor*.

468. Death of Aristides: birth of Socrates.
the "*just man's*" *reward*.

466. Revolt and subjugation of Naxos.
subject independent Naxos.

,, Battle of the Eurymĕdon: Ionia regains her independence.
a *splendid naval engagement*.

465. Revolt of Thasos from the Athenian alliance.
east of *Macedonia* it *lies*.

464. The third Messenian War, which lasts ten years.
a *judgment* on the *unfaithful Spartans*.

462. Birth of Hippocrates, "the Father of Medicine."
the *science* of *medicine founded* by him.

461. Beginning of the administration of Pericles.
skilled in *numerous accomplishments*.

,, Herodotus, the historian, visits Egypt.
stores of *knowledge* are *collected*.

456. Death of Æschylus, the Father of Tragedy.
Æschylus the *illustrious poet*.

,, Battle of Œnophyta, in Bœotia.
success of the *allies* at *Œnophyta*.

449. Sophocles and Euripides, the tragic poets, flourish.
they *succeed Æschylus* as *tragedians*.

,, The Phœnician fleet signally defeated by the Athenians at Salamis in Cyprus.
they *sink* the *ships* of *Tyre*.

,, Death of Cimon in Cyprus.
sent to the *east* with his *triremes*.

B.C.
449. Athens attains her highest elevation.
supreme by a *series* of *victories.*
447. Battle of Chæronea, in Bœotia : Athenians defeated.
her *supremacy suddenly perishes.*
445. The thirty years' truce begins, which lasts only fourteen.
stript of her *supremacy* by *land.*
,, Phidias, the eminent sculptor, flourishes.
executed the *statue of Jupiter Olympus.*
440. Revolt and conquest of Samos.
Samos subdued expeditiously.
437. The Athenians send a colony to Amphipolis.
they *search* for *gold* at *Pangœus.*
435. War between Corinth and Corcyra about Epidamnus.
they *ask help* against the *Illyrians.*
433. The Athenians send a colony to Thurii, in Italy.
the expedition *joined* by the *king of historians.*
,, Alliance between Corcyra and Athens.
a *squadron goes* to their *help.*
432. Revolt and siege of Potidæa by the Athenians.
they *send* a *great fleet.*
431. The Peloponnesian War begins: lasts 27 years.
the *Spartan hatred culminates.*
430. A plague rages at Athens.
a *scourge heavily wastes* it.
429. Death of Pericles.
the *statesman* who *decorated Athens.*
427. Platæa taken and destroyed.
the *Spartans destroy Platæa.*
425. Capture of Sphacteria.
the *issue disastrous* to the *Lacedemonians.*
424. Battle of Delium : surrender of Amphipolis.
Socrates distinguished as a *soldier.*
423. Herodotus and Thucydides, the historians, flourish.
known as the *fathers* of *history.*
,, Thucydides banished: Alcibiades begins his career.
exile *saves* a *famous historian.*

B.C.

422. Battle of Amphipolis: Cleon and Brassidas slain.
   the *Spartans defeat* the *demagogue.*

421. Peace of Nicias: a fifty years' truce.
   Sparta forms a *confederacy* (with Athens).

418. Battle of Mantinea.
   the *Spartans beat* the *Argives.*

416. The Athenians conquer Melos.
   shocking butchery at *Melos.*

,, Age of Malachi: the Old Testament completed.
   the *Scriptures conclude* with *Malachi.*

415. Sicilian expedition under Nicias, Alcibiades, and Lamachus.
   sails under the *command of Alcibiades.*

413. Total defeat of the Athenians at Syracuse.
   the *Spartans conquer* under *Gylippus.*

412. Alcibiades quarrels with Agis, and befriends Tessaphernes.
   the *satrap confides* in a *deserter.*

411. Revolution at Athens: the four hundred.
   a *scheme* to *abolish* the *constitution.*

,, Battle of Cynossema: the Spartans defeated.
   the *Spartans beaten* at *Cynossema.*

410. Battle of Cyzicus.
   the *Spartan* (fleet) *captured* and *exterminated.*

407. Battle of Notium: return of Alcibiades to Athens.
   a *joyful welcome* at the *Piræus.*

406. Battle of Arginusæ.
   the *Spartans worsted* near *Mytilene.*

405. Battle of Ægospotami: Dionysius, Tyrant of Syracuse.
   the *Spartans win* under *Lysander.*

404. The Spartans capture Athens: end of the Peloponnesian War.
   she exercised a *seventy-five years' supremacy.*

SECT. 13.—The Spartan Supremacy (B.C. 404-371).

B.C.
404. Reign of Terror at Athens: the thirty tyrants.
shameful excesses and *assassinations.*

403. Thrasybulus expels the thirty: democracy restored.
he *succeeds* in *expelling* the *governors.*

401. Cyrus the Younger slain at the battle of Cunaxa.
Xenophon *joined* the "*Expedition of Cyrus.*"

400. Retreat of "the ten thousand."
a *sad* and *weary way.*

399. Death of Socrates: campaign of Thimbron in Asia.
hemlock is the *verdict* of the *Athenians.*

397. Campaign of Dercyllidas.
Greece against *Tissaphernes* and *Pharnabazus.*

396. Campaign of Agesilaus in Asia Minor.
Agesilaus outwits his *antagonist.*

395. Defeat and death of Tissaphernes.
they execute the *hypocritical Tissaphernes* at *last.*

394. Battles of Haliartus, Corinth, Cnidus, and Coronæa.
Haliartus turns the *scale.*

393. Conon rebuilds the walls of Athens and restores her maritime supremacy.
walls *gird Athens again.*

387. Peace of Antalcidas: the Greek colonies in Asia ceded to Persia.
Greece recognises Persian (supremacy).

382. Olynthian War: Phœbidas seizes the Cadmea of Thebes.
the *general resorts* to *fraud.*

378. War between Thebes and Sparta.
the *genius* of *Epaminondas revealed.*

371. Battle of Leuctra: the Lacedemonians defeated.
heroic Epaminondas conquers.

SECT. 14.—The Theban Supremacy (B.C. 371-361.)

B.C.
370. Megalopolis and Messene founded.
   a *great protection* against *war*.
368. Expedition of Pelopidas into Thessaly and Macedonia.
   exacts *hostages* from the *Macedonian regent*.
367. Pelopidas induces Persia to proclaim Thebes the head of Greece.
   the *great manifesto* of *Persia*.
366. Aristotle, the naturalist and philosopher, flourished.
   the *great naturalist* of *antiquity*.
362. Battle of Mantinea: death of Epaminondas.
   the *hero* of *Mantinea falls*.
   ,, Æschines the orator flourished.
   the *great antagonist* of *Demosthenes*.
361. Death of Agesilaus in Cyrene.
   the *Greeks embalm* his *body*.

SECT. 15.—The Macedonian Supremacy (B.C. 361-323).

B.C.
359. Philip ascends the throne of Macedon.
   as a *hostage* he *learned* his *tactics*.
358. Philip besieges Amphipolis and Pydna.
   he *gallantly labours* to *reduce* them.
357. The Social War begins: Philippi built.
   the *Greeks* in *alliance* with *Persia*.
   ,, The first Sacred or Phocian War.
   the *gods* in *alliance* with *Philip*.
356. Birth of Alexander the Great.
   the *great leviathan* of *antiquity*.
   ,, The chronology of the Arundelian Marbles ends.
   Greek legendary inscriptions.
352. Philip defeats the Phocians.
   the *Greek legions* are *defeated*.
   ,, Demosthenes delivers his first Philippic at Athens.
   the *grand eloquence* of *Demosthenes*.

B.C.
- **350.** The Olynthiac Orations of Demosthenes.
  the hopes of the Olynthians excited.
- **347.** Capture of Olynthus by Philip.
  won by the great shrewdness of Philip.
- ,, Plato, the greatest philosopher of antiquity, flourished.
  the great king of philosophers.
- ,, Praxiteles, the famous Athenian sculptor, flourished.
  the graceful statue of Aphrodite.
- **346.** Philip conquers Phocis, and ends the Sacred War.
  the galling sentence of the Amphictions.
- **342.** Philip's expedition to Thrace.
  the Hellespont seized with fright.
- **339.** Philip is compelled to raise the siege of Byzantium.
  the gallant Greeks victorious.
- **338.** Second Sacred or Locrian War: Battle of Chæronea.
  the Greek generals are routed.
- **337.** Congress at Corinth: Greece no longer independent.
  Greece henceforth a province.
- **336.** Philip is murdered at Ægæ by Pausanias.
  at Ægæ the generalissimo is murdered.
- ,, Alexander the Great succeeds to the throne of Macedon.
  the great hero a monarch.
- **335.** Thebes revolts, and is destroyed by Alexander.
  the great hero levels it.
- **334.** Battle of Granicus: Sardis and Ephesus taken.
  the Granicus hinders his journey.
- **333.** Battle of Issus, and defeat of Darius Codomannus.
  what heaps of gold and gems!
- **332.** Tyre and Gaza are captured by Alexander.
  walls great and high defend them.
- ,, Alexander conquers Egypt and builds Alexandria.
  the "gem" of the hero's "diadem."
- **331.** Battle of Arbela or Gaugamela.
  great havoc and carnage.
- ,, Babylon, Susa, and Persepolis captured.
  the hoarded gold is captured.

B.C.
330. Alexander marches to Ecbatana : the Persian Empire terminates.
the *great hero extinguished* it.

,, Philotas and Parmenio executed for treason : death of Darius : speech of Demosthenes *De Coroná.*
great generals executed.

,, Ægis, King of Sparta, defeated by Antipater.
the *Greeks* and *Ægis* are *worsted.*

329. Alexander conquers Bactria, and defeats the Scythians.
the Oxus *aggravates* his *difficulties* in *travelling.*

328. Alexander conquers Sogdiana : marries Roxana.
Oxyartes *gave* him his *daughter Roxana.*

327. Alexander invades India, and defeats Porus.
the *hero defeats Porus.*

326. Voyage of Nearchus down the Indus.
the *geographical discoveries* of *Nearchus.*

325. Mutiny of Alexander's army.
the *grand defence of Alexander.*

,, Death of Hephæstion.
Hephæstion dies lamented.

324. Demosthenes banished from Athens.
Ægina affords him an *asylum.*

323. Death of Alexander at Babylon : Philip Arrhidæus, his half-brother, becomes king.
the *hero dies* in *agony.*

SECT. 16.—From the Death of Alexander to the Conquest of Greece by the Romans (B.C. 323-146.)

B.C.
323. The Lamian War : defeat of Antipater.
the *Greeks defeat* the *general.*

322. Battle of Crannon : death of Demosthenes.
the *great Demosthenes destroys* himself.

321. Perdiccas marches against Ptolemy, but is assassinated.
the *general dies* by *conspirators.*

B.C.
321. Partition of the empire among Alexander's four generals (Antipater, Ptolemy, Seleucus, and Antigonus): Antipater obtains Greece.
the generals divide his conquests between them.

318. Death of Antipater, regent of Greece and Macedonia.
Greece bewails her regent.

317. Phocion is poisoned at Athens.
they grudge the cup of poison.

316. Cassander conquers Macedonia.
the general conquers Macedonia.

,, Cassander puts Olympia to death.
the general basely murders her.

311. Cassander murders Roxana and her son.
he is guilty of the basest acts.

307. Antigonus restores democracy at Athens.
the Greeks worship Poliorcetes.

306. Naval battle of Salamis: siege of Rhodes.
the Egyptians worsted in the engagement.

301. Battle of Ipsus, and death of Antigonus.
a great war concluded.

,, New partition of the empire: Cassander gets Greece and Macedonia; Ptolemy, Egypt and Syria; Seleucus, Upper Asia; Lysimachus, nearly all Asia Minor.
Greece is awarded to Cassander.

300. Antioch (on the Orontes) founded by Seleucus.
a great and wealthy city.

296. Demetrius Poliorcetes captures Athens.
dethrones the Athenian monarch.

294. Demetrius becomes King of Macedon and Greece.
Demetrius takes the sovereignty.

287. Demetrius dethroned by Pyrrhus, King of Epirus.
dethroned by his rival, Pyrrhus.

284. The Ætolian League formed: the Septuagint translation completed at Alexandria.
first rendering of the Scriptures.

B.C.
284. The Epicurean, Stoic, Peripatetic, and Academic schools flourish.
four renowned schools.

283. Death of Demetrius.
death of the *ruler* of *Greece.*

281. Battle of Corupedion, and death of Lysimachus.
he *fell* in the *rout* of *Corupedion.*

280. Assassination of Seleucus by Ptolemy Ceraunus, King of Macedonia.
a *dire retribution awarded* him.

279. The Gauls invade Thrace and Macedonia: Brennus, their king, slain.
a *formidable people threaten* them.

,, Ptolemy Ceraunus dies.
death of *Ptolemy* in *Thrace.*

272. Death of Pyrrhus, King of Epirus, at Argos.
death of *Pyrrhus* the *despot.*

264. Rome begins the first Punic War.
fights the *mistress* of the *seas.*

251. The Achæan League revived by Aratus of Sicyon.
the *formidable league* of *Achaia.*

244. Agis IV. attempts reforms in Sparta.
a *famous Spartan king.*

239. Archimedes, Eratosthenes, and Apollonius flourish.
a *famous geometrical trio.*

225. Cleomenes III. effects a revolution in Sparta.
a *devoted friend* of *liberty.*

221. Battle of Sellasia, between the Spartans and Achæans.
the *fatal defeat* of *Cleomenes.*

218. War between the Ætolian and Achæan leagues.
defeat of the *Achæans* and *Aratus.*

216. Philip of Macedon declares war against the Romans.
friendship between *Carthage* and *Macedon.*

213. Aratus poisoned by Philip.
death of the *Achæan general.*

B.C.
207. The Spartans defeated at Mantinea by Philopœmen.
  the *day* is *won* by *Philopœmen*.

197. Battle of Cynoscephalæ: the Romans defeat Philip.
  the *complete overthrow* of *Philip*.

196. Greece declared independent of Macedon by Flamininus, the Roman general.
  the *coming event* is *nigh*.

„ Date of inscription on the Rosetta stone.
  a *celebrated trilingual inscription*.

191. Defeat of Antiochus III., King of Syria, by the Romans.
  the *battle* of *Thermopylæ checks* him.

189. The Ætolian League crushed by the Romans.
  crushed and *ruined* for *ever*.

183. Philopœmen, "the last of the Greeks," captured and poisoned by the Messenians.
  they *capture* a *renowned general*.

179. Perseus, last king of Macedon, comes to the throne.
  the *accession* of *Perseus* to the *throne*.

168. Perseus defeated: Macedonia a Roman province.
  conquest of *Macedon* by the *Romans*.

167. Perseus carried prisoner to Rome.
  they *carry* the *monarch* a *prisoner*.

147. The Spartans appeal to the Romans agt. the Achæans.
  the *Achæans* and *Spartans quarrel*.

146. Hipparchus, the founder of astronomical science, flourished.
  the *chief astronomer* of *antiquity*.

„ Corinth destroyed by Mummius, the Roman general.
  Corinth sacked by *Mummius*.

„ Greece becomes a Roman province, under the name of Achaia.
  a *celebrated kingdom annihilated*.

CHAP. V.—HISTORY OF ROME.

(B.C. 2000—A.D. 476.)

WITH the exception of Greece, Italy was the first European country that attained to any considerable degree of civilisation. Notwithstanding the patient and laborious researches of modern ethnologists, considerable doubt still attaches to the question of its original inhabitants; though it is generally acknowledged that they belonged to the same great family of nations as the Greeks, both being descendants of the Pelasgi, a people of Northern India, who formed the first great wave of population that broke on the shores of south-eastern Europe, and that permanently covered Asia Minor, Thrace, Macedonia, Greece, and Italy. This migration appears to have commenced as early as about B.C. 2000, and to have been continued at intervals to about B.C. 1350. They must have entered Italy from the north, and have advanced southward, being pushed forward by fresh bodies of immigrants.

According to this view, the first inhabitants of Southern Italy were the most ancient in the peninsula; and these are the people who are known in history as the Siculians, Tyrrhenians, and Pelasgi. Next, in point of antiquity, were the inhabitants of Latium and the other parts of Central Italy, whose languages, though not identical, appear to have been only dialectically different from each other, and closely allied to those of the Siculi or first inhabitants. All these languages ultimately merged in the Latin, one of the most copious and refined of the great Indo-European family of tongues, and the twin-sister of the still nobler Greek.

In the valley of the Po we first find the Etruscans, who had likewise descended from the Alps, but who were subsequently driven forward (by the Gauls or Celts, who took possession of that territory) into the country now known as Tuscany, whose former inhabitants, the Tyrrhenians, they reduced to bondage.

Who the Etruscans were, remains a question of the greatest uncertainty; for though numerous inscriptions belonging to that people have been found, they remain wholly unintelligible. There are certain indications, however, that their language was a branch of the Indo-European group, and therefore allied, however remotely, to the Celtic, Teutonic, Sclavonic, and Greco-Latin families. From the numerous remains of their works of art, there can be no doubt that they had attained to a high civilisation while Rome was still in her infancy. Lastly, in the north-west of Italy (the modern Piedmont) were the Ligurians, whose origin is also uncertain, some writers supposing them to be Celts, others Iberians, and others still, Pelasgi.

Subsequent to the dawn of authentic history, the southern portion of the peninsula was colonised from different parts of Greece, and was in consequence named Magna Græcia; but the Greek immigrants, in common with all the other nations above enumerated, came in the course of time to lose their original languages, and, in the reign of Augustus, Latin was the spoken language of Italy from the one extremity of the peninsula to the other.

SECT. 17.—Italy from the Earliest Times to the Founding of Rome (B.C. 2000-753).

B.C.
2000. The Pelasgi from the east arrive in Italy and Greece.
a family wends its way westward.

1984. The Patriarch Abraham visits Egypt.
Abraham visits the ruler of Sebennytus.

1900. The Shepherd Kings begin to reign in Egypt.
their celebrated victories win our admiration.

1856. Argos, the most ancient city in Greece, founded.
colonise Argos, lordly Inachus.

1816. Pharaoh Aphophis, patron of Joseph, crowned king.
a celebrated ruler crowned at Memphis.

1791. Joseph arrives in Egypt.
his brethren persecute the type of Christ.

FACTS AND DATES.

B.C.

1769. Jacob and his family migrate to Egypt.
   the covenant people are nourished and trained.

1698. Death of Joseph.
   his body embalmed for the time of release.

1635. Birth of Moses.
   birth of Moses the Hebrew lawgiver.

1582. The chronology of the Arundelian Marbles commences.
   contain a lengthened record of dates.

1556. Athens founded by Cecrops, an Egyptian.
   Cecrops leaves the land of Mizraim.

1554. Exodus of the Israelites, and destruction of Sethos II.
   the cruel lord of the land is smitten.

1514. Death of Moses.
   buried by the Lord beyond the Jordan.

1453. First celebration of the Olympic Games.
   competitors strive at the Olympic Games.

1387. The Hellenes arrive in Greece, and expel the Pelasgi.
   the brave Hellenes rout the Pelasgi.

1364. The Iapygians, or oldest inhabitants of the north, a Pelasgic race, are driven southwards by the Umbri and Tyrrhenians, kindred nations.
   the aboriginal hordes move southwards.

1326. The Isthmian Games begin at Corinth.
   commencement of games of famous name.

1273. Tyre founded by a colony of Sidonians.
   the beautiful daughter of "Zidon the Great."

1184. The Trojan war ends : Æneas migrates to Italy.
   brave Achilles razes Ilium.

1181. Æneas arrives in Italy, and builds Lavinium.
   a celebrated chief erects a city.

1155. Ascanius, son of Æneas, founds Alba Longa.
   begins to build Alba Longa.

B.C.
1116. The Philistines capture the Ark: death of Eli.
a child called Ichabod by his mother.

1095. Saul crowned first king of Israel.
they choose a young tall leader.

1038. Cumæ (near Naples) founded, the most ancient Greek colony in Italy.
a colony of exiles from Greece arrives.

1004. Dedication of the Temple of Solomon.
accept our willing work, Jehovah!

985. The Rasena or Etruscans (possibly a Teutonic nation) descend from the Rhætian Alps and expel the Umbri from the north of Italy.
the Etruscans arrive from the Alps.

975. Dismemberment of the Israelitish empire.
ten parts are alienated.

853. Carthage founded by a Tyrian colony.
her ruins lie in heaps.

776. Date of the First Olympiad.
a prime epoch among the ancients.

SECT. 18.—From the Founding of Rome to the End of the Kingdom (B.C. 753-509).

B.C.
753. Rome founded by Romulus, who became its first king.
its position learned by augury.

747. Era of Nabonassar.
a primitive astronomical epoch.

741. Romulus slays Acron, King of Cænina.
the "opima spolia" are obtained.

734. Greek colonists found Syracuse and Agrigentum.
they plant Agrigentum in Sicily.

721. The Ten Tribes carried captive to Assyria.
Ephraim departs to the Caspian.

716. Numa Pompilius succeeds Romulus as king.
pontiffs begin now.

B.C.
714. The Greeks found colonies in Magna Græcia.
    the *planting* of *Croton* and *Sybaris.*

707. Tarentum founded by a colony from Sparta.
    planted by *exiles* from the *Peloponnesus.*

685. Locri founded by a colony from Locris.
    emigrants arrive from *Locris.*

673. Tullus Hostilius, third king of Rome.
    the *end* of a *peaceful age.*

667. Combat between the Horatii and Curiatii.
    a *novel* and *memorable plan.*

665. Alba Longa destroyed: the citizens transferred to Rome.
    they *annihilate ancient Alba.*

640. Ancus Martius, fourth king of Rome.
    engaged in a *series* of *wars.*

625. Fall of Nineveh.
    Nineveh destroyed by the *allies.*

624. Ancus Martius builds Ostia, at the mouth of the Tiber.
    Ancus founds Ostia.

616. Lucius Tarquinius Priscus, fifth king of Rome.
    many cities are *incorporated.*

608. The Gauls expel the Etrusci from the basin of the Po.
    invaders expel the *Rasena.*

588. The Jews carried captive to Babylon.
    the *Lord's residence* in *ruins.*

578. Servius Tullius, sixth king of Rome.
    laws for *popular rights.*

559. Cyrus founds the Medo-Persian empire.
    leads his *legions* to *victory.*

546. The Lydian monarchy overthrown by Cyrus.
    the *Lydian kingdom annihilated.*

538. Babylon destroyed by Cyrus and "Darius the Mede."
    the "*Lord* of *heaven's*" *revenge.*

B.C.
537. Tyrrhenian pirates and Carthaginians harass the Greek colonies of Magna Græcia.
the *land* is *harassed* by *pirates.*

534. Lucius Tarquinius Superbus, seventh king of Rome.
its *last haughty prince.*

531. Tarquin forms a league of 47 Latin cities.
Lucius heads the *confederacy.*

529. War with the Volsci.
Lucius defeats the *Volsci.*

521. Tarquin builds the Temple of Jupiter on the Capitoline Hill.
lays the *foundation* of the *capitol.*

515. Dedication of the Second Temple.
they *loudly bless* the *Lord.*

509. Tarquin expelled from Rome : end of the kingdom.
the *lieges expel* the *Tarquins.*

SECT. 19.—The Republic—From its Commencement to the First Punic War (B.C. 509-264).

B.C.
509. Republican government established under consuls (Brutus and Collatinus).
the *lieges expel* the *tyrants.*

508. Porsena, King of Clusium, aids Tarquin.
levies war against *Rome.*

„ First dictator appointed (Titus Lartius).
Lartius wields the *rod.*

498. Battle of Lake Regillus.
a *sad victory* to the *Romans.*

496. Tarquin dies at Cumæ.
succumbs to the *verdict* of *nature.*

494. First secession to Mount Sacer : Tribunes appointed.
establish tribunes on (Mount) *Sacer.*

488. Coriolanus leads the Volsci against Rome.
the women *save Rome* from *ruin.*

B.C.
- **486.** Spurius Cassius proposes the first Agrarian law.
  the senate revenges his meddling.
- **479.** The Fabii cut off by the Vejentes at the Cremera.
  they suddenly perish near Veii.
- **474.** Cumæ, at war with the Etruscans, is aided by Hiero of Syracuse.
  assisted by the power of Syracuse.
- **458.** The dictator Cincinnatus relieves Minucius, and makes the Æqui pass under the yoke.
  saves him from losing his army.
- **453.** The Syracusan navy ravages the coast of Etruria.
  the Isle of Elba is gained from them.
- **451.** Decemvirs first appointed.
  they settle the legal code.
- **449.** Second secession to Mt. Sacer: ten plebeian tribunes.
  a second set of tribunes.
- **445.** Third secession (to Mount Janiculum) anent the Marriage Law.
  the seceders succeed at last.
- **443.** Censors first appointed.
  they establish just government.
- **440.** Great famine at Rome.
  a serious scarcity exists.
- **439.** Cincinnatus dictator: Ahala murders Mælius.
  assassination of a horrid type.
- **437.** Cor. Cossus, the Roman general, slays in single combat Lars Tolumnius, King of Veii.
  second gaining of the ("spolia) opima."
- **426.** Fidenæ, an Etruscan city, destroyed.
  they sell Fidenates in the market.
- **414.** The Etruscans aid the Athenians against Syracuse and Sparta.
  their sceptre begins to shake.
- **405.** Siege of Veii, the greatest city in Etruria, begins.
  a siege of extraordinary length.
- **404.** First recorded Italian eclipse.
  they see a wondrous sight.

B.C.
- **396.** Veii taken by Camillus, after a ten years' siege.
  gains his *triumph* by *mining*.
- **394.** Camillus takes Falerii, another Etruscan city.
  the *horrid treachery* of a *schoolmaster*.
- **390.** Rome burned by Brennus, leader of the Gauls.
  Gallic tribes waste it.
- **387.** Dionysius of Syracuse attacks the Etrurian coasts.
  the *glory* of the *Rasena perishes*.
- **384.** Marcus Manlius hurled from the Tarpeian rock.
  hurled from a *rock* by the *senate*.
- **376.** The Licinian Rogations proposed.
  granting power to the *multitude*.
- **367.** The Licinian Rogations become law.
  great enactments are *passed*.
- **366.** L. Sextius, first plebeian consul : prætors instituted.
  governed by a *new magistrate*.
- **362.** Curtius leaps into the gulf in the Forum.
  the *gulf* is *nobly filled*.
- **361.** Story of Titus Manlius Torquatus.
  a *giant* and *Manlius* in *combat*.
- **356.** Rutilus, first plebeian dictator, defeats the Etrusci.
  a *great land engagement*.
- **„** Birth of Alexander the Great.
  the *great leviathan* of *antiquity*.
- **351.** First plebeian censor appointed.
  they *gradually loosen* their *bonds*.
- **349.** Story of Marcus Valerius Corvus.
  a *giant slain* by *Valerius*.
- **347.** Legal rate of interest reduced to 5 per cent.
  the *hopes* of the *usurers perish*.
- **343.** First Samnite War.
  the *haughty Samnites* are *humbled*.
- **340.** The great Latin War.
  great slaughter in the *war*.

B.C.
340. Battle of Mt. Vesuvius, and self-sacrifice of Decius.
the *general sacrifices* himself *willingly.*

337. First plebeian prætor appointed.
the *highest government* in the *people.*

336. Alexander ascends the throne of Macedon.
the *great hero* a *monarch.*

330. Fergus, first king of the Scots, comes from Ireland with an army.*
governs the *Hebrides* and the *west.*

329. Capture of Privernum : the Volsci subdued.
grand defeat of the *Volsci.*

326. Second or great Samnite War.
general defeat of the *enemy.*

323. Death of Alexander, the Great at Babylon.
the *hero dies* in *agony.*

322. The Tusculans and Privernatians demand to be enfranchised.
they *gain* the *franchise* by *force.*

321. The Romans defeated by the Samnites at the Caudine Forks.
a *great disaster* at *Caudium.*

318. P. Cursor defeats the Samnites at Luceria.
the *hostages* and *captives recovered.*

314. The Romans gain decisive victories over the Samnites.
great battles in *Samnium.*

304. The second Samnite War terminates.
the *great war subsides.*

300. The whole of central Italy is subject to Rome.
her *government* is *widely extending.*

298. Third Samnite War : the Samnites in coalition with the Etruscans, Umbrians, and Gauls.
a *formidable trio* against *Rome.*

---

* Fergus is said to have defeated the Britons and slain Coilus their king ; the Scots in gratitude entailed the crown on him and his posterity for ever. He and his successors reigned over the tribe till A.D. 357, when the kingdom became extinct, having existed nearly seven centuries.

B.C.
295. Battle of Sentinum, and self-sacrifice of Decius Mus.
  a famous victory over the *allies.*

290. Third Samnite War ends: the whole of Samnium subdued.
  final termination of the *war.*

281. War with Pyrrhus, King of Epirus.
  a foreigner ravages the *country.*

280. Pyrrhus defeats the Romans at Pandosia.
  a fearful reverse in *war.*

279. Pyrrhus defeats the Romans at Asculum.
  the *forces* of *Pyrrhus* are *victorious.*

274. Curius defeats Pyrrhus at Beneventum.
  defeats Pyrrhus with *ease.*

272. Rome is mistress of all Italy.
  defeats her *peninsular foes.*

SECT. 20.—The Republic—From the first Punic War to the End of the Third (B.C. 264-146).

B.C.
264. First Punic War commences in Sicily.
  she *fights* the *mistress* of the *seas.*

262. Victory of the Romans at Agrigentum.
  defeats the *enemy's forces.*

260. First naval victory at Mylæ in Sicily.
  the *fleet* of the *enemy worsted.*

256. Regulus defeats the Carthaginians in Africa.
  a fearful loss to the *enemy.*

255. Xanthippus, the Carthaginian general, defeats the Romans in Africa.
  his *fortune lay* in his *elephants.*

250. Victory of Metellus at Panormus: Regulus cruelly put to death by the Carthaginians.
  death of the *illustrious warrior.*

249. Claudius defeated at Drepanum by the Carthaginians.
  Drepanum sees his *overthrow.*

B.C.
241. Victory of L. Catulus at the Ægatian Islands.
destroys the *ships* of the *Carthaginians.*

„ First Punic War ended : Sicily a Roman province.
the *dominion* of *Sicily* is *ceded* to them.

238. Rome demands Corsica and Sardinia from Carthage.
the *demands* of the *grasping republic.*

„ The Carthaginian mercenaries in open revolt.
the *famous Hamilcar reduced* them.

229. The Romans send their fleet to Illyria anent pirates.
the *Adriatic freebooters vanquished.*

225. The Romans defeat the Boian Gauls in Etruria.
a *formidable foe alarms* her.

222. Marcellus kills Viridomarus, chief of the Galli Insubres, and obtains the "*spolia opima.*"
a *dauntless* and *daring deed.*

218. Placentia and Cremona founded.
founded by *colonists* from *Rome.*

„ Second Punic War begins : Fabius at Carthage.
the *dauntless behaviour* of the *Roman.*

„ Hannibal defeats the Romans at Ticinus and Trebia.
their *forces completely routed.*

217. Hannibal defeats the Romans at Lake Trasimenus.
Flaminius the *consul perishes.*

216. Hannibal defeats the Romans at Cannæ.
defeats the *consul Æmilius.*

„ Philip of Macedon declares war against the Romans.
friendship between *Carthage* and *Macedon.*

215. Hannibal defeated at Nola : First Macedonian War.
defeated by the *consuls* at *last.*

212. Syracuse retaken by the Romans : Archimedes burns their ships by burning glasses.
their *fleet* is *consumed* by *fire.*

211. Capua taken by the Romans.
a *frightful carnage* at *Capua.*

HISTORY OF ROME.   195

B.C.
207. Hasdrubal defeated at the Metaurus.
   a dauntless warrior perishes.
204. Scipio leaves Spain for Africa.
   Africa is wasted by Scipio.
203. Hannibal quits Italy to defend Carthage.
   the formidable warrior is gone.
202. Hannibal defeated at Zama : second Punic War ends.
   the formidable warrior is defeated.
200. Second Macedonian War begins.
   a four years' war.
197. Battle of Cynoscephalæ in Thessaly.
   the complete overthrow of Philip.
191. Syrian War : Antiochus defeated at Thermopylæ.
   the battle of Thermopylæ checks him.
189. Ætolian and Galatian wars : Ætolian league extinguished.
   the consul reduces the Ætolians.
184. Censorship of Marcus Porcius Cato.
   Cato the orator and statesman.
183. Death of Hannibal and Scipio Africanus.
   Carthage and Rome in grief.
179. Third Macedonian War.
   battles with Perseus and Cotys.
168. Perseus defeated at Pydna : Macedonia a Roman province.
   conquest of Macedon by the Romans.
149. Third Punic War begins.
   Cato's sentence triumphs.
147. The Spartans appeal to Rome against the Achæans.
   the Achæans and Spartans quarrel.
146. Corinth destroyed by Mummius.
   Corinth is sacked by Mummius.
   ,, Greece becomes a Roman province, and named Achaia.
   a celebrated kingdom annihilated.
   ,, Carthage destroyed by Scipio Africanus Minor.
   the Carthaginian kingdom annihilated.

SECT. 21.—The Republic—From the End of the Punic Wars to the Empire (B.C. 146-30).

B.C.
144. Revolt of the Celtiberi in Spain: the Numantian War.
commencement of a *sedition* in *Spain*.

141. Viriathus surprises the Roman proconsul.
the *consul's escape cut* off.

140. Cœpia bribes the soldiers of Viriathus to murder him.
bribes his *soldiers* to *execute* him.

134. First Servile War in Sicily.
commencement of a *great sedition*.

133. Numantia taken by Scipio.
the *besieged* are *harassed* with *hunger*.

„ Tiberius Gracchus, the tribune, put to death.
bitter hostility to *Gracchus*.

132. The consul Rupilius captures Eunus, the Servile leader.
he *captures* the *head disturber*.

129. Asia Minor becomes a Roman province.
bequeathed by the *dying Attalus*.

123. Gracchus, the tribune, proposes the Sempronian laws.
the *able defence* of *Gracchus*.

121. Death of Caius Gracchus, the tribune.
blamed for *founding* a *colony*.

113. Inroads of the Cimbri and Teutones.
bands of *Celts* and *Goths*.

111. The Jugurthine War commences.
the *consul Bestia bribed* by him.

107. First consulship of Marius.
a *consul* of *extraordinary popularity*.

106. Jugurtha taken prisoner.
Bocchus wilily ensnares him.

„ Birth of Cicero and Pompey.
a *couple* of *extraordinary men*.

B.C.
102. The Teutones defeated by Marius at Aquæ Sextiæ.
    the *battle* of *Aix finishes* them.

,, Second Servile War: Lucullus defeats the Sicilian slaves.
    a *bloody war* is *finished*.

101. The Cimbri defeated near Verona by Marius and Catulus.
    Catulus exterminates the *Cimbri*.

100. The tribune Saturninus slain.
    his *blood expiates* his *wickedness*.

,, Birth of Julius Cæsar.
    birth of an *extraordinary warrior*.

91. The Social or Marsic War.
    the existence of *Italy* in the *balance*.

88. Civil war between Marius and Sulla.
    a war between *rival rulers*.

86. Rome pillaged by Marius and Cinna.
    the *revenge* of *Marius*.

84. Mithridates defeated: first Mithridatic War ends.
    worsted at *Orchomenus* by *Sulla*.

83. Murena defeated by Mithridates on the Halys.
    he is worsted at the *river Halys*.

82. Sulla takes Rome and publishes his proscriptions.
    Rome is *decimated* by him.

81. Second Mithridatic War ends: Sulla defeats the Romans.
    the *Romans* are *conquered* by him.

78. Death of Sulla.
    an extraordinary *procession* at *Rome*.

74. The third or great Mithridatic War.
    warlike *preparations* in *Asia*.

72. Sertorius assassinated in Spain by Perperna.
    the *perpetrator* is *foiled*.

71. Servile insurrection: Spartacus defeated by Pompey and Crassus.
    extinguished by *Pompey* and *Crassus*.

B.C.
68. Diodorus Siculus visits Egypt, and writes his 'Historical Library' in Greek.
   a writer of *immense research*.
67. The Mediterranean pirates defeated by Pompey.
   extinguishes the *Mediterranean pirates*.
66. The great Mithridatic war ended.
   war with *Mithridates ended*.
65. Pontus becomes a Roman province.
   its *independence* is *lost*.
64. Pompey deposes Antiochus, and annexes Syria.
   expels *Antiochus* from *Syria*.
63. Palestine becomes tributary, and Jerusalem taken.
   the western *empire grasps* it.
62. Suppression of Cataline's conspiracy.
   his wicked *intentions* are *frustrated*.
60. Cæsar, Pompey, and Crassus form the first triumvirate.
   mighty warriors.
58. Banishment of Cicero.
   expel the *illustrious orator*.
,, Julius Cæsar begins his campaigns in Gaul: the Helvetii are subdued.
   in war and *literature renowned*.
55. Cæsar invades Britain.
   the warrior *lands* in *Albion*.
53. Crassus defeated and slain in Mesopotamia.
   a woeful *loss* at *Haran*.
52. Pompey sole consul.
   he wanted to be *elected dictator*.
51. Cæsar makes Gaul a Roman province.
   he extinguishes the *liberty* of the *Celts*.
49. Cæsar crosses the Rubicon.
   the *senators tremble*.
48. Cæsar defeats Pompey at Pharsalia: death of Pompey.
   they *slay* his *rival*.

B.C.
48. Cæsar aids Cleopatra, and burns Alexandria.
    Julius's revenge.
47. Cæsar defeats Pharnaces, son of Mithridates, in Pontus.
    extraordinary *success* in *Pontus.*
46. Cæsar in Africa : Battle of Thapsus, and death of Cato.
    he is *successful* in *Mauritania.*
,, Cæsar reforms the calendar.
    a year of *solar months.*
44. Cæsar assassinated at Rome by Brutus and Cassius.
    stabbed in the *senate-house.*
43. Second triumvirate—Octavius, Antony, and Lepidus.
    they *settle* the *globe* between them.
,, Reign of terror at Rome : Cicero assassinated.
    the whole *story* is *horrible.*
42. Brutus and Cassius defeated at Philippi.
    they experience a *sad fate.*
40. Herod the Great becomes king of Judæa.
    the *senate exalts* him.
37. The Romans take Jerusalem : a multitude of the inhabitants massacred.
    the wicked *Herod persecutes* them.
36. Sextus Pompey defeated in a naval engagement.
    he is worsted by *Agrippa* at *Naulochus.*
34. Octavius subdues the Dalmatians.
    an experienced *general subdues* them.
31. Battle of Actium : Antony and Cleopatra defeated.
    a woeful *humiliation* to *Cleopatra.*
30. Octavius enters Egypt : Antony commits suicide.
    the wretched *general expires.*
,, Octavius master of the Roman world : the republic ends.
    governs the *world.*

SECT. 22.—The Empire: its Rise and Progress, from Augustus to Aurelius (B.C. 30 – A.D. 180).

B.C.
29. Octavius's grand triumph: Temple of Janus closed.
    weary of deeds *of* violence.

„ Virgil, Horace, and Ovid flourish.
    a *famous trio.*

27. Octavius obtains the titles of Augustus and Emperor.
    wins the *favour* of the *people.*

24. War with the Dacian tribes.
    the *Dacians* are *subdued.*

23. Livy, the celebrated Roman historian, flourishes.
    a *distinguished historian.*

20. Porus, King of India, sends an embassy to Augustus.
    they wander to the *far west.*

17. Augustus revives the Secular Games at Rome.
    exhibits *beasts* of *prey.*

„ Herod rebuilds the Temple of Jerusalem.
    the wiles of a *crafty prince.*

15. The Rhæti, Norici, and Vindelici defeated by Drusus.
    a *campaign* beyond the *Alps.*

13. Augustus assumes the title of Pontifex Maximus.
    becomes the *head* (pontiff).

12. Drusus begins his campaign in Germany.
    beyond the *banks* of the *Danube.*

11. Herod builds the city of Cæsarea.
    he *builds Cæsarea.*

8. A census at Rome gives it 4,233,000 inhabitants.
    wonderful if *reliable.*

6. Dionysius of Halicarnassus writes his 'Roman Antiquities.'
    a writer of *antiquities.*

5. Birth of John the Baptist.
    walks in the ways of *Elijah.*

B.C.
4. Birth of CHRIST, four years before the common era.
  welcome the world's *Saviour*.

3. Death of Herod the Great.
  woe to the wicked *Herod*.

2. Augustus exhibits grand spectacles at Rome.
  their eyes are *delighted*.

A.D.
1. Birth of Christ, according to Dionysius Exiguus.
  Exiguus's wrong *computation*.

,, Caius Cæsar consul: peace concluded with the Parthians.
  a young *consul*.

2. Tiberius returns from Rhodes: Lucius Cæsar dies.
  expects to wear the *diadem*.

4. Tiberius overruns the countries of the Rhine and Weser.
  Westphalia is *subdued*.

6. Augustus makes Palestine a Roman province.
  extinguished its *nationality*.

7. Pannonia, Illyricum, and Dalmatia in revolt.
  war in *Pannonia*.

8. Jesus at Jerusalem, when twelve years of age.
  a young *reasoner*.

9. Hermann totally defeats Varus in Germany.
  exterminates the warrior *Varus*.

,, Ovid is banished by Augustus to Tomi.
  the exile of *Ovid*.

12. Tiberius and Germanicus, returning from Germany, obtain a triumph.
  an excitement *caused* by *fear*.

14. Augustus dies at Nola, aged 77 years.
  the weary *Cæsar sleeps*.

,, Tiberius, the second emperor, succeeds his stepfather.
  cruel and *sensual*.

16. Germanicus's third and last campaign in Gaul.
  an expedition to the *banks* of the *Ems*.

FACTS AND DATES.

A.D.

18. Herod Antipas builds Tiberias, on the Sea of Galilee.
    on its western *coast erected*.

19. Tiberius banishes the Jews from Rome.
    they are *banished* by *Tiberius*.

23. Drusus poisoned by his wife, instigated by Sejanus.
    a wife *destroys* her *husband*.

26. Pontius Pilate becomes procurator of Judæa.
    awed by the *fear* of *man*.

27. Jesus baptised by John the Baptist.
    a *dove appears*.

,, Tiberius retires from Rome to Capreæ.
    wallowed in *debauchery* and *pleasure*.

28. John beheaded by Herod.
    a *damsel's request* (Matt. xiv. 8).

31. Sejanus disgraced and put to death by Tiberius.
    a *hypocrite cut* off.

,, The crucifixion of our Lord.
    the *God-man crucified*.

32 Stephen, the first martyr, stoned.
    witness his *heavenly face*.

35.. Conversion of St Paul on his way to Damascus.
    witnessed a *heavenly light*.

36. Pontius Pilate and Caiaphas deposed.
    the *guiltiest* of *mankind*.

37. Death of Tiberius: Caligula the third emperor.
    he expires *hated* by his *people*.

,, Birth of Josephus, the Jewish historian.
    wrote the *history* of his *people*.

40. Caligula sets out for Gaul, intending to invade Britain.
    a *silly exploit*.

41. Caligula assassinated: Claudius the fourth emperor.
    he *succeeded Caligula*.

HISTORY OF ROME. 203

A.D.

43. Claudius invades Britain, and founds Colchester, the first Roman colony in Britain.
    he warred in Essex and Hants.

44. Claudius returns in triumph to Rome.
    they welcome their successful sovereign.

47. Claudius celebrates the Secular Games at Rome.
    they witness splendid pastimes.

,, A new census of the empire gives 5,984,000 males fit for military service.
    an exact summation of the people.

50. London, already existing, is colonised by the Romans.
    London walled-in by them.

51. Caractacus, King of the Silures, carried prisoner to Rome.
    the Welsh leader is betrayed.

,, Paul and Silas begin to preach the Gospel in Europe.
    Lydia is converted.

54. Claudius poisoned by his wife Agrippina.
    Xenophon and Locusta assist her.

,, Nero, the fifth emperor, succeeds Claudius.
    a wretched life of sensuality.

55. St Matthew writes his Gospel.
    exhibits our Lord's lineage.

59. Murder of Agrippina by Nero.
    allured by Otho's (wife).

60. Felix, recalled from Judæa, is succeeded by Festus.
    Nero expels him.

61. Boadicea, the British queen, defeated by Suetonius.
    an awful massacre of the Britons.

,, Paul arrives in Rome from Cæsarea.
    the missionary in the capital.

64. Nero sets fire to Rome, and blames the Christians.
    Nero himself kindled it.

,, First general persecution of the Christians.
    an awful massacre of the saints.

65. Nero murders Seneca, Lucan, and many others.
    murders Lucan.

A.D.

65. The Jewish rebellion in Judæa begins.
   a *mutiny* in the *land*.

66. Nero in Greece competes in public with musicians, tragedians, and charioteers.
   exploits *unworthy* of an *emperor*.

,, The Jewish War begins under Flavius Vespasian.
   a war *unparalleled* in *annals*.

67. Paul is imprisoned in Rome a second time.
   in the *Mamertine prison*.

,, Massacre of the Jews at Cæsarea, Ptolemais, &c.
   what *monstrous proceedings!*

68. Paul and Peter suffer martyrdom at Rome.
   executed by *Nero* at *Rome*.

,, Death of Nero, and accession of Galba.
   the execrable *Nero* is *removed*.

69. Galba, Otho, and Vitellius succeed Nero as emperors.
   an *unfortunate trio*.

,, Flavius Vespasian proclaimed ninth emperor at Alexandria.
   next after *Vitellius*.

70. Titus Vespasian, the Emperor's son, takes and burns Jerusalem, and disperses the Jews.
   what a *piteous wail!*

78. Agricola becomes Governor of Britain, and subdues Anglesea and North Wales.
   Wales a *province* of *Rome*.

79. Titus Vespasian tenth emperor of Rome.
   perishes by *violence*.

,, Pompeii and Herculaneum buried by an eruption of Mount Vesuvius: death of Pliny the elder.
   they *perish* by a *volcano*.

80. Great fire in Rome; many of the public buildings destroyed.
   its *ravages* are *awful*.

HISTORY OF ROME.

A.D.
81. Domitian the eleventh emperor, and last of the twelve Cæsars.
    a reign of *cruelty*.

85. Galcacus, the Caledonian General, defeated by Agricola near the Grampians.
    yields to *Rome* for a *little*.

95. Second general persecution: John banished to Patmos.
    tribulations are *allotted* them.

96. Nerva becomes twelfth emperor of Rome.
    the *twelfth emperor*.

97. Tacitus the historian and his friend Pliny the Younger flourish.
    Tacitus and *Pliny*.

98. Trajan becomes thirteenth emperor of Rome.
    Trajan restores the empire.

100. The third general persecution of the Christians.
    the *Christians wantonly exterminated*.

102. Trajan commences his wars in Dacia.
    begins to *war* in *Dacia*.

105. Trajan builds a stupendous bridge across the Danube, near Orsova.
    a *bridge* of *extraordinary length*.

106. Dacia subjugated and made a Roman province: the column of Trajan erected.
    conquers Wallachia and *Moldavia*.

114. Trajan leaves Rome to make war on the Armenians and Parthians.
    a *celebrated campaign* in the *east*.

115. Trajan captures Ctesiphon, the Parthian capital.
    captures the *capital* of their *land*.

,, Insurrection of the Jews in Cyrene, Egypt, Cyprus, &c.
    a *bloody butchery* of the *lieges*.

117. Adrian, fourteenth emperor.
    a *calm career* of *peace*.

A.D.
119. Adrian visits Gaul, Germany, and Britain.
begins his *celebrated travels.*

121. Adrian builds a wall from the Eden to the Tyne.
builds a *fortified barrier.*

123. Adrian visits Spain, Africa, Greece, &c.
from *Britain* to *Africa* and *Greece.*

131. The Jewish War begins, which lasts five years.
commencement of a *great calamity.*

136. Jerusalem destroyed: Ælia Capitolina built on its site.
bestows on it a *heathenish name.*

138. Antoninus Pius the fifteenth emperor.
a *calm* and *gentle reign.*

140. Dublin (anciently named Aschcled) probably erected.
called Aschcled of *yore.*

143. Antoninus builds a wall between the Forth and Clyde.
built on the *site* of *Agricola's.*

158. Celsus, Lucian, and Arrian write against Christianity.
Celsus, Lucian, and *Arrian.*

161. Aurelius Antoninus, sixteenth emperor: Verus his associate.
a *consistent unwavering character.*

162. The Parthians revolt, but are defeated by Verus.
conquers Mesopotamia afresh.

166. The northern barbarians begin to invade the Empire.
bands of *invaders menace* it.

167. A dreadful pestilence spreads over the Empire.
the *Christians massacred* for the *plague.*

169. Verus expires at Altinum in Venetia.
a *combination* of *innumerable vices.*

174. War with the Quadi and Marcomanni: the thundering legion.
the *Christians pray* for *success.*

177. The Christians persecuted at Lyons and Vienne.
Bishop Pothinus perishes.

Sect. 23.—Decline and Fall of the Empire; or from Commodus to Augustulus (A.D. 180-476).

A.D.
180. Commodus the seventeenth emperor.
   cruel, rapacious, and *wanton.*
183. Lucilla attempts to assassinate the Emperor.
   Commodus rescued by the *guards.*
189. Famine and pestilence in Rome: death of Cleander.
   a *cry* is *raised* for a *victim.*
192. Commodus strangled by his domestics.
   they *bribe* an *athlete* to *destroy* him.
193. Pertinax, eighteenth emperor, reigns three months.
   they *choose* a *virtuous governor.*
   „ Didius Julianus, nineteenth emperor, reigns two months.
   bribes the *troops* with his *gold.*
   „ Septimius Severus, twentieth emperor.
   contends with *two generals.*
194. Severus marches to the East against Niger: Battle of Issus.
   becomes victorious in the *east.*
196. Byzantium destroyed after a three years' siege.
   Byzantium overthrown by the *Emperor.*
197. Fifth general persecution of the Christians.
   cruelly tortured by *persecutors.*
   „ Severus, in Gaul, defeats and slays his rival Albinus.
   a *courageous veteran perishes.*
198. Severus returns to the East, and makes war with the Parthians.
   Ctesiphon taken and *ravaged.*
202. Severus prohibits the Christians from disseminating their doctrines.
   an *edict* to *exterminate* the *faith.*
208. Severus in Britain at war with the Caledonians: erects a wall from the Solway to the Tyne.
   formidable warriors resist him.

A.D.
211. Death of Severus at Eborăcum (York): accession of Caracalla, twenty-first emperor.
dies at *Eborăcum* in *Britain*.

212. Caracalla murders his brother Geta.
a *fierce* and *cruel fratricide*.

215. Caracalla orders a general massacre of the Alexandrians.
a *frightful butchery* at *Alexandria*.

217. Caracalla is murdered, and is succeeded by Macrinus, twenty-second emperor.
the *detestable Caracalla perishes*.

218. Macrinus, defeated at Antioch, is slain in Bithynia.
the *fugitive coward is ruined*.

„ Elagabalus, the twenty-third emperor, chosen by the army in Syria.
the *foulest character* on *record*.

220. Death of Tertullian.
death of a *famous writer*.

222. Alexander Severus, twenty-fourth emperor.
a *despot deserving* our *affection*.

„ Urban I. becomes Bishop of Rome.
a *fearless defender* of the *faith*.

226. A revolt in Persia, under Artaxerxes.
a *distant dependency* of the *empire*.

232. Alexander gains a great victory over Artaxerxes.
a *decisive* and *glorious day*.

234. Revolt in Gaul: Alexander proceeds thither.
a *defection* of the *Gauls suppressed*.

235. Severus marches against the Germans, but is assassinated.
dies by the *hands* of his *legions*.

„ Maximin, a Thracian of mean origin, succeeds him as twenty-fifth emperor.
a *daring herdsman elected*.

„ Sixth general persecution of the Christians.
the *fury* of the *heathen let* loose.

A.D.
238. The two Gordians, rival emperors at Carthage.
   in *Africa* the *Gordians* are *rivals*.

,, Maximin assassinated: Maximus and Balbinus elected twenty-eighth and twenty-ninth emperors.
   a *dual government* at *Rome*.

,, Maximus and Balbinus assassinated: Gordian III. thirtieth emperor.
   forebodings of *general ruin*.

242. Gordian defeats the Persians: recovers Mesopotamia.
   defeats his *eastern foes*.

244. Gordian assassinated, and Philip the Arabian elected thirty-first emperor.
   the *discontented soldiers assassinate* him.

248. Rome completes her 1000th year: great Secular Games.
   a *famous secular era*.

249. Revolt of Mœsia and Pannonia: Philip slain: Decius becomes thirty-second emperor.
   defeated and *slain* at *Verona*.

251. Gothic invasion: Decius slain: Gallus becomes thirty-third emperor.
   they *defeat* the *legions* at *Abrutum*.

,, Peace with the Goths purchased by promise of an annual payment.
   a *disgraceful league* with *barbarians*.

253. Æmilianus thirty-fourth, and afterwards Valerian thirty-fifth, emperor.
   he *fights legions* of *Goths*.

254. Death of Origen, Bishop of Alexandria.
   death of the *Alexandrian scribe*.

257. The empire invaded by barbarians on all sides.
   the *Franks* and *Allemanni appear*.

,, Eighth general persecution: Cyprian put to death.
   Africa laments her *apostle*.

260. Valerian, made prisoner by the Persians, is succeeded by Gallienus, thirty-sixth emperor.
   they *defeat* the *emperor* by a *wile*.

o

FACTS AND DATES.

A.D.
262. The Germans invade Italy, and reach Ravenna.
formidable nations from the *Danube*.

264. Odenathus of Palmyra, one of "the Thirty Tyrants," repels the Persians, and is honoured with the title of Augustus.
Odenathus monarch of the *East*.

265. War, pestilence, and famine ravage the empire.
war and *famine* in *many lands*.

267. Odenathus murdered by his queen, Zenobia, who assumes the title of empress of the East.
Odenathus murdered by *Zenobia*.

268. Claudius II. thirty-seventh emperor: pardons Aureolus, one of "the Thirty Tyrants."
dispenses mercy to his *rival*.

269. Claudius defeats the Goths and Heruli at Naissus.
destroys many thousands.

270. Death of Claudius: Aurelian thirty-eighth emperor.
famous in *peace* and in *war*.

271. Aurelian invites the Goths to settle in Dacia.
Dacia peopled by *barbarians*.

272. Aurelian defeats Zenobia, who is captured next year.
the *famous Zenobia defeated*.

„ Ninth general persecution.
the *designs* of the *persecutors frustrated*.

273. Tetricus, tyrant of Gaul, defeated at Chalons by Aurelian.
defeats the *potentate* of *Gaul*.

274. Great triumph of Aurelian: Zenobia and Tetricus among the captives.
a *famous procession* in *state*.

275. Aurelian, on his way to the East, is assassinated.
dies by the *perfidy* of a *lieutenant*.

„ Tacitus, thirty-ninth emperor, defeats the Alani.
defeats the *powerful Alani*.

276. Probus, fortieth emperor, succeeds Tacitus.
distinguished for the *purity* of his *morals*.

A.D.
277. Probus defeats the Sarmatians, Goths, and Germans.
    defeat of the *Poles* by *Probus*.
278. Probus erects forts from the Danube to the Rhine.
    forts protect the *realm*.
279. Saturninus, governor of the East, proclaimed emperor at Alexandria.
    forced by the *popular verdict*.
280. Proculus and Bonosus head a revolt in Gaul, but are defeated.
    a *formidable revolt extinguished*.
281. Probus celebrates a great triumph at Rome.
    the *due reward* of a *conqueror*.
282. Probus assassinated by his troops at Sirmium.
    the *fiery rage* of "the *ditchers*."
  ,, Carus, forty-first emperor, defeats the Sarmatians.
    their *formidable army* is *defeated*.
283. Carus marches against Persia, but is killed near Ctesiphon: Carinus and Numerian succeed him.
    dies in a *raging hurricane*.
284. Diocletian forty-second emperor: era of Diocletian.
    a *famous era* in the *East*.
286. Maximian, forty-third emperor, associated with Diocletian: the period of partition begins: Diocletian takes the East, Maximian the West.
    they *divide* the *Roman empire*.
  ,, The Northmen attack the empire in the West, and the Persians in the East.
    the *frontiers ravaged* by *invaders*.
287. Carausius, a Roman general, usurps the sovereignty in Britain.
    defies the *Roman power*.
290. Carausius compels Maximian to acknowledge the independence of Britain.
    (Britain) *free* for *ten years*.
292. Two emperors and two Cæsars (Galerius and Constantine) govern the empire between them.
    the *former* a *twofold division*.

A.D.
295. Alexandria in Egypt taken by Diocletian.
Diocletian takes Alexandria.

296. Britain recovered to Rome by Constantius.
her *freedom vanishes* in a *moment.*

298. Diocletian at war with Persia.
famous victories in *Armenia.*

302. Tenth general persecution.
a *general extermination decreed.*

,, Diocletian and Maximian celebrate the last triumph.
its *glory* is *extinguishing fast.*

305. The emperors Diocletian and Maximian resign: Constantius and Galerius succeed as forty-fourth and forty-fifth emperors.
the *Augusti* are *willing* to *leave.*

306. Death of Constantius in Britain: is succeeded by Constantine the Great, forty-sixth emperor.
the *great Western emperor.*

310. Maximian put to death by Constantine.
the *great Constantine executes* him.

,, Galerius dies of a loathsome disease.
Galerius, base and *cruel.*

312. Constantine defeats Maxentius.
the *great Constantine defeats* him.

,, Constantine becomes a convert to Christianity.
a *great cross descried* by him.

313. Edict of Milan: Christianity tolerated everywhere.
a *glorious change* in its *history.*

314. Licinius, emperor of the East, resigns to Constantine all his European possessions.
he *grants* to *Constantine* their *sovereignty.*

321. Constantine commands Sunday to be observed by all his subjects.
the *holy day* to be *observed.*

322. Constantine victorious in Dacia and Sarmatia.
the *Goths* of the *Danube* are *defeated.*

324. Licinius put to death at Thessalonica by Constantine.
his *great adversary* is *slain.*

HISTORY OF ROME.

A.D.
- **324.** Constantine sole emperor in the East and West.
  a great date in *sacred* (history).
- „ Christianity becomes the religion of the State.
  the *holy faith established.*
- **325.** Council of Nice, the first General Council.
  they *agree* in *defining* the "*Logos.*"
- **326.** Athanasius introduces Monachism into the West.
  a *great advocate* of *Monachism.*
- **330.** Byzantium becomes the capital of the empire, and is named Constantinople.
  the *glory* is *gone* from the *West.*
- **332.** Great victories obtained over the Goths by Constantine.
  the *Goths* are *grievously defeated.*
- **334.** Multitudes of Sarmatians settle in Illyria and Italy.
  a *great host* of *Sarmatians.*
- **337.** Constantine submits to baptism by Eusebius, an Arian.
  a *great historian performs* it.
- „ Death of Constantine: Constantine II., Constantius II., and Constans, his sons, share the empire.
  a *great gap* is *produced.*
- **340.** Civil war breaks out: the eldest brother killed: Constans emperor of the West.
  a *great* and *sanguinary war.*
- **348.** Constantius II. defeated at Sangara by the Persians.
  a *humiliation sustained* by the *Romans.*
- **350.** Constans murdered: Magnentius usurps the throne.
  a *gross life* of *wantonness.*
- **351.** Magnentius signally defeated by Constantius at Mursa.
  a *great loss* in the *battle.*
- **354.** Gallus put to death by Constantius II.
  Gallus laid-hold-of and *slain.*
- **356.** Athanasius, Bishop of Alexandria, expelled from his see.
  gained his *laurels* at *Nice.*
- **361.** Constantius II. dies: Julian the Apostate succeeds.
  a *grave misfortune* to *Christianity.*
- „ Julian permits the Jews to rebuild the Temple.
  a *grant* to *annoy* the *Christians.*

A.D.
363. Julian marches from Antioch against the Persians.
  the *heat* of *midsummer harasses* him.

,, Death of Julian: Jovian, fifty-first emperor, favours the Christians.
  his *government* is *mild* and *gentle.*

364. Death of Jovian: Valentinian becomes emperor of the West; Valerius, of the East.
  the *great empire is severed.*

368. The Allemanni cross the Rhine, but are defeated.
  the *Germans menace Rome.*

370. Valens concludes a peace with the Visigoths.
  the *Goths peaceably withdraw.*

375. Death of Valentinian: Gratian and Valentinian II. emperors of the West.
  his *heirs* are *peaceably elected.*

376. Valens allows the Goths, who are hard pressed by the Huns, to settle in Thrace.
  the *Goths protected* by the *emperor.*

378. The Goths signally defeat the Romans at Adrianople.
  the *Goths prevail* over the *Romans.*

379. Theodosius the Great, emperor of the East, advances Christianity.
  heathenism persecuted in *turn.*

382. Theodosius concludes a peace with the Goths.
  the *Goths* are *restored* to *friendship.*

383. Maximus assumes the purple in Britain: invades Gaul.
  Gratian is *routed* in *Gaul.*

,, The Huns overrun Mesopotamia, but are defeated.
  the *Huns* are *routed* by the *Goths.*

387. Maximus aspires to be sole emperor of the West.
  grasps the *reins* of *power.*

388. Theodosius defeats and slays Maximus.
  his *greed* is *righteously revenged.*

391. Great massacre at Thessalonica, by order of Theodosius.
  a *grievous event* in the *circus.*

,, Ambrose, Archbishop of Milan, compels Theodosius to do penance.
  a *great triumph* to the *Church.*

HISTORY OF ROME. 215

A.D.
392. Valentinian II. slain, and the empire of the West bestowed on Eugenius.
   a gross outrage by a *Frank*.
393. Theodosius gives the title of Augustus to Honorius.
   Honorius is voted "Augustus."
394. Eugenius slain: Theodosius sole emperor.
   Eugenius vanquished and slain.
395. Death of Theodosius: the empire permanently separated into East and West, under Arcadius and Honorius.
   the *great Theodosius* is *lamented*.
 ,, Alaric, King of the Visigoths, overruns Thrace, Macedonia, and Greece.
   Greece overrun by *Alaric*.
403. Stilicho defeats Alaric at Pollentia, near Turin.
   Stilicho worsts the *Goths*.
406. The Vandals, Suevi, Burgundians, and Alani invade Italy and Gaul.
   the *Sclavonian* and *Wendish invasion*.
407. Death of Chrysostom, patriarch of Constantinople.
   he *sinks* on his *way* to *Pityus*.
408. Stilicho put to death by Honorius.
   Stilicho executed at *Ravenna*.
409. Attalus appointed emperor by Alaric and the Senate.
   the *Senate welcome Attalus*.
 ,, The Vandals, Suevi, and Alani invade Spain.
   the *Suevi* and *Wends overrun* it.
410. Rome sacked by the Goths for six days.
   they *sack* the *capital* of the *West*.
 ,, Death of Alaric, who is succeeded by Adolphus.
   a *king concealed* in an *excavation*.
412. Adolphus concludes a treaty with Honorius.
   a *shameful bargain* with *Adolphus*.
414. Adolphus invades Spain.
   shocking barbarities and *slaughter*.
418. Britain acknowledged to be independent by Rome.
   the *sovereignty* of *Britain recognised*.

A.D.

418. Kingdom of the Visigoths established on both sides of the Pyrenees.
kings of a *conquering race.*

,, Pharamond founds the kingdom of the Franks in Gaul.
their *king* is the *celebrated Pharamond.*

423. Death of Honorius: usurpation of Johannes.
Johannes follows Honorius.

425. Valentinian III. proclaimed emperor of the West.
a *king five* (years) *old.*

426. Illyricum, Pannonia, and Noricum ceded to the East.
separated finally from the *empire.*

429. Genseric, King of the Vandals, invades Africa.
king of the *ferocious Vandals.*

430. Death of Augustine, Bishop of Hippo.
the *saintly Augustine expires.*

439. Conquest of Africa by the Vandals completed.
the *savage Genseric overruns* it.

443. The Huns, under Attila, cross the Danube, and lay waste the Roman empire.
savage Scythian hordes.

449. The Jutes, Angles, and Saxons arrive in Britain.
the *Jutes* and *Saxons* in *Thanet.*

451. Battle of Chalons-sur-Marne, defeat of Attila, and death of Theodoric I., King of the Visigoths.
killed while *leading* his *cavalry.*

452. Attila invades Italy: foundation of the city of Venice.
situated in a *lagoon* on the *Adriatic.*

453. Death of Attila, "the Scourge of God."
seas of *liquid gore.*

454. Ætius assassinated by Valentinian III.
assassinates its *last saviour.*

455. Genseric pillages Rome, but spares the citizens.
spares the *lives* of the *lieges.*

457. Kingdom of Kent (first of the Saxon Heptarchy) founded by a tribe of Jutes under Hengist.
a *kingdom* of *limited proportions.*

A. D.
460. Genseric destroys the Roman fleet at Carthagena.
   the *ships* of *Majorian exterminated.*
461. Leo the Great claims to be Vicar of Christ.
   sets-up an *impious claim.*
468. Euric the Visigoth drives the Romans out of Spain.
   Spain independent of *Rome.*
475. Romulus Augustulus last Roman emperor.
   in the *series* of *potentates* the *last.*
476. Rome taken by Odoacer the Goth, and extinction of the Western empire.
   her *stupendous power* is *ended.*

PERIOD II.—HISTORY OF THE MIDDLE AGES.

CHAP. VI.— FROM THE FALL OF THE ROMAN EMPIRE TO THE DISCOVERY OF AMERICA (A.D. 476-1492).

[The substance of this Introduction is mainly derived from the ' General History of the World,' by Charles Von Rotteck, Professor of History in the University of Freiburg. London: Longman & Co. 1842.]

THE wonderful pictures of a twilight age, the lofty figures of Greece and Rome, and the glimmering life-sparks of a declining world, have now finally disappeared; while another race, another theatre, another tone of action and passion, appear in their room. Here, from the dark forests of the north, and there, from the solitudes of the Arabian desert, nations hitherto unknown, or slumbering in dead repose, overflow, like huge ocean billows, the mighty Roman world. The long-decayed foundation shakes, and the structure, now shattered in all its parts, falls with an astounding crash. What the human mind had created in many centuries, what the toil of many generations had nurtured, what lengthened experience had perfected and established—the monuments of the power, genius, and virtue of the ancient world—were suddenly overwhelmed in ruins. Considering, however, its incurable internal corruption, this fate was unavoidable, and scarcely deserves our regret; for all that was beautiful and great had long since been abandoned, and every germ of a nobler life had now been stifled. The nations of the West, now disgracefully fallen from their ancient virtue and splendour, crawled in the dust, despising freedom as a tale of the past, neither desiring nor expecting anything better than servitude. The race had become so incurably corrupt, that it is impossible to suppose that it could ever elevate itself to its former level. The one solitary element of hope or stability that remained—the preserving salt of pure Christianity—had now lost its savour and its energy, and had become a gross, inert superstition. Heaven could endure the revolting spectacle no longer; for though the forbearance of God is infinite in extent, it is finite in duration. The day of reckoning had come, and a terrible doom was inevitable. As the Antediluvian world was destroyed by a flood of waters, so the mighty empire of Rome was inundated by a destructive flood of barbaric nations, that carried all before them. "The fountains of the great deep were broken up, and the windows of heaven were opened." Before the close of the fifth century the throne of the Cæsars was prostrated; Odoacer the Goth, and Theodoric the Eastgoth, extended their sceptres over Italy and Rome, both of which had already experienced repeated plundering from the Westgoths, Vandals, and Huns. Barbarian nations had taken possession of all the provinces of the Western empire; the Vandals, of Africa; the Alani, Suevi, and Westgoths, of Spain; the last-mentioned, also of Southern Gaul; the Burgundians, of the countries around the Saone; the Allemanni, of the Upper Rhine; the Franks, of northern and eastern Gaul; the Jutes, Angles, and Saxons, of Britain; the Rugii and Heruli, of Noricum and its environs; the Goths, of the Rhætian and Illyrian countries. The Eastern empire had also to see the greater part of its provinces desolated by the barbarians. The Goths, before proceeding further west, had ravaged the countries of the Danube and the Hæmus, while the Gepidæ had established themselves in Pannonia. After the Goths came the terrible Huns, whose appearance in Europe had been the principal signal of these great movements, and who drove before them, or carried in their train, a concourse of tribes as far as the Po and the Loire; and the Huns were followed, in turn, by the Bulgari, Avari, Ugri, Chasari, and other savage tribes.

These tumultuary migrations continued in the sixth century, and did not cease in the seventh and eighth. New swarms succeeded, supplanted, and drove away the older, or were driven away by them. The pastoral nations of Asia already enumerated, then the Sclaves, variously divided and immensely extended, and afterwards new German tribes, established themselves in the Roman, or in the Old-German and Sarmatian countries. The kingdoms of the Saxons, Frieslanders, Thuringians, and Bavarians arose, or were more accurately defined. The Longobards seized upon Upper Italy; Wendic and Sclavonic, Turkish and Tartar races, wandered about, confusedly mingled together and mutually hostile, in the vast countries between the Black Sea and the Baltic. There is no revolution recorded in the pages of history which has proved so important and imposing, whether in extent, character, or results, as this great NORTHERN MIGRATION OF NATIONS.

But let us glance at that mysterious land, that great magazine of nations, where spring the inexhaustible fountains which have thus, from time to time, desolated the civilised countries, and revolutionised the world. From the Caspian Sea to the Hoang-ho, and from the Altai Mountains to the Himalayas, stretches one unbroken gigantic plateau, named High Asia, the most elevated and immense on the surface of the globe. In ancient times this great table-land was almost wholly unknown, and even at the present day it has been very imperfectly explored; but some idea of its magnitude may be formed from the fact that here originate nearly all the giant rivers of Asia—the Indus, Ganges, Brahmaputra, Yang-tse-kiang, Hoang-ho, Amour, Lena, Yenisei, and Oby. The natural properties of this rugged and inhospitable region have imperiously determined the character and pursuits of its inhabitants. If we compare the description which Herodotus gives of the ancient Scythians with that of the pastoral nations of the great desert as handed down by the Chinese annalists, or the testimonies of the Roman and Byzantine writers concerning the great migrations of nations which took place in their own day with the descriptions of European travellers who passed through High Asia in the middle ages, we shall discern the most wonderful uniformity of condition and manners among the numberless nations of this boundless region—a uniformity which remains indelibly stamped on them till the present day. All the roughness which the untamed state of man, living under a northern sky, can produce, is and ever has been the character of the Scythian hordes. Strangers to agriculture, partly from the nature of their country and partly from disinclination, they have ever been restricted for food and raiment to the breeding of cattle and to the chase—occupations incompatible with the luxuries, or even the conveniences, of civilisation. Familiar with want and hardship, accustomed to the slaughter of animals wild and tame, the northern nomad acquires a hardiness of body and mind which harmonises him with his climate. Hunting and travelling are his daily occupations, and, in fact, the sum of his life. Abandoning his whole nature to savage affections, no one is so adapted to violence, or so disposed to war. The possession of the horse, which they manage with marvellous dexterity, greatly increases the formidable character of these warlike hordes, thus carried along from their impregnable fastnesses, with the speed of the wind, to the most distant plains of an unprepared or effeminate enemy. Such were the diverse and multinomial swarms of Scythians, Sarmatians, and Germans which, at the commencement of this era, moved along the frontiers of the Roman empire, like the threatening clouds of a tempest, and by their contemporaneous shock fulfilled the destiny which had long hung over her!

SECT. 24.—From Romulus Augustulus to Charlemagne (A.D. 476-800).

A.D.
476. Extinction of the Western empire by the Goths.
   the *succeeding period* is *medieval*.

„ Odoacer founds the Gothic kingdom of Italy.
   a *king* in *place* of an *emperor*.

A.D.
481. Clovis establishes the kingdom of France.
　　　the *judicious reign* of *Clovis.*
486. Clovis defeats the Romans at Soissons.
　　　are *severely routed* in the *north.*
489. The Ostrogoths, under Theodoric the Great, seize Italy.
　　　the *Ostrogoths rule* in *Italy.*
493. Death of St Patrick, the patron saint of Ireland.
　　　the *saint* who *turned* them to *God.*
496. Clovis routs the Allemanni, and embraces Christianity.
　　　ascribes his *victory* to the *Most-High.*
507. Clovis defeats Alaric, King of the Visigoths, at Poitiers.
　　　Alaric expires at *Poitiers.*
511. Death of Clovis: his kingdom divided among his sons.
　　　leaves his *conquests* to his *children.*
514. Arthur, king of the Silures, leads the Britons against the Saxons.
　　　leads them against "*Cerdic* the *Saxon.*"
525. Time first computed in Italy from A.D. 1 (the Christian era) by Dionysius Exiguus.
　　　the year of our *Lord,* according to *Denys* the *Little.*
534. Belisarius overthrows the Vandals in Africa.
　　　the *illustrious general* of *Justinian.*
553. Belisarius and Narses recover Italy from the Ostrogoths.
　　　the *labours* of *illustrious generals.*
563. St Columba, from Ireland, founds a monastery at Iona, and converts the Scots to Christianity.
　　　a *lonely monastery* in the *Hebrides.*
568. The Lombards seize a great part of Northern Italy.
　　　the *Lombards invade* the *realm.*
571. Birth of Mohammed at Mecca.
　　　the *lying prophet* is *born.*
582. The Saxon Heptarchy completed in England by the creation of Mercia into a kingdom.*
　　　aliens our *realm divide.*

* The seven kingdoms forming the Saxon Heptarchy were as follow:—
1. KENT, comprising the present county of Kent, founded 457 by a tribe

A.D.
596. Augustine, with forty monks, arrives in England, to convert the Saxons to Christianity.
a *large troop* of *missionaries.*

612. Mohammed publishes the Koran.
the *Mohammedan Bible* is *forged.*

622. Era of the Hegira, or the Prophet's flight from Mecca.
Mohammed's famous flight.

632. Death of Mohammed, who is succeeded in the Caliphate by Abubekr, his father-in-law.
Mohammed's greater flight.

634. Syria invaded by the Saracens under Khaled.
the *Mohammedans gain Syria.*

„ Omar succeeds Abubekr in the Caliphate at Medina.
Omar the *greatest Khalif.*

637. Jerusalem taken by the Saracens: Omar builds a mosque on the site of the Temple.
a *mosque* on the *hill of Zion.*

640. The Saracens take Alexandria and burn the library.
Omar's savage whim.

644. Othman succeeds Omar in the Caliphate.
Mohammed's secretary succeeds.

655. Ali becomes Caliph of Arabia, and Moawiah, of Egypt.
Mohammed left it to *Ali.*

672. The Saracens besiege Constantinople ineffectually.
the *Mohammedans opposed effectually.*

685. The Britons, being totally vanquished by the Saxons, retire into Wales and Cornwall.
the *invaders rule* the *land.*

of Jutes under Hengist. 2. SUSSEX, founded 490 by a tribe of Saxons under Ella, and comprising Surrey and Sussex. 3. WESSEX, founded by a tribe of Saxons under Ida in 495, contained Hants, Wilts, Somerset, Dorset, and Devon. 4. ESSEX, founded in 527 by a tribe of Saxons, included our present Essex and Middlesex. 5. EAST ANGLIA (Norfolk, Suffolk, Cambridge), founded in 570 by a tribe of Angles under Uffa. 6. NORTHUMBRIA (Northumberland, Durham, York), founded in 547 by a tribe of Angles under Ida. 7. MERCIA (situated between Wales and the other kingdoms), founded in 582, and formed by different migrations inland of the other settlers.

A.D.
691. Pepin, father of Charles Martel, rules France.
  a mayor of the *third Clovis.*

697. The Republic of Venice is governed by Doges.
  the *merchants* of *Venice* in *power.*

714. The Moors conquer Spain, and terminate the empire of the Visigoths.
  the *prowess* of the *Caliphs* in *Spain.*

 ,, Charles Martel governs France.
  Pepin's courageous son.

726. Leo, emperor of the East, forbids image-worship.
  zealously denounces the *image.*

730. Leo is excommunicated by Pope Gregory II.
  Pope Gregory excommunicates him.

732. Charles Martel defeats the Saracens at Poitiers.
  at *Poitiers* he *grievously defeats* them.

736. Leo destroys all the images : is opposed by the Pope.
  a *pope* the *guardian* of *images.*

741. Edinburgh founded by Edwin, King of Northumbria.
  the *queen* of *Scotia's cities.*

746. A three years' pestilence in Europe and Asia.
  a *pestilence sweeps* away *many.*

 ,, The Scriptures translated into Saxon verse by Cædmon.
  parts of *Scripture* in *metre.*

750. The dynasty of Abbassides begins at Damascus.
  the *powerful line* of *Abbassides.*

751. Pepin begins the Carlovingian dynasty in France.
  "*Pepin le Bref.*"

763. Bagdad, founded by Almansor, becomes the capital of the Caliphate instead of Damascus.
  the *powerful metropolis* of *Haroun-al-Raschid.*

768. Charlemagne ascends the throne of France.
  a *powerful monarch rules* it.

774. Charlemagne overthrows the Lombard kingdom.
  the *pretensions* of the *Pope sustained.*

786. Haroun-al-Raschid, Caliph of the Saracen empire.
  portrayed in the '*Arabian Nights.*'

A.D.
787. The Danes or Normans first land in England.
   pirates arrive in *Purbeck.*

800. Charlemagne crowned emperor of the West.
   exalted to *rule* the *Western world.*

SECT. 25.—From Charlemagne to the Norman Conquest (A.D. 800-1066).

A.D.
803. Death of Irene, empress of the East.
   Irene expires through *grief.*

807. Haroun-al-Raschid courts the alliance of Charlemagne.
   Arabian wisdom at its *perfection.*

808. The Normans, under Godfrey, invade France.
   an *era* in *Western Europe.*

814. Death of the Emperor Charlemagne.
   the *renowned Charlemagne sleeps.*

 ,, The Caliph Almamon greatly encourages learning.
   a *renowned Caliph* of the *Saracens.*

827. End of the Heptarchy, and establishment of Monarchy in England under Egbert.
   roving Danes plague him.

836. Ethelwulf, second king of England.
   he *routs* the *Gothic invaders.*

843. The Picts and Scots united under Kenneth II., and the country henceforth called Scotland.
   an *era* in *Scottish history.*

851. The Danes, or Normans, invade England.
   resist the *lawless bands.*

855. Tithes first granted to the priests in England.
   they *receive* a *large allowance.*

856. Paris plundered by the Northmen—Eric, their king, slain.
   Eric the *lawless Northman.*

858. Ethelbald, third king of England.
   he *rules* the *land* with *rigour.*

860. Ethelbert, fourth king of England.
   Ragnar the *Northman* is *wrecked.*

A.D.
861. The Norwegians discover Iceland.
roving Norwegians in *Iceland.*
862. John Scotus, a celebrated Irish writer, flourishes.
"*Erigena*" *of noble fame.*
,, Ruric, the Norman, founds the Russian monarchy.
the *Russian monarchy founded.*
,, The Greek and Latin Churches separate.
Rome encounters a *defeat.*
863. St Giles's Church, Edinburgh, erected.
erection of *ancient* (St) *Giles.*
866. Ethelred, fifth king of England.
roving Northmen multiply.
869. Eighth General Council held at Constantinople.
the *Roman Emperor attended* it.
871. Alfred the Great, sixth king of England.
routs the *pirates* in *battle.*
875. Charles the Bald crowned emperor of Germany.
received it from the *Pope* for a *largess.*
886. University of Oxford founded by Alfred.
rears a *renowned university.*
889. The Magyars under Arpad arrive in Hungary.
a warlike *race arrives* from the *Volga.*
891. Alfred institutes trial by jury, and divides England into counties, hundreds, and tithings.
reform in the *trial* of *criminals.*
898. Algebra introduced into Spain by the Saracens.
Arabians transport it into *Europe.*
901. Civil war in France and Germany.
torn by *warlike contests.*
,, Edward the Elder, seventh king of England.
vanquishes Wales and *Cambria.*
906. The Normans under Rollo settle in Normandy.
a *valiant warrior invades* it.
914. Westminster Abbey built by Ethelbert.
a *venerable abbey established.*
915. Cambridge University restored by Edward the Elder.
various colleges for *learning.*

P

A.D.
923. The Moors in Spain defeated by the Christians.
a terrible defeat in Granada.

925. Athelstane, eighth king of England.
translates the divine law.

926. Rise of the English Order of Freemasons.
Athelstane its first master.

936. The Saracen empire divided into seven kingdoms.
terminates the grandeur of the Mussulmans.

941. Edmund the Magnificent, ninth king of England.
an outlaw slays him at a banquet.

947. Edred, tenth king of England.
a terrible sickness paralysed him.

955. Edwy, eleventh king of England.
vexed by a learned liege.

959. Edgar the Peaceful, twelfth king of England.
his territory is lined by the Thames.

,,   Edgar extirpates wolves out of England and Wales.
the tribute is levied in vermin.

961. Church-bells first used in England.
Turketel's musical chimes.

962. Otho I. succeeds Charlemagne as emperor of the West.
Otho, a monarch of fame.

975. Edward the Martyr, thirteenth king of England.
treacherously poisoned by Elfrida.

978. Ethelred the Unready, fourteenth king of England.
vanquished by a powerful rival.

981. Vladimir, first Christian monarch of Russia.
turned the Russians to Christ.

982. Greenland discovered by a Norwegian from Iceland.
a tempestuous region discovered.

987. Hugh Capet founds the third dynasty in France.
the third race of princes.

991. Arabic numerals brought into Europe by the Saracens.
of vast value in computation.

A.D.
994. Sweyn, King of Denmark, sails up the Thames.
Ethelred attacked by *Sweyn.*

1000. Paper first made of cotton rags.
cotton wondrously woven for *writing.*

1002. The Danes cruelly massacred by Ethelred.
he *basely exterminates* the *warlike Danes.*

1004. Churches begin to be built in the Gothic style.
churches executed in a *wondrous style.*

1013. The Danes, under Sweyn, get possession of England.
a *cruel expiation* for *cunning* and *guilt.*

1016. Edmund Ironside, the fifteenth king of England.
chosen by the " *Witan*" to *contest* the *monarchy.*

1017. Canute the Dane, sixteenth king of England.
Canute a *wise* and *crafty prince.*

1025. Musical notes invented by Guido Aretino.
characters expressing duration or *length.*

1028. Norway conquered by Canute of England.
Canute wins a *double realm.*

1036. Harold Harefoot, the seventeenth king of England.
Canute wanted Hardicanute to be *monarch.*

1039. Duncan I., King of Scotland, murdered by Macbeth, who usurps the throne.
his *cruel wife hastens* the *tragedy.*

1040. Hardicanute, eighteenth king of England.
from *brutal excess* the *king expires.*

1042. The Saxon line of kings restored: Edward the Confessor, nineteenth king.
a "*confession*" that *yielded* the *saddest fruit.*

,, Decimals invented in France about this time.
a *curious way* of *estimating* the *difference.*

1043. Manco Capac founds Cuzco, the capital of the Incas.
civilises wild and *savage hordes.*

1046. Three rival popes in Rome at the same time.
a *bloody contest* for the *sacred mitre.*

1049. Leo IX. the first pope that maintained a standing army.
the *bloody wars* of the *Saviour's vicars!*

228   FACTS AND DATES.

A.D.
1054. The great schism between the Eastern and Western Churches completed.
the Church of the West in lasting schism.

1056. The Turks take Bagdad and overturn the empire of the Caliphs.
Bagdad wrested from the line of Mohammed.

1057. Malcolm III. (Canmore), son of Duncan, nineteenth king of Scotland.
the crown is won at Lumphanan from Macbeth.

1066. Harold II., the twentieth king of England.
conquering William invades England.

„ Battle of Hastings: William the Conqueror the twenty-first king.
the battle is won by Norman invaders.

SECT. 26.—From the Norman Conquest to the Accession of the Plantagenets—the Norman Period (1066-1154).

A.D.
1070. William establishes feudalism in England.
the conqueror wickedly perfects his extortions.

1072. Surnames first used by the Norman nobility.
the conqueror's wile to perfect the distinction.

1079. The Court of Exchequer established in England.
a court to expedite pecuniary trusts.

1080. The Doomsday Book begins to be compiled.
compiled by William for regulating his extortions.

1086. Toledo, in Spain, wrested from the Saracens, becomes the capital of Castile.
the Christians at war with Arabs and Moors.

1087. William II. (Rufus), twenty-second king of England.
the Crusaders want to recover Palestine.

„ War between England and France.
he confidently expects to rout Philip.

1093. Donald Bane usurps the Scottish throne.
the Celts win the throne for a Highlander.

A.D.
1094. Duncan II., natural son of Malcolm, aided by William II., becomes twenty-first king of Scotland.
consents to *wield* a *vassal's sceptre.*

1096. The First Crusade begins under Peter the Hermit.
the *Crusaders want* to *vanquish* "the *infidels.*"

,, The first duel fought in England.
the *combat* is *expected* to *vindicate* the *innocent.*

,, Heraldry introduced into Europe by the Crusaders.
the *Crusaders wear visible emblems.*

1098. Edgar, twenty-second king of Scotland.
the *crown* is *won* for him by *Atheling's army.*

,, The Orkneys, Shetland, and the Hebrides subjected to Norway.
they *capture* the *West,* with *Thule* and *Orkney.*

1099. Jerusalem taken by Godfrey de Bouillon: frightful massacre of Mussulmans and Jews.
the *Crusaders win* a *triumphant victory.*

1100. Henry I. (Beauclerc), twenty-third king of England.
a *colony* of *craftsmen weave* in *Wales.*

1107. Alexander I., brother of Edgar, twenty-third king of Scotland.
they *crown* the *brother* of the *expiring prince.*

1118. The Order of Knights Templars instituted.
the *crusaders begin* a *chivalric order.*

1123. The ninth General Council, or first Council of Lateran.
clerical celibacy first agreed on.

1124. David I., twenty-fourth king of Scotland.
the *Church canonised* her *devoted saint.*

1128. Holyrood Abbey, in Edinburgh, built by King David.
a *celebrated abbey* by *David erected.*

1135. Stephen (de Blois), twenty-fourth king of England.
civil-wars cause him *great alarm.*

1139. Portugal, recovered from the Moors, becomes a kingdom under Alphonso I.
the *Crusaders combine* to *give* him the *throne.*

A.D.

1140. The canon law introduced into England.
: the *canons of councils supreme* in the *West*.

1141. The Guelphs and Ghibelines contend.
: *curious burdens issue* from a *castle*.

1147. The Second Crusade under Conrad III. of Germany and Louis VII. of France.
: *Conrad's crusade* is the *second* to *Palestine*.

" Spanish literature begins with "the Cid," a romance.
: the *Cid commences Spanish poetry*.

1151. Gratian, a Benedictine monk, collects the canon law.
: *codifies* the *canon law* at *Bologna*.

1153. Malcolm IV., grandson of David, twenty-fifth king of Scotland.
: *converts* the *chiefs* into *loyal Highlanders*.

1154. Henry II., twenty-fifth king of England, begins the Plantagenet line.
: *Becket caused* him *labour* and *sorrow*.

SECT. 27.—From the Accession of the Plantagenets to the End of the Crusades (1154-1291).

A.D.

1156. Moscow founded by Juric I., Duke of Kiev.
: *builds* the *capital* of a *large empire*.

1157. Henry II. permitted by the Pope to conquer Ireland.
: *obtains* a *bull* from a *lying Pope*.

1164. Thomas-à-Becket condemned by the Council of Clarendon: trial by jury perfected in England.
: *Becket condemned* by an *English jury*.

1165. William I. (the Lion), brother of Malcolm, twenty-sixth king of Scotland.
: *confer* the *crown* on a *noble lion*.

1172. Henry II. takes possession of Ireland.
: *bishops* and *abbots promise* him *fealty*.

1180. Glass windows begin to be used in England.
: *bright beams* to *readers welcome*.

1187. Jerusalem taken from the Christians by Saladin.
: a *brave conqueror retakes Zion*.

HISTORY OF THE MIDDLE AGES. 231

A.D.
1189. Richard I. (Cœur de Lion), Philip of France, and Frederick, begin the THIRD CRUSADE.
the Crusade begun by Richard was the third.

1190. The Teutonic Order of Knights instituted.
a badge conferred for valiant exploits.

1199. John (Lackland), twenty-seventh king of England.
content to accept the throne of a vassal.

1200. Riga, capital of Livonia, built.
built on the Düna for exporting wheat.

1202. The Fourth Crusade sets out from Venice.
the Crusaders' fourth expedition departs.

„ Algebra first employed in Italy by Leonardo of Pisa.
a curious device to express figures.

1203. Pope Innocent III. establishes the Inquisition.
a court formed to exterminate heretics.

1204. France recovers Normandy, Anjou, and Maine.
the colonial dependencies wrested from John.

„ The Crusaders seize and plunder Constantinople.
the Crusaders force it on their way to Asia.

1205. First regular Parliament in England convoked.
the barons demand an extension of liberty.

1208. John empowers the Londoners to elect their mayor and aldermen.
the citizens first exercise their right.

1209. The Pope anathematises King John of England.
a bloody despot excommunicated by the Vicar.

1210. The Albigenses cruelly persecuted by the Inquisition.
a cruel edict causes their extermination.

„ First war between Genoa and Venice.
begins the furious contest of years.

„ Zenghis Khan, founder of the Mogul empire, enters China, and subdues five Chinese provinces.
breaks through the formidable Chinese wall.

1214. Birth of Roger Bacon, the English philosopher.
Bacon the founder of British science.

„ Alexander II., twenty-seventh king of Scotland.
carries on a furious contest with John.

A.D.
1215. Twelfth General Council (fourth Council of Lateran).
    the *Council determines* to *condemn* the *Albigenses.*

,,   Magna Charta signed by King John at Runnymede.
    a *charter defining British liberty.*

1216. Henry III., twenty-eighth king of England.
    contends with the *Dauphin* for the *crown* of *England.*

1218. The Fifth Crusade, under Andrew II. of Hungary.
    the *Crusaders' fifth abortive raid.*

,,   Zenghis Khan invades Persia.
    begins his *fearful career* of *rapine.*

1220. Astronomy and geography introduced into England.
    at *Cambridge* they are *first fully expounded.*

1223. Death of Philip III. of France.
    the *breadth* of *France* was *doubled* by *Augustus.*

1225. Louis VIII. joins a crusade against the Albigenses.
    a *crusade formed* to *destroy* the *Albigenses.*

1227. Death of Zenghis Khan: succeeded by his son, Oktai.
    cease the *devastations* of the *formidable Zenghis.*

1231. First charter granted to Cambridge University.
    Cambridge first granted a *charter.*

1234. Coal first discovered in England, near Newcastle.
    coal first heats our *stoves.*

1236. Leaden pipes for conveying water invented.
    convey the *fluid* in *hollow pipes.*

,,   Russia overrun by more than a million Mongol Tartars under Batu Khan.
    the *country devastated* by *hordes* of *Mongols.*

1239. The Tartars invade Poland and Hungary.
    the *country devastated* by *hordes* of *Tartars.*

1240. Tin mines first discovered in Germany.
    Cornwall formerly supplied the *world.*

1241. The Hanseatic League formed.
    a *confederacy formed* for the *safety* of *commerce.*

1242. The Mongols invade Siberia, and make Tobolsk their capital.
    the *Czar's dominions* in *Asia flooded* by them.

A.D.
1245. **Thirteenth General Council (Council of Lyons).**
condemns Frederick the *Second* at *Lyons.*

1246. **Saladin II. introduces the Mamelukes into Egypt.**
his *body defended* by " *slaves*" or *Mamelukes.*

1248. **Sixth Crusade under Louis IX. of France.**
the *Crusaders defeated* by *Sultan Turau.*

1249. **Alexander III., twenty-eighth king of Scotland, succeeds his father, Alexander II.**
celebrated in our *first Scottish verse.**

,, **The Mamelukes revolt in Egypt, and seize the throne.**
Bibar, their *first Sultan*, was a *Turk.*

1250. **Kublai Khan, a descendant of Zenghis, becomes chief of the Mongols.**
a *bloody despot leads* them to *war.*

,, **Roger Bacon invents magnifying and burning glasses.**
Bacon forms lenses for the *eye.*

1253. **The Arabic numerals introduced into England.**
counting by *digits learned* from the *hand.*

1254. **Alphonso the Wise publishes his astronomical tables.**
a *celebrated friend* of *literature* and *science.*

1258. **The Tartars seize Bagdad, and terminate the empire of the Caliphs.**
the *Caliphate destroyed* by an *alien race.*

,, **The King of Aragon cedes Languedoc and Provence to France.**
cedes to *France* her *legitimate rights.*

---

* Alexander III. was long affectionately remembered in Scotland, and the old Chronicle of Wynton has preserved the following verses about him, which are extremely interesting, as being the most ancient specimen of the Scottish dialect now extant :—

" Quhen Alexandyr oure King was dede,
dat Scotland led in luwe and le,
Away wes sons of ale and brede,
of wyne and wax, of gamyn and gle.
Oure gold was changed into lede.
Chryst, born into virgynyte,
Succour Scotland and remede,
dat stad is in perplexyte."

A.D.
1260. Kublai Khan overruns part of China, and makes Pekin the capital instead of Nanking.
China devastated by *Mongol warriors.*

1263. Alexander III. repels an invasion of the Norwegians, and compels them to resign the Hebrides.
bravely defeats their *monarch Haco.*

,, The Seljukian Turks cross the Bosphorus, and settle west of the Black Sea.
bands of *foreigners* and *northern hordes.*

1265. The House of Commons first summoned to convene.
the *best defence* of the *nation's liberties.*

,, Battle of Evesham : Leicester defeated.
the *barons defeated* with *Montford of Leicester.*

,, Birth of Dante, the illustrious Italian poet.
birth of *Dante, memorable* in *literature.*

1270. The eighth or last Crusade, under Louis IX.
the *Crusaders fail* in their *quixotic expeditions.*

1271. Marco Polo, a Venetian, travels to the East.
a *bold adventurer proceeds* to " *Cathay.*"

1272. Edward I., the twenty-ninth king of England.
the *Countess* of *Flanders quarrels* with *Edward.*

1274. Marco Polo arrives at the court of Kublai Khan.
a *celebrated adventurer presented* to the *Khan.*

,, Death of Thomas Aquinas, the famous Schoolman.
the *celebrated divine, Aquinas* the *Schoolman.*

1279. The whole of China subdued by Kublai Khan, who founds the Yuen dynasty.
China a *dependency* of the *powerful Tartars.*

1282. Conquest of Wales by Edward I. of England.
the *Cymri* are *forced* to *resign* their *freedom.*

,, The Sicilian Vespers: the French massacred in Sicily.
a *bloody deed* of *reckless daring.*

,, The Zuider Zee united to the North Sea.
the *briny flood rushes* into *Flevo.*

1286. Death of Alexander III.: Bruce and Baliol compete for the crown.
they *choose Edward* as *arbiter* in the *matter.*

A.D.
1291. End of the Crusades: Ptolemais, &c., surrender to the Sultan of Egypt.
the Crusades are finished by the taking of Acre.

SECT. 28. — From the End of the Crusades to the Death of Richard II. (A.D. 1291-1399).

A.D.
1294. Boniface VIII. becomes Pope of Rome.
Boniface, the fiery Vicar of Jesus.

1295. Marco Polo returns, and writes his 'Travels.'
China described by a traveller in the land.

1296. Edward I. invades Scotland, and penetrates to Elgin.
crafty Edward travels to Morayshire.

,, Battle of Dunbar: the Scots are defeated by the Earl of Warrenne.
Baliol defeated by a valiant Englishman.

1298. Battle of Falkirk: Wallace defeated by Edward.
the battle of Falkirk a taunt and reproach.

,, The Ottoman Empire founded in Asia by Othman.
the bloody founder of Turkish rule.

1300. Windmills first used in Western Europe.
begin to grind with wind for water.

1302. The mariner's compass introduced into Europe by Gioja of Amalfi.
the compass guides through watery fields.

1303. The Scots defeat the English near Roslin.
Comyn gallantly extinguishes a host.

1304. Birth of Petrarch, the Italian poet.
birth of a great writer of "sonnets."

1305. Sir William Wallace beheaded at Westminster.
our country's hero executed in London.

1306. Robert Bruce murders Comyn, and becomes thirty-first king of Scotland.
"the Bruce" is guilty of wilful murder.

1307. Edward II., thirtieth king of England.
the accomplished Gaveston weakens his popularity.

A.D.
1307. Establishment of Swiss independence: story of William Tell.
the *cruel Gessler warned* by a *patriot*.

1308. The seat of the Popes transferred to Avignon for seventy years.
beginning of their *ignominious exile* from *Rome*.

1310. Rhodes taken by the Knights of St John.
a *celebrated Grecian colossus* of *yore*.

1311. Gaveston, the favourite of Edward II., beheaded.
the *accomplished Gaveston cruelly beheaded*.

1312. Order of the Knights Templar abolished by the Pope.
accused them of *guilt* of the *blackest dye*.

1313. Birth of Boccaccio.
Boccaccio, a *highly celebrated Genoese*.

1314. Bruce defeats the English at Bannockburn.
Bannockburn's glorious battle in *Scotland*.

1315. Battle of Morgarten: the Swiss defeat the Austrians.
a *brave handful contending* for *liberty*.

1316. First exercise of the "Salic Law" in France.
the *crown* to be *heired* by *boys* and *men*.

1318. The Scots invade Ireland: defeated by the English.
Bruce's host is beaten in *Ireland*.

1320. Lace first manufactured in Flanders.
costly gear for *female wear*.

1321. Abulfeda, the Saracen prince of Hamah, finishes his 'Arabian Geography.'
Abulfeda of *Hamah describes* his *country*.

1322. Walter Lollard, founder of a sect, burned for heresy at Cologne.
they *commit* a *holy father* to the *flames*.

„ Battle of Mühldorf, between Frederick III. of Germany and Louis V. of Bavaria.
the *Bavarian host defeats Frederick*.

1324. Truce of 13 years between England and Scotland.
cessation of *hostilities* between *Edward* and the *Scotch*.

„ Birth of Wycliffe.
Britain gets first the *Scriptures*.

A.D.
1327. Edward III., thirty-first king of England.
  begins with a *general dispensation* of *pardon*.

1328. Birth of Chaucer, the father of English poetry.
  Chaucer our *great father* of *rhyme*.

,, Philip VI. commences the fourth dynasty in France.
  the *brilliant glories* of the *French realm*.

1329. David II., thirty-second king of Scotland.
  beware of the *guile* of *Edward* the *Third!*

1333. Edward III. defeats the Scots at Halidon Hill.
  the *carnage* is *great* at *Halidon Hill*.

1334. Edward Baliol driven from the throne of Scotland.
  Baliol's government is *hateful* to the *Scotch*.

1344. Gold coins come into general circulation in England.
  coins of *gold* are *used* for *silver*.

1346. Battle of Cressy between Edward III. and Philip.
  Cressy the *glory* of the *kings* of *England*.

,, Cannon and gunpowder first employed by the English in the Battle of Cressy.
  their *cannon greatly assist* the *English*.

,, The Scots invade England: are defeated at Durham.
  a *bloody havoc* of the *Scotch invaders*.

,, Windsor Castle rebuilt by Edward III.
  built for a *home* to the *kings* of *England*.

1348. The Black Death, a terrible plague, sweeps over the three continents.
  a *calamity* from *heaven smites* the *earth*.

,, General massacre of the Jews, as the alleged cause of the plague.
  a *cry against* the *scattered remnant*.

1349. The Order of the Garter instituted by Edward III.
  a *blue garter* of *spangled velvet*.

1353. The Turks first enter Europe, under Solyman.
  they *cross* the *Hellespont*, and *land* at *Gallipoli*.

1356. Battle of Poitiers: great victory over the French.
  " the *Black-Prince*" gains his *laurels now*.

A.D.
1360. Amurath, the Turk, overruns Eastern Europe from the Danube to the Adriatic.
a courageous general marches westward.

„ Peace of Bretigni: Edward releases King John of France from captivity.
crowns of gold in millions for an exile.

1362. Law pleadings changed from Norman-French to English.
clients hear their native dialect.

„ Adrianople becomes the capital of the Turkish empire in Europe.
begin to govern their empire from Adrianople.

1363. Death of Baliol: David II. acknowledges Edward of England his heir, should he have no issue.
a cause of great misery and grief.

1364. Charles V. (the Wise), King of France.
Charles gets Navarre from Spain.

1367. Battle of Najera: the Black Prince restores Peter the Cruel to the throne of Castile.
the crown is gained at Najera for Peter.

1369. Third great pestilence in England.
the cloud hovered over England thrice.

1370. Birth of John Huss, the Bohemian Reformer.
birth of a great protesting witness.

1371. Robert II., the thirty-third king, begins the Stuart dynasty in Scotland.
Bruce's heir at Perth is crowned.

1372. The combined fleets of France and Spain defeat the English at Rochelle.
a celebrated hold of the Protestants of France.

1374. Truce of Bruges: England cedes to France nearly all her French possessions.
Charles gets-back the possessions of his sires.

1376. Death of "the Black Prince."
they bewail the glory and pride of England.

HISTORY OF THE MIDDLE AGES. 239

A.D.
1377. Richard II., a minor, son of the Black Prince, thirty second king of England.
a council governs in place of the prince.

,, Pope Gregory XI. returns to Rome from Avignon.
changes the home of the papal pontiffs.

1378. The schism of double popes at Rome and Avignon now begins.
beginning of the ugly papal rivalry.

1380. Charles VI. (the Insane) ascends the throne of France.
a cloud hovers over the royal youth.

,, Wycliffe translates the Scriptures into English.
the book of God is rendered by Wycliffe.

,, Tamerlane, descendant of Zenghis Khan, takes Herat.
a celebrated hero in rapine and war.

1381. Wat Tyler's insurrection in England.
a blacksmith heads the rebel band.

1384. Tamerlane subdues Persia and High Asia.
barbaric hordes ravage the steppes.

1387. Tamerlane conquers Turkestan and Siberia.
barbaric hordes ravage the plain.

1388. Battle of Otterburn (or "Chevy Chase") between Douglas and the Percies.
a battle of great and romantic renown.

1389. Boniface IX. becomes pope at Rome.
Boniface ignores his rival at Avignon.

1390. Robert III., thirty-fourth king of Scotland.
bands of Highlanders valiant in war.

1396. Sultan Bajazet defeats the Christians in Bulgaria.
Bajazet gains a victory at Nicopolis.

1397. Union of Calmar—Norway, Sweden, and Denmark united under Margaret.
begins to govern a vast peninsula.

1399. Tamerlane overruns India and seizes Delhi.
conquest of Hindostan by Timur the Tartar.

SECT. 29.—From the Death of Richard II. to the Accession of Edward IV.—The Lancastrian Period (1399-1461).

A.D.
1399. Henry IV., thirty-third king of England, begins the Lancastrian dynasty.
Bolingbroke gains the *vacant throne.*

1400. Owen Glendower raises a rebellion in Wales.
behold the *standard* of *Owen,* a *Welshman!*

1401. First persecution of the Lollards in England.
they *burn Sawtree* in *wanton cruelty.*

1402. Battle of Homildon Hill: the Percies defeat Douglas.
the *courageous Scotch woefully defeated.*

,, Battle of Angora, between the Osmanlees and Tartars.
Bajazet, the *Sultan, yields* to his *foe.*

1403. Battle of Shrewsbury: the rebellion ended.
the *battle* of *Shrewsbury—Owen* and *Hotspur.*

1405. Death of Tamerlane, on his way to conquer China.
China escapes the *wanton leveller.*

,, Siege of Berwick: great guns first used in England.
cannon are *used* the *walls* to *level.*

1406. James I., a captive in England, is proclaimed thirty-fifth king of Scotland.
the *captive king* an *exile* in *England.*

1407. John of Burgundy assassinates the Duke of Orleans.
cruel John's execrable perfidy!

1409. Council of Pisa deposes the two rival popes.
the *Church, scandalised, excommunicates* the "*vicars.*"

1411. St Andrews University (first in Scotland) founded.
our *celebrated Scottish colleges begin.*

,, Sigismund, Emperor of Germany.
crafty Sigismund calls a *Council.*

1413. Henry V., thirty-fourth king of England: the Lollards again persecuted.
a *black spot* in the *character* of *Henry.*

1414. Council of Constance (seventeenth General) condemns John Huss and Jerome of Prague.
courageous Jerome consigned to the *stake.*

A.D.
1415. Battle of Agincourt: Henry totally defeats the French.
Charles the *Sixth* the *battle loses.*

1418. The Canary Islands, discovered by a French vessel in 1330, are colonised by the Portuguese.
the *Canaries slowly colonised* by *Europeans.*

1420. Madeira discovered by the Portuguese.
a *beautiful island adorned* with "*wood.*"

,, Treaty of Troyes between Henry V. and Charles VI. of France.
the *crown* and *sceptre* of *France* are *won* by him.

1422. Death of Henry V. and of Charles VI.
Charles the *Sixth*, or the *Fatuous, dies.*

,, Henry VI. crowned King of England and France.
a *child succeeds* to a *double dominion.*

,, James I. of Scotland liberated by the English.
the *captive king* is *freed* from *durance.*

1424. The French and Scotch defeated at Verneuil.
Bedford severely defeats the *Scots.*

1429. Joan of Arc raises the siege of Orleans.
the *brave Joan defeats* the *victors.*

1431. Joan burned as a witch by the English at Rouen.
they *burn Joan* of *heroic celebrity.*

,, Council of Basle (eighteenth General Council).
the *council seeks* to *heal* the *breach.*

,, The Azores discovered by Vanderberg of Bruges.
the "*Açores*" are *seen* with "*hawks*" *abounding.*

1434. Cosmo di Medici, founder of the family of that name, rules the republic of Florence.
a *celebrated savant governs* the *state.*

1435. Treaty of Arras between Charles VII. and the Duke of Burgundy.
Charles secures a *great ally.*

,, *f.* Blind Harry, author of 'Sir William Wallace.'
begins our *Scottish heroic literature.*

1436. Paris retaken by the French from the English.
Charles the *Seventh gains* it from the *English.*

Q

A.D.
1436. Printing by movable wooden types invented.
   the *celebrated Koster* of *Haerlem invented* them.
1437. James I. assassinated at Perth : James II. succeeds him as thirty-sixth king of Scotland.
   basely assassinated by *Graham* at *Perth.*
1439. "The Pragmatic Sanction :" Charles VII. summons a national synod at Bourges.
   Charles the *Seventh* and *Eugenius* at *variance.*
1440. Guttemberg improves printing by *cutting* metal types.
   books scatter knowledge widely.
1441. Copenhagen made the capital of Denmark, Norway, and Sweden.
   Copenhagen on the *Sound* the *Scandinavian capital.*
1444. Guttemberg and Faust print the Mazarin Bible.
   the *Bible spreads* the *knowledge* of *salvation.*
  ,, Don Pedro of Portugal proposes to send an embassy to "Prester John," King of Abyssinia.
   a *Christian king* of *sable skin !*
  ,, Great battle of Varna between Amurath II. and Vladislaus, King of Hungary : great slaughter of the Christians.
   on the *Black Sea* the *savages slaughter* them.
1446. Great inundation of the sea in Holland : 100,000 persons perish at Dort.
   the *boisterous sea swamps* the *Netherlands.*
  ,, Frederick III. of Germany declares war against Switzerland.
   the *Cantons* of *Switzerland* at *issue* with the *emperor.*
1449. Cape Verd Islands discovered by the Portuguese.
   a *curious scene,* the *seas* are *"verdant !"*
1450. Jack Cade's insurrection at Blackheath.
   a *" cad"* strikes the *Londoners* with *wonder.*
  ,, University of Glasgow founded by Bishop Turnbull.
   a *college* for the *spread* of *learning* in the *west.*
1453. Constantinople taken by the Turks : end of the Eastern Empire.
   the *capital* of the *East lost* by the *Greeks.*

A.D.
1453. The English lose all their possessions in France, except Calais.
Calais is *still left* to *Henry.*

1454. Venice and Genoa conclude a peace with the Turks.
commercial states in *league* with the *strangers.*

1455. Battle of St Albans, first in the "Wars of the Roses."
a *contest severe,* which *lasted long.*

1458. Matthew Corvinus, King of Hungary.
the *conqueror* of *Austria elected* to *rule.*

1460. Death of James II. of Scotland: accession of James III., thirty-seventh king.
the *courageous king* is *mortally wounded.*

,, Battle of Northampton; Henry VI. taken prisoner.
the *celebrated "king maker" worsted* him.

,, Battle of Wakefield; the Duke of York slain.
in *battle* he is *slain* by *Margaret* at *Wakefield.*

SECT. 30.—From the Accession of Edward IV. to the Discovery of America (1461-1492).

A.D.
1461. Edward IV., thirty-sixth king of England, begins the "York" dynasty.
a *courageous soldier, enterprising* and *bloody.*

,, Death of Charles VII. by voluntary starvation: Louis XI. succeeds him.
commits suicide the *unfortunate Charles.*

1462. Storming of Mentz by Adolphus: the art of printing extends to other places.
the *celebrated storming* of *Mentz* by *Adolphus.*

,, Ivan III. founds the present Russian monarchy.
courageous John, the *northern despot.*

1465. League against Louis XI. of France.
the *barons scheme* to *menace Louis.*

1467. Birth of Erasmus at Rotterdam.
the *brightest "star* of the *Netherlands" appears.*

1468. Orkney and Shetland ceded by Denmark to Scotland.
brave seamen of *Norwegian origin.*

A.D.
1470. Edward IV. attainted, and Henry VI. restored to the throne.
a couple of *kings opposed* in *war*.

1471. Caxton introduces printing into England, and begins with Cicero's "De Officiis."
Caxton succeeds in *printing Cicero*.

1473. Study of the Greek language introduced into France.
classical scholars appear from *Greece*.

1475. Edward IV. invades France: peace of Pacquigny.
the *crafty king pays* for it *liberally*.

1478. The conspiracy of the Pazzi against the Medici at Florence suppressed.
the *conspirators joined* by the *Pope* of *Rome*.

1479. Ferdinand and Isabella unite the kingdoms of Aragon and Castile.
a *celebrated king* and *queen* on the *throne*.

,, Russia freed from the Tartar yoke by Ivan Basilowitz, the first Czar.
the *Czar assumes* his *present title*.

1480. The Inquisition revived in Spain by Ferdinand.
a *bloody jurisdiction revived* in the *west*.

1481. African slavery commenced by the Portuguese.
cargoes of *slaves arrive* from *Congo*.

,, Bajazat II., Emperor of the Turks.
Bajazet the *Second reigns* at *Constantinople*.

1483. Edward V. and Richard III., thirty-seventh and thirty-eighth kings of England.
the *crown* is *usurped* by *Richard* of *Gloucester*.

,, Birth of Martin Luther at Eislében in Saxony.
born at *Eisleben*, the *Reformer* of *Germany*.

1485. Battle of Bosworth; Richard III. is killed.
the *brave usurper* is *routed* in *Leicester*.

,, Henry VII., the thirty-ninth king of England, begins the Tudor dynasty, and unites the houses of York and Lancaster.
a *better king rules* the *land*.

A.D.
1485. Vienna and Lower Austria taken by Matthias Corvinus, King of Hungary.
Corvinus seizes and *rules* the *land.*

1486. The Cape of Good Hope unconsciously doubled by Bartholomew Diaz, a Portuguese.
the "*Cape of Storms*" its *original name.*

1487. Cavilham, a Portuguese, travels to India by Suez.
Cavilham seeks the *renown of Portugal.*

,, Simnel's rebellion in Ireland.
the *obscure Simnel is routed* and *pardoned.*

1488. James IV. becomes thirty-eighth king of Scotland.
an *active king rules* the *realm.*

,, The "Great Harry," first English ship of war, built.
they *build* a *ship* at the *royal arsenal.*

,, Sea-charts first brought to England by Bartholomew Columbus to illustrate his brother's ideas.
the *circular shape* of the *earth is revealed.*

1490. Will. Grocyn, first Professor of Greek at Oxford.
classical knowledge is *taught* at *Oxford.*

1492. The Moors expelled from Granada.
conquest of the *Saracens* by *valiant Ferdinand.*

PERIOD III.—MODERN HISTORY.

CHAP. VII.—FROM THE DISCOVERY OF AMERICA TO THE PEACE OF WESTPHALIA (A.D. **1492-1648**).

We have at length emerged from the darkness of ancient times, have passed the dim twilight of the Middle Ages, and have arrived at the clear sunshine of Modern History. This last and greatest, though at the same time the shortest, period of human history, is mainly distinguished from the two preceding by the following marked characteristics : 1. The theatre of history, the field of action, has, by the discovery of a new world, become suddenly and vastly enlarged, embracing now, for the first time, all parts of the earth's surface, and all the races of our species.

2. The subjects that occupy the historian's attention are greatly multiplied, history being no longer a chronicle of great battles, and the exploits of kings and heroes, but an expounder of the principles that lead to true national greatness, and of the progress of civilisation in all lands. 3. This is pre-eminently the age of *literature, science,* and *art,* as well as of *inventions* of all kinds, though at first we find all these only in their germs and rude beginnings. 4. It is the period of legislation, administration, and progressive reform in the methods of governing—the period of statistics, politics, and finances, and of *social science* generally. 5. Similarly, it is the period of widespread enlightenment of the masses—of the elevation of those classes of society that were previously trodden down and despised. 6. It is the period of the establishment and maintenance of colonies, and of extensive and world-wide commerce. 7. Finally, it is the period when all things are being tested, sifted, and tried to their foundations; when all that is false in religion, science, and philosophy, is sure to be exposed; and when all that is true and genuine will be allowed to shine in its native colours.

Modern History consists of three great periods: the first extends from the discovery of America, and the great Reformation in Germany (events that were nearly contemporaneous), to the Peace of Westphalia; the second, from that event to the French Revolution; and the third, from the French Revolution to the present time.

The authorities most frequently consulted in this division of our labours have been Rotteck's 'General History of the World;' Russell's 'Modern Europe;' Alison's 'History of Europe;' Macaulay's 'History of England;' Guizot's 'History of Civilisation;' Hallam's 'Literature of Europe;' Haydn's 'Dictionary of Dates;' and the 'Penny Cyclopædia.'

SECT. 31.—From the Discovery of America to the Reformation (A.D. 1492-1517).

A.D.
1492. Columbus, with three Spanish vessels, sails to St Salvador, and thus discovers a new world.
Columbus sails on a *voyage* of *fame.*

MODERN HISTORY. 247

A.D.
1492. Columbus, on his first voyage to America, discovers the variation of the needle.
Columbus sees it *vary* in *dip.*

,, The Jews expelled from Spain and Portugal.
the *children* of *Judah violently dispersed.*

1493. Pope Alexander VI. grants to Spain all lands that may be discovered west of the Azores, and to Portugal all lands east of them.
the *boundary stretches* from (St) *Vincent* to *Graciosa.*

,, Columbus finds wild cotton in Hispaniola.
cotton seen on *trees* in *Hispaniola.*

1494. King's College, Aberdeen, founded by James IV.
the *Aberdonians study theology* and *science.*

,, John Cabot, sent out by Henry VII. of England, discovers Newfoundland.
the *icy shores* of " *Vista*" are *seen* by him.

1495. Columbus, on his second voyage, discovers Jamaica and Puerto Rico.
Columbus sees vast islands.

1497. Vasco de Gama, a Portuguese, doubles the Cape.
a *bold sailor visits Zanguebar.*

,, John and Sebastian Cabot plant the English flag in Labrador, Nova Scotia, and Virginia, the first part of the continent seen by Europeans.
the *Cabots survey* a *vast peninsula.*

1498. Columbus, on his third voyage, discovers Trinidad and the river Orinoco.
Columbus sees a *vast river.*

,, Death of Charles VIII. of France: Louis XII. succeeds.
Charles is *succeeded* by the *valiant Orleans.*

,, Savonarola burned by Pope Alexander VI. for preaching against the vices of the clergy.
they *burn Savonarola* for *testifying* against *Rome.*

1499. Canada discovered by John and Sebastian Cabot.
the *Cabots seize* a *vast territory.*

,, Amerigo Vespucci discovers Venezuela.
a *boasting subaltern visits Venezuela.*

A.D.
1499. Columbus sent to Spain in chains by Bobadella.
  the *courageous sailor* a *victim* to *avarice*.
1500. Pinzon, a Spaniard, discovers the river Amazon.
  he *beholds* the *leviathan* of the *world's waters*.
1501. Cabral, a Portuguese, discovers the coast of Brazil.
  Cabral lands on *wide Brazil*.
1502. Columbus discovers Central America.
  Columbus learns the *way* to *Darien*.
1503. The Spanish colonists compel the aborigines to work in the mines.
  the *Caribs* are *lashed* while *working* for *gold*.
  „ Goa Factory, in India, founded by the Portuguese.
  begin to *lay* the *walls* of *Goa*.
  „ Luther discovers the Vulgate in the library of Erfurth.
  a *Bible* in *Latin*, the *Word* of *God!*
1504. The French expelled from Naples, which is henceforth under the yoke of Spain.
  continues long under the *yoke* of *Spain*.
1506. Death of Columbus, at Seville, in his 59th year.
  Columbus lands on a *world unknown*.
  „ The sugar-cane introduced from the Canaries into the West Indies.
  begin to *elevate* the *West Indies*.
  „ St Peter's Church at Rome begun by Bramante.
  they *build* a *large* and *wondrous monument*.
  „ Lisbon made the capital of Portugal by Emanuel.
  beautiful Lisbon exalted by *Emanuel*.
  „ Birth of George Buchanan, the Scottish historian.
  born a *learned writer* of *annals*.
1507. Almeida discovers Madagascar and Ceylon.
  the *bold Almeida wins* them to *Portugal*.
  „ Copernicus conceives the true theory of the solar system.
  Copernicus learns our *world's position*.
1508. African slaves first imported into the Spanish colonies.
  a *cruel law* of *wrong* and *rapine*.

A.D

1508. League of Cambray, by which Venice cedes to Spain her Neapolitan possessions.
the Cambray league wounds the republic.

1509. Henry VIII. ascends the throne of England.
binds the Lancastrians and Yorkists to the throne.

,, Birth of John Calvin, the famous Reformer.
Calvin, the learned writer and theologian.

1510. Balbao establishes the first Spanish settlement on the western continent (Darien).
begins a little colony in the west.

1511. Velasquez, a Spaniard, conquers Cuba.
the Caribs lament the conquest of Cuba.

1512. Ponce de Leons, a Spaniard, discovers Florida and the Gulf Stream.
observes a land with beautiful "flowers."

1513. Balbao crosses the Isthmus of Darien to the Pacific.
Balbao lights on an ocean great.

,, Battle of Flodden Field between English and Scots: James IV. slain: James V., thirty-ninth king, succeeds him.
a battle long celebrated in Galloway.

,, "The Battle of Spurs," between English and French.
called also the Battle of Guinegate.

1514. Joan Diaz de Solis enters the Rio de la Plata.
Buenos lies on the banks of the estuary.

1515. Francis I. of France defeats the Swiss at the great Battle of Marignan.
a courageous leader crosses the Alps.

1516. Death of Ferdinand of Spain, and accession of Charles of Germany.
Charles lays-claim to both empires.

,, Cardinal Wolsey becomes papal legate in England.
a cardinal legate of boundless ambition.

SECT. 32.—From the Reformation in Germany to the Death of Luther (A.D. 1517-1546).

A.D.
1517. Martin Luther begins the Reformation in Germany.
courageous Luther *braves* the *Pope.*

,, Ferdinand Cordoba, a Spaniard, sails from Cuba, and explores Yucatan.
Cordoba lands on a *broad peninsula.*

1518. The Mexicans teach the Spaniards cochineal-dyeing.
the *colonists learn* a *curious art.*

,, Barbarossa, the Algerine pirate, slain.
Barbarossa, the *lawless corsair, routed.*

,, Reuchlin appointed Professor of Hebrew and Greek at Wittenberg.
a *celebrated linguist,* the *companion* of *Erasmus.*

1519. Cortez sent by Velasquez to conquer Mexico.
Cortez lands on a *civilised territory.*

,, Charles I. of Spain becomes Emperor of Germany as Charles V.
begins a *long conflict* with *Turkey.*

,, Zwingle raises the standard of reform in Switzerland.
courageous Ulrich, a *champion* of the *truth.*

1520. Death of Selim, Sultan of Turkey, who is succeeded by Solyman the Magnificent.
Christendom alarmed with *fear* of *war.*

,, Interview between Henry VIII. and Charles V.
Charles is *allured* to *Dover* by *Wolsey.*

,, Magellan discovers the Strait bearing his name.
he *cautiously leads* his *fleet westward.*

1521. Magellan discovers the Philippines, where he is killed.
the *courageous leader falls* in *battle.*

,, Magellan's fleet discovers Borneo, Celebez, the Moluccas, and circumnavigates the globe.
they *curiously lose* a *day* in their *course.*

,, Adrian VI. becomes Pope of Rome.
the *cardinals elect Adrian* to be their *chief.*

A.D.
1521. Henry VIII. wins the title of "Defender of the Faith" by writing against Luther.
   a bloody libertine defends the Church.

,, Luther outlawed at the Diet of Worms.
   courageous Luther a fearless confessor.

,, Cortez completes the conquest of Mexico.
   conquers a large district of country.

1522. Death of Gawin Douglas, an early Scottish poet.
   commencement of our literature by Douglas of Dunkeld.

,, Luther translates the New Testament into German.
   converts the Latin into the dialect of "Fatherland."

1523. Gustavus Vasa offered the throne of Sweden.
   the crown is laid at the feet of Gustavus.

1524. Sweden and Denmark embrace the Reformed religion.
   beginning of Lutheranism in Denmark and Sweden.

1525. "War of the Peasants" in Germany.
   beginning of a lengthened feud with the Lutherans.

,, Battle of Pavia between Charles V. of Germany and Francis I. of France.
   a contest which loses to Francis his liberty.

,, Tyndale publishes his English New Testament.
   the British learn the divine law.

1526. Prussia receives the Reformed faith.
   in Berlin the Lutherans denounce the mass.

,, Treaty of Madrid: Francis cedes to Charles V. Burgundy, Naples, &c.
   Charles in league with Francis at Madrid.

,, Battle of Mohacz between Louis of Hungary and Solyman the Magnificent.
   the brave Louis dies at Mohacz.

,, Pizarro invades the empire of Peru in the reign of Huano Capac, its twelfth emperor.
   Capac the last of the dynasty of the Incas.

1527. Rome taken and plundered by Charles V. of Germany: the Pope taken prisoner.
   a Bourbon leads the Father to prison.

A.D.
1528. Council of Bern : controversy between the Catholics and Lutherans.
the bold *Lutherans* defeat *the* Romanists.

„ Patrick Hamilton begins the Reformation in Scotland, and is burned at St Andrews.
his blood laid *the* foundation *of our* Reformation.

1529. Diet of Spires against the Huguenots : the Reformers first termed Protestants.
the courageous Lutherans defend *the* truth.

1530. Death of Cardinal Wolsey.
the crafty legate hastily expires.

„ League of Smalcald between the Protestant princes of Germany.
a *celebrated league* of *German worthies*.

1531. Rupture between Henry VIII. and the Pope: Henry becomes "Head of the Church" in England.
acknowledged by the *legislature* the "*Head* of the *Church*."

1532. Archbishop Cranmer disapproves of Henry's marriage with Queen Catharine.
Catharine loses Henry's affection.

„ Treaty of Nuremberg : Charles V. grants liberty of conscience to the Lutherans.
Charles allows the *Huguenots freedom.*

1533. Henry VIII. marries Anne Boleyn, a Protestant.
Boleyn is elevated *to the* highest honour.

1534. Lima, in Peru, founded by Pizarro.
the building *of* Lima *by a* gold-hunting Spaniard.

„ Cuzco, capital of the Incas, taken by Pizarro.
Cuzco at last *is* gained *by Spain.*

1535. Jacques Cartier, a Frenchman, explores Canada.
the Canadian lakes *at the* head *of (St)* Lawrence.

1536. The monasteries of England suppressed by Henry.
confiscates the *lands* and *goods* of the *monks*.

„ Henry places a copy of Coverdale's Bible in every church in England.
the Bible *at* length *given to* England.

A.D.
1536. Ann Boleyn beheaded by Henry.
: the *base licentious Henry murders* her.

,, Death of Erasmus at Basle.
: his *controversy* with *Luther* a *great misfortune.*

1537. Friendly relations established between the followers of Luther and Zwingle.
: the *boisterous Lutherans agree* with *Zwingle.*

,, Macao granted as a settlement to the Portuguese.
: *China allows* a *haven* to *Portugal.*

1538. Treaty of Nice between Charles V. and Francis I.
: *Charles* in *league* with his *greatest rival.*

1539. Socinus begins to propagate his opinions.
: a *bold* and *learned heretic* of *Italy.*

,, The bloody statute of six articles passed in England.
: *bloody laws* to *hurt* the *truth.*

1540. Order of the Jesuits founded by Ignatius Loyola.
: *crafty Loyola* is *supported* by *Xavier.*

1541. The Spaniards form their first settlement in Chilè.
: they *begin* to *lay Santiago* de *Chilè.*

,, Expedition of Charles V. against the Algerines.
: *Charles loses* his *ships* in *Barbary.*

1542. The Portuguese accidentally discover Japan.
: the *civilised land* of *Japan discovered.*

,, Ireland made a kingdom by Henry VIII.
: *converts* a *lordship* into a *kingdom fair.*

,, Death of James V. of Scotland, and accession of Mary Queen of Scots, fortieth sovereign.
: *begins* a *life* of *shame* and *disaster.*

1543. Henry VIII. marries Catharine Parr, his sixth wife.
: *Catharine,* the *last, survived* her *husband.*

1544. Charles V. concludes a treaty with Francis I.
: *Charles leagues* with the *King* in *Oise.*

1545. Council of Trent, the last General Council.
: *Calvinism* and *Lutheranism judged illegal.*

1546. George Wishart suffers martyrdom at St Andrews.
: *confessing* his *Lord,* he *suffers martyrdom.*

254   FACTS AND DATES.

A.D.
1546. Death of Martin Luther.
cease thy *labours, star* of the *morning !*

SECT. 33.—From the Death of Luther to the Accession of Queen Elizabeth (A.D. 1546-1558).

A.D.
1547. Death of Henry VIII., and accession of Edward VI.
the *council elects Seymour Protector.*

,, Battle of Pinkey : Seymour defeats the Scots.
the *battle* is *lost* by the *Scots* at *Pinkey.*

,, Charles V. defeats the Protestants at Muhlberg, and takes the Elector of Saxony prisoner.
the *bold Elector* of *Saxony* a *prisoner.*

1548. Charles V. grants "the Interim" to the Protestants.
the *bold Elector* his *sanction refuses.*

1549. Insurrection in England, headed by Ket.
the *Catholic lieges join* his *tribunal.*

1550. The Koh-i-nor diamond discovered in Golconda.
a *brilliant luminary* to *lighten* our *Exhibition.*

1552. Treaty of Passau between Charles V. and the Protestants.
Charles allows the *Lutherans freedom.*

1553. Michael Servetus burnt for heresy at Geneva.
they *burn* a *learned* and *eloquent heretic.*

,, Death of Edward VI. : accession of " Bloody Mary."
cruel laws the *lieges gall.*

1554. Lady Jane Grey beheaded.
a *beautiful lady led* to the *scaffold.*

,, Mary marries Philip of Spain, son of Charles V.
came to *lament* her *alliance* with a *Spaniard.*

1555. Cranmer, Ridley, Latimer, Hooper, and many others, suffer martyrdom.
Cranmer and *Latimer leal* to the *Lord.*

1556. Charles V. abdicates in favour of Ferdinand I.
Charles elects to *live* in a *monastery.*

MODERN HISTORY. 255

A.D.
1556. Philip II. crowned King of Spain, the Netherlands, and the Indies.
  his *cruelty leads* to *lasting misery*.

1557. Philip II. defeats the French at the decisive battle of St Quentin.
  he *bravely leads* his *legions* to *Picardy*.

1558. Queen Mary of Scotland marries the Dauphin of France, afterwards Francis II.
  a *brief alliance leading* to *ruin*.

,, Calais, our last French possession, lost to England.
  Calais is *lost*, the *last remaining*.

,, Death of "Bloody Mary:" accession of Elizabeth.
  a *bright luminary* to *lighten* the *realm*.

   SECT. 34.—From the Accession of Queen Elizabeth to James I. of England (A.D. 1558-1603).

A.D.
1560. John Knox appointed minister of Edinburgh.
  a *bold* and *eloquent minister* of the *Word*.

,, First General Assembly of the Church of Scotland.
  the *Church legislates* by *ministers* of the *Word*.

,, Papal authority in Scotland abolished: Presbyterianism established.
  they *abolish all mummeries* in *worship*.

1561. Mary Queen of Scots arrives from France.
  celebrates an *illegal mass* in her *chapel*.

,, Knox attempts to convert the Queen.
  boldly lays down his *Master's commands*.

,, Conference of Poissy between the Lutherans and Calvinists.
  Calvinists and *Lutherans meet* in *conference*.

1562. Sir J. Hawkins introduces slaves into the W. Indies.
  a *captain* of *Elizabeth introduced* them from *Africa*.

1563. Battle of Dreux between the Huguenots and Romanists.
  crafty Elizabeth encourages the *Huguenots*.

1564. Birth of W. Shakespeare, dramatist and tragedian.
  birth of the *illustrious* and *immortal Shakespeare*.

A.D.
1564. Birth of Galileo, the Italian astronomer.
    a bright luminary in the *morning* of *science.*

,, Knox's Liturgy enjoined in the Church of Scotland.
    a curious liturgy enjoined by the *Assembly.*

,, Death of John Calvin at Geneva.
    Calvin, the *learned methodiser* of *Scripture.*

,, David Rizzio becomes Secretary to Queen Mary.
    the *bitter lot* of *Mary's secretary.*

1565. Mary Queen of Scots marries Darnley.
    betrothed to a *licentious noble lord.*

1566. Revolt of the Netherlands against Philip II.
    his *bigotry leads* to an *insurrection* in the *Netherlands.*

,, Rizzio murdered by Darnley and others.
    the *banished lords murder* the *musician.*

1567. Murder of Darnley by the Earl of Bothwell.
    a cruel lord murders the *prince.*

,, Abdication of Mary: James VI. proclaimed king.
    they *carry* to *Leven Mary* a *prisoner.*

1568. Death of Philip Melanchthon the Reformer.
    the *celebrated* and *learned Melanchthon rests.*

,, Duke of Alva tyrannically rules the Netherlands.
    cruel Alva the *Netherlands rules.*

,, Battle of Langside: Mary escapes to England.
    at the *battle* of *Langside Mary* is *routed.*

1570. Terrible inundation in the Netherlands.
    countless lives perish by *water.*

,, Assassination of the Earl of Murray by Hamilton of Bothwellhaugh.
    a *conspirator levels* his *piece* from a *window.*

1571. Birth of Kepler, the celebrated German astronomer.
    what a *beautiful ellipse* is a *planet's course!*

,, Great victory over the Turks at Lepanto by the combined fleets of Spain, Venice, and Rome.
    the *Crescent* at *last pales* before the *Cross.*

,, Parliament ratifies the Thirty-nine Articles.
    brief and *luminous principles* of *Christianity.*

MODERN HISTORY.

A.D.
1572. Massacre of St Bartholomew begins at Paris.
    the *cruel lust* of *Popery displayed.*

,, Death of John Knox, the Scottish Reformer.
    the *courageous leveller* of *Popery dies.*

,, Camöens publishes the 'Lusiad' at Lisbon.
    Camöens's Lusiad, an *epic* of *fame.*

1573. Venice cedes Cyprus to Turkey, after which her power begins to decline.
    when *Cyprus* was *lost* her *power* was *gone.*

1574. Siege of Leyden by the armies of Spain.
    the *beginning* of *Leyden's protracted siege.*

,, Death of Charles IX. : accession of Henry III.
    they *choose* to *elect* a *Polish king.*

1575. Tasso completes his 'Gerusalemme Liberata.'
    behold the *illustrious poet* a *lunatic !*

1576. Death of Maximilian II. of Germany: accession of Rodolphus II.
    his *accession alarms* the *Protestants* of the *empire.*

1577. The "Catholic League" headed by Philip of Spain.
    the *Catholic League* is *protected* by *Philip.*

1578. Queen Elizabeth engages to support the revolted provinces of the Netherlands.
    cautious Elizabeth protects the *rebels.*

1579. The Republic of Holland commences by the Union of Utrecht.
    the *celebrated League* of the *Provinces* at *Utrecht.*

1580. Portugal subdued by Philip II. of Spain.
    brave Lusitania reduced by *war.*

,, Sir Francis Drake circumnavigates the globe.
    a *captain* of *Elizabeth rounds* the *world.*

1582. Pope Gregory XIII. reforms the Calendar, and introduces the New Style into Italy.*
    the *calendar altered* by *retrenching days.*

---

* This event is one of the greatest importance in modern history, for by it the ever-increasing deviation of the Julian calendar from the true reckoning was arrested, the equinoxes and solstices brought back to the days in which they had taken place in A.D. 325, and every new deviation prevented for the longest future.

FACTS AND DATES.

A.D.
1582. The Gowrie Conspiracy: James VI. imprisoned.
abandon Lennox and *Arran*, the *favourites !*

„ James VI. founds the University of Edinburgh.
a *college* for *learning* the *arts* in *Edinburgh.*

1584. William, Prince of Orange, assassinated at Delft.
the *champion* of *liberty ruthlessly assassinated.*

„ Sir W. Raleigh takes possession of Virginia for England.
a *colony leaves* for our *earliest settlement.*

1587. Mary Queen of Scots beheaded at Fotheringay Castle.
crafty Elizabeth's remorseless policy.

1588. Destruction of the Spanish Armada.
blessed be the *Lord*, the *Armada* is *ruined !*

1589. Henry III. of France murdered: accession of Henry IV. (the Great).
the *country* at *last* is *restored* to *tranquillity.*

1590. Battle of Ivry, which ruins the Catholic League.
the *Catholic League* at *Ivry* expires.

1591. Dublin University founded by Queen Elizabeth.
called by *Elizabeth* "*Trinity College.*"

1594. Galileo discovers the isochronism of the pendulum.
observes that the *lengths* of the *times* are the *same.*

1596. Cadiz taken by the English under Essex.
Cadiz is *levelled* by the *victorious English.*

1598. The English commence whale-fishing at Spitzbergen.
for *common oil* they *voyage* to *Russia.*

„ Edict of Nantes, granting toleration to the Protestants.
a *celebrated law* of *toleration ratified.*

„ Death of Philip II. of Spain.
a *cruel* and *lawless tyrant arrested.*

„ Earl of Tyrone's rebellion in Ireland.
a *bold liberator attempts* a *rebellion.*

1600. The English East India Company established.
a *company* of *merchants yearning* for *wealth.*

„ The Second Gowrie Conspiracy.
a *crafty manœuvre well executed.*

1601. Earl of Essex beheaded in the Tower.
a *brave nobleman, wilful* and *capricious.*

MODERN HISTORY. 259

A.D.
1602. The Dutch seize the Portuguese Indian settlements.
their colonial empire extended by the *Dutch.*

1603. Death of Queen Elizabeth : accession of James I. (VI. of Scotland).
a *curious end* to *worldly greatness.*

SECT. 35.—From the Accession of James I. to the Accession of Charles I. (A.D. 1603-1625.)

A.D.
1604. The Hampton Court conference.
a *conference* for *union* which *widens* the *schism.*

„ Death of Socinus, the celebrated Unitarian.
an *able Unitarian yields* his *spirit.*

„ Barbadoes colonised, England's first West Indian colony.
commence our Indian western settlements.

„ Silk first manufactured in England.
we *begin* to *manufacture webs* of *silk.*

1605. The Gunpowder Plot discovered.
a *bloody method* to *extirpate* the *legislators.*

1606. Virginia begins to be colonised by Britain.
colonists from *England wander* to *America.*

„ The Australian continent discovered by the Dutch.
a *beautiful new world* at the *antipodes.*

1608. Quebec founded by the French.
the *chief emporium* of a *wealthy region.*

1609. Galileo invents the telescope.
observes new worlds through his *telescope.*

„ Kepler discovers his first two "laws."
a *celebrated mathematician exults* in *triumph.*

1610. The Hudson Sea discovered by Hudson, in search of a north-west passage to the Pacific.
the *captain enters* a *cheerless expanse.*

„ The Moors finally expelled from Spain by Philip II.
the *courageous Moors* are *cruelly expelled.*

1611. The present translation of the Bible completed.
the *Bible* an *inestimable boon* to *Britain.*

A.D.
1611. The title of Baronet originated, and sold by James I.
confers on *Nicholas Bacon* a *baronetcy*.

„ Gustavus Adolphus ascends the throne of Sweden.
accession of a *monarch celebrated* for *bravery*.

1612. The Bermudas colonised by Sir George Somers.
colonists from *England cross* the *deep*.

„ First English factory in India established.
British India begins with a *factory*.

1613. Sir W. Raleigh publishes his 'History of the World.'
a *celebrated nobleman composes* a *history*.

1614. Baron Napier invents logarithms.
a *celebrated mathematician* the *boast* of *Scotland*.

1616. Death of William Shakespeare.
the *brightest name* in *Britain's annals*.

1618. Commencement of the Thirty Years' War in Germany.
begins a *memorable* and *bloody era*.

„ The Synod of Dort begins its sittings.
the *clergy meet* and *condemn* the *Arminians*.

„ Kepler announces his third law of planetary motions.
observes a *new* and *curious ratio*.

1619. Batavia built and settled by the Dutch.
Batavia their *emporium* of *commerce* and *trade*.

„ Harvey discovers the circulation of the blood.
the *blood* of *animals circulates* in their *veins*.

1620. The Puritans emigrate to New England.
the *cheerful Mayflower* our *fathers wafted*.

„ Bacon publishes his 'Novum Organum.'
Bacon ends his *famous work*.

„ Battle of Prague: defeat of the Elector-Palatine.
the *brave Maximilian defeats* him in *war*.

„ African slaves introduced into New England.
the *cause* of *innumerable disasters* and *woes*.

1621. Death of Philip III. of Spain: accession of Philip IV.
accession of a *mild despotic bigot*.

„ Willebrod Snell discovers the refraction of light.
observes the *angle*, and *discovers* the *cause*.

A.D.
1621. New York founded by Dutch colonists.
called Amsterdam by the Dutch colonists.

1622. Bellows for smelting employed in the Hartz mines.
bellows employed for fanning the flame.

1623. The Fatal Vespers in London: a Roman Catholic priest killed, with one hundred of his auditors.
the Catholics mourn the death of a host.

SECT. 36.—From Charles I. to the Peace of Westphalia (A.D. 1625-1648).

A.D.
1625. Charles I. of England accedes to the throne.
the beginning of England's fight for liberty.

,, Hackney coaches first used in London.
cabs and omnibuses fly through London.

1626. Protestant league against the Emperor, Ferdinand II.
a Catholic emperor our faith endangers!

1628. Charles I. grants his assent to the Petition of Right.
the Commons of England demand their rights.

1629. The Bahamas settled by the British.
its capital, Nassau, is famed for turtles.

1631. Magdeburg captured by Tilly, generalissimo of the Catholic League.
capture of Magdeburg, and great carnage.

,, Battle of Leipsic: defeat of Tilly by G. Adolphus.
his cruel antagonist by Gustavus conquered.

1632. Gustavus Adolphus killed at the battle of Lutzen.
the chivalrous monarch, Gustavus, dies.

1633. Galileo obliged by the Inquisition to recant his astronomical tenets.
is cited by inquisitors for horrible heresies!

1634. France and Spain begin a twenty-five years' war.
begin a momentous and grievous struggle.

,, The French Academy instituted by Cardinal Richelieu.
a congress of those most honoured in science.

1636. Death of Santorio, inventor of the air thermometer.
the celebrated inventor of our heat measurer.

A.D.
1638. The Solemn League and Covenant subscribed.
　　　the *commons* and *nobles* for *God* are *earnest*.
　,,　Harvard University, the oldest in the United States, founded.
　　　the *celebrated University* of *Harvard erected*.
1639. Bagdad taken from the Persians by the Turks.
　　　Bagdad is *menaced* by *hordes* of *Turks*.
1640. Portugal throws off the Spanish yoke.
　　　Braganza independent of the *Spanish yoke*.
　,,　The Long Parliament begins in England.
　　　they *oblige* the *monarch* to *stop* his *exactions*.
1641. Charles signs the League and Covenant at Edinburgh.
　　　they *compel* the *monarch* to *sign* the *covenant*.
　,,　Irish rebellion, and massacre of the Protestants.
　　　the *Catholics massacre* them in *savage cruelty*.
　,,　The Earl of Strafford beheaded.
　　　a *celebrated minister sentenced* to the *block*.
1642. Birth of Sir Isaac Newton, and death of Galileo.
　　　the *brightest names* in *scientific discovery*.
　,,　Civil war in England: battle of Edgehill.
　　　begin the *mighty struggle* at *Edgehill*.
　,,　Death of Cardinal Richelieu.
　　　a *celebrated minister* of *state's demise*.
　,,　Tasman discovers Van Diemen's Land and New Zealand.
　　　a *bold navigator sent* by the *Dutch*.
1644. Battles of Marston Moor and Newbury.
　　　Cromwell massacres the *king's soldiers*.
1645. Archbishop Laud beheaded.
　　　a *celebrated minister* to the *scaffold* is *led*.
　,,　Battle of Philiphaugh between the Covenanters and the Marquis of Montrose.
　　　cruel Montrose is *surprised* by *Leslie*.
　,,　Battle of Naseby decisive against Charles.
　　　Cromwell at *Naseby succeeds* to his *laurels*.
　,,　Battle of Nordlingen: Turenne defeats the Imperialists.
　　　by his *skilful manœuvres* he *slays* their *legions*.

A.D.
1647. The "Society of Friends" begins in England.
called by their *enemies* the *sect* of the *Quakers*.
1648. Peace of Westphalia: the present system of European States established.
begin a *number* of *States* in *Europe*.

CHAP. VIII.—FROM THE PEACE OF WESTPHALIA TO THE FRENCH REVOLUTION (A.D. 1648-1789).

THE period embraced by the last chapter was marked by a multitude of great events, the most celebrated of which were the discovery of a new hemisphere by Columbus, and the rediscovery by Luther of a grand principle in theology of perhaps equal importance. That period terminated with the times of Charles I. of England, when, according to Macaulay, the hazardous game began on which were staked the freedom and destinies of the English people—when the great statesmen of the land resolved to place their present and future kings in such a situation that they must either rule in conformity with the wishes of the nation, or make outrageous attacks on the most sacred principles of the Constitution. After a protracted contest, Charles ratified, in the most solemn manner, that celebrated law known as the "Petition of Right," a law which forms the second great charter of our liberties. By ratifying that law, he bound himself never again to raise money without the consent of Parliament; never again to imprison any person except in the course of law; and never again to subject his people to the jurisdiction of courts-martial. Within three weeks, however, after the signing of this solemn compact, it became evident that Charles had no intention of fulfilling any part of its terms. A violent conflict followed, resulting in the ignominious death of the unhappy monarch, in miseries innumerable to the nation during the reign of his two successors, and finally, in the great Revolution of 1688.

The execution of Charles, or rather the Peace of Westphalia which immediately preceded it, commences the period on which we are now entering. That celebrated Peace properly marks the advent of a new era, seeing that by it the principle of a "balance of power" in Europe was first recognised, the religious and political rights of the German States established, and the independence of the Swiss Confederation acknowledged by Germany. It was signed at Münster, in Westphalia, October 24, 1648, the contracting powers being France, Germany, and Sweden. Spain was not a party to it, as she and France still remained at war. The balance of power—the great principle established by this treaty—has ever since formed the palladium of the smaller States of Europe, though it was soon imperilled by the aspiring ambition of Louis XIV.

It were needless to trace the many striking events which give character to this period, more especially as they will be found sufficiently indicated in the following sections. Though shorter in duration, it will bear favourable comparison with any previous period. In England we have Cromwell and the Commonwealth, the restoration of Charles II., the atrocities that marked his reign, and the great revolution; in Western Europe we have the career of the grasping and arrogant Louis XIV., the Revocation of the Edict of Nantes, the war of the Spanish succession, and the capture of Gibraltar by the English; in Northern Europe, Charles XII., Peter the Great, and the still greater Frederick of Prussia; in politics we have the Peace of Utrecht and of Breda, the Treaties of Aix-la-Chapelle and Versailles, and the legislative union of England and Scotland; in war, many great battles, both by land and sea; in philosophy we have Kant in Germany, and Locke in England; in literature, the brilliant names of John Milton, John Bunyan, and John Owen; and in science, Sir Isaac Newton, James Watt, and the distinguished Swedish botanist, Linnæus.

SECT. 37.—From the Peace of Westphalia to the Revolution in England (A.D. 1648-1688).

A.D.
1649. Charles I. of England beheaded.
    Charles of England slain as a *traitor.*

  ,,   The Commonwealth begins in England.
    the *Commons* of *England swear* to be *true.*

A.D.
1649. Cromwell captures Drogheda and Wexford.
   the *Catholics* are *massacred* in the *southern towns.*

1650. The Marquis of Montrose put to death at Edinburgh.
   cruel Montrose by *Leslie executed.*

,, Cromwell defeats the Scots at Dunbar.
   Cromwell encounters Leslie in *war.*

,, Death of Descartes, mathematician and philosopher.
   a *celebrated mathematician leaves* the *world.*

1651. Charles II. crowned at Scone; defeated at Worcester.
   the *crowned monarch loses* the *battle.*

,, Charles II. escapes to Normandy.
   the *crowned monarch leaves* the *country.*

1652. First war between the English and Dutch.
   a *bloody engagement lamented* by the *Dutch.*

1653. The Dutch fleet destroyed by Admiral Blake.
   a *bloody engagement* off *La Hague.*

,, Oliver Cromwell made Lord Protector.
   the *Commonwealth* of *England elect* their *head.*

1654. A new Parliament is convened at Westminster.
   the *Commons* of *England* in *London assemble.*

1655. The English take possession of Jamaica.
   a *colony* of *England* in a *low latitude.*

1657. Admiral Blake burns a Spanish fleet at Teneriffe.
   burns their *navy laden* with *plate.*

1658. Death of Cromwell: Richard Cromwell Protector.
   Cromwell merits our *lasting regard.*

1659. Peace of the Pyrenees between France and Spain.
   conclude a *matrimonial alliance* by *treaty.*

,, Aurung Zebe, "the Great Mogul," Emperor of Delhi.
   the *chief Mogul elevated* to the *throne.*

1660. Charles II. of England restored to the throne.
   Charles, "the *merry monarch," welcomed.*

,, Isaac Newton enters the University of Cambridge.
   Cambridge the *immortal Newton welcomes.*

1661. Death of Cardinal Mazarin, minister of Louis XIV.
   Cardinal Mazarin the *eminent counsellor.*

A.D.
1661. Corporation and Test Act passed against the Presbyterians.
    an *act nefarious* for its *means* and *objects*.

,, Marquis of Argyle beheaded for treason.
    a *celebrated name* in the *annals* of the *Covenanters*.

1662. Charles II. sells Dunkirk to France for £500,000.
    Charles's need necessitates the *deed*.

,, The Royal Society incorporated by Charles II.
    charters an *institute unrivalled* in *fame*.

,, French Academy of Inscriptions instituted.
    the *Academy* of *Inscriptions* and *Medals founded*.

,, Act of Uniformity; 2000 English clergymen ejected.
    conscientious ministers imprisoned and *fined*.

,, Death of Pascal, author of the 'Provincial Letters.'
    the *brightest name* in the *annals* of *France*.

1663. Steam pump, for raising water, invented by the Marquis of Worcester.
    commencement of the *mightiest invention* of the *age*.

1664. The Conventicle Act passed.
    a *cruel inhuman measure sanctioned*.

1665. Great plague in London: 8000 persons cut off in a week.
    a *contagious* and *mortal malady* in *London*.

1666. Great fire in London; 13,000 houses consumed.
    consumes a *multitude* of *mansions* in the *metropolis*.

,, Four days' conflict between the English fleet and the united squadrons of France and Holland.
    a *bloody engagement* with *united navies*.

,, The 'London Gazette,' the oldest newspaper in England, published.
    begins our *unrivalled metropolitan newspapers*.

,, Battle of Pentland Hills: the Covenanters routed.
    the *Covenanters mercilessly murdered* in *myriads*.

1667. Peace of Breda, which confirms to England Pennsylvania, New York, and New Jersey.
    confirms to *England New-York* and *Pennsylvania*.

,, Milton publishes his famous 'Paradise Lost.'
    the *celebrated Milton's immortal poem*.

MODERN HISTORY. 267

A.D.
1668. Treaty of Aix-la-Chapelle between France and Spain.
   a compact memorable in the *annals* of *Europe*.

1669. Clarendon banished: formation of the "Cabal."
   a cabal of *ministers noted* for *treachery*.

,, Newton invents the differential and integral calculus.
   the *celebrated Newton's novel talisman*.

,, Great eruption of Mount Etna, which continues forty days.
   Calania mourns her *many thousands*.

,, Candia taken by the Turks from Venice.
   Candia included in the *empire* of *Turkey*.

,, Phosphorus discovered by Brandt of Hamburg.
   a chemical ingredient of *immense value*.

1670. The bayonet invented at Bayonne, in France.
   a Bayonnese invents a *powerful weapon*.

1672. Louis XIV. conquers a great part of Holland.
   a beautiful instance of *patriotic fortitude*.

,, The Mississippi discovered by Father Marquelte, a Frenchman.
   the *basin* of the *Mississippi* of *peerless dimensions*.

1673. Death of Molière, the French comic poet.
   a comedian endures the *penalty* of *hypochondria*.

,, Battle of Choczin: the Poles totally defeat the Turks.
   a *battle memorable* in *Polish history*.

1674. Death of John Milton.
   our *choicest English poet slumbers*.

,, John Sobieski, the last independent king of Poland.
   a celebrated name 'mong *Polish sovereigns*.

1675. Royal Observatory of Greenwich founded.
   we *calculate* the *meridian* of *places* from *London*.

,, Turenne, the French general, slain at Sassbach.
   a brave marshal parts with *life*.

1676. Pope Innocent XI. assumes the tiara.
   the *cardinals meet* and *appoint Innocent*.

,, Calico-printing first practised in England.
   calico now printed in *England*.

268   FACTS AND DATES.

A.D.
1677. Bunyan publishes his 'Pilgrim's Progress.'
  Bunyan's immortal 'Pilgrim' published.

1678. Popish plots in England instigated by Titus Oates.
  a crafty malcontent a pension receives.

1679. The *Habeas Corpus* Act passed in England.
  a charter of immense practical value.

,, The Long Parliament dissolved : Danby impeached.
  the Commons imprison the premier in the Tower.

,, Battle of Drumclog : Claverhouse defeated.
  the Covenanters for once prove victorious.

,, Battle of Bothwell Bridge : the Covenanters defeated.
  their cruel enemies pursue them with vengeance.

,, Peace of Nimeguen bet. France and United Provinces.
  conclude at Nimeguen a peaceful treaty.

1680. Carolina established as a British colony.
  Carolina memorable in the recent war.

,, The political distinction of "Whig" and "Tory" begins in England.
  the Conservatives name their rivals " Whigs."

1681. London first lighted with oil lamps.
  causes immense rejoicings in the capital.

1682. Peter the Great ascends the throne of Russia.
  the Czar who made Russia formidable.

1683. The Rye-House Plots : Lord Russel and Algernon Sydney executed.
  clandestine meetings in the Rye-House held.

,, Siege of Vienna : the Turks defeated by the Poles.
  a countless multitude routed by the Germans.

1684. Treaty of Ratisbon : peace between France, Spain, and Germany.
  the cautious emperor restores Strasbourg.

1685. Death of Charles II. : accession of James II.
  a Catholic monarch restrains our liberty.

,, Battle of Sedgemoor between the Royalists and the Duke of Monmouth.
  the banner of Monmouth, " Religious Liberty."

A.D.
1685. Revocation of the Edict of Nantes by Louis XIV.
bands of *emigrants arrive* in *London.*

1686. League of Augsburg against France.
a *contract meant* to *restrain ambition.*

1687. Sir Isaac Newton completes his 'Principia.'
the *celebrated Newton reveals* his *philosophy.*

SECT 38.—From the English Revolution to the Peace of Utrecht (1688-1713).

A.D.
1688. The Revolution in England: James II. abdicates.
benefits innumerable result from the *revolution.*

„ Death of John Bunyan.
composed an *immortal religious romance.*

1689. Accession of William and Mary: Toleration Act.
the *charters* of *England renewed* on *oath.*

„ Battle of Killiecrankie, and death of Claverhouse.
a *bloody malignant receives* his *verdict.*

„ Episcopacy abolished in Scotland, and Presbyterianism established.
the *Covenanters now rejoice* in *turn.*

„ Siege of Londonderry by James II.
the *brave Enniskilliners resist* the *tyrant.*

1690. Battle of the Boyne: total defeat of James II.
a *bloody engagement terminates* the *war.*

1692. Massacre of Glencoe by order of William III.
a *bloody massacre tarnishes* his *fame.*

„ Battle off La Hague between France and the Allies.
in a *bloody engagement* they *vanquish* the *French.*

„ Battle of Steinkirk: the French defeat the Allies.
a *battle memorable* among the *victories* of *France.*

1694. Mary, Queen of England, dies.
the *career* of *Mary terminates* by *small-pox.*

„ Bank of England established, the first in the land.
the *Bank* of *England* in *Threadneedle Street.*

1695. Namur taken from the French by William III.
the *capture* of *Namur vexes Louis.*

A.D.
1695. Dryden publishes his translation of Virgil.
   the *celebrated Æneid* of *Virgil* is *launched.*
1696. Peter the Great takes and fortifies Azov.
   Cossack incursions terminate now.
  ,,   Newcoming invents the atmospheric steam-engine.
   a *curious, new,* and *valuable invention.*
1697. Peace of Ryswick : wars of the Grand Alliance cease.
   conclude in the *Netherlands* a *treaty* of *peace.*
  ,,   Battle of Zenta : the Turks totally defeated.
   a *bloody engagement* with the *Turks* at *Zenta.*
  ,,   Charles XII. ascends the throne of Sweden.
   Charles mounts the *throne* at *Upsala.*
1698. Peter the Great visits England, and labours in the docks at Deptford.
   a *celebrated monarch toils* in an *arsenal.*
  ,,   The Scots attempt to found a colony at Darien.
   a *bubble* of *emigration terminates* in *ruin.*
  ,,   Secret treaty of the Hague for the partition of the Spanish dominions.
   the *court* of *Madrid* in a *violent rage.*
1699. Peace of Carlowitz between Austria and Turkey.
   concludes a *memorable treaty* with *Turkey.*
1700. Accession of Philip V. of Spain : the Spanish war of succession.
   the *accession* of *Philip excites* a *war.*
  ,,   Charles XII. defeats the Russians at Narva.
   Charles and *Peter* at *war* for *years.*
  ,,   Death of Dryden, the poet.
   a *British poet* of *excellence expires.*
1701. Charles XII. defeats the Poles near Riga.
   the *courageous Poles* by a *youth* are *beaten.*
  ,,   Death of James II. at St Germains.
   an *object* of *pity expires abroad.*
1702. Death of William III. : accession of Queen Anne.
   the *court* of this *queen* for " *wits* " is *famous.*
  ,,   England at war with France and Spain.
   our *beautiful queen* at *war* with *France.*

A.D.
1703. Peter the Great founds St Petersburg.
Czar Peter in *want* of a *harbour*.

1704. Battle of Blenheim : the Duke of Marlborough defeats the French and Bavarians.
Britain presents the *warrior* with an *estate*.

„ Gibraltar taken from Spain by Sir George Rooke.
a *celebrated promontory wrested* from *Spain*.

„ Death of Locke, the celebrated English philosopher.
a *celebrated philosopher* at *Wrington sleeps*.

1706. Battle of Ramilies : Marlborough defeats the French.
the *Belgian populace witness* the *engagement*.

„ Birth of Benjamin Franklin at Boston.
a *celebrated patriot* in the *War* of *Independence*.

1707. Legislative union between England and Scotland.
a *common Parliament extends* our *power*.

„ Charles XII. invades Poland, and places Stanislaus on the throne.
Charles and *Peter* at *war* in *Poland*.

„ Battle of Almance : the Allies defeated by the French and Spaniards.
Berwick in the *Peninsular war prevails*.

„ Death of Aurung Zebe, "the Great Mogul."
a *celebrated prince* for *wealth* and *power*.

1708. Battle of Oudenarde : Marlborough and Eugene defeat the French.
blast the *Pretender's expectation* of *reigning*.

„ The English take Sardinia and Minorca from Spain.
Britain prosecutes the *war resolutely*.

1709. Battle of Poltowa : Charles XII. signally defeated by Peter the Great.
the *Czar* at *Poltowa wins* a *victory*.

„ Battle of Malplaquet : the French defeated by Marlborough and Prince Eugene.
the *brave prince* a *wounded victor*.

1710. St Paul's Cathedral, in London, completed.
the *cathedral* of (St) *Paul* was *built* by *Wren*.

A.D.
1710. The Sacheverell riots in London.
a churchman preaches against *Bolingbroke* and *Oxford*.

1711. Capitulation of the Pruth bet. Russia and Turkey.
the *capitulation* of the *Pruth accomplished* by *Catharine*.

,, The 'Spectator' begins to be published in London.
a *celebrated periodical begins* in the *capital*.

1713. Peace of Utrecht: end of the war of the Spanish succession: Nova Scotia ceded to Britain by France.
a *celebrated peace concluded* in *Holland*.

SECT. 39.—From the Peace of Utrecht to the Treaty of Aix-la-Chapelle (1713-1748).

A.D.
1713. Death of Queen Anne: George I. (Elector of Hanover) accedes to the throne.
a *childless queen changes* the *succession*.

1715. Rebellion in Scotland: battles of Sheriffmuir and Preston.
the *champions* of the *Pretender beaten* by the *Elector*.

,, Accession of Louis XV. of France.
called by the *people* "*Beloved Louis.*"

1716. Prince Eugene's campaign against the Turks.
Belgrade and *Peterwardein change masters*.

1717. The pianoforte invented by Schröder of Dresden.
Broadwood's pianos & *Collard's preferred*.

1718. Charles XII. killed at the siege of Frederickshall.
the *champion* of *Protestantism brave* and *romantic*.

1719. Death of Addison the essayist, and of Flamsteed the astronomer.
our *choicest prose contributor vanishes*.

,, Quadruple alliance: Britain, France, Austria, and Holland against Spain.
Britain a *party* to a *celebrated treaty*.

1720. The Mississippi and South Sea bubbles burst.
bubbles of *peerless advantage explode*.

A.D.
1720. Ruins of Pompeii and Herculaneum discovered.
   the *city* of *Pompeii's famous excavations.*
1721. Sir Robert Walpole becomes Prime Minister.
   a *celebrated politician* his *administration begins.*
  ,, ,, Inoculation for small-pox introduced into England.
   a *course practised* at *first* on *criminals.*
1722. Last execution for witchcraft in Scotland (at Dornoch).
   believed to be *possessed* by *foul demons.*
  ,, Death of the Duke of Marlborough.
   a *courageous Protestant* of *distinguished fame.*
1723. Death of Sir Christopher Wren.
   his *country* is *proud* of his *distinguished genius.*
1725. Death of Peter the Great: accession of Catharine.
   the *Czar Peter* of *fame illustrious.*
1726. Great earthquake at Palermo: 6000 lives lost.
   the *city* of *Palermo fearfully menaced.*
1727. Death of George I.: accession of George II.
   our *beloved prince dies* of *apoplexy.*
  ,, Death of Sir Isaac Newton.
   a *celebrated philosopher departs* in *peace.*
1728. Great fire in Copenhagen: 650 houses destroyed.
   a *city* in *Zealand* by *fire* is *ravaged.*
  ,, Congress of Soissons.
   crafty politicians in *France arrive.*
  ,, Béhring Strait discovered: Asia found to be separate from the New World.
   a *chasm appears dividing* the *Russias.*
1729. Treaty of Seville, bet. Britain, France, and Spain.
   they *contract* in the *Peninsula* a *famous treaty.*
  ,, The city of Baltimore, in Maryland, founded.
   on the *banks* of the *Patapsco* they *found* a *town.*
1730. Earthquake in China: 100,000 perish in Pekin.
   the *citizens* of *Pekin* are *greatly excited.*
1731. Treaty between Britain, Spain, and Germany.
   Britain, the *Peninsula,* and *Germany concur.*

s

A.D.
1732. Birth of George Washington, the American patriot.
   birth of a *patriot* to *guide* its *destinies.*

" Linnæus, the Swedish naturalist, sets out for Lapland.
   the *botanist* of *Upsal gathering flowers!*

" The Jesuits expelled from China.
   the *Chinese persecute* the *holy fathers.*

" Potatoes begin to be cultivated in Scotland.
   they *cultivate potatoes* in the *gardens* of *Edinburgh.*

1734. Commercial treaty between Britain and Russia.
   commerce and *peace are helpful to states.*

1736. The Porteous Riot in Edinburgh.
   Captain Porteous hanged by the *mob.*

" Francis, Duke of Lorraine, marries Maria Theresa, daughter of Charles VI.
   the *beautiful Queen* of *Hungary* is *married.*

" Death of Fahrenheit, inventor of the thermometer.
   a *celebrated philosopher* and *heat measurer.*

" Kouli Knan (Nadir Shah) becomes King of Persia.
   the *celebrated Persian hero enthroned.*

1737. War between Germany and Turkey.
   a *Christian prince humbled* by the *Porte.*

1738. Nadir Shah subdues Afghanistan.
   the *celebrated Persian hero reduces* it.

" The Russians invade the Crimea.
   the *Crimea penetrated* by *hosts* of *Russians.*

" John Wesley begins to found the sect of Methodists.
   a *celebrated preacher heads* a *reform.*

1739. War between Britain and Spain: capture of Puerto Bello.
   capture of *Puerto* by the *gallant Vernon.*

" Peace of Belgrade, humiliating to Austria.
   Belgrade passes from *Germans* to *Turks.*

" Nadir Shah invades India, and plunders Delhi.
   carries to *Persia* its *hoarded treasures.*

" Clayton produces carburetted hydrogen (coal-gas).
   Clayton's primitive gas evolved.

A.D.

1740. Death of Charles VI., who is succeeded by Maria Theresa: war of the Austrian succession.
   her accession plunges Austria in war.

,, Frederick II. (the Great) becomes King of Prussia.
   an acute politician and sage writer.

1741. Cartagena (S. America) bombarded by Ad. Vernon.
   bombards a principal Spanish city.

,, Linnæus founds the Academy of Sciences.
   the botanist of Upsal establishes an academy.

1742. Charles VII. (of Bavaria), Emperor of Germany.
   Charles is proclaimed sovereign at Frankfort.

,, Peace of Breslau between Austria and Prussia.
   Breslau passes from Austria to Frederick.

,, The Grenville Administration in England begins.
   begins to be Premier a statesman of fame.

1743. George II. defeats the French at Dettingen.
   Britain's prestige sustained by George.

,, France plans an invasion in favour of the Chevalier.
   a bold pretender sanguinely hopes.

,, Peace of Abo between Sweden and Russia—the Duke of Holstein to succeed Ulrica.
   Britain promotes the succession of Holstein.

1744. Britain declares war against France.
   Britain prepares for a sanguinary struggle.

,, Admiral Anson completes his voyage round the world.
   Britain promotes a successful sailor.

,, Death of Alexander Pope, the English poet.
   a brilliant poet and splendid scholar.

,, Mr Pelham becomes Prime Minister of England.
   Chatham or Pitt serves as a subaltern.

1745. The quadruple alliance between Britain, Austria, Holland, and Poland.
   Britain, Poland, and Austria allied.

,, The Pretender lands in the Highlands of Scotland.
   Charles the Pretender supported by Lochiel.

A.D.
1745. Battle of Prestonpans, between the Pretender and Sir John Cope.
the *chivalrous prince succeeds* in *Lothian.*

,, Francis I. (of Lorraine) becomes Emperor of Germany.
they *crown* the *petty sovereign* of *Lorraine.*

1746. Battle of Falkirk : the Chevalier victorious.
the *chivalrous prince* by *success intoxicated.*

,, Battle of Culloden : the Pretender totally defeated by the Duke of Cumberland.
Cumberland quenches the *Jacobite insurrection.*

,, Dreadful earthquake in Peru—Lima destroyed.
the *coast* of *Peru shaken* and *inundated.*

,, Princeton College, New Jersey, founded.
the *College* of *Princeton established* in *New-England.*

1747. Great naval victories over the French at Cape Finisterre and Belleisle.
the *citizens* of *Paris* are *seized* with a *panic.*

,, Lords Lovat, Kilmarnock, and Balmerino beheaded.
they *behead* the *Pretender's stanch partisans.*

,, The indigo plant first cultivated in the United States.
calico printing successfully prosecuted.

1748. Death of James Thomson, the Scottish poet.
the *celebrated poet* of " the *Seasons* " *rests.*

,, Peace of Aix-la-Chapelle between England, France, Spain, Austria, and Holland.
concord among the *principal states* of *Europe.*

SECT. 40.—From the Peace of Aix-la-Chapelle to the American War of Independence (A.D. 1749-1774).

A.D.
1749. League between the Pope and the Venetians against the Algerines.
bands of *pirates* are *sunk* by the *Venetians.*

1750. Commercial treaty between Great Britain and Spain.
commerce and *peace* in *lieu* of *war.*

A.D.
1751. Arcot, in India, captured by Lord Clive.
Clive proves himself an *illustrious commander*.

1752. The New Style adopted in England.
the *calendar passes* over *eleven days*.

,, Franklin proves the identity of lightning and electricity.
the *clouds* are *proved* to be *electric* by *Franklin*.

,, China-ware first manufactured in England.
china produced of *elegant forms*.

1753. The British Museum established in Montagu House.
a *collection* of the *productions* of *all* the *globe*.

1754. Great earthquake at Cairo.
the *colossal pyramids* alone *escape*.

1755. Samuel Johnson publishes his English Dictionary.
a *celebrated epoch* in our *living language*.

,, Great earthquakes in Portugal and South America.
the *cities* of *Quito* and *Lisbon* are *levelled*.

,, Britain and Prussia at war with France, Austria, and Russia—the Seven Years' War.
Britain and *Prussia allied* from *interest*.

,, Minorca taken from Britain by the French.
Byng pusillanimously loses Minorca.

,, Calcutta captured by the Nabob of Bengal.
the *British prisoners* are *alive entombed*.

1757. Battle of Plassey: the Nabob of Bengal signally defeated by the British.
Clive procures his *laurels* at *Plassey*.

,, Damiens, a lunatic, attempts to assassinate Louis XV.
the *cruel prince* a *lunatic punishes*.

,, The Austrians defeated by the Prussians at Lieberk.
beaten by the *Prussians* at *Lieberk* and *Prague*.

,, The Austrians and French defeated by the Prussians at Rosbach.
the *courageous Prussians* their *laurels procure*.

1758. Cape Breton taken from the French by the British.
a *British possession* by *Lawrence retaken*.

278   FACTS AND DATES.

A.D.
1758. Britain seizes the French possessions in Senegambia.
capture the *possessions* of *Louis* on the *river*.

1759. Quebec taken from the French by General Wolfe.
we *capture Quebec*, but *lose* the *victor*.

,, The French defeated by the Allied army under Prince Ferdinand at Minden, Westphalia.
the *courageous prince* and the *allies victorious*.

,, The French fleet destroyed by Admiral Boscawen.
Boscawen procures at *Lagos* a *victory*.

,, Admiral Hawke defeats the French fleet near Brest.
the *British Parliament loudly triumphs*.

1760. Canada wrested by Britain from France.
Canada passes to *new owners*.

,, Lord Clive returns to England, laden with booty.
created a *peer* for his *Indian exploits*.

,, Death of George II., and accession of George III.
accession of a *prince* of *inflexible will*.

,, The Prussians defeat the Austrians at Torgau.
a *brave Prussian's noble exploit*.

1761. The first canal in Britain constructed.
Brindley plans the *Manchester canal*.

,, Pondicherry captured from the French.
capture of *Pondicherry* by an *English commodore*.

,, War between Britain and Spain — the Bourbon "Family Compact."
a *compact* to *promote* the *interests* of *Bourbons*.

1762. Manilla and Havana taken by the English from Spain.
conquest of the *Philippines* by an *English fleet*.

1763. Seven Years' War ends: peace at Paris: our national debt increased by £75,000,000.
Britain at *peace* with her *neighbours again*.

,, Watt greatly improves Newcomen's steam-engine.
the *ablest practical invention* of the *age*.

,, Hargraves invents the spinning-jenny.
a *curious application* of *machinery* to *hand-looms*.

,, Accession of Catharine II. to the throne of Russia.
a *celebrated patroness* of *men* of *genius*.

A.D.
1764. Byron sets out on his voyage round the world.
   on the *coasts* of *Patagonia* he *encounters storms*.

" The King of Oude defeated by the English at Buxar.
   a *celebrated potentate* of *India subdued*.

" A duty imposed on all American goods brought to England.
   an *Act* of *Parliament* of *momentous issue*.

" Accession of Stanislaus II., last king of Poland.
   Catharine's paramour made a *sovereign*.

1765. Joseph II., Emperor of Germany.
   a *cautious prince, moderate* and *liberal*.

" The American Stamp Act: the colonies rebel.
   an *Act* of *Parliament* to *mutiny leads*.

1766. The Stamp Act repealed, but the *right* of taxing maintained.
   colonial patriots murmur at the *measure*.

" Bruce begins his travels in Asia Minor, Abyssinia, &c.
   Bruce proceeds on a *memorable mission*.

" The Isle of Man purchased from the Duke of Athol.
   the *British purchase Mona* for *money*.

1767. Wallis and Carterel's discoveries in the South Seas.
   Carterel proceeds on a *mission* to the *Pacific*.

1768. Cook explores New Holland and New Zealand.
   Cook proceeds on a *mission* of *research*.

" Royal Academy established by Sir Joshua Reynolds.
   the *Academy's president* an *eminent artist*.

" Corsica ceded to France by the Genoese.
   the *Corsicans prefer* the *empire* to the *republic*.

1769. Napoleon I. born at Ajaccio, in Corsica.
   born the *prince* of *ambitious tyrants*.

1770. Euler publishes his Algebra at St Petersburg.
   the *Academy* of *Petersburg published* the *work*.

1771. Death of Gray, author of "Elegy in a Country Churchyard."
   a *beautiful poem perpetuates* his *celebrity*.

A.D.
1772. First partition of Poland between Russia, Prussia, and Austria.
    the *celebrated partition* of *Poland determined* on.

1773. Captain Cook sets out on his second voyage.
    Cook proceeds to the *Pacific again*.

,, Society of the Jesuits abolished by Clement XIV.
    abolished by the *papal pontiff, Ganganelli.*

SECT. 41.—From the American War to the French Revolution (A.D. 1774-1789).

A.D.
1774. The American War of Independence begins.
    begin their *quarrel* with the *parent state.*

,, Warren Hastings first Governor-General of India.
    the *British Parliament appoints* him *supreme.*

,, Death of Oliver Goldsmith, the distinguished Irish poet and naturalist.
    a *celebrated poet quits* the *scene.*

,, Death of Louis XV.: accession of Louis XVI.
    began as a *powerful* and *popular king.*

1775. Battle of Bunker's Hill, near Boston.
    colonial patriots purchase their *laurels.*

,, General Washington appointed Commander-in-Chief of the colonial forces.
    a *courageous patriot appointed* their *leader.*

1776. The American Declaration of Independence.
    colonial patriots publish their *manifesto.*

,, General Howe takes Long Island, New York, and part of New Jersey.
    bombards the *principal ports* of the *insurgents.*

,, Necker becomes Director of Finance in France.
    a *celebrated Protestant appointed minister.*

1777. Battle of Brandywine: capture of Philadelphia.
    the *British prevail* at *Philadelphia* in *Pennsylvania.*

,, Battle of Saratoga: General Burgoyne, with all his army, surrenders to the colonists.
    colonial patriots prove their *zeal.*

A.D.
1778. France recognises the independence of the British colonies: Britain declares war against France.
Britain opposed by a *powerful rival.*

,, Spain offers to mediate between Britain and the colonies.
the *British Parliament proudly refuses* it.

,, Death of Linnæus, the eminent Swedish botanist.
the *botanist* of *Upsal quietly rests.*

1779. Spain declares war against Britain, and, along with France, besieges Gibraltar.
Britain opposed by a *powerful trio.*

,, Captain Cook, on his third voyage, is killed at Hawaii, in the Sandwich Islands.
the *captain perishes* in the *perilous voyage.*

1780. Sir G. Rodney defeats the Spanish fleet off Cape St Vincent.
Britain is *proud* of *Rodney,* her *warrior.*

,, Charleston, South Carolina, surrenders to the British.
the *colonial patriot army worsted.*

,, Lord George Gordon Riots in London.
a *crowd* of *Protestant rioters executed.*

1781. Cornwallis defeats the colonial army at Guildford.
the *colonial patriot army beaten.*

,, Cornwallis surrenders to the united American and French army at Yorktown.
the *cowardly peer retires* from the *contest.*

,, Necker is succeeded by Calonne as Finance Minister.
the *celebrated Protestant resigns* his *charge.*

,, Sir W. Herschell discovers the planet Uranus.
the *beautiful planet Uranus observed.*

,, Immanuel Kant publishes his 'Critic of Pure Reason.'
the '*Critic* of *Pure Reason*' *composed.*

1782. Elliot gallantly defends Gibraltar against the powerful armaments of France and Spain.
the *British persistently resist* their *efforts.*

,, Rodney defeats the French fleet off Dominica.
created a *peer* for *routing* the *French.*

A.D.

1782. Wedgewood invents the pyrometer for measuring the heat of furnaces.
a clay pyrometer is reduced in dimensions.

1783. Treaty of Versailles: Britain acknowledges the independence of the United States.
her colonial possessions relinquished grudgingly.

„ William Pitt becomes Prime Minister of England.
a celebrated Parliamentary orator at the helm.

1784. Peace concluded between Great Britain and Holland.
they cede their possessions in the remote seas.

„ Peace between the English and Tippoo Sahib in India.
conclude a peace with Rajah Sahib.

„ First aerial voyage in England by Vincent Leonardi.
his balloon appears as it rises in the sky.

„ Mail-coaches supersede post-horses in England.
a Bristol patriot reforms the system.

1785. The Queen of France loses her popularity: "the diamond necklace."
the accomplished queen ruined by Lamotte.

1786. Warren Hastings impeached in Parliament.
a bold Parliamentary orator impeaches him.

„ Lord Cornwallis appointed Governor-General of India.
Cornwallis appointed to rule in India.

„ Death of Frederick the Great: accession of Frederick-William to the throne of Prussia.
a capricious potentate ruined by indolence.

„ Commercial treaty between England and France.
commerce appeases the rivalry of nations.

1787. The colony of New South Wales established.
our convicts proceed to a remote penitentiary.

„ Wilberforce and Clarkson denounce slavery.
the British Parliament roused by their pleadings.

„ The Assembly of Notables meets at Versailles.
Colonne proposes to restore the equipoise.

1788. Brienne retires, and Necker is recalled by Louis.
the Catholic prelate relieved of the reins.

A.D.
1788. Death of Prince Charles Edward at Rome.
    the *chivalrous Pretender retires* to his *rest.*
,,   The Quakers of Philadelphia emancipate their slaves.
    conscientious Quakers restore them their *rights.*

CHAP. IX.—FROM THE FRENCH REVOLUTION TO THE PRESENT TIME (A.D. 1789-1869).

It would be difficult to find in any age or country an event of a purely secular nature that can vie in importance with the French Revolution. We have now in these pages surveyed several thousand leading events—events belonging to all countries of the globe, and to the seven millenniums that have elapsed since human history began; but, laying aside the Universal Deluge, the Call of Abraham, and the Birth of Christ (all of which partake of the *supernatural*), we have nowhere discovered an event which, in the interests that were at stake, the passions brought into play, or the magnitude of the results, can fairly compare with this tremendous revolution. The mighty empires of ancient times were founded or overthrown with much noise and bloodshed, but, generally speaking, each of them left the world and the human race very much as it found them. Originating in the avarice or ambition of the individual actors, they were carried into effect by mere physical force, and not by intellect, reason, or justice. Or if, in later ages, we detect intellectual and moral *ideas* at work—as in the achievements of Mohammed, Hildebrand, and the Crusaders—we see them assuming the degenerate forms of fanaticism and superstition. Nowhere did the conquerors make an indelible impression on the race, or ameliorate the condition of society. Some great inventions and discoveries—as the arts of writing and of printing, the variation of the needle, and the law of gravitation—have, indeed, produced mighty and manifold changes, but in every instance these changes have been silent, slow, and gradual; whereas the great revolution which ushered in the present age, and which has given tone and character to all its main events, burst on the world with all the suddenness of a volcano, shaking to its foundations the country in which it occurred, and darkening the heavens of all civilised lands.

SECT. 42.—From the Meeting of the States-General to the Death of Louis XVI. (A.D. 1789-1793).

A.D.
1789. The States-General convoked to meet at Versailles.
a celebrated quarrel which ruins thrones.

,, The States-General assume the title of " the National Assembly."
an Abbé proposes to repair to Tennis-Court.

,, The Bastile broken open, and the Governor massacred.
begins the popular "reign of terror."

,, The princes and chief nobility leave France.
Condé and the princes retire voluntarily.

,, The National Assembly adopts the declaration of " the Rights of Man."
the culminating point of the era of tumult.

,, Washington becomes first President of the U. States.
a celebrated patriot raised to authority.

,, The Federal Constitution accepted by all the States.
the coloured people remain in vassalage.

1790. France divided by the National Assembly into eighty-five departments.
change is paramount every where.

,, Louis swears fidelity to the new Constitution.
the common people in thousands witness it.

,, Titles of nobility and monastic establishments abolished in France.
the convents pulled down and titles exscinded.

,, The National Guard (of 300,000 citizens) instituted.
the citizens of Paris trained to war.

,, Death of George Howard and of Benjamin Franklin.
celebrated for philanthropy in their various walks.

A.D.
1791. Mirabeau becomes President of the National Assembly.
    becomes their *President* at a *trying crisis.*

,, The King and royal family escape from Paris, but are captured at Varenne.
    the *citizens* of *Paris* in the *Tuilcries confine* them.

,, Riots in Birmingham: Dr Priestley's house destroyed.
    chastise Priestley the *atheistical chemist!*

,, Death of John Wesley, the founder of Methodism.
    an *able* and *zealous teacher* of *Christianity.*

,, Galvani discovers electro-magnetism.
    a *curious play* at *telegraphic communication.*

1792. Death of Leopold II.: accession of Francis II.
    accedes to *power* during a *violent ferment.*

,, The Allied army (Prussian, Austrian, and Dutch) cross the French frontiers.
    they *came* to *quell* the *tumult* in *France.*

,, The Tuileries attacked: the Swiss Guard massacred.
    the *beautiful queen* in *violent dismay.*

,, The Allied army defeated by Dumouriez.
    boldly punishes the *violators* of the *frontier.*

,, The National Convention (Robespierre, Murat, and Danton) constituted.
    accession to *power* of *violent demagogues.*

,, Louis deposed by the National Convention: France declared a Republic.
    the *blood* of the *prince vociferously demanded.*

,, France offers support to all nations desiring liberty.
    a *call* to the *peoples* to *overthrow despotism.*

1793. Louis condemned to death by the Convention.
    consign their *prince* a *victim* to the *guillotine.*

SECT. 43.—From the Death of Louis XVI. to the Election of Napoleon as First Consul (A.D. 1793-1799).

A.D.
1793. France declares war against Britain and Holland.
    they *begin* the *quarrel* by *attacking Holland.*

A.D.
1793. The English and Dutch fleets defeated by the French off Cape St Vincent.
they begin the quarrel by tarnishing our glory.

,, The Queen condemned to death by the Convention.
the beautiful queen a victim to the guillotine.

,, Napoleon Buonaparte first distinguishes himself at the siege of Toulon.
begins to appear the terror of the age.

1794. Howe defeats the French fleet off Ushant.
a British peer victorious at sea.

,, Robespierre and twenty of his partisans guillotined.
the cruel paragon of tyranny suffers.

,, Battle of Warsaw: destruction of Polish independence.
the courageous Poles vanquished by Suwarrow.

,, Death of Edward Gibbon, author of 'History of Decline and Fall of the Roman Empire.'
brilliantly portrays its various stages.

1795. The French overrun Holland: the Stadtholder escapes.
brave Pichegru victorious in the Low-Countries.

,, Mungo Park sets out on his first African expedition.
the celebrated Park travels to Ludamar.

,, Cape Colony and Ceylon taken by the English.
their colonial possessions are taken by Elphinstone.

,, Maynooth College, Ireland, founded and endowed.
Catholic priests vociferate for liberty!

,, Peace concluded at Basle between France and Prussia.
concludes with Prussia a treaty of alliance.

,, The French Royalists rebel against the Convention: are suppressed by Napoleon Buonaparte.
Buonaparte proves a victorious leader.

,, Final partition of Poland between Russia, Austria, and Prussia.
the courageous Poles outlive their liberty.

1796. Napoleon commences his Italian campaign.
Buonaparte proves victorious at Montenotte.

A.D.
1796. Napoleon defeats the Austrians at Lodi.
    the bridge is passed by the victorious Napoleon.

,, Death of Robert Burns, the national poet of Scotland.
    his beautiful poems his truest monument.

,, Treaty of Ildefonso between France and Spain.
    they conclude a peace vexatious to England.

1797. Admiral Jervis defeats the French and Spanish fleets off Cape St Vincent.
    Britain's prestige vindicated in Portugal.

,, Commercial panic in England : the Bank of England stops payment.
    bank paper in temporary payment.

,, Mutiny of the English fleets at Spithead and the Nore.
    the British Parliament in terrible panic.

,, Death of Edmund Burke, statesman and orator.
    the British Parliament's truest pride.

,, Great naval victory by Admiral Duncan over the Dutch off Camperdown.
    Britain is proud of her valiant peer.

,, Peace of Campo Formio between France and Austria: the latter cedes the Low Countries and the Ionian Islands to France.
    Buonaparte's perfidy to Venice appears.

,, Napoleon returns from Italy to Paris.
    Buonaparte proclaimed the victorious " Pacificator."

1798. Napoleon suppresses the Papal Government, and imprisons the Pope.
    the Catholic pontiff vacates Rome.

,, Napoleon embarks for Egypt, and takes Alexandria.
    Buonaparte proceeds from Toulon with an army.

,, Battle of the Pyramids : Buonaparte defeats Murad Bey, and enters Cairo.
    battle of the Pyramids, a terrible rout!

,, Battle of the Nile : Nelson totally defeats the French.
    Buonaparte paralysed by a tremendous reverse.

,, Rebellion in Ireland under Lord Fitzgerald.
    Catholics and Protestants in treasonable revolt.

FACTS AND DATES.

A.D.
1799. Bass and Flinders prove Tasmania an island.
boldly pass between *Victoria* and *Tasmania*.

,, Seringapatam taken by Sir David Baird: Tippoo Sahib killed.
Baird prevails over the *valiant Tippoo*.

,, Siege of Acre: Napoleon defeated by Sir S. Smith.
checks the *progress* of the *triumphant victor*.

,, Death of George Washington, first President of the United States.
they *bury* the *President* at *Vernon, Virginia*.

,, Napoleon, in Paris, is proclaimed "First Consul."
Buonaparte placed at the *top* of the *tree*.

SECT. 44.—From the Election of the First Consul to the Battle of Austerlitz (A.D. 1799-1805).

A.D.
1800. The Nabob of Surat resigns his government to the British.
British rule extending widely.

,, Napoleon crosses the Alps into Italy with an army of 50,000 men.
his *chariot rides* on the *wings* of the *wind!*

,, Battle of Marengo: Napoleon defeats the Austrians.
Buonaparte's rule is *widely extended*.

,, Battle of Hohenlinden: the Austrians signally defeated by the French.
the *brave republicans win* in the *war*.

,, Death of William Cowper, poet, author of 'The Task.'
Cowper at *rest*, and *weary* of the *world*.

,, Seat of Government of United States changed from Philadelphia to Washington.
the *capital removed wisely* to *Washington*.

1801. Legislative Union of Great Britain and Ireland.
Britain and *Ireland* are *wedded* in *bonds*.

,, Treaty of Luneville between Germany and France.
the *course* of the *Rhine*, her *western boundary*.

A.D.
1801. Pitt resigns the premiership : accession of Addington.
   a brief rest in an extraordinary career.

   ,, Abercromby defeats the French at Alexandria.
   the bold Republicans expelled the country.

   ,, Paul I. assassinated : accession of Alexander I.
   the Czar of Russia expires in blood.

   ,, First regular census of the United Kingdom taken : population, 15,942,646.
   begin to reckon by exact census.

   ,, Nelson destroys the Danish fleet at Copenhagen.
   " Britannia rules the waves" bravely !

   ,, Convention between England and Russia—Alexander withdraws from the Northern League.
   the Czar resolves to withdraw from the Confederacy.

   ,, The Surrey tram-railway, the first in Britain.
   cars run from Wandsworth to Croydon.

   ,, Ceres, the first of the minor planets, discovered by Piazzi at Palermo.
   Bode's rule is wonderfully confirmed.

1802. Peace of Amiens between Britain, France, and Spain.
   Britain rests in her war with France.

   ,, Napoleon elected First Consul for life.
   the Corsican rules by the will of France.

   ,, Cape Colony restored to the Dutch by England.
   Britain restores the extremity of Africa.

   ,, Ohio enters the American Union as the 17th State.
   the colossal Republic extends her domain.

1803. Tasmania established as a penal colony.
   convicted rogues exported to Hobart-Town.

   ,, Louisiana purchased from France by the States.
   cotton is raised and exported hence.

   ,, Britain renews the war with France.
   Britain renews the war in haste.

   ,, The French overrun Hanover.
   Buonaparte resumes the war in Hanover.

   ,, Delhi retaken by General Lake from the Mahrattas.
   Britain resists the warlike Holcar.

T

290 FACTS AND DATES.

A.D.
1804. Mungo Park sets out on his 2d voyage of discovery.
   bravely returns to explore the *Joliba*.

,, Duke d'Enghien murdered by order of Napoleon.
   Buonaparte rues his *wrath* and *jealousy*.

,, Napoleon crowned "Emperor of the French."
   Buonaparte reigns in the *West supreme*.

,, Pitt reappointed Prime Minister of England.
   called to *reoccupy* his *wonted station*.

,, Spain declares war against England.
   Britain resumes the *war* with *Spain*.

1805. Third coalition against France, of England, Russia, Austria, and Sweden.
   Britain and *Russia* in *willing alliance*.

,, Napoleon, at Milan, is proclaimed "King of Italy."
   the *crown* of *iron is wrested* from *Lombardy*.

,, Napoleon prepares an armament to invade England.
   he *comes* to *ravage* our *western land*.

,, Battle of Trafalgar: Nelson destroys the French and Spanish fleets, but is mortally wounded.
   "*Britannia rules* the *waves*" alone.

,, Battle of Austerlitz—the Allies signally defeated.
   Buonaparte regains his *wonted laurels*.

SECT. 45.—From the Battle of Austerlitz to Napoleon's Retreat from Moscow (A.D. 1805-1812).

A.D.
1806. Cape Colony seized by the English from the Dutch.
   Baird restores our *wonted mastery*.

,, Death of Pitt, and of his rival, C. J. Fox.
   the *British realm* in *weeds* of *mourning*.

,, Napoleon makes his brothers, Joseph and Louis, kings of Naples and Holland respectively.
   the *brothers reign* by the *will* of *Napoleon*.

,, The "Confederation of the Rhine" formed, with Napoleon as Protector.
   the *Confederation* of the *Rhine* his *willing instrument*.

MODERN HISTORY. 291

A.D.
1806. Sir J. Stuart defeats the French at Maida, in Calabria.
   our *chivalrous regiments worst* him at *Maida.*
,, The King of Prussia declares war against Napoleon.
   a *celebrated ruler* at *war* with *Napoleon.*
,, Battle of Jena: the power of Prussia annihilated.
   blood and *ruin* in the *wake* of *Napoleon.*
,, Napoleon issues his famous Berlin Decrees.
   Buonaparte's revenge for the *exploits* of our *navy.*
1807. Battle of Eylau: Napoleon defeats the Russian army.
   Buonaparte routs them at *Eylau,* in *Prussia.*
,, Treaty of Tilsit between France, Russia, and Prussia.
   compels them to *ratify* his *worst proceedings.*
,, Conspiracy of the Prince of Asturias against the King of Spain.
   the *Corsican resorts* to *extreme perfidy.*
,, Copenhagen bombarded, and the Danish fleet seized by the British under Cathcart and Gambier.
   Cathcart receives his *wages* from *Parliament.*
,, Treaty of Fontainebleau for the partition of Portugal between France and Spain.
   Braganza is *ruined* by a *wily opponent.*
,, The royal family of Portugal escapes to Brazil.
   the *brave regent* an *exile* from *Portugal.*
1808. The French, under Murat, enter Madrid.
   Buonaparte resolves to *extend* his *rule.*
,, Treaty of Bayonne: Charles IV. cedes to Napoleon Spain and the colonies.
   Buonaparte's rapacity excites a *revolt.*
,, The Spanish patriots solicit aid from Britain.
   Britain resolves on an *expedition* of *resistance.*
,, Wellington lands at Mondego Bay to resist Napoleon.
   courageous Arthur Wellesley arrives.
,, Battle of Vimiera: Wellington defeats the French.
   the *'British army wholly routs* them.
,, Convention of Cintra: the French army allowed to retire safely to France.
   the *brave Arthur Wellesley resigns.*

A.D.
1809. Battle of Coruna : Sir John Moore defeats the French, but is killed in the hour of victory.
Coruna reminds us of Wolfe's verses.

,, Battles of Ratisbon, Abensburg, and Eckmühl: Napoleon defeats the Austrians.
Buonaparte receives a wound in the victory.

,, Battle of Wagram : the Austrians totally defeated.
completely routs them at Wagram, near Vienna.

,, Battle of Talavera : Wellington routs the French.
completely routed by Wellington at Talavera.

,, Collingwood defeats the French fleet in the Mediterranean.
Britannia rules the waves victoriously.

1810. Napoleon having deposed Josephine, marries Maria Louisa of Austria.
Buonaparte resorts to a base expedient.

,, Louis Buonaparte abdicates the throne of Holland, which is now incorporated with France.
a brief reign of care and wretchedness.

,, The French defeated by Wellington at Busaco.
Buonaparte's army beaten by Wellington.

,, Napoleon burns all British merchandise in France.
Buonaparte resolves to burn our exports.

,, Mauritius captured from the French by General Abercromby.
a colony rich in cotton and wheat.

1811. Regency of the Prince of Wales (George IV.) commences.
a careless heir his country's care.

,, General Graham defeats the French at Barossa.
compelled to retire from the bloody conflict.

,, Maria Louisa delivered of a son—styled "King of Rome."
Buonaparte's heir born to care.

,, Battle of Albuera : the French totally defeated.
an achievement remarkable for British courage.

A.D.
1811. Serious riots in Nottingham: the weavers resist the introduction of machinery.
bands of *rioters convulse* the *country*.

1812. Ciudad Rodrigo stormed and taken by the British.
Ciudad Rodrigo captured by the *Duke*.

,, Capture of Badajos by the Duke of Wellington.
capture of a *renowned border fortress*.

,, The United States declare war against Great Britain.
our *cousins resent* the *blockade* of *France*.

,, Napoleon invades Russia with a force of 498,000 men.
Buonaparte rushes on his *coming destiny*.

,, Battle of Salamanca: Madrid taken by Wellington.
the *conqueror receives* a *badge* of *distinction*.

,, Battle of Borodino: fearful carnage on either side.
both armies at *Borodino decimated*.

,, The Americans invade Canada, but, after several sanguinary battles, are compelled to surrender.
the *British army beats* them at *Detroit*.

,, Moscow burned by the Russian authorities: 11,000 houses consumed.
a *conflagration ruinous* to *Buonaparte's destiny*.

SECT. 46.—From Napoleon's Retreat from Moscow to the Battle of Waterloo (A.D. 1812-1815).

A.D.
1812. Battle of the Berezina: Napoleon loses 20,000 men.
Buonaparte's retreat is *covered* with *disaster*.

,, Napoleon deserts his army, and returns to Paris.
Buonaparte reaches his *capital* in *disguise*.

1813. Concordat of Fontainebleau between Napoleon and the Pope.
Buonaparte's ruse with his *Catholic Holiness*.

,, Sixth coalition against France—England, Russia, Prussia, Austria, and Sweden.
the *countries* of *Europe combine against* him.

,, Napoleon quits Paris for the seat of war in Germany.
Buonaparte renews the *campaign* in *Germany*.

A.D.
1813. Battles of Lutzen, Bautzen, Wurtzchen: Napoleon defeats the Allies.
Buonaparte redeems his character as a general.

,, Battle of Vitoria: Wellington defeats the French.
a battle ruinous to Buonaparte's hopes.

,, Battle of the Pyrenees: Wellington defeats Soult.
is completely routed by the British general.

,, Wellington and the Peninsular army enter France.
the Bidassoa is reached by our brave hero.

,, Battle of Leipsic: Napoleon defeated by the Allies.
Buonaparte's ruinous campaign in Germany.

,, Revolution in Holland: the Prince of Orange resumes his crown.
a bloodless revolution breaks-out in Holland.

,, The Allied army crosses the Rhine, and invades France.
they cross the Rhine, a countless host.

1814. Treaty of Kiel between Britain, Sweden, and Denmark: Denmark cedes Norway to Sweden, and receives back her colonies.
the colonies restored by the brave Swedes.

,, Surrender of Paris to the Allied army.
Buonaparte ruined, his capital surrenders!

,, Battle of Toulouse: Marshal Soult defeated by Wellington.
completely repulses the courageous Soult.

,, Napoleon abdicates, but retains the title of Emperor.
Buonaparte resigns his crown and kingdom.

,, Napoleon transported to Elba in the British frigate "Undaunted."
Buonaparte retires to a cheerless solitude.

,, Louis XVIII. enters Paris as King of the French.
the Bourbons regain their crowns and sceptres.

,, Peace of Paris: France restored to her original limits.
Christendom resounds with boundless joy.

A.D.
1814. The Sovereigns of Russia and Prussia visit England.
Britain resounds with a *cry of jubilee.*

,, Washington, capital of the United States, captured, and the capitol burned.
the *British reduce* the *capitol to ashes.*

,, General Ross defeats the Americans at Baltimore.
courageous Ross in *battle* is *killed.*

,, Congress of Vienna : the Allies ratify the Treaty of Paris.
the *bounds* of *European countries settled.*

,, Peace of Ghent between Britain and the U. States.
concord restored between *Britain* and the *States.*

1815. Battle of New Orleans : the British defeated by General Jackson.
the *British repulsed* with *considerable loss.*

,, Napoleon escapes from Elba, and arrives at Cannes with 1000 men.
Buonaparte returns, to the *consternation of all.*

,, Louis XVIII. escapes from Paris : Napoleon resumes the crown.
Buonaparte returns, to the *confusion of Louis.*

,, Battles of Ligny and Quartrebras.
Blucher is *routed* in the *battle* of *Ligny.*

,, Battle of Waterloo : Napoleon totally defeated by Wellington and Blucher.
Buonaparte is *ruined* by the *combined Allies.*

SECT. 47.—From the Battle of Waterloo to the Accession of George IV. (A.D. 1815-1820).

A.D.
1815. The Allied army again returns to Paris.
the *capital re-entered* by the *brave Allies.*

,, Napoleon surrenders to Captain Maitland of the "Bellerophon."
he *claims* at *Rochefort British leniency.*

,, The Holy Alliance between Russia, Prussia, and Austria.
the *Czar originates* a *curious alliance.*

A.D.
1815. Napoleon arrives at St Helena.
Buonaparte removed to a cheerless isle.

,, Second Peace of Paris between France and the Allies.
compelled to restore the contents of the Louvre.

,, Murat, ex-king of Naples, and Marshal Ney, shot.
a base recompense to brave leaders.

1816. Marriage of Princess Charlotte of Wales to Leopold of Saxe-Coburg, afterwards King of Belgium.
betrothes the heir of the crown of England.

,, The Argentine Confederation shakes off the Spanish yoke.
the colonists resolve to become independent.

,, Algiers bombarded by a British fleet, and slavery abolished in Algeria.
Britain restores the captives magnanimously.

,, The Elgin Marbles purchased by Parliament.
celebrated records in the British Museum.

1817. Death of Princess Charlotte of Saxe-Coburg.
Britain regrets the beloved princess.

,, Marquis of Hastings overthrows the Mahratta and Pindaree power in India.
a British ruler conquers the Pindarees.

1818. Marriage of the Duke of Clarence (William IV.), and of the Duke of Kent (father of Queen Victoria).
the citizens rejoice, and the bells ring.

,, Congress of Aix-la-Chapelle decrees the removal from France of the Army of Occupation.
the British return, with the consent of Richelieu.

,, Battle of Maypu; Chilé becomes independent of Spain.
the Chilians raise their colony to a republic.

,, Velocipedes first introduced into England from Germany.
bicycles run on our common roads.

,, Death of Queen Charlotte, wife of George III.
Charlotte rests from the cares of royalty.

MODERN HISTORY. 297

1819. Birth of Queen Victoria, daughter of the Duke of Kent.
   Britain rejoices at the *birth* of *Victoria.*

,, First passage of the Atlantic by steam from New York to Liverpool.
   a *celebrated era* in *commerce* and *trade.*

,, Monster Reform Meeting in Manchester; many persons killed.
   a *cry* to *reform* the *constituency* in *towns.*

,, Death of Marshal Blucher of Prussia.
   a *cross* of *iron* his *badge* of *triumph.*

SECT. 48.—From the Accession of George IV. to the Accession of William IV. (A.D. 1820-1830).

A.D.
1820. Death of George III., and accession of George IV.
   continued to *reign fifty-nine years.*

,, Revolution in Spain against Ferdinand VII.
   the *Bourbons repress freedom* of *worship.*

,, Duke de Berri assassinated in France by Louvel.
   the *Bourbons' reign* in *France* is *execrated.*

,, The Cato conspiracy, and attempt to murder the British Cabinet.
   the *conspirators arrested* and *duly executed.*

,, Revolutions in Naples and Piedmont suppressed by Austria.
   where *Bourbons reign freedom expires.*

,, The trial of Queen Caroline commences.
   the *citizens* are *roused* to *fearful excitement.*

1821. Florida ceded by Spain to the United States.
   the *colossal republic Florida acquires.*

,, Battle of Carobobo: New Granada, Ecuador, and Venezuela shake off the Spanish yoke.
   the " *Columbian Republic* " *formed* by *Bolivar.*

,, The Greek Revolutionary War commences.
   a *cry* for *refuge* from *despotic cruelty.*

,, Death of Napoleon Buonaparte at St Helena.
   Buonaparte released from his *dreary captivity !*

A.D.
1821. Coronation of George IV. : Queen Caroline vainly attempts to gain admission into Westminster Abbey.
Caroline refused admission to the *ceremony.*

,, Funeral of Queen Caroline : great riot in London.
the *citizens resent* the *despot's conduct.*

1822. The Greeks declare their independence of Turkey.
a *cry resounds* of *freedom* from *despotism.*

,, Mexico becomes independent of Spain : Augustine I. elected Emperor.
the *colony rebels*, and *demands* to be *free.*

,, Brazil becomes independent of Portugal : Don Pedro elected Emperor.
Brazil rejects the *domination* of a *despot.*

,, Death of Lord Castlereagh : Canning becomes Foreign Secretary.
a *celebrated orator directs* our *affairs.*

1823. The French invade Spain to support Ferdinand VII.
the *Cortes resists* the *despot's government.*

,, Free Trade commences in England.
our *commerce rendered free* by *Huskisson.*

,, The Spanish Constitution abolished, and absolutism restored.
the *Bourbon's rule* is *despotic* and *grievous.*

,, Belzoni, the famous Egyptian traveller, dies.
Belzoni renowned for *discoveries* in *Egypt.*

1824. New London Bridge founded.
constructed by *Rennie*, a *famous Scotchman.*

,, Death of Lord Byron at Mesolonghi.
Byron rests on a *foreign shore.*

,, Burmese war : Rangoon captured by the British.
they *capture Rangoon*, on a *delta situated.*

,, Battle of Ayacucho : Peru and Bolivia become independent of Spain.
Bolivar rids them of the *domination* of *Spain.*

1825. The Great Erie Canal, 370 miles long, opened.
the *canal of Erie* of *formidable length.*

A.D.
1825. Great Britain acknowledges the independence of the South American republics.
Britain recognises the *friends* of *liberty.*

,, First steam voyage from England to India.
a *celebrated era dawns* on the *land.*

,, Algiers nearly destroyed by an earthquake, and Blida ruined.
a *celebrated earthquake devastates Algeria.*

,, Death of Alexander I. of Russia, and accession of Nicholas I.
the *champion* of *order* and *defender* of *legitimacy.*

,, The Egyptian army, under Ibrahim Pacha, lands in the Morea.
a *celebrated ruler devastates* the *land.*

,, John Quincy Adams becomes President of the United States.
cradled in *revolution,* a *friend* of *liberty.*

,, Commercial panic in England: seventy banking establishments fail.
a *commercial reaction frightens* the *land.*

1826. Revolt of Bhurtpur, and its capture by the British.
Bhurtpur revolts from the *dominion* of *England.*

,, The great Suspension Bridge over the Menai Strait constructed by Telford.
a *bridge* of *iron* by a *famous engineer.*

,, Peace with Burmah: several provinces ceded to England.
they *cede Aracan* to the *dominion* of *England.*

,, Revolt of the Janissaries at Constantinople: 15,000 of them slain.
abolition of the *order,* by *firman* of *Mahmoud.*

,, Mesolonghi besieged and taken by the Turks.
they *bravely resist* the *despot* at *Mesolonghi.*

,, Russia declares war against Persia, and defeats the Shah in several battles.
she *cedes Erivan* to the *dominion* of *Nicholas.*

A.D.

1826. Treaty of Akerman: Turkey cedes to Russia freedom of the Black Sea.
cedes to *Russia freedom* of *navigation.*

1827. Treaty of London between England, France, and Russia, for the independence of Greece.
Britain, Russia, and *France* are *parties* to it.

,, Death of Canning: Lord Goderich, Prime Minister.
Canning, the *orator, dies* in *peace.*

,, Battle of Navarino: the Turkish fleet destroyed by the allied squadrons of England, France, and Russia.
Codrington ruins the *fleet* of the *oppressor.*

1828. Duke of Wellington becomes Premier, and Sir R. Peel Home Secretary.
the *Conservatives rule* the *affairs* of the *realm.*

,, Russia declares war against Turkey for declining to acknowledge the independence of Greece.
the *Czar* of *Russia defends* their *rights.*

,, Corporation and Test Acts repealed in England.
acts repealed in *favour of Romanists.*

,, London University opened.
Bell reads the *first oration.*

,, The Turkish army evacuates the Morea.
Ibrahim's army forced to *retire.*

1829. Civil war threatened in Ireland: Catholic Emancipation Act passed.
the *Catholics relieved,* and *danger averted.*

,, Capture of Adrianople by the Russians.
they *capture* a *renowned fortress* in *Turkey.*

,, Treaty of Adrianople: Turkey concedes the independence of Greece, and grants to Russia freedom of traffic.
they *cede* to *Russia freedom* of *traffic.*

,, The colony of Western Australia established.
the *colony receives* the *desperately vicious.*

,, York Minster set on fire by an insane person.
consumes the *roof* of a *famous temple.*

SECT. 49.—From the Accession of William IV. to the Accession of Victoria (A.D. 1830-1837).

A.D.
1830. Death of George IV., and accession of William IV.
confer the *reins* of *government* on *William.*

,, Algiers taken by the French, and Algeria erected into a French province.
a *city renowned* for *ages won* by them.

,, The "Three Days' Revolution" in Paris: Charles X. expelled.
the *Bourbon's rule goads* them to *excesses.*

,, Louis Philippe, Duke of Orleans, crowned King of the French.
they *crown Orleans* of *heroic exploits.*

,, Belgium asserts its independence of Holland.
Belgium revolts from the *dominion* of *William.*

,, Opening of the Manchester and Liverpool Railway, the first great railway in Britain.
begins an *era* in the *history* of the *world.*

,, Revolution in Warsaw against Russia.
they *begin a revolution* in the *government* of *Warsaw.*

1831. Prince Leopold of Saxe-Coburg chosen King of the Belgians.
the *Belgians request* him to *govern* their *country.*

,, Russia suppresses the insurrection in Warsaw.
the *Czar* of *Russia governs* them *cruelly.*

,, New Granada, Ecuador, and Venezuela become separate states.
the *Columbian Republic* is *hastily broken.*

,, The great cholera of 1832 makes its first appearance in Sunderland.
the *cruel ravages* of the *great cholera.*

,, The "British Association for the Advancement of Science" (instituted by Sir D. Brewster) holds its inaugural meeting at York.
Brewster arrives with *Herschel* and *Babbage.*

A.D.
1832. Poland becomes an integral part of Russia.
    the *Czar* of *Russia governs* it *despotically.*

,, The cholera appears in Paris: 1000 deaths the first week.
    the *cholera rages grievously* in *France.*

,, The Reform Bill passed by the English Parliament.
    a *bill* to *repress* the *government* of the *few.*

,, Otho of Bavaria elected King of Greece.
    a *Bourbon rules* in *Greece despotically.*

,, Death of Sir Walter Scott.
    cease thy *romance, genius* of *fiction!*

,, Death of Goethe, the great German poet.
    the *chief romance* of *Goethe* is " *Faust.*"

1833. The Zollverein, or Germanic Customs League, formed.
    a *common rate* on *goods* in *Germany.*

,, Death of Ferdinand VII. of Spain: Isabella succeeds under a regency.
    the *Bourbon's rule* a *humiliating history.*

,, The English Factory Act, limiting the hours of labour, passed.
    an *Act* to *restrain* the *greed* of *gain.*

1834. Slavery abolished in the British colonies: £20,000,000 paid by Parliament to the slave-owners.
    a *bright era* in the *history* of *slavery.*

,, The Poor Law Amendment Bill passed.
    the *benevolent restrained* from *giving spontaneously!*

,, British Houses of Parliament destroyed by fire.
    a *conflagration ruins* the *home* of our *Senate.*

,, The Chinese Government interdict the opium trade.
    Christians reproved by *heathens* for *smuggling!*

,, Death of S. T. Coleridge, poet, philosopher, and theologian.
    Coleridge rests in his *grave, slumbering.*

1835. Death of Francis I. of Austria: accession of Ferdinand I.
    begins to *rule* his *German lieges.*

A.D.
1835. Fieschi, inventor of the "infernal machine," attempts to assassinate Louis Philippe.
a Corsican robber hazards his life.

„ Municipal Corporation Reform Bill passed.
the citizens rejoice at greater liberty.

„ Great fire at New York: 20,000,000 dollars' worth of property destroyed.
the citizens rush in great alarm.

1836. The colony of South Australia settled by the British.
a colony rich in agriculture and mines.

„ Lord Auckland becomes Governor-General of India.
a celebrated earl governs India.

„ The Spanish Constitution of 1812 accepted by the Queen Regent.
the constitution revived agreed to at Madrid.

„ The Portuguese Constitution of 1820 accepted by Donna Maria.
the Constitution revived agreed to by Maria.

„ San Sebastian stormed by the British: the Carlists repulsed.
the Carlists repulsed by a gallant Englishman.

„ A balloon, with three persons, ascends from London, and arrives at Weilburg in Nassau.
a celebrated aeronaut to Germany navigates.

1837. Van Buren becomes President of the United States.
Buren rules, their eighth President.

„ The U. States recognise the independence of Texas.
the colossal republic grasping at power.

„ The Emperor of China allows a British commissioner to reside at Canton.
the celestial ruler grants his permission.

„ Death of William IV., and accession of Queen Victoria, WHOM GOD PRESERVE!
begin to reign, our gracious Queen!

SECT. 50.—From the Accession of Queen Victoria to the Repeal of the Corn Laws (A.D. 1837-1846).

A.D.
1837. The Duke of Cumberland becomes King of Hanover, and abrogates the old Constitution.
constitutional rule in *Hanover paramount.*

,, Rebellion in Montreal.
the *Canadian rebellion* is *headed* by *Papineau.*

1838. Death of Talleyrand, the eminent French diplomatist.
a *brilliant* but *erring genius* at *rest.*

,, Slavery abolished by the Anglo-Indian Government.
the *bondmen released* by the *Governor's orders.*

,, Treaty of commerce between England and Turkey.
commercial regulations by *Government ratified.*

,, Battle of Prescott: the Canadian rebellion repressed.
the *Canadian rebels* are *grievously routed.*

,, Great famine in the North-west Provinces of India.
the *crops* of *rice* on the *Ganges* are *ruined.*

1839. Aden, in Arabia, captured by the English.
we *capture* in *Arabia* a *haven* for our *troops.*

,, The Governor of Canton seizes all the opium belonging to the British.
Chinese regulations grossly outraged.

,, The Affghan war: a British force occupies Candahar.
the *British arms* at *Ghuznee victorious.*

,, Abdul Medjid becomes Sultan of Turkey.
Abdul reigns over a *gigantic territory.*

,, The United States Bank, and many others, suspend payment.
the *colossal republic* is *greatly troubled.*

1840. New Zealand established as a British colony.
coal, iron, silver, and *wool.*

,, The Emperor of China prohibits all trade and intercourse with England for ever.
commercial relations suspended for *aye!*

MODERN HISTORY. 305

A.D.
1840. The penny-postage system introduced by Mr Rowland Hill.
cheap rates a *successful experiment.*

,, Marriage of Queen Victoria with Prince Albert of Saxe-Coburg.
a *cousin* of the *reigning Sovereign weds* her.

,, Thiers and Guizot become successively Ministers of Foreign Affairs in France.
celebrated orators and *statesmen exalted.*

,, Edward Oxford attempts to assassinate the Queen.
beware of the *ruthless assassin, Oxford.*

,, The remains of Napoleon Buonaparte are removed from St Helena to Paris.
his *bones return,* amid *jubilant exclamations.*

1841. Canton taken by the British, and ransomed by the Emperor.
Canton ransomed by the *Sovereign* of *China.*

,, Amoy taken by the British.
a *British royal squadron captures* it.

,, Sir Robert Peel becomes Prime Minister.
a *Conservative Reformer steers* our *course.*

,, Birth of Albert Edward, Prince of Wales.
birth of an *heir,* to the *joy* of the *country !*

,, Dispute with the United States regarding the brig "Creole."
a *brig arrives* with *slaves* at the *Bahamas.*

,, Insurrection at Cabool against the English.
Burnes is *ruthlessly assassinated* at *Cabool.*

1842. The British evacuate Cabool under a convention, but are treacherously attacked by the Affghans.
a *British army savagely destroyed.*

,, Sir R. Peel's Bill, imposing an income tax, passed.
an "*Act to repeal sundry duties !*"

,, General Sale defeats Akhbar Khan at Jelallabad.
the *British army* the *Khan defeats.*

U

A.D.
1842. The Ashburton Treaty, defining the boundary between the British dominions and the United States, ratified.
the boundaries of realms scientifically determined.

„ Treaty of Nankin between China and Great Britain.
consuls to reside at Shanghae and Foo-Choo.

„ The Affghan war concluded: the British evacuate Affghanistan.
the British retire from Akhbar's dominions.

1843. The Disruption of the Church of Scotland, and formation of the Free Church.
a celebrated era in Scottish history.

„ Battle of Meanee: Scinde annexed to British India.
the British arms successful at Hyderabad.

„ The Mahratta war in India: Gwalior invaded by the British.
the British army successful in Gwalior.

1844. Daniel O'Connell found guilty of sedition, and imprisoned.
O'Connell arraigned for seditious speeches.

„ Hayti (St Domingo) becomes an independent republic.
Britain recognises the struggling state.

„ Sir Robert Peel's Bank Charter Act passed.
a certain ratio between issue and specie.

1845. Texas annexed to the U. States: war with Mexico.
the colossal republic succeeds to a legacy.

„ Sir J. Franklin sets out on his third Arctic expedition.
in the cheerless regions of snow he lies.

„ Great meeting of the Anti-Corn-Law League in Manchester.
Corn-Law Reformers support the League.

1846. Battle of Sobraon: Lord Gough signally defeats the Sikhs.
the British army slays a myriad.

A.D.
1846. Great railway panic in England.
: a *consequence* of the *railway speculation mania*.

„ Pope Pius IX. raised to the pontifical chair.
: a *cardinal raised* to *supreme eminence*.

„ Famine in Ireland, caused by the failure of the potato crop.
: *crowds* of *Irishmen sink* or *emigrate*.

SECT. 51.—From the Repeal of the Corn Laws to the Accession of Louis Napoleon as Emperor of the French (A.D. 1846-1852).

A.D.
1846. The Corn Laws repealed, and Free Trade established.
: the *Corn-Laws repealed*, to the *joy* of the *nation*.

„ Sir Robert Peel resigns the Premiership.
: the *Conservative ranks sink* to a *minority*.

„ Austria absorbs the republic of Cracow.
: the *Cracow republic* to *Austria annexed*.

1847. Death of Dr Thomas Chalmers.
: the *brilliant ornament* of *Scottish Presbyterianism*.

„ Death of Mendelssohn, the celebrated composer.
: *composed oratorios* of *singular pathos*.

1848. Charles Albert grants his subjects a liberal Constitution.
: his *country regenerated* by *salutary reforms*.

„ Louis Philippe prohibits a Reform banquet in Paris.
: *begins* a *revolution* which *swept* over *Europe*.

„ Revolution in Vienna: Ferdinand grants a liberal Constitution.
: *concedes Reform*, and *saves* the *realm*.

„ Insurrection at Berlin against the Government.
: the *cry* for *Reform spreads* through *Europe*.

„ Lombardy and Venice revolt against Austria.
: *courageous reformers sigh* for a *republic*.

„ The Provisional Government of France abolishes slavery.
: an *act* to *remove* a *spot* from the *realm*.

A.D.
1848. Upper California ceded to the United States by Mexico.
   the colossal republic seeks to "organise" it.

,, Rebellion in Ireland: the *Habeas Corpus* Act suspended.
   O'Brien raises the signal of revolt.

,, Pope Pius IX. quits Rome in disguise, and flees to Gæta.
   "Christ's representative" escapes from Rome.

,, Louis Napoleon elected President of the French Republic.
   chief of the republic, but a king in reality.

,, Ferdinand I. of Austria abdicates in favour of his nephew, Francis Joseph.
   crown the heir of the Austrian realm.

1849. The Constituent Assembly at Rome divests the Pope of his temporal power, and proclaims a Republic.
   bold reformers shake his throne.

,, The Pope implores the aid of the Roman Catholic powers of Europe against his own subjects.
   accuses them of rebelling against Jesus' Vicar.

,, Lord Gough totally defeats the Sikhs at Gujerat.
   the British arms are signally victorious.

,, The Punjab annexed to British India.
   the conquered region is subject to Victoria.

,, Battle of Novara: the Austrians defeat the Sardinians.
   brave Radetsky the Sardinians vanquishes.

,, Charles Albert abdicates in favour of his son, Victor Emanuel.
   Charles resigns the sceptre to Victor.

,, Rome surrenders to a French army, after a siege of thirty days.
   the city of Rome is stormed by the Vicar.

,, The temporal authority of the Pope re-established.
   a Catholic army sustains his throne.

MODERN HISTORY. 309

A.D.
1849. Peace between Sardinia and Austria.
concord resumed 'tween Joseph and Victor.

,, Battle of Temeśwar: the Hungarian army surrenders to the Russians.
the courageous Russians storm Temeswar.

1850. Rebellion in China begins in the province Kwang-si.
the Chinese rebellion a lengthened war.

,, Death of the poet Wordsworth.
in Cumberland rests the illustrious Wordsworth.

,, Death of Sir Robert Peel.
Conservative, Radical, Liberal, and Whig!

,, Roman Catholic hierarchy attempted to be established in England.
the country roused from its lethargy of years.

,, Fugitive Slave Bill passed by the American Congress.
the colossal republic legalises wickedness.

,, Death of Louis Philippe, ex-king of the French, in England.
Claremont receives the last of the exile.

1851. Census of the United Kingdom: pop. 27,724,849.
the census of Ireland alarms the country.

,, Opening of the Great Exhibition in Hyde Park.
a celebrated rendezvous for all countries.

,, Telegraphic communication first established between France and England.
communications received by electric cable.

,, The "Coup d'Etat:" Paris in a state of siege.
a Buonaparte ruins the liberties of his country.

,, Census of the United States: pop. 23,191,876.
the census returns are lower than Britain.

1852. The motto, "Liberté, Fraternité, Egalité," abolished in France.
bury the remains of your lost freedom!

,, Death of Thomas Moore, the poet.
the bard of Ireland's lamented death.

,, Second Burmese war: Rangoon taken by the British.
Britain receives a large dependency.

FACTS AND DATES.

A.D.
1852. Death of the Duke of Wellington.
        the *celebrated Irishman's lamented decease.*

,, Louis Napoleon elected Emperor of France.
        the *citizens rush* to *elect* a *despot !*

SECT. 52.—From the Accession of Louis Napoleon to the Secession of the Confederate States of America (A.D. 1852-1861).

A.D.
1853. The Czar issues a manifesto against Turkey.
        the *Czar* of *Russia alarms* the *Governments.*

,, A Russian army enters the Danubian Principalities.
        the *Czar's army* is *led* by *Gortschakoff.*

,, A Congress of the Great Powers assembles at Vienna.
        commissioners rush to *allay* a *hurricane !*

,, Turkey formally declares war against Russia.
        the *Crescent* is *raised* with *loud huzzas !*

,, The Russians destroy the entire Turkish fleet at Sinope.
        Constantinople raises a *lamentable howl.*

1854. The Allied fleet enters the Black Sea.
        Abdul requests the *Allies' assistance.*

,, The Queen reviews the Baltic fleet at Spithead.
        calmly reviews her *leviathan ships.*

,, England and France declare war against Russia.
        they *beard* the *roaring lion* of *Scythia.*

,, The Crystal Palace opened at Sydenham.
        crowds resort from *London* to *Kent.*

,, Bomarsund surrenders to Sir Charles Napier.
        completely reduces the *Aaland Isles.*

,, Battle of the Alma: the Russians defeated.
        the *courageous Raglan leads* our *soldiers.*

,, Prince Menschikoff sinks the Russian fleet in the harbour of Sebastopol.
        a *crafty Russian lessens* our *success.*

,, Battle of Balaclava.
        a *chivalrous earl* his *laurels secures.*

A.D.
1854. Battle of Inkermann: the Russians severely defeated.
   a battle renowned for the legions of slain.

1855. Death of the Emperor Nicholas: accession of Alexander II.
   the Czar resigns his lease of life.

,, Industrial Exhibition opened at Paris.
   a collection of the riches of all lands.

,, Kertch and Yenikaleh taken by the Allies.
   both are reduced by the illustrious Lyons.

,, Death of Lord Raglan.
   courageous Raglan lamented lies!

,, Fall of Sebastopol: the French capture the Malakhoff.
   the courageous Russians leave in alarm.

1856. Oude annexed to British India.
   the British resolve at last to annex it.

,, Birth of the Prince Imperial of France.
   birth of an heir to Louis Napoleon!

,, Treaty of Paris: peace ratified between Russia, Turkey, Great Britain, France, and Sardinia.
   they contrive by articles to limit his empire.

1857. The Indian rebellion begins at Meerut: the sepoys shoot their officers, and massacre all Europeans.
   the obvious result of our lax policy.

,, First news of the mutiny reaches England.
   the British read an alarming page.

,, The mutineers seize Delhi, and proclaim as king a descendant of the Great Mogul.
   chief of the religion of "Allah" proclaimed.

,, Cawnpore surrenders to Nana Sahib, who cruelly butchers the garrison and other Europeans.
   a cruel rebel's lawless proceedings.

,, General Havelock defeats Nana Sahib, and retakes Cawnpore.
   Cawnpore restored to loyalty and peace.

,, Delhi recaptured by General Wilson: the king taken prisoner.
   the chiefs of the rebels are led to prison.

A. D.
1857. The British Presidency of Lucknow relieved by Sir Colin Campbell.
the Campbell's arrive, list to the pibroch!

1858. Marriage of the Princess Royal of England to Prince Frederick William of Prussia.
betrothed to the heir of an illustrious realm.

„ Orsini attempts to assassinate the French Emperor.
crafty Orsini's lawless revenge.

„ Sir Colin Campbell finally captures Lucknow, and suppresses the Indian rebellion.
the bloody rebellion at last repressed.

„ Atlantic Telegraph, from Valencia to Newfoundland, completed.
the cable rests on an elevated ridge.

„ Treaty of commerce bet. Japan and Britain ratified.
a British earl, with his largess, received.

„ The Queen of England becomes Empress of India.
begins to reign over a loyal region.

1859. The Punjab and North-West Provinces erected into Presidencies.
basins of rivers of largest type.

„ An Austrian army crosses the Ticino, and invades Piedmont.
they cross the river that limits their territory.

„ France declares war against Austria.
Buonaparte resolves to liberate Italy.

„ The French defeat the Austrians at Magenta.
the courageous armies of Louis and Victor.

„ Lombardy annexed to the kingdom of Sardinia.
a beautiful region 'mong the lakes of Italy,

„ Battle of Solferino; total defeat of the Austrians.
carries renown to Louis and Victor.

„ Treaty of Villafranca between France and Austria.
their battles result in a lasting treaty.

„ Peace of Zurich bet. France, Austria, and Sardinia.
they confirm the articles of the late treaty.

A.D.
1859. Death of Lord Macaulay, the English historian.
the *brilliant ornament* of *literature vanishes.*

1860. Treaty of commerce bet. France and Great Britain.
our *commerce receives* a *mighty extension.*

,, Tuscany, Parma, and Modena annexed to Sardinia; and Savoy and Nice ceded by Sardinia to France.
both are *regarded* as the *Emperor's wages.*

,, Garibaldi arrives at Marsala, in Sicily, and captures Palermo.
a *chivalrous reformer lands* in the *west.*

,, Second Chinese war.
the *Chinese repulsed* by our *men* of *war.*

,, Francis II. flees from Naples: Garibaldi enters.
the *chivalrous reformer's unparalleled exploits!*

,, Pékin invested by the Allied troops.
the *celestial regions menaced* by *war.*

,, Abraham Lincoln elected President of the United States.
a *critical era* in the *annals* of the *West.*

,, South Carolina secedes from the United States.
the *citizens rush* in *intense excitement.*

SECT. 53.- From the American Secession to the Present Time (A.D. 1861-1869).

A.D.
1861. Seven Southern States secede from the Union.
boldly resolve to *maintain* the *conflict.*

,, The seceding States elect Jeff. Davis, President.
the *city* of *Richmond* their *new capital.*

,, The Emperor of Russia emancipates the serfs.
the *Czar resolves* to *emancipate* the *bondmen.*

,, Fort Sumpter, Charleston, taken by the Secessionists.
beginning of an *era* of *mourning* and *bloodshed.*

,, President Lincoln proclaims the blockade of the Southern ports.
a *blockade* to *repress Northern commerce.*

A.D.

1861. Death of Count Cavour, the Sardinian Prime Minister.
Cavour, the arm of Emanuel, broken!

„ Britain, France, and Spain sign a convention against Mexico.
the *contractors resolve* to *menace* their *coasts.*

„ Mason and Slidell violently taken from the English mail-steamer, "Trent," and carried to Boston.
the *British* are "*riled*" by the *Americans' conduct.*

„ Death of Prince Albert.
the *country regards* it as a *national calamity.*

1862. Engagement between the "Merrimac" and "Monitor."
a *Confederate ram amazes* the *Federals.*

„ The French army defeats the Mexicans at Coimbres.
the *battle rages* between the *Mexicans* and *French.*

„ Great distress in the manufacturing districts.
caused by the *raw material failing.*

„ Second International Exhibition opened in London.
the *catalogue arranged* under *many divisions.*

„ The "Alabama," a Confederate cruiser, is built in England, and stealthily leaves for the Azores.
a *Confederate rover* from *England departs.*

„ The U.S. Senate decrees the total abolition of slavery.
a *celebrated era* in *American freedom.*

„ Otho I. abdicates the throne of Greece.
the *Bavarian retires immensely disgusted.*

1863. The Prince of Wales marries the Princess Alexandra.
the *British realm unanimously agree.*

„ Greece elects Prince William of Denmark to be king.
a *boy received* as *monarch* of *Greece.*

„ Maximilian of Austria elected sovereign of Mexico.
they *choose* the *Archduke Maximilian* of *Germany.*

„ Arrival of Grant and Speke from the head-waters of the Nile.
a *celebrated era* in the *annals of geography.*

MODERN HISTORY. 315

A.D.
1863. Battle of Gettysburg—a three days' conflict.
the Confederates retire with unquenched hopes.

,, Death of Frederick VII. of Denmark: accession of Christian IX.
Christian rejected as monarch of Holstein.

,, First Fenian convention held at Chicago.
blustering Irishmen menace Great-Britain.

,, Terrible conflagration in a church at Santiago-de-Chilè.
the Chilian Republic immersed in grief.

1864. The Ionian Islands finally ceded to Greece.
Britain resolves on a magnanimous sacrifice.

,, The "Alabama" captured and sunk by the Federals.
clamorous rejoicings in the Northern States.

,, Fall of Savannah: end of Sherman's expedition.
a celebrated raid ends at Savannah.

1865. Death of Richard Cobden.
a celebrated reformer mourned by all.

,, Capture of Richmond: end of the American rebellion.
a bloody rebellion ended at last.

,, President Lincoln assassinated by Wilkes Booth.
a cause of regret to the nation at large.

,, The cattle plague commences in England.
beginning of rinderpest in the markets of London.

,, Death of Lord Palmerston.
a brilliant orator by England lamented.

,, Insurrection in Jamaica suppressed by Governor Eyre.
boldly repressed it by martial law.

,, Steevens, the notorious Fenian, escapes from prison.
a cunning rebel manages to elude us.

,, Death of Leopold I., King of the Belgians.
the Belgian realm mourns for Leopold.

1866. The Queen thanks Mr Peabody, an American merchant, for his extraordinary liberality.
Britain remembers his unparalleled munificence.

A.D.
1866. The Prussian army enters Holstein.
    a bloody rupture menaces the North.

,, Battle of Sadowa: the Prussians signally defeat the Austrians.
    Bismark routs his enemy with needle-guns.

,, Battles of Kissengen and Gerscheim: the Bavarians defeated.
    the Bavarians routed in many engagements.

,, Peace between Prussia and Austria: Prussia to annex Hanover, Nassau, Electoral Hesse, &c.; Austria to be excluded from the German Confederation.
    Bismark rapaciously annexes Nassau.

1867. The "North-German Confederation" meets at Berlin.
    Bismark reigns in the new Parliament.

,, The Emperor Maximilian routed and executed.
    they betray the royal Maximilian at Queretaro.

,, New Reform Bill receives the royal sanction.
    confers on the ratepayers unwonted power.

,, An English expedition leaves Bombay for Abyssinia.
    comes to rescue unfortunate prisoners.

,, Russian America transferred to the United States.
    acquires Russian America by purchase.

,, Five Fenian prisoners sentenced to death at Manchester.
    a band of rebels at Manchester punished.

1868. The remains of Maximilian arrive at Trieste.
    the body of the royal Maximilian arrives.

,, Death of Charles Kean, the celebrated actor.
    an actor of real merit arrested.

,, Death of Sir David Brewster.
    celebrated for his researches in nature and art.

,, President Johnson impeached by the American Congress.
    Congress resolves to impeach the ruler.

,, Resignation of Lord Derby: Mr Disraeli, Prime Minister.
    a brilliant orator meekly retires.

MODERN HISTORY. 317

A.D.
1868. Attempt to assassinate the Duke of Edinburgh at Sydney.
 a coward's revolver aimed at royalty.

,, Mr Gladstone moves resolutions to disestablish the Irish Church.
 begins to redress a manifest wrong.

,, Magdala captured by Sir Robert Napier: Theodore slain, and the captives rescued.
 the captives recovered, Magdala reduced.

,, Revolution in Spain: flight of Queen Isabella, and the formation of a Provisional Government.
 the Bourbons ruin the morals of the realm !

,, Death of Prof. Schönbein of Baden, the discoverer of ozone, and inventor of gun-cotton.
 a chemist, remarkable for invention, rests.

,, Reverdy Johnson, United States ambassador, arrives in England with full powers to settle the " Alabama claims."
 the bargain, ratified by their minister, they reject !

,, General Grant elected President of the United States.
 bravely rules a united realm.

,, The Disraeli Ministry resign: the Gladstone Ministry succeed.
 a bold-reformer our nation rules.

1869. The Postmaster-General authorised by Parliament to acquire and maintain the various lines of electric telegraph.
 a cheaper rate for messages by telegraph.

,, Insurrection in Cuba against the Provisional Government of Spain.
 the Cuban rebellion mars their triumph.

,, The Irish Church disestablished and disendowed.
 the Churches in Ireland now on their trial.

,, The Suez Canal, uniting the Mediterranean and Red Seas, opened.
 a canal and railway minimise the time.

INDEX.

AARON, 73
Abbassides, 223
Abdon, 75
Abednego, 85, 162
Abensburg, 292
Abercromby, 289, 292
Aberdeen Univ., 247
Abijah, 81
Abimelech, 75
Abiram, 73
Abo, 275
Abraham, 71, 72, 90, 91, 92, 139, 140
Abrutum, 269
Absalom, 77
Abubekr, 222
Abulfeda, 236
Abydos, 137, 139
Abyssinia, 46, 242, 316
Academic Sch., 182
Academy, Fr, 261
Academy of Inscriptions, 266
Academy, Royal, 279
Accad, 154
Achæan League, 182
Achæans, 170, 183, 195
Achala, 183, 195
Aches, 137, 156
Achilles, 170
Achish, 76
Achoris, 149
Achthoes, 67, 139
Acid, sulphuric, 21, 23
Aconcagua, 51
Acre, 235, 288
Acron, 187
Acts, 103
Adam, 69, 70, 137
Adams, J. Q., 299
Addington, 289
Addison, 272
Aden, 55, 304
Adolphus, 215, 243
Adolphus, Gust., 260, 261
Adrian, 205, 206
Adrian, Pope, 250
Adrianople, 214, 238, 300

Ægæ, 179
Ægatian Isles, 194
Ægis, 180
Ægospotami, 176
Æmilianus, 209
Æmilius, 194
Æneas, 170, 186
Æqui, 190
Ærial voyage, 282
Æschines, 178
Æschylus, 174
Ætolian League, 181, 182, 183, 195
Ætolian war, 195
Afghan war, 304, 305, 306
Afghanistan, 43, 44
Africa, 88, 46, 47, 57, 193, 195, 199, 206, 216, 221
Africanus (Scipio), 151, 195
Agag, 76
Agamemnon, 170
Agassiz, 32
Agesilaus, 166, 177, 178
Agincourt, 241
Agis, 176, 182
Agrarian laws, 190
Agricola, 204, 205
Agrigentum, 187, 193
Agrippa, 103
Agrippina, 203
Agua, Mt, 49
Ahab, 78, 81
Ahalah, 190
Ahasuerus, 86, 165
Ahaz, 83
Ahaziah, 79, 82
Ahijah, 78
Aix-la-Chapelle, 267, 276, 296
Ajaccio, 279
Akerman, 300
Alabama, 314, 315
Alabama claims, 317
Alani, 210, 215, 218
Alaric, 117, 215, 221
Alaska, 47, 48
Alba Longa, 186, 188
Albans, St, 243
Albert, 305, 314

Albert, Charles, 307
Albigenses, 110, 231, 232
Albinus, 103
Albuera, 292
Alciblades, 175, 176
Alcohol, 22
Alderman, 231
Alexander Balas, 151
Alexander (Gt.), 87, 149, 178, 179, 180
Alexander I. (Rus.), 289, 299
Alexander I. (Scot.), 229
Alexander II. (Egy.) 151, 152
Alexander II. (Rus.), 311
Alexander II. (Scot.), 231, 233
Alexander III. (Scot.), 233, 234
Alexander VI., 247
Alexandra, 314
Alexandria, 12, 87, 114, 115, 117, 149, 150, 152, 179, 181, 199, 204, 208, 209, 211, 212, 213, 287, 289
Alfred (Gt.), 225
Algebra, 225, 231, 279
Algeria, 46, 47, 296, 301
Algerines, 253, 276
Algiers, 296, 299, 301
Ali, 222
Alleghanies, 48
Allemanni, 209, 214, 218, 221
Alma, 310
Almamon, 224
Almance, 271
Almansor, 223
Almeida, 55, 248
Alphonso, 229, 233
Alps, 187, 200
Altinum, 206
Alva, Duke of, 256
Alyattes, 163
Amalek, 76

Amalfi, 235
Amasis, 148
Amaziah, 82
Amazon, 51, 55, 248
Ambrose, 109, 117, 214
Amenemes, 139, 140, 156
Amenephthes, 143
Amenophis, 142, 145
America, 55, 246, 247, 248
America, Central, 48, 55, 248
America, N., 38, 47, 48, 49
America, S., 38, 49, 50, 51, 56
American Indians, 35
American secession, 313
American war, 280
Amerigo-Vespucci, 247
Amiens, 289
Ammonites, 75
Amon, 84
Amorites, 142
Amos, 79
Amosis, 142
Amour, 45
Amoy, 305
Amphictions, 179
Amphipolis, 175, 176, 178
Amuntimæus, 140
Amurath, 238, 242
Amyrtæus, 148, 166
Ananias, 100
Anaxagoras, 4
Ancus Martius, 188
Andes, 51
Andrew II., 232
Andrews, St, 240, 252, 253
Angles, 216, 218
Anglesea, 204
Angora, 240
Anicetus, 112
Animal worship, 137
Animals, 32, 33
Anjou, 231
Anna, 88

Anne, Queen, 270, 272
Anson, 57, 275
Antalcidas, 149, 166, 177
Ante-Nicene Fathers, 106
Anthropomorphites 117
Antichrist, 97
Antigonus, 87, 149, 150, 181
Antimony, 16, 18, 19
Antioch, 101, 102, 116, 181, 208, 214
Antiochus Epiph., 87, 151
Antiochus (Great), 88, 150, 195, 198
Antiochus III., 183
Antipas, Herod, 89, 98, 202
Antipater, 88, 149, 180, 181
Antisana, 50
Antoninus Pius, 206
Antony, 152, 199
Aphophis, 67, 141
Aphrodite, 179
Apis, 137
Apollinaristic controversy, 116
Apollonius, 182
Apologies, 112, 113
Aquæ Sextiæ, 197
Aquileia, 109
Aquinas, Th., 234
Arabia, 43, 44, 222
Arabian dyn., 145, 157
Arabian Nights, 223
Arabic Geog., 236
Arabic numerals, 226, 233
Aragon, 233, 244
Ararat, 44
Aratus, 182
Arbaces, 163
Arbela, 167, 179
Arc, Joan of, 241
Arcadius, 215
Archelaus, 89, 97
Archimedes, 182, 194
Archons, 170, 171
Arcott, 277
Arcturus, 13
Aretino, 227
Argentine Confed., 50, 296
Arginusæ, 176
Argonautic exped., 145, 170
Argos, 169, 171, 182
Argyle, Marq., 266
Arian controversy, 109, 115

Aristarchus, 4
Aristides, 173, 174
Aristobulus, 88
Aristogeiton, 172
Aristomenes, 171
Aristotle, 178
Arius, 116
Arjish, 44
Ark, 70, 76, 77
Armada, 258
Armais, 142
Armenia, 212
Armenians, 205
Arminians, 260
Arnobius, 108, 115
Arpad, 225
Arphaxad, 71
Arran, 258
Arras, 241
Arrhidæus, 180
Arrian, 112
Arsenic, 16, 18, 19
Arses, 167
Artaphernes, 165, 173
Artaxerxes, 86, 148, 149, 166, 208
Articles, XXXIX., 256
Artillery, 26
Arundel Marbles, 144, 157, 169, 178
Arvad, 140, 142
Aryans, 137, 156, 163
Asa, 78, 81
Ascanius, 186
Ascension, the, 99
Aschled, 206
Asculum, 193
Ashburton, 306
Ashdod, 147, 159
Asia, 33, 43, 44, 45, 57
Asia Minor, 101, 103, 181, 198
Asia, Upper, 181
Asnapper, 160
Assembly, General, 255
Asses, 141, 142
Asshur-akh-iddina, 160
Asshur-bani-pal, 158, 160
Asshur-dani-pal, 158
Asshur-emit-ili, 160
Association, Brit., 301
Assyria, 80, 146, 157
Astronomy, 1, 183, 232, 233
Asturias, 291
Astyages, 162, 164
Athaliah, 82
Athanasius, 108, 116, 213

Athelstane, 226
Athenagoras, 107
Athens, 102, 107, 144, 169, 177, 180, 181
Athol, 279
Athotes, 137
Atlantic, 297
Attalus, 196, 215
Attica, 144
Attila, 118, 216
Auckland, 303
Augsburg, 269
Augustine, 109, 117, 216, 222, 298
Augustulus, 217
Augustus, 88, 97, 152, 210, 212
Auletes (Ptol.), 152
Aurelian, 114, 210
Aurelius Anton., 206
Aureolus, 210
Austerlitz, 290
Australasia, 52
Australia, 38, 52, 53, 57, 259, 279
Australian Alps, 53
Austria, 39, 40, 245, 307, 316
Austrian suc., 275
Austrians, 236, 308, 312
Avignon, 236, 239
Ayacucho, 298
Azores, 54, 241, 247, 314
Azov, 270

BAAL, 78
Baasha, 78, 81
Babel, 71, 154
Babylon, 85, 86, 136, 149, 156, 161, 162, 167, 179
Babylonia, 157, 164
Bacon, Francis, 260
Bacon, Roger, 231, 233
Bactria, 180
Badajos, 293
Baden, 39
Bagdad, 223, 228, 262
Bagoas, 167
Bahamas, 261
Baird, 288
Bajazet, 239, 240
Bajazet II., 244
Balaam, 74
Balaclava, 310
Baladan, 83
Balak, 74
Balbao, 56, 249
Balbinus, 209
Baliol, 234, 237, 238
Balloon, 282, 303

Balmerino, 276
Baltic, 310
Baltimore, 273, 295
Bane, Donald, 228
Bank Charter Act, 306
Bank of England, 269, 287
Bank, U. S., 304
Bannockburn, 236
Baptism, 113
Baptist (John), 89, 98, 200
Barak, 75
Barbadoes, 259
Barbarossa, 250
Bardesanes, 112
Barium, 18
Barnabas, 101
Baronet, 260
Barossa, 292
Bartholomew Diaz, 245
Bartholomew, St., 257
Basil, 108
Basilides, 112
Basilowitz, 244
Basle, 110, 253, 286
Bass, 288
Bastile, 284
Batavia, 57, 260
Bats, 83
Batu Khan, 232
Batuta, John, 54
Bautzen, 294
Bavaria, 39
Bavarians, 316
Bayonet, 267, 291
Bayonne, 267, 291
Beauclerc, 229
Becket, 230
Bedford, 241
Behring, Str., 57, 273
Belesys, 161
Belgians, 315
Belgium, 301
Belgrade, 274
Belibus, 160
Belisarius, 221
Belleisle, 276
Bellenden Ker, 53
Bellerophon, 295
Bellows, 261
Bells, 226
Beloochistan, 43, 44
Belshazzar, 86, 162, 164
Belus, 167
Belzoni, 298
Beneventum, 193
Bengal, 277
Benhadad II., 78, 158
Benhadad III., 79, 81

Benjamin, 74
Ben Nevis, 41
Berenice, 152
Berezina, 293
Berlin, 12, 291, 307, 316
Bermudas, 260
Bern, Council of, 252
Bernice, 103
Berosus, 87, 137, 155, 156, 167
Berri, Duke de, 297
Berwick, 240, 271
Beryllium, 13
Bessel, 5, 12
Bestia, 196
Bethlehem, 92
Bhurtpur, 299
Bible, 242, 252, 259
Biela's comet, 11
Birds, 32, 33
Birmingham, 285
Bismark, 316
Bismuth, 16, 19, 20
Bithynia, 208
Black Death, 237
Blackheath, 242
Black Prince, 237, 238
Black Sea, 234, 300, 310
Blake, 265
Blanc, Mt., 41
Blenheim, 271
Blida, 299
Blind Harry, 241
Blockade, 313
Blois, Stephen de, 229
Blood, circ. of, 260
Bloody Mary, 254, 255
Bloody statute, 253
Blucher, 295, 297
Blue Mts., 53
Boadicea, 203
Bobadella, 248
Boccaccio, 236
Bochus, 137
Bœotia, 174, 175
Boian Gauls, 194
Boleyn, Anne, 252, 253
Bolivar, 297, 298
Bolivia, 50, 51, 298
Bologna, 230
Bolor Tagh, 44
Bomarsund, 310
Bombay, 316
Boniface VIII., 235
Bonosus, 211
Booth, Wilkes, 315
Borneo, 56, 250
Borodino, 293
Boron, 16, 19, 21

Boscawa, 278
Boston, 314
Botany, 27
Bothwellhaugh, 256
Bothwell, 256
Bothwell Bridge, 268
Bouillon, 229
Bourbons, 278, 297
Boyne, 269
Brahmapootra, 45
Brahmins, 35
Bramante, 248
Brandt, 267
Brandy, 21
Brasidas, 176
Brazil, 50, 55, 248, 298
Breda, 266
Brennus, 182, 190
Brest, 278
Bretigni, Peace of, 238
Breton, Cape, 277
Brewster, 316
Brienne, 282
Britain, 118, 198, 202, 203, 204, 215, 216, 275, 285, 305, 312, 313, 314
British empire, 39, 40
British Isles, 38, 40
British Museum, 277
Britons, 192, 203, 221, 222
Bromine, 19, 21
Brörsen's comet, 11
Bruce, 234, 235, 236, 279
Bruges, 238
Brutus, 189, 199
Bryant, 53
Bubastis, 137, 146
Buchanan, George, 268
Buddhists, 35
Bug, 42
Bulgaria, 239
Bunker's Hill, 280
Bunyan, 268, 269
Buren, Van, 303
Burgoyne, 280
Burgundians, 215
Burgundy, 240, 241, 251
Burke, 287
Burmah, 299
Burmese war, 293, 309
Burns, 287
Busaco, 292
Butschetje, 41
Byron, Lord, 298
Byzantium, 165, 173, 179, 207, 213

CABAL, 267
Cabool, 305
Cabots, 55, 247
Cabral, 55, 248
Cabs, 261
Cade, Jack, 247
Cadiz, 258
Cadmium, 18
Cadmus, 169
Cædmon, 223
Cænina, 187
Cæsar, C., 201
Cæsar, Jul., 152, 197, 198, 199
Cæsar, Luc., 201
Cæsars, 211
Cæsarea, 89, 103, 104, 114, 200, 204
Cæsium, 18
Caiaphas, 98, 99
Caille, De la, 5, 8
Cainan, 64, 70
Cairo, 277, 287
Calah, 71, 154
Calais, 243, 255
Calania, 267
Calcium, 16, 19
Calculus, 267
Calcutta, 277
Caledonians, 207
Calendar, 199
Calico-printing, 267
California, 308
Caligula, 100, 202
Caliphs, 222, 223, 228, 233
Callistus, 113
Calmar, Union of, 239
Calonne, 271
Calvin, 249, 256
Calvinism, 109, 110, 255
Cambodia, 45
Cambray, 249
Cambria, 225
Cambridge University, 225, 232
Cambyses, 148, 164
Camillus, 191
Camoëns, 257
Campbell, Colin, 312
Camperdown, 287
Campo Formio, 287
Cana, 93
Canaan, 67, 74, 144, 169
Canada, 47, 48, 55, 56, 247, 252, 278, 293
Canadian rebellion, 304, 305
Canals, 147, 278, 317
Canary Isles, 54, 241, 248
Candahar, 304

Candia, 267
Canmore, Mal., 228
Cannæ, 194
Cannes, 295
Canning, 298, 300
Cannon, 237, 240
Canon law, 230
Canton, 240, 303, 305
Canute, 227
Capac, H., 251
Capac, M., 227
Cape of Good Hope, 54, 55, 245, 247
Cape Verd Islands, 54, 242
Capella, 13
Capet, H., 226
Capitolina, Ælia, 112, 206
Capitoline Hill, 189
Cappadocia, 157
Capreæ, 202
Captivity, 61, 80, 83, 85
Capua, 194
Caracalla, 113, 208
Caractacus, 203
Carausius, 211
Carbon, 16, 19, 21
Carboniferous syst., 29, 34
Carchemish, 161
Carians, 211
Caribs, 248, 249
Carlists, 303
Carlowitz, 270
Carobobo, 297
Carolina, 268, 313
Caroline, Queen, 297, 298
Carlovingian dyn., 223
Carmel, 78
Cartagena, 275
Carterel, 57, 270
Carthage, 82, 88, 107, 108, 113, 146, 170, 171, 182, 187, 194, 195, 209
Carthagena, 217
Carthaginians, 180, 193
Cartier, Jacq., 56, 252
Carus, 211
Caspian, 81, 163
Cassander, 181
Cassiodorus, 100
Cassius, 190, 199
Castile, 228, 238, 244
Castlereagh, 298
Cataline, 198
Catechist, 113
Catharine, 252, 253, 273, 278
Cathay, 136, 234

Cathcart, 291
Catholic League, 257, 258, 261
Catholica, 36, 252
Cato, 195, 199
Cato Conspir., 297
Cattle Plague, 315
Catulus, 194, 197
Caucasian race, 35
Caudine Forks, 192
Cavilham, 55, 245
Cavour, Ct., 314
Cawnpore, 311
Caxton, 244
Cechous, 137, 156
Celebez, 56, 250
Celsus, 112, 206
Celtiberi, 196
Celts, 36, 168, 196
Censors, 99, 190, 191
Census, 289
Centauri, alpha, 12, 13
Ceraunus, Ptol., 182
Cerdic, Sax., 221
Ceres, 289
Cerium, 18
Cerinthus, 111
Ceylon, 55, 243, 286
Chæronea, 175, 179
Chalcedon, 109, 118
Chaldæa, 137, 145
Chaldæan dyn., 156, 161
Chalmers, Th., 307
Chalons, 210, 216
Charlemagne, 223, 224, 226
Charles I. (Eng.), 261, 262, 264
Charles I. (Sp.), 250
Charles (Bald), 225
Charles (Germ.), 249
Charles II. (Eng.), 265, 266, 268
Charles V., 238, 252, 253, 254
Charles VI., 239, 241, 275
Charles VII., 275
Charles IX., 257
Charles X., 301
Charles Edward, 283
Charles Martel, 223
Charleston, 281, 313
Charlotte, 296
Charta, Magna, 232
Charts, sea, 245
Chaucer, 237
Chebar, 85, 161
Chedorlaomer, 72
Chemical equiv., 19
Chemistry, 13
Cheops, 138
Chephrenes, 138
Chevalier, 275, 276

Chevy Chase, 239
Chicago, 315
Chilè, 50, 51, 56, 253, 296
Chimborazo, 51
China, 43, 44, 54, 136, 231, 234, 240, 273, 302, 303, 304
China-ware, 277
Chlorine, 18, 19, 21
Chlorus, Const., 115
Choczin, 267
Cholera, 301, 302
Christ, 89, 97, 99
Christian IX., 315
Christianity, 115, 213, 221
Christians, 36, 101, 226, 230, 242
Chromium, 18
Chronicles, 86
Chronology, 58, 64, 89, 92, 139
Chrysostom, 103, 117
Church of England, 106
Church of Scot., 256
Church bells, 226
Church, Irish, 317
Churches, 114
Churches, Greek and Lat., 225
Churches, Gothic, 227
Cicero, 196, 198, 199, 244
Cid, 230
Cilicia, 102
Cimbri, 196, 197
Cimon, 174
Cincinnatus, 190
Cinna, 197
Cintra; Convention, 291
Circulation of blood, 260
Ciudad Rodrigo, 293
Civil war, 225, 262
Clarence, 296
Clarendon, 230, 267
Clarkson, 282
Claudius, 101, 193, 202, 203, 210
Claverhouse, 268, 269
Clayton, 274
Cleander, 207
Cleisthenes, 173
Clement, 107, 111
Cleomenes III., 182
Cleon, 176
Cleopatra, 151, 152, 199
Clinton, 66
Clive, 277, 278

Clovis, 221
Clusium, 189
Clyde, 206
Cnidus, 166, 177
Coaches, hackney, 261
Coal, 232
Coal-gas, 274
Coal-measures, 29, 34
Cobalt, 16, 18
Cobden, 315
Cochineal dyeing, 250
Codomannus, Dar., 167, 179
Codrington, 300
Codrus, 170
Cœle-Syria, 149
Cœpia, 196
Cœur de Lion, 231
Coilus, 192
Coimbres, 314
Coins, 171, 237
Colchester, 203
Colchis, 145, 170
Cold, 21
Coleridge, 302
Colladon, 24
Collatinus, 189
Collingwood, 292
Cologne, 236
Colonisation, Egypt, and Canaan, 136
Colonists, 160
Colony, C., 286, 289, 290
Colorado, 49
Colossians (Ep.), 103
Columba, St., 221
Columbia, 49, 297, 301
Columbus, Barth., 245
Columbus, Christ., 55, 246, 247, 248
Column of Trajan, 205
Comets, 10
Commerce, treaty of, 313
Commodus, 207
Commons, House of, 234
Commonwealth, 264
Compass, mariner's, 54, 235
Communion, 99
Comyn, 235
Concordat, Fontainebleau, 293
Confederates, 314
Confederation, N. Ger., 316
Conflagration, 315
Confusion of tongues, 136

Congo, 244
Congress, 179, 310
Coniah, 85, 161
Conon, 177
Conqueror (Willm.), 228
Conquest, Norman, 228
Conrad III., 230
Conservatives, 268
Conspiracy, Gowrie, 258
Constance, 110
Constans, 213
Constantine, 115, 116, 211, 212, 213
Constantinople, 109, 110, 116, 213, 215, 222, 231, 242, 299
Constantius, Cæs., 212, 213
Continents, 37, 38
Conventicle Act, 266
Convention, 289, 314
Cook, 57
Cook, Mt., 54
Cope, 276
Copenhagen, 242, 273, 289, 291
Copernicus, 248
Coponius, 97
Copper, 16, 19, 21, 23
Coptos, 139-
Corcyra, 175
Cordoba, Ferd., 250
Corinth, 102, 104, 166, 170, 175, 177, 183, 195
Corinthians (Epist.), 102
Coriolanus, 189
Corn-laws, 307
Cornelius, 100
Cornwall, 222, 232
Cornwallis, 281, 282
Coroná (oration), 180
Coronea, 166, 177
Corporation Act, 266, 300, 303
Corsica, 194, 279
Cortez, 250, 251
Coruna, 292
Corupedion, 182
Corvin, Math., 243, 245
Cosmo di Medici, 241
Cossus, Cor., 190
Cotopaxi, 51
Cotys, 195
Councils, 109, 110
Counties, 225
Coup d'Etat, 309

INDEX.

Covenanters, 262, 266, 268
Coverdale's Bible, 252
Cowper, Wm., 288
Cracow, 307
Cradle Mt., 54
Cranmer, 252, 254
Crannon, 180
Crassus, 88, 197, 198
Creation, 69
Cremera, 190
Creole, 305
Cressy, 237
Cretaceous syst., 29, 34
Crete, 104
Crimea, 274
Crocodilopolis, 139, 141
Crœsus, 172
Cromwell, 262, 265
Croton, 188
Crucifixion, 99
Crusaders, 229, 231
Crusades, 229, 230, 231, 232, 233, 234, 235
Cryptogamia, 28
Crystal Palace, 310
Ctesiphon, 207, 211
Cuba, 55, 56, 249, 250, 317
Culloden, 276
Cumæ, 187, 189
Cumberland, Duke of, 276, 304
Cunaxa, 86, 106
Cuninghame, 63
Curiatii, 188
Curius, 193
Curtius, 191
Cush, 154
Cushites, 140, 145
Cuzco, 227, 252
Cyaxares, 86, 161, 163
Cygnus, 12, 13
Cylo, 172
Cymri, 234
Cynoscephalæ, 183
Cynossema, 176
Cyprian, 108, 114
Cyprus, 101, 151, 152, 159, 174, 205, 257
Cyrene, 148, 152, 162, 178, 205
Cyril, 108, 109, 117
Cyrus (Eld.), 85, 86, 148, 162, 164, 188
Cyrus (Younger), 86, 166
Cyzicus, 176
Czar, 244, 310

DACIA, 205, 210, 212

Dacians, 200
Dalmatia, 199, 201
Damascus, 83, 100, 223
Damiens, 277
Danby, 268
Danes, 224, 227
Daniel, 85, 86, 161
Danish America, 47
Dante, 234
Dauton, 285
Danube, 42, 200, 211, 216
Danubian Princip., 310
Dapsang peak, 45
Darien, 56, 249, 270
Darius Codomannus, 167, 179, 180
Darius Hystaspes, 86, 148, 165
Darius(Mede), 86, 164
Darius Nothus, 166
Darnley, 256
Dathan, 73
David, 76, 77
David I., 229
David II., 237, 238
Davidson, 25
Davis, Jef., 813
Day, St J. Vincent, 7
Deacons, 100
Deborah, 75
Decemvirs, 190
Decimals, 227
Decius, 114, 192, 193, 209
Defender of the Faith, 251
Deioces, 163
Delagoa Bay, 54
Delambre, 5
Delany, 3
Delft, 258
Delhi, 239, 274, 289, 311
Delium, 175
Delta, 142, 144, 145
Deluge, 61, 65, 70, 136, 169
Demetrius, 181, 182
Democracy, 173, 181
Demosthenes, 178, 179, 180
Denmark, 39, 40, 227, 239, 242, 243, 251, 314, 315
Deptford, 270
Deputations, 85
Derby, 316
Dercyllidas, 177
Descartes, 265
Dettingen, 275
Deucalion, 169
Devonian system, 29, 34

Diamond (Koh-i-nor), 254
Diamond necklace, 282
Diaz, Bartholomew, 245
Diaz, Juan de Solis, 249
Dictator, 191
Didius, Julianus, 207
Dido, 82
Didymium, 18
Differential calculus, 267
Diocletian, 114, 115, 211, 212
Diodorus, 152, 198
Dionysius, 107, 114, 176, 191, 200
Dionysius Exiguus, 97, 221
Dispersion, 71, 136
Disputation, 101
Disraeli, 316, 317
Disruption, 306
Distress, 314
Dnieper, 42
Doges, 223
Dominica, 281
Domitian, 105, 205
Don, 43
Donati's comet, 11
Donatist, 115
Don Pedro, 242
Doomsday, 228
Dorians, 170
Dort, 242, 260
Douglas, 239, 240
Douglas, Gawin, 251
Douro, 42
Dover, 250
Draco, 171
Drake, Sir Francis, 257
Drepanum, 193
Drogheda, 265
Druinclog, 268
Drusilla, 102
Drusus, 200, 202
Dryden, 270
Dublin, 206, 258
Duels, 229
Dumouriez, 285
Dúna, 231
Dunbar, 235
Duncan, Admiral, 287
Duncan I., 227, 228
Duncan II., 229
Dunkeld, 251
Dunkirk, 266
Durham, 237
Dutch, 57, 259, 260, 265, 287, 290
Dwina, 42

Dyads, 15, 16, 17

EARTHQUAKE, 88, 277
Earth's surface, 22
Easter, 112
East India Co., 258
Ebenezer, 76
Eborăcum, 208
Ebro, 42
Ecbatana, 163, 180
Eckmühl, 292
Eclipse, 190
Ecuador, 50, 297, 301
Eden, the, 206
Edgar the Peaceful, 226
Edgar (Scotland), 229
Edgehill, 262
Edicts, 113, 212, 258
Edinburgh, 24, 223, 255, 258
Edinburgh, Duke of, 317
Edmund Ironside, 227
Edmund (Magnificent), 226
Edom, 82, 83
Edred, 226
Edward(Confessor), 227
Edward (Elder), 225
Edward (Martyr), 226
Edward I., 234, 235
Edward II., 235
Edward III., 237, 238
Edward IV., 243, 244
Edward V., 244
Edward VI., 254
Edwin 223
Edwy, 226
Egbert, 224
Eglon, 74
Egypt, 46, 72, 89, 119, 136, 137, 152, 157, 164, 179, 181, 197, 205, 222, 233, 235, 287
Ehud, 74
Eisleben, 244
Elagabulus, 208
Elah, 78
Elam, 155, 163
Elba, 190, 294, 295
Elbe, 42
Elburz, 41, 44
Eleazar, 73
Elector-Palatine, 260
Electricity, 27, 277

Electric telegraph, 317
Electro-magnetism, 285
Elementary substances, 17, 13, 20
Elgin, 235
Elgin Marbles, 296
Eli, 75
Eliakim, 85
Elijah, 78, 79, 32
Elisabeth, 255, 257, 259
Elisha, 79
Elkanah, 76
Elliot, 281
Elon, 75
Elvira, Conn. of, 115
Elymas, 101
Emancipation, Act of, 300, 313
Emperor, 200
Encke, 5
Encke's comet, 10, 11
Enghien, Duke d', 290
England, 38, 57, 224, 227, 228, 232, 310, 314, 315, 317
England, New, 260
English, 314, 316
Enoch, 70
Enos, 70
Epaminondas, 178
Ephesians (Ep.), 103
Ephesus, 102, 109, 118, 179
Ephræm, 108
Ephraim, 81
Epicurean School, 182
Epidamnus, 175
Epiphanes, 87, 151
Epiphanius, 108
Epirus, 104
Episcopacy, 269
Equator, 12, 51
Erasmus, 243, 253
Eratosthenes, 182
Erbium, 18
Erech, 154
Erfurth, 248
Eric, 224
Erie Canal, 298
Erigena, 225
Erivan, 299
Eruptions, 267
Esarhaddon, 81, 84, 160
Esau, 72
Essex, 258
Esther, 86, 165
Ethelbald, 224
Ethelbert, 224
Ethelred, 225

Ethelred (Unready), 226, 227
Ether, 22
Ethiopia, 35, 81, 84, 144, 145
Ethnography, 35
Etna, 41, 267
Etruria, 190, 191, 194
Etruscans, 185, 186, 188, 190, 191
Eugene, 271, 272
Eugenius, 215, 242
Euler, 279
Eunuch, Ethiopian, 100
Eunus, 196
Euphrates, 45, 147, 153
Euric, 217
Euripides, 174
Europe, 36, 37, 38, 41, 42, 263
Eurymedon, 166, 174
Eusebius, 108, 114, 213
Eutyches, 118
Eutychian controversy, 109
Everest, 45
Evesham, 234
Evil-Merodach, 162
Exchequer, Court of, 228
Exhibition, 309, 311, 314
Exiguus, 97, 221
Exodus, 73, 144
Eylau, 291
Eyre, 315
Ezekiel, 85, 161
Ezra, 86, 166

FABII, 190
Fabius, 194
Factory, 260
Factory Act, 302
Fahrenheit's thermometer, 21, 274
Falerii, 191
Falkirk, 235, 276
Falling bodies, 26
Family compact, 278
Famine, 190, 207, 210, 307
Fauna (Europe), 33
Faust, 242
Faye's comet, 3, 11
Federals, 284, 315
Felix, 102, 103, 203
Fenians, 315, 316
Ferdinand I. (Austria), 302, 307, 303
Ferdinand II. (Germany), 261
Ferdinand, Prince, 278

Ferdinand II. (Sp.), 55, 244, 249
Ferdinand VII. (Spain), 297, 298, 302
Fergus, 192
Fernandez Cortez, 56
Ferns, 28
Festus, 103, 203
Feudalism, 228
Fidenæ, 190
Fieschi, 303
Finisterre, 276
Fires, 204, 266
Fishes, 32, 33
Fitzgerald, 237
Fixed stars, 11, 12
Fizeau, 25
Flamininus, 183
Flamsteed, 272
Flanders, 234, 236
Flavius, Vespasian, 204
Fleets, 290, 310
Flinders, 288
Flodden Field, 249
Floras, 27, 28
Florence, 241, 244
Florida, 56, 249, 297
Fluorine, 18, 19
Fontainebleau, 291, 293
Forth, 206
Forum, 191
Fossil botany, 29, 30
Fossil zoology, 34
Fotheringay Castle, 258
Foucault, 3, 6, 25, 27
Four hundred, 176
Fugitive Slave Bill, 309
Fulgentius, 109
Fusing-point of metals, 23
France, 39, 40, 221, 223, 226, 228, 234, 303, 309, 310, 311, 312, 313, 314
Franchise, 192
Francis I. (Austria), 302
Francis I. (France), 249, 251, 253
Francis II. (France), 255, 285
Francis Joseph, 302
Francis I. (Lorraine), 274, 276
Francis II. (Naples), 313
Franklin, Benjamin, 271, 277, 284

Franklin, Sir J., 306
Franks, 209, 216
Frederick (Barbarossa, Ger.), 231
Frederick VII. (Denmark), 315
Frederick III. (Germany), 236, 242
Frederick the Great (Prussia), 275, 282
Frederick - William (Prussia), 282, 312
Frederickshall, 272
Freemasons, 226
Freezing - point of liquids, 21
Free Trade, 298, 307
French colonists, 57
Friends, Society of, 263

GAETA, 303
Galatian war, 195
Galatians (Ep.), 102
Galba, 104, 204
Galcacus, 205
Galerius, 115, 211
Galilee, 89, 202
Galileo, 4, 256, 258, 259, 261, 262
Gallienus, 209
Galli Insubres, 194
Gallio, 102
Gallipoli, 237
Gallus, 209, 213
Galvani, 285
Gama, Vasco de, 247
Gambier, 291
Games, 200, 203, 209
Ganges, 45
Garibaldi, 313
Garonne, 42
Garter, order of, 237
Gases, 16, 17, 24
Gath, 76
Gaugamela, 167, 179
Gaul, 198, 202, 206, 207, 208, 211, 214, 215, 216
Gauls, 182, 188, 191, 192, 194
Gaveston, 235, 236
Gaza, 109, 179
Gazette, Lond., 266
General Assembly, 255
Geneva, 254
Genoa, 231, 243
Genseric, 118, 216, 217
Gentiles, 100
Geography, 37, 232, 236
Geological botany, 29

Geological zoology, 34
Geology, 59, 60, 61
George I., 272, 273
George II., 273, 275, 278
George III., 278, 297
George IV., 292, 297, 298, 301
German Confed., 316
Germanicus, 201
Germans, 208, 211, 220
Germany, 3, 29, 33, 200, 206, 232, 240
Gerscheim, 316
Gerusalemme Lib., 257
Gessler, 236
Geta, 208
Gethsemane, 99
Gettysburg, 315
Ghent, 295
Ghibelines, 230
Gibbon, 286
Gibraltar, 271, 281
Gideon, 75
Gilboa, 76
Gilead, 80, 159
Giles, St, 225
Gioja, 54, 235
Gipsies, 36, 37
Gladstone, 317
Glasgow Univ., 242
Glass, 160, 230
Glasses, 233
Glencoe, 269
Glendower, 240
Gnosticism, 112
Goa Factory, 55, 248
Goderich, 300
Godfrey, 224, 229
Gœppert, 29
Goethe, 302
Gold, 16, 19, 23
Gold coins, 237
Goldsmith, 280
Goliath, 76
Gomorrah, 72
Gonzales, 54
Good Hope C., 5, 54, 55, 245
Gordians, 209
Gordon riots, 281
Goshen, 73
Gospels, 116
Gothic invasion, 209
Gothic kingdom, 220
Gothic style, 227
Goths, 196, 210, 211, 213, 214, 218, 220
Gough, Lord, 306
Gowrie Conspiracy, 258
Gozan, 81

Gracchi, 196
Graciosa, 247
Graham, 242, 292
Grampians, 205
Granada, 245
Granadian Confed., 49, 50
Grand Alliance, 270
Granicus, 167, 179
Granite, 26
Grant, 314, 317
Gratian, 214, 230
Gratus, Val., 98
Gravity, 26
Great Harry, 245
Greece, 4, 33, 39, 40, 167, 181, 183, 300, 302, 314, 315
Greek, 244, 250
Greek Church, 26, 225
Greek revolution, 297, 298
Greenland, 47, 226
Greenwich, 5, 6, 267
Gregories, 105, 107, 108, 109, 223, 239, 257
Grenville, 275
Grey, 279
Grocyn, 245
Guelphs, 230
Guiana, 50
Guido Aretino, 227
Guinea, 47
Guinegate, 249
Guizot, 305
Gujerat, 308
Gulf Stream, 56, 249
Gun-cotton, 317
Gunpowder, 237
Gunpowder Plot, 259
Gustavus Adolph., 261, 262
Gustavus Vasa, 251
Guttemberg, 242
Gwalior, 306
Gylippus, 176

HABAKKUK, 84
Habeas Corp., 268, 308
Habor, 81
Hackney - coaches, 261
Haco, 234
Haerlem, 242
Hague treaty, 270
Halah, 81
Hales, 69
Haliartus, 166, 177
Halicarnassus, 148, 200
Halidon Hill, 237
Halley's comet, 11

Halys, 163
Ham, 136, 137
Hamah, 236
Haman, 86, 165
Hamilcar, 194
Hamilton, B., 256
Hamilton, P., 252
Hampton Ct. Conf., 259
Hannibal, 194, 195
Hanover, 289, 304, 316
Hanseatic League, 232
Hants, 203
Haran, 72, 198
Hardicanute, 227
Harefoot, Har., 227
Hargrave, 278
Harmodius, 172
Harold, 227, 228
Haroun-al-Raschid, 223, 224
Harry, Blind, 241
Hartz mines, 261
Harvard Univ., 262
Harvey, 260
Hasdrubal, 195
Hastings, 228
Hastings, Marq. of, 296
Hastings, Warren, 280, 282
Havanna, 278
Havelock, 311
Hawke, 278
Hawkins, 255
Hayti, 306
Hazael, 79, 82, 158
Head of Church, 252
Heathens, 35
Heber, 71
Hebrew, 62, 63, 250
Hebrews (Epistle), 103
Hebrides, 102, 229, 234
Hebron, 71, 76, 91, 136
Hegesippus, 107, 112
Hegira, 222
Heights of mts., 41, 44, 48, 50
Helen, 170
Heliogabalus, 113
Heliopolis, 136, 137, 150
Hellenes, 145, 168, 169
Hellespont, 237
Helvetii, 198
Henderson, 5, 6
Henfrey, 29
Hengist, 216
Henry of Castile, 54
Henry I., 229

Henry II., 230
Henry III., 232, 257, 258
Henry IV., 240, 258
Henry V., 240, 241
Henry VI., 241
Henry VII., 55, 244, 247
Henry VIII, 249, 250, 251, 252, 253, 254
Hephæstion, 180
Heptarchy, 216, 221, 224
Heracleopolis, 138
Heraclidæ, 170
Heraldry, 229
Herat, 239
Herculaneum, 204, 273
Hermann, 201
Hermias, 107
Hermit, Peter, 229
Hernandez Cordoba, 56
Herods, 88, 89, 98, 101, 199, 200
Herodotus, 4, 65, 148, 174, 175
Herschel, 10, 281, 301
Heruli, 210
Hesiod, 171
Hesse, Elector., 316
Hezekiah, 83, 147, 160
Hiel, 78
Hierapolis, 107
Hiero, 190
Hieroglyphic, 120, 137
Hilary, 108
Hill, Row., 305
Himalaya, 45
Hindoo-Koosh, 44
Hindustan, 43, 44
Hipparchus, 172, 173, 183
Hippias, 172
Hippo, 109, 117, 216
Hippocrates, 174
Hippolytus, 113, 114
Hispaniola, 55, 247
Historical Lib., 198
History of World, 260
Hittites, 142
Hoang-ho, 45
Hohenlinden, 288
Holland, 242, 257, 267, 285, 286, 290, 292, 294, 301
Holstein, 275, 316
Holy Alliance, 295
Holyrood Abbey, 229
Homer, 171

Homildon Hill, 240
Honorius, 215, 216
Hood, Mt., 49
Hooper, 254
Hophra, 147, 148, 162
Horace, 200
Horntii, 188
Hosea, 79
Hoshea, 80
Hotspur, 240
Howard, 284
Howe, 280, 286
Huano Capac, 56, 251
Hudson Bay, 57, 259
Huguenots, 252, 255
Humboldt, 28
Hungarian army, 309
Hungary, 225, 232, 243
Huns, 118, 214, 216
Huskisson, 293
Huss, John, 110, 238
Hycsos, 139
Hydrogen. 15, 16, 17, 18, 19
Hyrcanus, 88
Hystaspes, Dar., 148

Iapygians, 186
Ibzan, 75
Iceland, 225, 226, 253
Ichabod, 76
Iconium, 101
Idumea, 88
Ignatius, 107, 111
Ignatius Loyola, 253
Ildefonso, treaty of, 287
Iliad, 171
Illyria, 175, 194
Illyricum, 201, 213, 216
Inachus, 169
Inarus, 148, 166
Incandescence, 23
Incas, 227, 251, 252
Income-tax, 305
Independence, Declaration of, 280
Independence, War of, 280
India, 55, 180, 184, 200, 239, 245, 248, 260, 299, 303, 304, 3 8, 311, 312
India Co., East, 258
India, Further, 43, 44, 45
Indian Mutiny, 311
Indies, West, 48, 49, 248, 255
Indigo, 276

Indium, 18
Indo-European, 184
Indus, 45, 152, 163, 180
Infernal machine, 303
Inkermann, 301
Innocent III., 231
Innocent XI., 267
Inoculation, 273
Inquisition, 231, 244, 261
Inscriptions, 266
Insects, 28
Insubres, Galli, 194
Interest, 191
Interim, 254
Interregnum, 79, 80
Inundation, 242
Iodine, 18, 19
Iona, 221
Ionia, 165, 174
Ionian Isles, 287, 815
Iota, 18
Ipsus, 150, 181
Ireland, 39, 40, 221, 230, 236, 245, 258, 300, 307, 308
Irenæus, 107, 113
Irene, 224
Iridium, 18, 19
Irish Church, 317
Irish Rebellion, 262, 287
Iron, 16, 18, 19, 21, 23
Ironside, Edmund, 227
Irrawaddy, 45
Iryphon, 88
Isaac, 72
Isabella, 244, 302, 317
Isaiah, 83
Iscariot, 99
Ishmael, 72
Israel, 84
Issus, 167, 179, 207
Isthmian Games, 170
Italy, 33, 39, 40, 192, 210, 213, 215, 220, 221
Iva-lush, 158
Ivan Basilowitz, 244
Ivan III., 243
Ivry, battle of, 258

Jack Cade, 247
Jackson, 295
Jacob, 72, 141
Jacques Cartier, 252
Jair, 75
Jamaica, 247, 265, 315

James I., 240, 241, 242, 259, 260
James II., 242, 243, 268, 270
James III., 243
James IV., 245, 247, 249
James V., 249, 253
James VI., 256, 258, 259
Janiculum, Mt., 190
Janissaries, 299
Jannes, 141
Janus, 200
Japan, 43, 44, 56, 253, 312
Japheth, 70
Jardin des Plantes, 28
Jared, 70
Jason, 145, 170
Jeezeh, 9, 136
Jehoahaz, 79, 84
Jehoash, 79, 82
Jehoiakim, 85, 161
Jehoram, 79, 81, 82
Jehoshaphat, 81
Jehu, 79
Jellalabad, 305
Jena, 291
Jephthah, 75
Jeremiah, 84
Jericho, 74, 78, 99
Jeroboam, 77, 78, 79, 146
Jerome, 108, 110, 117
Jersey, New, 266
Jerusalem, 77, 85, 87, 88, 98, 101, 104, 149, 162, 196, 199, 204, 206, 222, 229, 230
Jerusalem Delivered, 257
Jervis, 287
Jesuits, 253, 287
Jesus Christ, 89, 98
Jewish war, 204, 206
Jews, 86, 87, 202, 229, 237, 247
Jezreel, 79
Joan of Arc, 241
Job, 72, 140
Joel, 83
Johannes, 216
John, 232, 240
John (Baptist), 89, 98
John Knox, 255, 256, 257
John, Prester, 242
John, St. 100, 105
Johnson, Reverdy, 317
Johnson, Sam., 277
Jomard, 8
Jonab, 79, 158

Jonathan, 76, 88
Joppa, 100
Jordan, 74, 99
Joseph, 72, 141
Joseph II., 279
Josephine, 292
Josephus, 100
Joshua, 74
Josiah, 84, 147, 161
Jotham, 83
Jovian, 214
Jubilee, 74, 75, 76, 81, 82, 83, 84
Judæa, 86, 88, 104, 199
Judah, 72, 81
Judas, 87, 99
Judges, 74
Jugurtha, 196
Julian, 116, 213, 214, 216
Julian Calendar, 257
Julianus, Did., 207
Julius Cæsar, 197
Jupiter, 6, 9, 10, 25
Jupiter, temple of, 189
Juric, 230
Jury trial, 225, 230
Justin Martyr, 107, 112
Jutes, 118, 216, 218

Kant, 281
Kean, 316
Kenneth II., 224
Kent, 216
Kent, Duke of, 296
Kepler, 2, 9, 45, 256, 259, 260
Kertch, 311
Kesh, 146
Ket, 254
Khaled, 222
Khan, Akhbar, 305
Khan, Batu, 282
Khan, Kublai, 233, 234
Khan, Zenghis, 231, 232
Kiel, 294
Kiev, Duke of, 230
Kileh-Shergat, 157
Killiecrankie, 269
Kilmarnock, 276
King's College (Aberdeen), 247
Kissingen, 316
Kirjath-jearim, 77
Knights of St John, 236
Knights Templars, 229, 236
Knights (Ten.), 231
Knox, Jn., 255, 256, 257

Konjakofski, 41
Korah, 73
Koran, 222
Kordofan, 46
Kosciusko, Mt., 58
Koster, 242
Kouli Khan, 274
Kuen-Lun, 45

LABRADOR, 55
Labynetus, 162
Lace, 236
Lachish, 160
Lackland, John, 231
Lactantius, 108
Ladô, 165, 173
Lagos, 278
La Hague, 265, 269
Lake, Gen., 289
Lamachus, 176
Lamech, 70
Lamian war, 180
Lamps, oil, 268
Lancastrian dyn., 240, 244, 249
Langside, 256
Languedoc, 233
Lanthanum, 18
La Plata, 56
Lartius, Titus, 189
Lateran, 110
Latimer, 254
Latin Church, 225
Latin lan., 184
LatinScriptures, 113
Latin war, 191
Laud, Archbp., 262
Lavinium, 186
Law of Moses, 84
Law pleadings, 238
Lawrence, St, 49
Lazarus, 99
Lead, 16, 18, 19, 23
Leaden pipes, 223
League and Covenant, Solemn, 262
League, Haus., 232
Lebanon, 44
Leicester, 234
Leipsic, 261, 294
Lena, 45
Lennox, 258
Leo (Emperor of East), 223
Leo (Great), 109, 118
Leo IX, 227
Leonardi, Vincent, 282
Leonardo of Pisa, 231
Leons, Ponce de, 249
Leopold I. (Belgium), 296, 301, 315
Leopold II. (Ger.) 285

Lepanto, 256
Lepidus, 199
Lepsius, R., 66
Leslie, 262, 265
Leuctra, Battle of, 177
Leven, Loch, 256
Levi, 73
Leyden, 257
Lias, 29, 34
Licinian Rogations, 191
Licinius, 115, 212
Lieberk, 277
Light, 27, 260
Lightning, 277
Ligny, battle of, 295
Lima, 56, 252, 276
Lincoln, 313, 315
Lindlay, 28
Lindsay, Mt., 53
Linnæus, 28, 274, 275, 281
Liquids, 21, 22
Lisbon, 248
Lithium, 18, 21
Liturgy, 256
Liverpool Mts., 53
Livonia, 231
Livy, 200
Lochiel, 275
Locke, 271
Locri, 188
Locrian war, 179
Locris, 188
Locusts, 151
Lodi, 287
Logarithms, 260
Loire, 42
Lollards, 240
Lollard, Walter, 236
Lombard kingdom, 223
Lombardy, 221, 307, 312
London, 203, 261
London Bridge, 298
Londoners, 231
London (Treaty), 300
London University, 300
Londonderry, 269
Longimanus, 86, 166
Long Island, 280
Long Parliament, 262, 268
Lord's Day, 112
Lord's Supper, 99
Lot, 72
Louis V. (Bavaria), 236
Louis VII. (France), 230
Louis VIII. (France), 232

Louis IX. (France), 233, 234
Louis XI. (France), 243
Louis XIV., 265, 267, 269
Louis XV., 272, 277, 280
Louis XVI., 280, 284, 285
Louis XVIII., 294
Louis (Hungary), 251
Louisiana, 289
Louvel, 297
Lovat, 276
Low Countries, 287
Lucan, 203
Luceria, 192
Lucian, 112
Lucilla, 207
Lucius Tar. Priscus, 188
Lucius Tar. Superbus, 189
Lucknow, 312
Lucullus, 197
Luke, St, 90, 103
Luneville, 288
Lusiad, 257
Luther, 4, 244, 248, 250, 251, 254
Lutheranism, 251
Lutherans, 252, 253, 255
Lutzen, 261
Lycopolis, 115
Lycurgus, 171
Lydia, 102, 163, 164, 172
Lyons, 107, 112, 206
Lyons, Council of, 110
Lysias, 103
Lysimachus, 181, 182
Lystra, 101, 102

MACAO, 56, 253
Macaulay, 312
Macbeth, 227
Maccabees, 87
Macedon, 86, 87
Macedonia, 102, 103, 165, 168, 173, 178, 181, 182, 183, 215
Macedonian wars, 194, 195
Macedonius, 116
Machpelah, 73
Mackenzie, 49
Macrinus, 208
Madagascar, 46, 47, 248
Madeira, 54, 241, 312
Madrid, 251, 291, 293
Mælius, 190

Magdala, 317
Magdalena, 51
Magdeburg, 261
Magellan, 56, 250
Magenta, 312
Magi, the, 62
Magna Charta, 232
Magna Græcia, 185, 188, 189
Magnentius, 213
Magnesium, 18, 19, 21
Magyars, 225
Mahalaleel, 70
Mahratta war, 296, 306
Maida, 291
Mail-coaches, 282
Maine, 231
Maitland, 295
Malachi, 86
Maladetta, 41
Malakoff, 311
Malays, 35
Malaysia, 52, 53
Malcolm III., 228, 229
Malcolm IV., 230
Malplaquet, 271
Malta, 103
Mamelukes, 233
Mamertine prison, 104
Mammals, 32, 33, 34
Manasseh, 84, 160
Manchester, 297, 306, 316
Manco Capac, 227
Manetho, 150, 155
Manganese, 18, 21
Man, Isle of, 279
Manichæus, 114
Manifesto, 310
Manilla, 278
Manlius, 191
Mantinea, 176, 178, 183
Maories, 35
Marathon, 148
Marcellus, 100, 194
Marcion, 112
Marcomanni, 112, 206
Marco Polo, 54, 234, 255
Mardonius, 173
Marengo, 288
Margaret (Norway), 239
Maria, Donna, 303
Maria Louisa, 292
Maria Theresa, 274, 275
Marignan, 249
Mariner's compass, 235

328 INDEX.

Marius, 196, 197
Mark, St, 102
Marlborough, 273
Marocco, 46, 47
Marquette, Father, 267
Marriage law, 190
Mars, 2, 5, 9, 10
Marsala, 313
Mars' Hill, 102
Marsic wars, 197
Marston Moor, 262
Martel, Charles, 223
Mary, 90
Mary, Bloody, 254, 255
Mary II., 269
Mary Queen of Scots, 253, 255, 256, 258
Mason, 314
Matthew Corvinus, 243, 245
Matthew, St, 90, 102
Mauritius, 292
Maxentius, 212
Maximian, 114, 115, 211, 212
Maximilian II. (Germany), 257
Maximilian (Mex.), 316
Maximin, 208, 209
Maximinus, 114
Maximus, 209, 214
Mayflower, 260
Maynooth College, 286
Mayor, 231
Maypu, 296
Mazarin Bible, 242
Mazarin, Card., 265
Meanee, 306
Mecca, 221, 222
Medals, 266
Medes, 81
Media, 162, 163
Median dynasty, 137, 156
Medici, 244
Medicine, father of, 174
Medina, 222
Mediterranean, 317
Medjid, Abdal, 304
Medo-Persian empire, 85, 163, 164
Meerut, 311
Megalopolis, 178
Megiddo, 84, 161
Melanchthon, 256
Melaneres, 141
Melos, 176
Memnon, 142
Memphis, 67, 71, 137, 142, 156
Menahem, 80, 158

Menai Strait, 299
Menam, 43
Mencheres, 138
Mendelssohn, 307
Mendes, 137
Menelaus, 170
Menes, 71, 123, 137
Menschikoff, 310
Menthesuphis, 139, 156
Mentz, 243
Mercia, 221
Mercury, 9, 16, 18, 20, 21, 23, 27
Merodach-adan-akhi, 158
Merodach-Baladan, 83, 159, 160
Merrimac, 314
Meshach, 85, 162
Mesolonghi, 298, 299
Mesopotamia, 72, 74, 85, 155, 163, 198, 209, 214
Messene, 178
Messenians, 183
Messenian wars, 171, 174
Metals, 23
Metaurus, 195
Metellus, 193
Methodism, 285
Methodists, 274
Methuselah, 70
Mexicans, 250
Mexico, 48, 250, 298, 306, 308, 314
Micah, 83
Michael Servetus, 254
Micronesia, 53
Midian, 73, 75, 144
Middle ages, history of, 217
Milan, 109, 115, 190
Milan, edict of, 212
Miletius schism, 115
Miletus, 103, 104, 165, 173
Milk, 21
Miltiades, 173
Milton, 266, 267
Minden, 278
Mines, 248
Minor, Asia, 181
Minorca, 271, 277
Minucius, 190
Mirabeau, 284
Miriam, 73
Mississippi, 49, 57, 267
Mississippi bubble, 272
Mithridatic wars, 197, 198

Mizpeh, 76
Mizraim, 71, 137, 138
Mizraites, 71
Mnemon, Artaxerxes, 166
Moab, 145
Moabites, 74, 79, 142
Moawiah, 222
Modern history, 245
Mœris, 138, 140, 141
Mœsia, 209
Mogul, Great, 265, 271, 311
Mohacz, 251
Mohammed, 221, 222
Mohammedans, 36, 37
Moldavia, 205
Molière, 267
Moluccas, 250
Molluscs, 32, 33
Molybdenum, 18
Monachism, 213
Monads, 15, 17
Monarchianism, 112
Monarchy (England) 224
Monasteries, 252, 284
Mondego Bay, 291
Mongols, 35, 36
Mongol Tartars, 232, 233
Monitor, the, 314
Monmouth, Duke of, 268, 271
Monophysite doct., 118
Monothelites, 110
Montagu House, 277
Montanism, 112
Montenotte, 286
Montreal, 304
Montrose, Marquis of, 262, 265
Moon, 9
Moore, 292, 309
Moors, 223, 226, 229, 245, 259
Morea, 299, 300
Morgarten, 236
Moscow, 230, 293
Moses, 73, 74, 143, 144, 145
Mosses, 28
Motion of stars, 13
Mühlberg, 254
Mühldorf, 236
Mummius, 183, 195
Mummy, 146
Murad Bey, 287
Murat, 291, 296
Murena, 197

Murray, Earl of, 256
Mursa, 213
Muschelkalk, 31
Musical notes, 227
Mussulmans, 226, 229
Mutineers, 311
Mycalè, 165, 173
Mycenæ, 170
Mylæ, 193
Mytilene, 176

NAAMAN, 79
Nabonassar, 158, 187
Nabonidas, 162
Nabopolassar, 85, 161, 163
Naboth, 78
Nadab, 78
Nadir Shah, 274
Naissus, 210
Najera, 238
Nana Sahib, 311
Nanking, 234, 306
Nantes, Edict of, 258, 269
Nanur, 269
Naomi, 75
Napier, 260, 310, 317
Naples, 248, 251, 290, 297
Napoleon Buonap., 279, 286, 287, 288, 290, 291, 292, 293, 294, 295, 296, 297, 305
Napoleon, Louis, 308, 310, 312
Naphtha, 22
Narses, 221
Narva, 270
Naseby, 262
Nassau, 261
Natal, 46
National Assembly, 285
National Con., 285, 286
National Guard, 284
Naulochus, 199
Navarino, 200
Navarre, 238
Naxos, 174
Nazareth, 89, 98
Nazianzen, 108
Nearchus, 180
Nebuchadnezzar, 85, 147, 148, 161
Necho, Ph., 84, 147, 161
Necker, 280, 281, 282
Nectanebo, 149

INDEX.   329

Needle, variation of, 247
Negro race, 35
Nehemiah, 86, 166
Nelson, 49, 237, 269, 290
Neo-Cæsarea, 107
Neptune, 9, 10, 26
Neriglissar, 162
Nero, 102, 103, 104, 203, 204
Nerva, 105, 205
Nestorius, 109, 117, 118
Netherlands, 39, 40, 255, 256, 257
Neva, 42
Nevada, 41
Nevis, Ben, 41
New Brunswick, 47, 48
Newburg, 262
Newcastle, 232
Newcombe, 3, 6
Newcomen, 270, 278
New England, 260
Newfoundland, 47, 48, 247, 312
New Granada, 297, 301
New Jersey, 266, 277, 280
New Orleans, 295
New South Wales, 52, 57, 282
New style, 257, 277
Newton, 262, 265, 267, 269, 273
Newton's comet, 11, 26, 27
New York, 261, 266, 280, 303
New Zealand, 52, 53, 57, 262, 279, 304
Ney, Marshal, 296
Nice, 109, 110, 116, 253, 313
Nicholas, 311
Nicias, 176
Nickel, 16, 18, 20, 21
Nicodemus, 93
Nicolas, 299
Nicopolis, 104, 239
Niger, 207
Nigritia, 46, 47
Nile, 119, 237, 314
Nimeguen, 263
Nimrod, 71, 136, 156
Nineveh, 71, 79, 84, 147, 158, 161, 163
Ninus, 145, 157
Niobium, 18
Nitrogen, 16, 18, 20

Noah, 70, 137
Noetus, 114
Nola, 194, 201
Nordlingen, 262
Nore, 237
Norici, 200
Noricum, 216
Norium, 18
Norman Conquest, 223
Normandy, 225, 231, 265
Normans, 224, 225
Northampton, 242
Northmen, 115, 211, 224
Northumbria, 223
Norway, 39, 41, 227, 229, 239, 242
Norwegians, 225, 234
Notables, 282
Notes, musical, 227
Nothus, Dar., 166
Notium, 176
Nottingham, 293
Nova Scotia, 47, 48, 272
Novara, 308
Novation, 114
Novum Organum, 260
Nubia, 46, 140, 144
Numantia, 196
Numa Pompil., 187
Number of stars, 11, 12
Numerals, 226, 233
Numerian, 211
Nuremberg, 252
Nyssa, 108

OATES, T., 268
Observatory, Green., 267
Oby, 45
Occupation, Army of, 296
Oceania, 38
Ochus, 149, 166
O'Connell, 306
Octavius, 152, 199, 200
Odenathus, 210
Oder, 42
Odoacer, 217, 220
Œdipus, 170
Œnophyta, 174
Ogyges, 169
Ohio, 289
Oise, 253
Oktai, 232
Old Testament, 86
Olympia, 181
Olympiad, First, 80, 83, 171

Olympic Games, 145, 169
Olynthiac orations, 178
Olynthian war, 177
Olynthus, 165, 173, 179
Omar, 222
Omnibuses, 261
Omri, 78
On, 136
Oolitic syst., 29, 34
Ophir, 81
Ophites, 112
Opium, 304
Orange, William of, 258, 294
Orchomenus, 197
Organum, Nov., 260
Origen, 107, 108, 113, 117
Orinoco, 51, 55
Orkneys, 229, 243
Orleans, 240, 241, 301
Orontes, 181
Orsini, 312
Orsova, 205
Osburn, W., 66, 67, 69, 119
Osiris, 138
Osmanlees, 240
Osmium, 18
Osorkhon I., 81, 146
Ostia, 188
Ostrogoths, 221
Othman, 222, 235
Othniel, 74, 145
Otho, 203, 204, 226, 302, 314
Othoes, 140
Otterburn, 239
Ottoman emp., 235
Oude, 279, 311
Oudenarde, 271
Ovid, 200, 201
Oxford, Edwd., 305
Oxford, 225, 245
Oxus, 180
Oxyartes, 180
Oxygen, 16, 18, 20
Ozone, 317

PACHA IBRAH., 299
Pacific, 56, 57
Pacific colonies, 47
Pacificator, 237
Pacquigny, 244
Padan-aram, 73
Paganism, 117
Palæozoic rocks, 31
Palermo, 273, 313
Palestine, 71, 104, 198, 201, 228
Palladium, 18
Palmerston, 315

Palmyra, 210
Pandosia, 193
Pangæus, 175
Pannonia, 201, 209, 216
Panormus, 193
Papal authority, 255
Paper, 227
Papias, 107
Papua, 52, 53
Papuans, 35
Paradise Lost, 266
Paraguay, 50
Parana, 51
Paris, 6, 24, 170, 224, 241, 285, 294, 295, 296, 301, 309, 311
Paris, Peace of, 278
Park, Mungo, 57, 286, 290
Parliament, 231, 262, 263, 317
Parliament Houses, 302
Parma, 313
Parmenio, 180
Paropamisan Mts., 44
Parr, Cath., 253
Parthians, 201, 205, 206, 207
Partition of emp., 115, 181, 211, 215
Pascal, 266
Passau, 254
Passover, 84, 99
Patmos, 105
Patrick, St, 221
Paul, 101, 102, 104, 114, 203, 204, 289
Pausanias, 174
Pavia, 251
Pazzi, 289
Pazzi Consp., 244
Peabody, 315
Pedro, Don, 242, 298
Peel, 300, 305, 306, 307, 309
Pekah, 80
Pekahiah, 80
Pekin, 234, 313
Pelagian, 117, 118
Pelagius, 109, 116
Pelasgi, 71, 145, 156, 167, 168, 169, 185
Peleg, 71
Pelham, 275
Pelopidas, 178
Peloponnesian war, 170, 175, 176
Peloponnesus, 4
Pelops, 170
Pendulum, 258
Peniel, 73
Pennsylvania, 266

Penny Post, 305
Pentateuch, 73
Pentecost, 99
Pentland Hills, 266
Pepin, 233
Peræa, 89
Percies, 239, 240
Perdiccas, 180
Pergamos, 112
Pericles, 174, 175
Peripatetic Sch., 182
Peruvian system, 29, 34
Perperna, 197
Persecutions, 100, 103, 105, 110, 111, 210, 240
Persepolis, 167, 179
Perseus, 170, 183, 195
Persia, 43, 44, 180, 208, 211, 212, 239, 299
Persian invas., 165
Persians, 81, 115, 148, 209, 210, 211
Pertinax, 207
Peru, 50, 56, 251, 252, 276
Perzoletti, 54
Peshito, 113
Pestilence, 206, 207, 210, 223, 233
Petchora, 42
Peter, 99, 100, 101, 104, 204
Peter (Cruel), 238
Peter (Great), 268, 270, 273
Peter (Hermit), 229
Peter's, St (Rome), 248
Petition of Right, 261
Petrarch, 235
Petrie, 3, 6, 7, 63, 135
Pharamond, 216
Pharaoh, 84, 137
Pharisees, 88
Pharnabazus, 177
Pharnaces, 199
Pharsalia, 198
Phidias, 175
Phidon, 171
Philadelphia, 280, 288
Philemon (Ep.), 103
Philip (Arabian), 209
Philip Arrhid., 180
Philip (Evang.), 100
Philip (France), 228, 231, 232, 237
Philip (Maced.), 86, 178, 182, 183, 194
Philip (Spain), 255,

256, 257, 258, 259, 260, 270
Philippe, Louis, 301, 303, 307, 309
Philiphaugh, 262
Philippi, 102, 178
Philippians (Ep.), 103
Philippic orats., 179
Philippines, 56, 250
Philistines, 75, 82, 83
Philites, 138, 156
Philopater, 150, 183
Philosophy, nat., 23
Philotas, 180
Phinehas, 74
Phiops, 73, 139, 141
Phocian war, 178
Phocis, 179, 181
Phœbidas, 177
Phœnicia, 87, 149, 152
Phœnicians, 138, 174
Phosphorus, 16, 18, 20, 267
Phraortes, 163
Phutim, 137, 142
Physcon, 151
Pianoforte, 272
Pichegru, 286
Picts, 224
Piedmont, 297, 312
Pilate, 98, 100, 202
Pilgrim's Progress, 267
Pindaree, 296
Pinkey, 254
Pinzon, 248
Pipes, lead, 232
Pirates, 189, 194, 198
Pisa, 110, 231
Pisidia, 101
Pisistratus, 172
Pitt, 282, 289, 290
Pityns, 215
Pius IX., 307, 308
Pizarro, 251, 252
Placentia, 194
Plague, 266, 315
Planetary motion, 260
Planetoids, 9, 10
Planets, 9, 10
Plantagenets, 230
Plants, 27, 28, 29
Plassey, 277
Plata, river, 249
Platæa, 165, 173, 175
Platinum, 18, 20
Plato, 179
Plenty, years of, 141
Plebeian Consul, 191
Pliny, 27, 111, 205
Po, 42, 188
Poissy, 255
Poitiers, 108, 221, 223, 237

Poland, 13, 232, 267, 286, 302
Polaris, alpha, 13
Poles, 211, 267, 263
Poliorcetes, 181
Pollentia, 215
Polo, Marco, 234, 235
Poltowa, 271
Polycarp, 107, 112
Polycrates, 172
Polynesia, 52, 53
Pompeii, 204, 273
Pompey, 88, 190, 197, 198
Ponce de Leons, 249
Pondicherry, 278
Pontianus, 114
Pontifex Max., 200
Pontiffs, 187
Pontus, 198, 199
Poor-Law Bill, 302
Popes, 236, 275, 287
Popes, three, 227
Popish riots, 268
Popocatepetl, 49
Porsena, 189
Porteous riots, 274
Porto Rico, 55
Ports, 313
Portugal, 33, 39, 40, 229, 247, 257, 262
Portuguese, 241, 244
Porus, 180, 200
Potassium, 18, 20, 21
Potatoes, 274
Potato famine, 307
Pothinus, 112, 206
Potidea, 175
Powalky, 3, 6
Powers, great, 316
Prætors, 191, 192
Pragmatic sanction, 242
Prague, 260
Praxitiles, 179
Presbyterianism, 255
Presbyterians, 266, 269
Prescott, 304
President, 313, 316, 317
Prester John, 242
Preston, 272
Prestonpans, 276
Pretender, 275, 276
Priam, 170
Priestly, Dr, 285
Prince Edward Isle, 47, 48
Princess Royal, 312
Princeton Coll., 276
Principia, 269
Printing, 242, 243
Prisoners, 316

Privernum, 192
Probus, 210, 211
Procopius, 109
Proculus, 211
Procurator, 97
Prodigies, 104
Prophet's flight, 222
Proscriptions, 197
Protector, Lord, 265
Protestant League, 261
Protestants, 36, 37, 252, 254, 258, 262
Provence, 233
Provincial Govt., 317
Provincial Letters, 266
Prussia, 39, 40, 251, 291, 316
Pruth, 272
Psammeticus, 147
Psempses, 137
Ptolemais, 104, 204, 235
Ptolemies, 4, 87, 149, 150, 151, 180, 181, 182
Puerto Bello, 274
Puerto Rico, 247
Pul, 80, 158, 163
Pump, steam, 266
Punic wars, 88, 193, 194, 195
Punjaub, 308, 812
Purbeck, 224
Puritans, 260
Pydna, 178, 195
Pyramid, Gt., 3, 7, 8, 9, 71, 136, 138
Pyramids, battle of the, 287
Pyrenees, 41, 216, 265, 294
Pyrometer, 282
Pyrrhus, 181, 182, 193
Pythagoras, 148, 172

QUADI, 206
Quadruple Alliance, 272, 275
Quakers, 263, 283
Quatrebras, 295
Quebec, 57, 259, 278
Queensland, 52, 53
Quentin, St, 255

RABSHAKEH, 84, 160
Races of men, 35, 36
Rachel, 73
Raglan, Lord, 311
Ragnar, 224
Railway, first, 201
Railway panic, 307
Raleigh, 57, 258, 260

Ramah, 76
Rameses I., 142
Rameses II., 143
Ramilies, 271
Ramoth-Gilead, 79, 81
Ramsay, 81
Rangoon, 298, 309
Raphia, 150
Rasena, 187, 191
Raspina, 109
Ratisbon, 288, 292
Ravenna, 210, 215
Rebekah, 72
Rebellion, Indian, 312
Rebellion, Irish, 308
Rebellion, Judæan, 104
Reformation, 250, 252
Reform Bill, 316
Refraction of light, 260
Regillus, 189
Regions, unexplored, 46, 47
Regulus, 193
Rehoboam, 77, 81
Rehoboth, 71, 154
Religions, 35, 36, 37
Rennie (C.E.), 298
Rephia, 150
Reptiles, 32, 33
Republic, Italian, 308
Republic, Roman, 189, 199
Restoration, the, 265
Resurrection, 99
Retreat (of 10,000), 177
Reuben, 72
Reuchlin, 250
Revelation, Book of, 105
Revolution, 269
Revolution (Comets) 11
Revolution (Planets), 9, 10
Reynolds, 279
Rezin, 80, 159
Rhaeti, 200
Rhaetian Alps, 187
Rhine, 42, 201, 211, 214
Rhine, Confederation of, 290
Rhodes, 181, 201, 236
Rhodium, 16, 18
Rhone, 42
Richard I., 231
Richard II., 239
Richard III., 244

Richelieu, Cardinal, 261, 262
Richmond, 313, 315
Ridley, 254
Riga, 231, 270
Right, Petition of, 261
Rio Grande del Norte, 49
River-basins, 42, 45, 49. 51
Rizzio, 256
Robespierre, 285, 286
Robert II., 238
Robert III., 239
Rochelle, 238
Rodney, 281
Rodolphus II., 257
Rodrigo, Ciudad, 293
Rogations, Licinian, 191
Roger Bacon, 231, 233
Rollo, 228
Romanists, 255
Romans, 103, 182
Rome, 80, 83, 103, 117, 187, 191, 215, 217, 256, 308
Romulus, 80, 187
Romulus Aug., 217
Rooke, 271
Rosbach, 277
Roses, Wars of, 243
Rosetta Stone, 150, 183
Roslin, 235
Ross, Gen., 295
Rotteck, 217
Rotterdam, 243
Rouen, 241
Roxana, 180, 181
Royal Observatory, 24
Royal Society, 266
Rubicon, 198
Rubidium, 18
Rufinus, 109
Runnymede, 232
Rupilius, 196
Ruric, 225
Russel, Lord, 268
Russia, 5, 89, 41, 226, 232, 244, 293, 313
Russian America (Alaska), 47
Russian monarchy, 225, 243
Russian wars, 310
Ruth, 75
Ruthenium, 18
Rutilus, 191
Rye House Plots, 268
Ryswick, 270

SABACO, 146
Sabellian controversy, 114
Sacheverell riots, 272
Sacer, Mt., 189, 190
Sacred War, 178
Sadducees, 87
Sadowa, 316
Sahara, 46, 153
Saïs, 146, 147
Saites, 138, 140
Saladin, 230
Saladin II., 233
Salamanca, 293
Salamis, 108, 165, 173, 174, 181
Sale, Gen., 305
Salic Law, 236
Salt, 16
Salvador, San, 246
Salwen, 45
Samaria, 78, 80, 84, 160
Samaria, woman of, 98
Samnite war, 191, 192, 193
Samos, 172, 175
Samosata, Paul, 114
Samson, 75, 76
Samuel, 76
Sanction, Pragmatic, 242
San Francisco, 51
Sangara, 213
Sanhedrim, 100
San Salvador, 246
Sanscrit, 168
Santiago de Chili, 253, 315
Santorio, 261
Sapphira, 100
Saracens, 113, 222, 223, 224, 225, 226, 245
Saracus, 84, 147, 160
Sarah, 72
Sardanapalus I., 158
Sardanapalus II., 160
Sardinia, 194, 271, 308, 309, 311
Sardis, 172, 173, 170
Sardo - Corsican Mts., 41
Sargon, 159, 163
Sarmatia, 211, 212, 213, 229
Saskatchewan, 49
Sassbach, 267
Saturn, 9, 10
Saturninus, 112, 197, 211
Saul, 76, 100
Savannah, 315

Savonarola, 247
Savoy, 313
Sawtree, 240
Saxons, 118, 216, 218, 222, 227
Saxony, 254
Schism of Churches, 228
Schism of Popes, 239
Schönbein, 317
Schoolman, 234
Schools, 182
Schröder, 272
Science, Academy of, 275
Scinde, 306
Scipio, 151, 195, 196
Sclavonian Invasion, 168, 215, 219
Scotland, 28, 38, 40, 224
Scots, 192, 221, 224
Scott, Sir Walter, 302
Scotus, John, 225
Scourge of God, 216
Scriptures, 84, 223, 236, 239
Scyros, 174
Scythians, 137, 156, 163, 180, 216, 220
Sea charts, 245
Sebastian, San, 303
Sebastopol, 310, 311
Sebennytus, 137, 138, 140
Secessions, 189, 190, 313
Secular games, 200, 203, 209
Sedgemoor, 268
Seine, 42
Sejanus, 202
Selenium, 16, 18
Seleucus, 149, 150, 181, 182
Selim, 250
Seljukian Turks, 234
Sellasia, 182
Semiramis, 158
Semneh, 140
Sempronian Law, 196
Seneca, 203
Senegambia, 46, 47, 278
Sennacherib, 81, 83, 84, 147, 159
Sentinum, 193
Senucheres, 139
Sephuris, 137
Sepoys, 311
Septuagint, 87, 15
Serapis, 117
Serfs, 313

Seringapatam, 288
Sermon (Lord's 1st), 98
Sertorius, 197
Servetus, 254
Servile Wars, 196, 197
Servius Tullius, 188
Sesortosis, 140
Sesostris, 143
Sestos, 173
Seth, 70
Sethos I., 142, 143
Sethos II., 67, 144
Seven against Thebes, 170
Seventy disciples, 99
Seven wise men of Greece, 172
Seven Years' War, 277, 278
Severus, Alexr., 113, 208
Severus, Sept., 113, 207, 208
Seville, 273
Sextius, 191
Sextus Pompey, 199
Seymour, 254
Shadrach, 85, 162
Shakespeare, 255, 260
Shallum, 80, 84
Shalmaneser, 80, 83, 158, 159
Shamas, Iva, 158
Shamgar, 75
Sheba, Queen of, 77
Shebek I., 146
Shebek II., 80, 147
Shepherd Kings, 139, 142, 144
Sheriffmuir, 272
Sherman, 315
Sheshouk, 77, 146
Shetland, 229, 243
Shinar, 71
Shishak, 77, 81, 146
Shrewsbury, 240
Siberia, 43, 44, 232, 239
Sicilian Expedition, 176
Sicilian Vespers, 234
Sicily, 193, 194, 196, 313
Siculus, 198
Sicyon, 182
Sidonians, 75
Sigismund, 240
Sikhs, 306, 308
Silk, 259
Silicon, 16, 18, 20
Silures, 203, 221
Siluria, 29, 30, 31, 34
Silver, 18, 20, 23

Silver coins, 171
Simnel, 245
Sinai, 73
Sinope, 310
Siphtha, 143
Sirius, 12, 13
Sirmium, 211
Sixtus II., 114
Skageslöestinden, 41
Slavery, 302, 304, 307, 314
Slavery, African, 244, 248
Slaves, 255, 260, 283
Slidell, 314
Smalcald, 252
Smallpox, 273
Smelting, 261
Smerdis, 164, 165
Smith, Sir S., 288
Smyrna, 107, 112
Smyth, 3, 7, 9
Snell, Willebrod, 260
So. 80, 147
Sobieski, John, 267
Sobraon, 306
Social War, 178, 197
Society of Friends, 263
Society, Royal, 266
Socinus, 253, 259
Socrates, 174, 175, 177
Sodium, 18, 20, 21, 23
Sodom, 72
Sogdiana, 180
Soissons, 221, 273
Solar sys., 1, 4, 248
Solemn League and Covt., 262
Solferino, 312
Solis, Joan Diaz de, 249
Solomon, 77, 146
Solon, 148, 172, 173
Solway, 207
Solyman, Magnificent, 250, 251
Solymites, 144, 145
Somers, Sir Geo., 260
Sophocles, 174
Soris, 137
Soter, Ptol., 150
Soudan, 46, 47
Soult, 294
Sound, 24
South Australia, 303
South Sea bubble, 272
Spain, 33, 39, 40, 56, 104, 195, 196, 197, 206, 215, 217, 223, 225, 226, 247, 249,

255, 256, 257, 259, 290, 291, 297, 298, 314, 317
Spanish literature, 230
Spanish succession, 270, 272
Sparta, 166, 182, 188, 190
Spartacus, 197
Spartans, 195
Specific gravity, 20
Spectator, 272
Speke, 314
Sphacteria, 175
Sphynx, 138
Spinning-jenny, 278
Spires, Diet of, 252
Spithead, 287, 310
Spitzbergen, 258
Spolia opima, 187, 190, 194
Spurs, Battle of, 249
St Albans, 243
St Andrews, 252
St Andrews University, 240
St Bartholomew Massacre, 257
St Columba, 221
St Giles, 225
St Helena, 296, 297, 305
St Luke, 103
St Mark, 102
St Matthew, 102
St Patrick, 221
St Paul's Cathedral, 271
St Petersburg, 5, 271
St Peter's (Rome), 248
St Quentin, 255
St Vincent, 247, 281, 286, 287
States-Gen., 284
Stamp Act, 279
Stanislaus, 271, 279
Stars, distance of, 12
Stars, motion of, 13
Stars, number, 11
Statute, Bloody, 253
Steam-engine, 270, 276
Steam-pump, 266
Steam voyage, 297
Steinkirk, 269
Stephen, 100
Stephen de Blois, 229
Stilicho, 215
Stoic School, 182
Stone, 3, 6

Strafford, Earl, 262
Strontium, 18
Stuart Dynasty, 238
Stuart, Sir J., 291
Style, new, 257
Stylites, Simon, 118
Succoth, 142
Suetonius, 208
Suevi, 215, 218
Suez, 245
Suez Canal, 317
Sugar-cane, 248
Sulla, 197
Sulphur, 16, 18, 20, 22
Sultan, 238
Sumpter, Fort, 313
Sun, 1, 10
Sunday observance, 115, 212
Superbus, 189
Suphis, 138, 156
Supper, Lord's, 99
Surat, Nabob of, 288
Surnames, 228
Surrey train-railway, 289
Susa, 167, 179
Susiana, 160
Suspension Bridge, 299
Sweden, 39, 41, 239, 242, 251, 260
Sweyn, 227
Swiss, 236
Swiss guard, 285
Swiss independence, 236
Switzerland, 39, 40, 242, 250
Sybaris, 188
Sydenham, 310
Sydney, 317
Sydney, Algernon, 268
Sylla, 197
Symeon, Bp., 111
Syphoas, 140
Syracuse, 176, 187, 190, 194
Syria, 181, 183, 195, 198, 208, 222
Syriac Script., 113
Syrian dynasty, 146
Syrians, 78, 79, 80, 82, 87

TACHOS, 149
Tacitus, 205, 210
Tagus, 42
Talavera, 292
Talleyrand, 304
Tallow, 22
Tamerlane, 239, 240
Tanis, 71, 137, 146

Tantalum, 18
Tarentum, 188
Tarpeian rock, 191
Tarquin, 172, 188
Tarquinius, 189
Tarsus, 101
Tartars, 86, 219, 232, 233, 239, 244
Tasman, 262
Tasmania, 52, 53, 57, 288, 289
Tasso, 257
Tatian, 107, 112
Taylor, John, 7
Telegraph, 25, 309, 312, 317
Telford, 299
Tell, Wm., 236
Telurium, 18
Temeswar, 309
Temperature, mean, 22
Templars, Knights, 229
Temple, 77, 82, 84, 85, 86, 88, 98, 99, 103, 162, 165, 213, 222
Temple, Jupiter's, 189
Teneriffe, 265
Terah, 71
Terbium, 18
Terror, reign of, 177
Tertiary System, 30, 32, 34
Tertullian, 107, 113
Tertullus, 103
Test Act, 266, 300
Testament, New, 251
Testament, Old, 86
Tetrads, 15, 16
Tetrarch, 89
Tetricus, 210
Teutones, 168, 196, 197
Teutonic Knights, 231
Texas, 303, 306
Thales, 172
Thallium, 18
Thames, 227
Thanet, 118, 216
Thapsus, 199
Thasos, 174
Thaumaturgus, Gregory, 107, 108
Theban war, 170
Thebes, 139, 140, 141, 142, 151, 156, 169, 177, 178, 179
Themistocles, 174
Theodore, 317
Theodoric I., 216, 218, 221

Theodosius (Great), 116, 117, 214, 215
Theophilus, 107, 117
Thermometer, 261
Thermopylæ, 165, 173, 183, 195
Theseus, 170
Thessalonians, Ep., 102
Thessalonica, 212
Thessaly, 178, 195
Thian Shan Mts., 45
Thiers, 305
Thimbron, 177
Thirty-nine Articles, 256
Thirty tyrants, 210
Thirty years' truce, 175
Thirty years' war, 260
This, 71
Thomas à Becket, 230
Thomson, James, 276
Thomson, Sir W., 25
Thorium, 18
Thoth, 137
Thouoris, 143
Thrace, 165, 168, 173, 170, 182, 214, 215
Thrasybulus, 177
Thucydides, 175
Thurii, 175
Tiber, 188
Tiberias, 98, 202
Tiberius (Emp.), 98, 100, 201, 202
Tiberius Gracchus, 196
Tibni, 78
Ticino, 312
Ticinus, 194
Tierra-del-Fuego, 51
Tiglath-Pileser I., 140, 158, 159
Tiglath-Pileser II., 80, 83, 157
Tigris, 45, 153, 155
Tilly, 261
Tilsit, 291
Time (computation of), 221
Timothy, 102
Timur, 54, 239
Tin, 18, 20, 21, 23
Tin mines, 232
Tippoo Sahib, 282, 288
Tirhakah, 84, 147, 160
Tirzah, 78
Tishbite, 78
Tissaphernes, 176, 177

Titanium, 18
Tithes, 224
Titus, 104
Tobolsk, 232
Tocantius, 51
Tolah, 75
Toledo, 228
Toleration Act, 269
Tolumnius, Lars, 190
Tomi, 201
Torgau, 278
Tories, 268
Torquatus, 191
Toulon, 286, 287
Toulouse, 294
Trafalgar, 290
Tragedy, 174
Trajan, 105, 111, 205
Tramway, 289
Transfiguration, 99
Trasimenes, 194
Treaty of Troyes, 241
Trebia, 194
Trent, 110, 314
Triads, 15, 16
Triassic System, 29, 31, 34
Tribunes, 189, 190
Tripoli, 46, 47
Trinity College, 258
Triumph, 212
Triumvirate, 198, 199
Troas, 102
Trojan War, 75, 145, 186
Troy, 170
Truce (Eng. and Scot.), 236
Truce, 30 years', 175
Tryphæna, 152
Tudor Dyn., 244
Tuileries, 285
Tulbanop, Mt., 54
Tullus Hostilius' 188
Tungsten, 18
Tunis, 46, 47
Tupungato, 51
Turenne, 262, 267
Turin, 215
Turkestan, 43, 44, 239
Turketel, 226
Turkey, 33, 43, 237, 256, 257, 268, 298, 300, 310, 311
Turks, 228, 234, 256, 257
Turnbull, Bishop, 242
Turpentine, 21
Tuscany, 184, 313
Tusculans, 192
Twenty-five years' War, 261

Tycho Brahe, 4
Tyler, Wat, 239
Tyne, 206, 207
Types, mov., 242
Tyre, 75, 82, 145, 159, 161 162, 170, 174, 179
Tyrone, Earl of, 258
Tyrrhenians, 184, 186, 189

ULPHILAS, 116
Ulrica, 275
Umbri, 186, 187
Umbrians, 192
Uniformity, Act of, 266
Union, Legislative, 271, 288
Unitarians, 259
United Kingdom, 309
United States, 6, 48, 49, 293, 295, 298, 308, 309, 313, 314, 316, 317
Upper Asia, 181
Ur, 90, 156
Urals, 41
Uranium, 18
Uranus, 9, 10, 281
Urban I., 113, 208
Urich, 250
Uruguay, 50
Usercheres I., 137
Ushant, 286
Usher, 66, 67
Utrecht, 257, 272

VALENCIA, 312
Valens, 214
Valentine, 112
Valentinian, 117, 214, 215, 216
Valerian, 114, 209
Valerius, 214
Valerius Corvus, 191
Valerius Gratus, 98
Vanadium, 18
Vandals, 118, 215, 216, 218, 221
Vanderberg, 241
Van Diemen's Land, 262
Varenne, 285
Variation of needle, 247
Varna, 242
Varus, 201
Vasa, Gust., 251
Vasco de Gama, 55, 247
Vashti, 165
Vega, 12
Veii, 190, 191
Vejentes, 190

INDEX.

Velasquez, 55, 249, 250
Velocipedes, 296
Velocities, 26
Venetia, 206
Venezuela, 49, 247, 297, 301
Venice, 216, 223, 231, 243, 249, 256, 257
Venus, 1,3,5,6,9,10
Verd, C., Isls., 242
Verneuil, 241
Vernon, 274, 275
Verona, 197, 209
Versailles, 282, 284
Verse, Scottish, 233
Vertebrata, 32, 33
Verus, 206
Vespasian, Flavius, 104, 105, 204
Vespasian, Titus, 204
Vespers, Fatal, 261
Vespers, Sicilian, 234
Vespucci, Amerigo, 247
Vesuvius, Mt., 192, 204
Vicar of Christ, 217
Victor Emanuel, 308
Victoria, Queen, 297, 303, 305, 310, 312, 315
Vienna, 245, 268, 295, 307, 310
Vienne, 110, 112, 206
Villafranca, 312
Vimiera, 291
Vincent, St., 247
Vindelici, 200
Virginia, 57, 258, 259
Virgil, 200, 270
Viriathus, 196
Viridomarus, 194
Visigoths, 117, 214, 215, 216, 217, 221, 223
Vista, 247

Vistula, 42
Vitellius, 204
Vitoria, 294
Vladimir, 226
Vladislaus, 242
Volga, 43
Volsci, 189, 192
Vulcan, 9
Vulgate, 248
Vyse, Howard, 8

Wagram, 292
Wakefield, 243
Wales, 204, 222, 225, 234, 240
Wales, Prince of, 305, 314
Wall, Adrian, 206
Wall, Antonine, 206
Wall, Severus, 207
Wallace, 63, 69, 71, 235, 241
Wallachia, 205
Wallis, 279
Walpole, 273
Warenne, 235
Warsaw, 286, 301
Washington, G., 274, 280, 284, 288
Washington, U.S., 288, 295
Water, 18, 22, 24
Waterloo, 295
Watt, 278
Wax, 22
Wealden, 29, 34
Wedgewood, 282
Wellburg, 303
Wellesley, 291
Wellington, 291, 292, 293, 294, 300, 310
Wends, 215
Weser, 201
Wesley, 274, 285
Western Emp., 220
Western Australia, 300

West Indies, 248
Westminster Abbey, 225
Westphalia, 201, 263
Wexford, 265
Whale-fishing, 258
Whigs, 268
Wilberforce, 282
Wildenow, 28
Willebrod Snell, 260
William (Conqr.) 228
William I. (Scot.), 230
William II., 228, 229
William IV., 301, 303
William (Den.), 314
William (Orange), 258, 269, 270
Wilson, Gen., 311
Windows, glass, 230
Windsor Cast., 237
Windmills, 235
Winnecke, 5
Wise men of Greece, 172
Wishart, G., 253
Witan, 227
Witchcraft, 273
Wittenberg, 250
Wolfe, 278
Wolsey, 249, 252
Wolves, 226
Wood, 26
Worcester, 265, 266
Wordsworth, 309
World, Hist. of, 260
Worms, Diet of, 251
Wren, 271, 273
Wurtemberg, 40
Wurtzchen, 294
Wycliffe, 236, 239
Wynton Chronicle, 233

Xanthippus, 193
Xavier, 253
Xenophon, 86, 166, 203
Xerxes, 86, 148, 165, 166
Xois, 142
Xoites, 142

Yenikaleh, 311
Yenisei, 45
York, 208
York dynasty, 243, 244, 249
York-minster, 300
York, New, 261, 266
Yorktown, 281
Yttrium, 18
Yucatan, 56, 250
Yuen dynasty, 234

Zachariah, 80
Zama, 195
Zanguebar, 247
Zealand, New, 262
Zebe, Aurung, 265
Zechariah, 82, 83
Zedekiah, 85
Zenghis Khan, 231, 232
Zenobia, 210
Zenta, 270
Zephaniah, 84
Zerah, 81
Zero, 22
Zerubbabel, 86
Zidon, 75
Zinri, 78
Zinc, 18, 20, 21, 23
Zirconium, 18
Zoan, 71, 136, 146
Zollverein, 302
Zoology, 30
Zorah, 146
Zuider Zee, 234
Zurich, 312
Zwingle, 250, 253

THE END.

PRINTED BY WILLIAM BLACKWOOD AND SONS, EDINBURGH.

OPINIONS

OF SOME EMINENT EDUCATIONISTS IN EDINBURGH.

1. From JAMES DONALDSON, LL.D., Rector of the High School of Edinburgh.

I HAVE examined your very remarkable work on Chronology. The plan which you have devised seems to me to be extremely ingenious, and it is worked out with great success. The book is calculated to be of very great use in helping old and young to remember dates, and I have no doubt that, in some shape or other, it will be largely adopted in schools.

JAMES DONALDSON.

2. From JOHN CARMICHAEL, M.A., one of the Classical Masters of the High School of Edinburgh.

DURING the last seven years I have intimately known Dr Alexander Mackay, whose admirable treatises on Geography have secured for him a place in the first rank of our scientific men. His latest work is a Text-Book of Physical Science and Universal Chronology adapted for scholastic purposes, on a principle of *natural* Mnemonics. The book is planned with great ingenuity and practical skill; it contains a vast amount of accurate and well-digested information; and, in the hands of a competent teacher, must prove a most effective medium of instruction on the subjects of which it treats.

JOHN CARMICHAEL.

3. From MAURICE PATERSON, Esq., M.A., Rector of the Free Church Training College, Moray House.

I HAVE read with care the preface to your book, and have glanced over the whole of it. No one can fail to admire the great research displayed in it. Your system of Mnemonics is eminently simple; and to those who advocate this species of aid to the memory, it will approve itself as not capable of much improvement. . . . As a system of Chronology, accurate and simply arranged, the book could be recommended for reference in all schools, and in many prescribed as a text-book. . . . For the large class of persons who in these days have to pass examinations for the military and civil services, Home and

Indian, the Mnemonics would be invaluable. To teachers also, and others to whom it is of importance to have numerous dates ready at hand, the book would recommend itself. ... On the whole, I would hail the appearance of the book as a very valuable addition to our school literature.

MAURICE PATERSON.

4. From WILLIAM KENNEDY, Esq., M.A., Lecturer on History, Training College, Moray House.

I HAVE examined with care the MS. of your work entitled 'Facts and Dates.' You have collected and put into an easily teachable shape a vast mass of useful information, which teachers would find to be very valuable and suitable for their pupils. While in numerous schools the whole course which your book contains might be gone over with advantage, in almost every one some portion of it might be profitably studied. Your book will also supply a desideratum as a work of reference. The system of Mnemonics you have invented seems to me to be founded on just principles — *the fact to be remembered, so as to produce the date, being always associated directly with the person or event.* And in many instances this is done with an aptness and felicity truly admirable. It is, also, a decided advantage that the work can be used by the teacher whether he chooses to employ the system of Mnemonics or not. Hoping that, for the benefit of both teachers and pupils, your work may soon appear, I am, yours faithfully,

WILLIAM KENNEDY.

5. From GILBERT GRAHAM, Esq., Head Master, Practising School, Moray House.

I HAVE examined with much care your MS. of 'Facts and Dates.' As a system of Chronology it is exceedingly good, and gives evidence of immense labour and research. The part which you wish to be regarded as the distinguishing feature of the book—viz., the means you take to assist the memory in the almost illimitable range of science, geography, history (sacred and profane, ancient and modern), is on the whole about the most ingenious thing of a scholastic kind which I have met with. ... I believe your work will have an extensive circulation for other than educational purposes: it gives such unmistakable evidence of learning, research, accuracy, and ingenuity, besides being pervaded throughout—but particularly in the Scripture part—with an admirable spirit, that many engaged in teaching, as well as others, might consider it of much consequence to have it at hand as an invaluable book of reference.

GILBERT GRAHAM.

EDUCATIONAL BOOKS

PUBLISHED BY

WILLIAM BLACKWOOD AND SONS,

EDINBURGH AND LONDON.

◆

NEW WORKS ON GEOGRAPHY.

BY THE

Rev. ALEXANDER MACKAY,

LL.D. F.R.G.S.

I.

A MANUAL OF MODERN GEOGRAPHY, Mathematical, Physical, and Political. With a copious Index. Crown 8vo, pp. 760, price 7s. 6d.

This volume—the result of many years' unremitting application—is specially adapted for the use of Teachers, Advanced Classes, Candidates for the Civil Service, and proficients in geography generally.

II.

TWELFTH THOUSAND.

ELEMENTS OF MODERN GEOGRAPHY, for the Use of Junior Classes. Crown 8vo, pp. 300, price 3s.

The 'Elements' form a careful condensation of the 'Manual,' the order of arrangement being the same, the river-systems of the globe playing the same conspicuous part, the pronunciation being given, and the results of the latest census being uniformly exhibited. This volume is now extensively introduced into many of the best schools in the kingdom.

III.

TWENTY-EIGHTH THOUSAND.

OUTLINES OF MODERN GEOGRAPHY: A Book for Beginners. 18mo, pp. 112, price 1s.

These 'Outlines'—in many respects an epitome of the 'Elements'—are carefully prepared to meet the wants of beginners. The arrangement is the same as in the Author's larger works. Minute details are avoided, the broad outlines are graphically presented, the accentuation marked, and the most recent changes in political geography exhibited.

IV.

NINETEENTH THOUSAND.

FIRST STEPS IN GEOGRAPHY. 18mo, pp. 56, price 4d. Sewed, or 6d. in Cloth.

V.

GEOGRAPHY OF THE BRITISH EMPIRE. Price 3d.

DR MACKAY'S ELEMENTARY GEOGRAPHIES.

OPINIONS.

Sir RODERICK IMPEY MURCHISON, K.C.B., President of the Royal Geographical Society, in his Anniversary Address, 1864, says of the 'Elements':—"Among the elementary publications, I may direct attention to a useful little work, by the Rev. Alexander Mackay, entitled 'Elements of Modern Geography' (Blackwood and Sons). In a former Address I ventured to commend the 'Manual of Geography' by the same author; and the present production is an improved and careful epitome of that work, which can be recommended as a text-book to be used in the educational establishments of the country. . . . I cannot but admire the assiduity and research displayed in the preparation of this elementary treatise."

A. KEITH JOHNSTON, LL.D. F.R.S.E. F.R.G.S., H.M. Geographer for Scotland, Author of the 'Physical Atlas,' &c. &c.—"There is no work of the kind, in the English or any other language, known to me, which comes so near my *ideal* of perfection in a school-book, on the important subject of which it treats. In arrangement, style, selection of matter, clearness, and thorough accuracy of statement, it is without a rival; and knowing, as I do, the vast amount of labour and research you bestowed on its production, I trust it will be so appreciated as to insure, by an extensive sale, a well-merited reward."

English Journal of Education.—"Of all the Manuals on Geography that have come under our notice, we place the one whose title is given above (the 'Manual') in the first rank. For fulness of information, for knowledge of method in arrangement, for the manner in which the details are handled, we know of no work that can, in these respects, compete with Mr Mackay's Manual."

The London Weekly Review.—"The book (the 'Manual') is a most valuable repertory of the facts of the science, remarkably full and accurate in detail. We cordially and earnestly recommend it for the higher classes in schools, for colleges, and to a permanent place, for the purpose of reference, in the library."

Spectator.—"The best Geography we have ever met with."

Athenæum.—"Full of sound information, including the results of the most recent investigations, such as those of Captain Speke in Africa, and in every respect corresponding to the actual state of geographical knowledge, both physical and political."

Museum.—"We are glad to be able very strongly to commend the 'Elements' to the attention of teachers, as one of the best, one of the very good school-books of geography in existence. We can recommend it on account of its fulness, yet within manageable limits. Its information is the most recent. We have tested its accuracy, by comparison with independent sources of information within our reach, and that in connection with our own country, with Denmark, and the United States: we have in no case found any serious discrepancy. To accuracy and freshness of matter it adds terseness of style and clearness of arrangement,—the latter much aided by varieties of typography."

EDUCATIONAL PUBLICATIONS. 3

IMPROVED EDITIONS.

SCHOOL ATLASES
By A. KEITH JOHNSTON, LL.D., &c.
Author of the "Royal Atlas," the "Physical Atlas," &c.

I.
ATLAS OF GENERAL AND DESCRIPTIVE GEOGRAPHY.
A New and Enlarged Edition, suited to the best Text-Books; with Geographical information brought up to the time of publication. 26 Maps, clearly and uniformly printed in colours, with Index. Imp. 8vo. Half-bd., 12s. 6d.

II.
ATLAS OF PHYSICAL GEOGRAPHY,
Illustrating, in a Series of Original Designs, the Elementary Facts of GEOLOGY, HYDROGRAPHY, METEOROLOGY, and NATURAL HISTORY. A New and Enlarged Edition, containing 4 new Maps and Letterpress. 20 Coloured Maps. Imp. 8vo. Half-bound, 12s. 6d.

III.
ATLAS OF ASTRONOMY.
A New and Enlarged Edition, 21 coloured Plates. With an Elementary Survey of the Heavens, designed as an accompaniment to this Atlas, by ROBERT GRANT, LL.D., &c., Professor of Astronomy and Director of the Observatory in the University of Glasgow. Imp. 8vo. Half-bd., 12s. 6d.

IV.
ATLAS OF CLASSICAL GEOGRAPHY.
A New and Enlarged Edition. Constructed from the best materials, and embodying the results of the most recent investigations, accompanied by a complete INDEX OF PLACES, in which the proper quantities are given by T. HARVEY and E. WORSLEY, MM.A., Oxon. 23 Coloured Maps. Imp. 8vo. Half-bd., 12s. 6d.

"This edition is so much enlarged and improved as to be virtually a new work, surpassing everything else of the kind extant, both in utility and beauty."—*Athenæum.*

V.
ELEMENTARY ATLAS OF GENERAL AND DESCRIPTIVE GEOGRAPHY,
For the use of Junior Classes; including a MAP OF CANAAN and PALESTINE, with GENERAL INDEX. 8vo, half-bd., 5s.

"The plan of these Atlases is admirable, and the excellence of the plan is rivalled by the beauty of the execution. . . . The best security of the accuracy and substantial value of a School Atlas is to have it from the hands of a man like our Author, who has perfected his skill by the execution of much larger works, and gained a character which he will be careful not to jeopardise by attaching his name to anything that is crude, slovenly, or superficial."—*Scotsman.*

NEW ATLAS by A. KEITH JOHNSTON.

THE HANDY ROYAL ATLAS.

By ALEX. KEITH JOHNSTON, LL.D. &c.

Author of the 'Royal Atlas,' the 'Physical Atlas,' &c.

45 MAPS CLEARLY PRINTED AND CAREFULLY COLOURED, WITH GENERAL INDEX.

Imperial Quarto, price £2, 12s. 6d., half-bound morocco.

"This work has been constructed for the purpose of placing in the hands of the public a useful and thoroughly accurate ATLAS of Maps of Modern Geography, in a convenient form, and at a moderate price. It is based on the 'Royal Atlas,' by the same author; and, in so far as the scale permits, it comprises many of the excellences which its prototype is acknowledged to possess. The aim has been to make the book strictly what its name implies, a **Handy Atlas** —a valuable substitute for the 'Royal,' where that is too bulky or too expensive to find a place, a needful auxiliary to the junior branches of families, and a *vade mecum* to the tutor and the pupil-teacher.

"Is probably the best work of the kind now published."—*Times.*

"Not only are the present territorial adjustments duly registered in all these maps, but the latest discoveries in Central Asia, in Africa, and America, have been delineated with laborious fidelity. Indeed, the ample illustration of recent discovery, and of the great groups of dependencies on the British Crown, renders Dr Johnston's the best of all Atlases for English use."—*Pall Mall Gazette.*

"This is Mr Keith Johnston's admirable Royal Atlas diminished in bulk and scale, so as to be, perhaps, fairly entitled to the name of 'handy,' but still not so much diminished but what it constitutes an accurate and useful general Atlas for ordinary households."—*Spectator.*

"He has given us in a portable form geography posted to the last discovery and the last Revolution."—*Saturday Review.*

Fourth Edition, 1s. 6d.

ENGLISH PROSE COMPOSITION,

A PRACTICAL MANUAL FOR USE IN SCHOOLS.

BY

JAMES CURRIE, M.A.,

PRINCIPAL OF THE CHURCH OF SCOTLAND TRAINING COLLEGE, EDINBURGH.

"We do not remember having seen a work so completely to our mind as this, which combines sound theory with judicious practice. Proceeding step by step, it advances from the formation of the shortest sentences to the composition of complete essays, the pupil being everywhere furnished with all needful assistance in the way of models and hints. Nobody can work through such a book as this without thoroughly understanding the structure of sentences, and acquiring facility in arranging and expressing his thoughts appropriately. It ought to be extensively used."—*Athenæum, September 21, 1867.*

WORKS
ON
GEOLOGY AND PHYSICAL GEOGRAPHY.
By DAVID PAGE, LL.D. F.R.S.E. F.G.S.

GEOLOGY FOR GENERAL READERS. A Series of Popular Sketches in Geology and Palæontology. Second Edition, containing several new Chapters. Price 6s.

"This is one of the best of Mr Page's many good books. It is written in a flowing popular style. Without illustration or any extraneous aid, the narrative must prove attractive to any intelligent reader."—*Geological Magazine.*

HANDBOOK OF GEOLOGICAL TERMS, GEOLOGY, AND PHYSICAL GEOGRAPHY. Second Edition, enlarged. 7s. 6d.

INTRODUCTORY TEXT-BOOK OF GEOLOGY. With Engravings on Wood and Glossarial Index. Seventh Edition. 2s.

"Of late it has not been our good fortune to examine a text-book on science of which we could express an opinion so entirely favourable as we are enabled to do of Mr Page's little work."—*Athenæum.*

ADVANCED TEXT-BOOK OF GEOLOGY, Descriptive and Industrial. With Engravings, and Glossary of Scientific Terms. Fourth Edition, revised and enlarged. 7s. 6d.

"We have carefully read this truly satisfactory book, and do not hesitate to say that it is an excellent compendium of the great facts of Geology, and written in a truthful and philosophic spirit."—*Edinburgh Philosophical Journal.*

"We know of no Introduction containing a larger amount of information in the same space, and which we could more cordially recommend to the geological student."—*Athenæum.*

THE GEOLOGICAL EXAMINATOR. A Progressive Series of Questions, adapted to the Introductory and Advanced Text-Books of Geology. Prepared to assist Teachers in framing their Examinations, and Students in testing their own Progress and Proficiency. Third Edition. 9d.

INTRODUCTORY TEXT-BOOK OF PHYSICAL GEOGRAPHY. With Sketch-Maps and Illustrations. Third Edition. 2s.

"A work which cannot fail to be useful to all who are entering on the study of Physical Geography. We believe, indeed, that many will be induced to enter on the study from a perusal of this little work. The divisions of the subject are so clearly defined, the explanations are so lucid, the relations of one portion of the subject to another are so satisfactorily shown, and, above all, the bearings of the allied sciences to Physical Geography are brought out with so much precision, that every reader will feel that difficulties have been removed, and the path of study smoothed before him."—*Athenæum.*

ADVANCED TEXT-BOOK OF PHYSICAL GEOGRAPHY. With Engravings. 5s.

"A thoroughly good Text-Book of Physical Geography."—*Saturday Review.*

EXAMINATIONS ON PHYSICAL GEOGRAPHY. A Progressive Series of Questions, adapted to the Introductory and Advanced Text-Books of Physical Geography. 9d.

THE PAST AND PRESENT LIFE OF THE GLOBE. With numerous Illustrations. Crown 8vo, 6s.

CHIPS AND CHAPTERS. A Book for Amateurs and Young Geologists. 5s.

FORTIFICATION: FOR OFFICERS OF THE ARMY AND STUDENTS OF MILITARY HISTORY. By Lieut. HENRY YULE, Bengal Engineers. With Illustrations. 8vo, 10s. 6d.

"An excellent manual; one of the best works of its class."—*British Army Despatch.*

In post 8vo, price 5s.

ELEMENTARY ARITHMETIC. By Edward Sang, F.R.S.E.

This treatise is intended to supply the great desideratum of an intellectual instead of a routine course of instruction in Arithmetic.

In crown 8vo, price 5s.

THE HIGHER ARITHMETIC. By the same Author. Being a Sequel to 'Elementary Arithmetic.'

"We know, indeed, of no more complete philosophy of pure arithmetic than they contain; they are well worthy of Sir John Leslie's favourite pupil. It is almost needless to add, that we consider the reasoning of these volumes both thorough and close, and the expression of that reasoning uniformly simple and clear."—*Edinburgh Weekly Review.*

Price Sixpence, for the Waistcoat Pocket.

FIVE PLACE LOGARITHMS. Arranged by E. Sang, F.R.S.E.

TREATISE ON ARITHMETIC, with numerous Exercises for Teaching in Classes. By JAMES WATSON, one of the Masters of Heriot's Hospital. Foolscap, 1s.

AINSLIE'S LAND-SURVEYING. A New and Enlarged Edition, embracing RAILWAY, MILITARY, MARINE, and GEODETICAL SURVEYING. By W. GALBRAITH, M.A. In 8vo, with plates in 4to, price 21s.

"The best book on Land-Surveying with which I am acquainted."—WM. RUTHERFORD, LL.D. F.R.A.S., *Royal Military Academy, Woolwich.*

SIR WILLIAM HAMILTON'S LECTURES ON METAPHYSICS. Edited by the Rev. H. L. MANSEL, B.D. LL.D., Waynflete Professor of Moral and Metaphysical Philosophy, Oxford; and JOHN VEITCH, M.A., Professor of Logic and Rhetoric in the University of Glasgow. Fourth Edition. In 2 vols. 8vo, price 24s.

SIR WILLIAM HAMILTON'S LECTURES ON LOGIC. Edited by Professors MANSEL and VEITCH. Second Edition. In 2 vols. 8vo, price 24s.

INSTITUTES OF METAPHYSIC. The Theory of Knowing and BEING. By JAMES F. FERRIER, B.A. Oxon., late Professor of Moral Philosophy and Political Economy, St Andrews. Second Edition. Crown 8vo, price 10s. 6d.

DESCARTES ON THE METHOD OF RIGHTLY CONDUCTING THE REASON, and Seeking Truth in the Sciences; and his MEDITATIONS, and SELECTIONS from his PRINCIPLES OF PHILOSOPHY. In one vol., price 4s. 6d.

CHOIX DES MEILLEURES SCENES DE MOLIÈRE, avec des Notes de Divers Commentateurs, et autres Notes Explicatives. Par Dr E. DUBUC. Fcap. 8vo, price 4s. 6d.

Sixteenth Edition.

EPITOME OF ALISON'S HISTORY OF EUROPE, for the Use of Schools and Young Persons. Post 8vo, pp. 604, price 7s. 6d. bound in leather.

In compiling this Epitome, it has been specially held in view to omit or suppress no *fact* of the slightest importance, and to limit the abridgment to the condensation of the minor and accessory details; and it is trusted that an adherence to this rule, while it has produced a work in which the interest of the narrative never flags, has also secured a history of the time in all essential particulars as complete as the more voluminous records of it.

A Chronological Table has been added of all the principal events, so arranged as to give a clear idea of the order in which they succeed each other; and a full Table of Contents, containing a synopsis of the subjects treated of in the body of the work.

ATLAS to Epitome of the History of Europe. Eleven Coloured Maps, by A. Keith Johnston, LL.D. F.R.S.E. In 4to, price 7s.

School Edition, post 8vo, with Index, price 6s.

HISTORY OF FRANCE, from the Earliest Times to 1848. By the Rev. James White, Author of 'The Eighteen Christian Centuries.'

"This book makes an attempt to furnish a readable account of the country with which we are in closest neighbourhood, and yet of whose history the generality of us know less than of that of almost any other kingdom. It aims at something higher than a mere epitome, for it founds itself on a great deal of various reading, and gives results more than abstracts. At the same time it devotes sufficient space to any occurrences which seem to have a general bearing on the progress or character of the nation. But it does not profess to be very minute in its record of trifling or uninfluential occurrences, nor philosophic in searching out the causes of obscure events."—*Author's Preface.*

"Contains every leading incident worth the telling, and abounds in wordpainting, whereof a paragraph has often as much active life in it as one of those inch-square etchings of the great Callot."—*Athenæum.*

School Edition, post 8vo, with Index, price 6s.

THE EIGHTEEN CHRISTIAN CENTURIES. By the Rev. James White, Author of 'The History of France.'

"He has seized the salient points—indeed, the governing incidents—in each century, and shown their received bearing as well on their own age as on the progress of the world. Vigorously and briefly, often by a single touch, has he marked the traits of leading men; when needful, he touches slightly their biographical career. The state of the country and of society, of arts and learning, and, more than all, of the modes of living, are graphically sketched, and upon the whole with more fulness than any other division."—*Spectator.*

"By far the best historical epitome we have ever perused, and it supplies a great want in this knowing age."—*Atlas.*

ELEMENTARY TEXT-BOOK OF SCRIPTURE HISTORY. By Thomas Struthers. Part I. From the Creation to the Death of Moses. Price 6d.

A GLOSSARY OF NAVIGATION. Containing the Definitions and Propositions of the Science, Explanation of Terms, and Description of Instruments. By the Rev. J. B. Harbord, M.A., St John's College, Cambridge; Chaplain and Naval Instructor, R.N. In Crown Octavo, Illustrated with Diagrams, price 6s.

DEFINITIONS AND DIAGRAMS IN ASTRONOMY AND NAVIGATION. By the Same. Price 1s. 6d.

COMPARATIVE GEOGRAPHY. By Carl Ritter. Translated by W. L. Gage. Fcap., price 3s. 6d.

Just published, a New Edition, price 8s. 6d. cloth, with Engravings and Charts.

A HANDY BOOK
OF
METEOROLOGY.

BY

ALEXANDER BUCHAN, M.A.,
Secretary of the Scottish Meteorological Society.

EXTRACTS FROM REVIEWS OF FIRST EDITION.

"A very handy book this, for in its small compass Mr Buchan has stored more and later information than exists in any volume with which we are acquainted."—*Symons's Monthly Meteorological Magazine.*

"To those who wish to have a really 'handy' book on meteorology, clear, concise, and easy of reference, we should certainly recommend Mr Buchan's work."—*The Field.*

"We know of no modern English treatise on meteorology that can compare, in comprehensiveness and conciseness, originality and accuracy, with Mr Buchan's unpretending little manual."—*Nonconformist.*

"After a minute examination of Mr Buchan's book, we feel entitled to say that it is really the best and *handiest* book on the subject that we know; and we have studied a good many of them."—*Aberdeen Journal.*

"Admirably fitted for the object which it is designed to serve—that of assisting people who have not made scientific matters their especial study to form intelligent notions on the subject of which it treats."—*Weekly News.*

"A volume such as this, which explains not only all meteorological phenomena, so far as they are at present understood, but the method of using the various instruments required for the purpose of taking observations, and of repairing them when out of order, cannot fail to be widely appreciated."—*Weekly Despatch.*

"It is also well suited to be used as a text-book in educational establishments, where, we hope, the study of meteorology will be introduced in common with that of the kindred sciences."—*Farmer.*

"We do not know a better book on meteorology; and certainly it is by far the best book on that subject which we know for the horticulturist, the farmer, and, speaking generally, the unscientific reader. Every gardener of the least pretensions to an intelligent knowledge of his profession should not only possess it, but thoroughly master it."—*Gardeners' Chronicle.*

"We have placed it in the row of authorities on our table, ready for reference; for it is, most truly, what it is designated, 'A Handy Book.' It is one of those books, too few in number, which contain nothing but what is desirable to be in its pages, and all is told clearly and pleasantly, as no one can narrate except a writer who is thoroughly master of his subject. We have not often the pleasure of speaking thus of a publication, and every reader of the volume will assent to our opinion of its merits."—*Journal of Horticulture.*

RECENT WORKS ON THE GREAT PYRAMID.

LIFE AND WORK
AT
THE GREAT PYRAMID
DURING THE MONTHS OF JANUARY, FEBRUARY, MARCH, AND APRIL, A.D. 1865;

WITH
A DISCUSSION OF THE FACTS ASCERTAINED:

BY

Prof. C. PIAZZI SMYTH, F.R.S.S., L. & E.
AND ASTRONOMER-ROYAL FOR SCOTLAND.

In Three Volumes, Demy 8vo, pp. 1653.   Price 56s.

ILLUSTRATED WITH THIRTY-EIGHT PLATES AND SEVERAL WOODCUTS.

EDMONSTON & DOUGLAS, 88 PRINCES STREET, EDINBURGH; HAMILTON, ADAMS, & CO., LONDON.

OPINIONS OF THE PRESS.

"Few narrations of Egyptian travel are more entertaining; and we cannot fail to sympathise heartily with the author's zealous desire to pluck out the heart of this huge mystery of forty centuries ago, or to admire the spirit of enterprise, the courage, industry, and practical ingenuity which he displayed in so toilsome a task, entirely carried on at his own private expense for the advancement of scientific and antiquarian truth."—*Illustrated London News*, 8th June 1867.

"What most surprises me, is the general ignorance that prevails about this Pyramid subject. I had a visit yesterday from two Bishops, who had never so much as heard of it; but you may be sure that before they left me they *did* know something about it."—*American Letter*, December 1869.

"Recent discoveries and verifications concerning the Great Pyramid, by John Taylor, C. Piazzi Smyth, St John Vincent Day, and William Petrie —all within the last ten years—show it to be, at this moment, the most wonderful thing now in existence on the face of the Earth, next to the Bible itself."—*The Scattered Nation*, October 1869.

OF INTELLECTUAL MAN,

FROM A PRACTICAL AND ASTRONOMICAL POINT OF VIEW:

BY

PROF. C. PIAZZI SMYTH, F.R.S.S., L. & E.

WITH APPENDICES BY WILLIAM PETRIE, ESQ.

In One Volume, pp. 512. Price 9s.

EDMONSTON & DOUGLAS, EDINBURGH; HAMILTON, ADAMS & CO., LONDON.—1868.

OPINIONS OF THE PRESS.

"The whole scope of this clever book goes to prove that the progress of mankind after the great deluge was *downwards*, from a highly civilised state to the barbarism in which they are found by the early Greek historians, and that our present discoveries are only working up again towards the primeval standard of science and wisdom."—*The Voice upon the Mountains*, 1st Sept. 1868.

"This is simply a very natural sequel to the author's valuable work on the Great Pyramid of Egypt. The method of investigation here pursued to trace the intellectual antiquity of man is unquestionably scientific, because it is based on the deductions of practical astronomy, and as the author remarks, it is abundantly direct, because it deals only with the very contemporary remains of the time actually concerned."—*The Rock*, 17th July 1868.

A POOR MAN'S PHOTOGRAPHY AT THE GREAT PYRAMID,

DISCUSSED.

By C. PIAZZI SMYTH, F.R.S.S., L. & E.

12mo, price 2s. 6d.; by post, 2s. 8d.

H. GREENWOOD, 2 YORK STREET, COVENT GARDEN, LONDON.—1870.

Besides its special photographic disquisitions, this little work contains a full yet succinct account of the present state of the Great Pyramid question; points out how far modern observation has been successful in ascertaining the numerical values of the ancient building, assigns their several places of merit to different explorers, and shows both where theoretical ideas may safely be based, and where further excavations and more refined measurements by either governments or wealthy associations may be usefully directed.

**PLEASE DO NOT REMOVE
CARDS OR SLIPS FROM THIS POCKET**

LIBRARY

D
11
M22
1870
c.1
ROBA

www.ingramcontent.com/pod-product-compliance
Lightning Source LLC
Chambersburg PA
CBHW032046220426

43664CB00008B/885